THE GREAT BARRIER REEF

A GUIDE TO THE REEF, ITS ISLANDS AND RESORTS

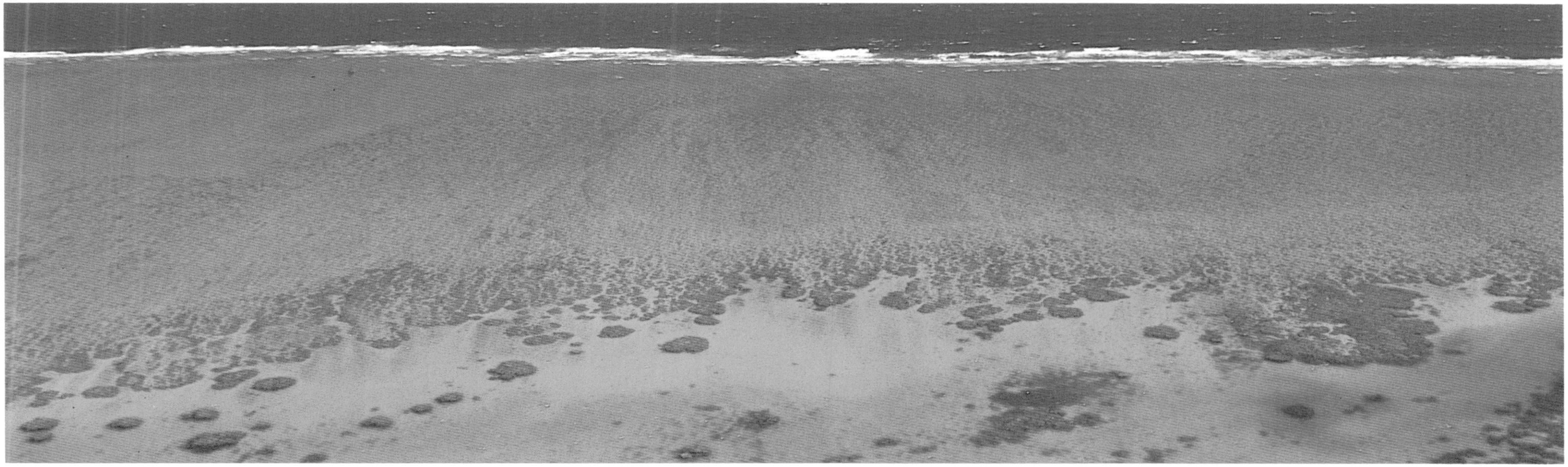

TEXT AND PHOTOGRAPHY BY DAVID HEENAN

GLENMEDE

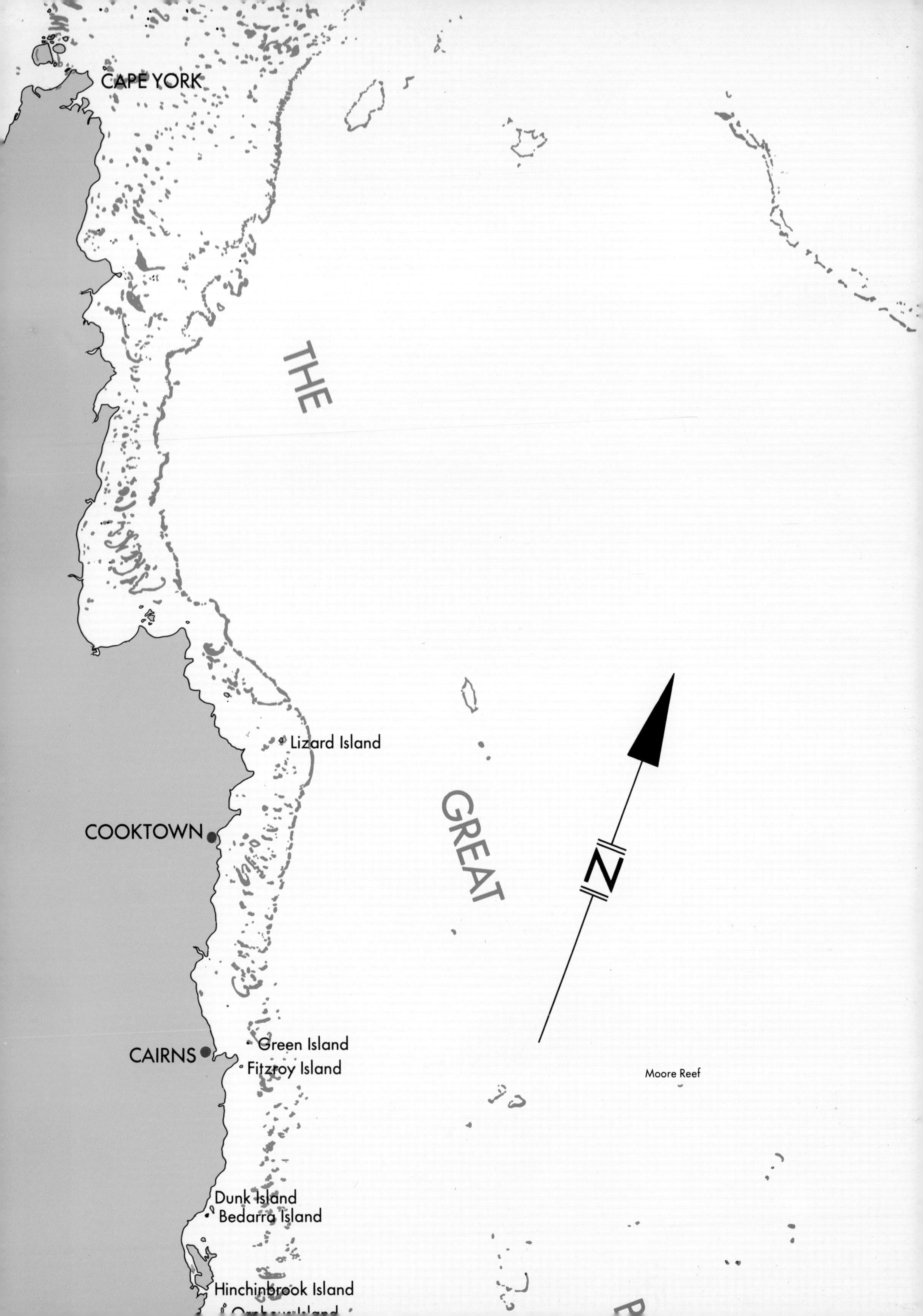

CAPE YORK
THE
Lizard Island
COOKTOWN
GREAT
N
Green Island
CAIRNS
Fitzroy Island
Moore Reef
Dunk Island
Bedarra Island
Hinchinbrook Island

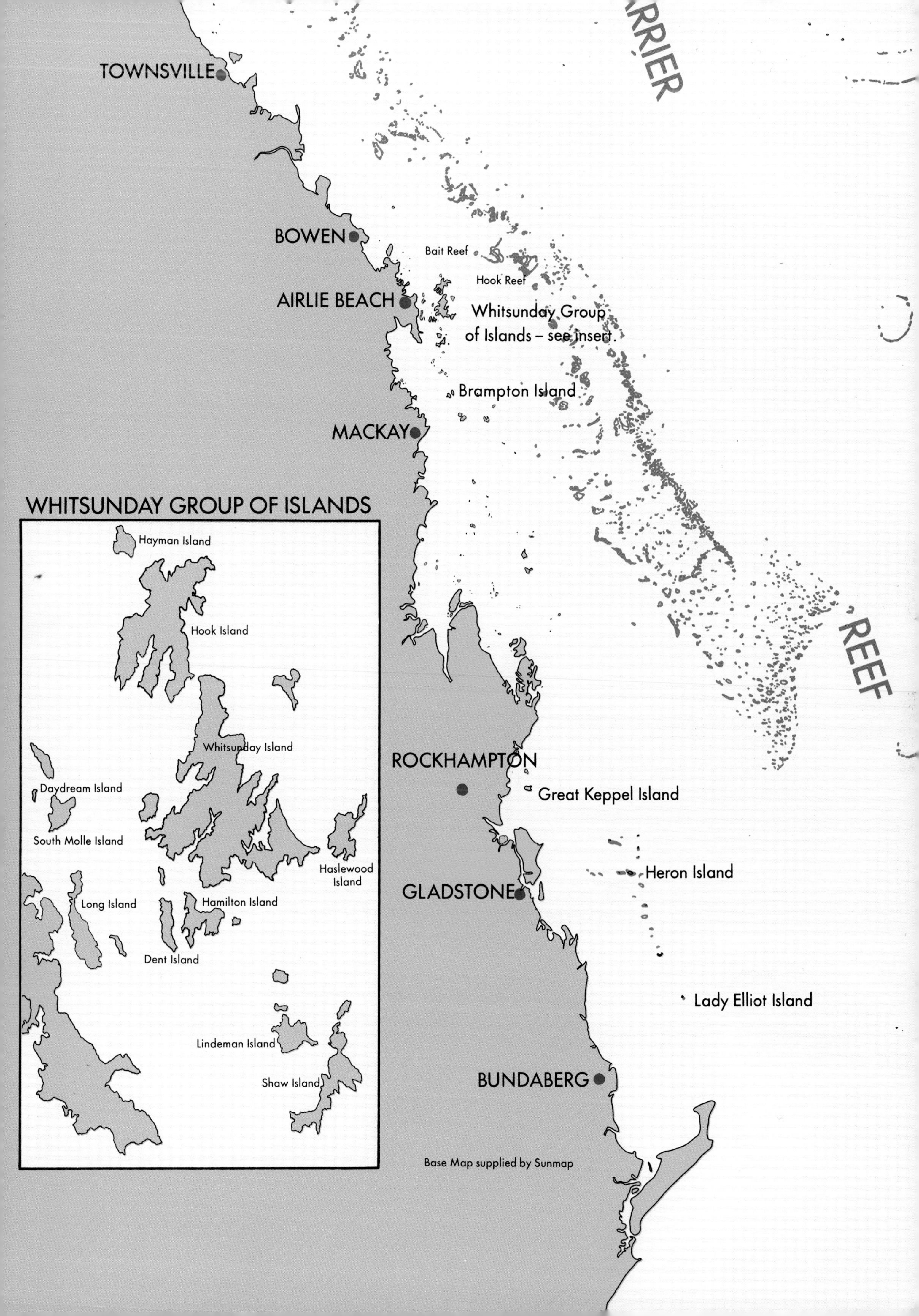

TOWNSVILLE
BARRIER
BOWEN
Bait Reef
Hook Reef
AIRLIE BEACH
Whitsunday Group
of Islands – see insert.
Brampton Island
MACKAY
WHITSUNDAY GROUP OF ISLANDS
Hayman Island
Hook Island
Whitsunday Island
Daydream Island
South Molle Island
Haslewood
Island
Long Island
Hamilton Island
Dent Island
Lindeman Island
Shaw Island
REEF
ROCKHAMPTON
Great Keppel Island
Heron Island
GLADSTONE
Lady Elliot Island
BUNDABERG
Base Map supplied by Sunmap

Published by
Glenmede Pty. Ltd.
P.O. Box 98
Wilberforce
NSW 2756 Australia
Telephone: (045) 751491

First published 1990

National Library of Australia
Card Number ISBN 0 7316 5785 3

Designer - Dennis Veal of Prime Design, Brisbane
Production Manager - Katrina Hergstrom, Prime Design
Typeset by Philip Taylor and Robyn Lowe, Prime Type, Brisbane
Printed by Dai Nippon Printing Co. Ltd., Tokyo, Japan
Written and produced using a Macintosh graphics system

ERRATUM
(Related to the chapters on Dunk and Daydream Islands.)
The colour image on Page 46 belongs on Page 54 and vice versa.

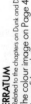

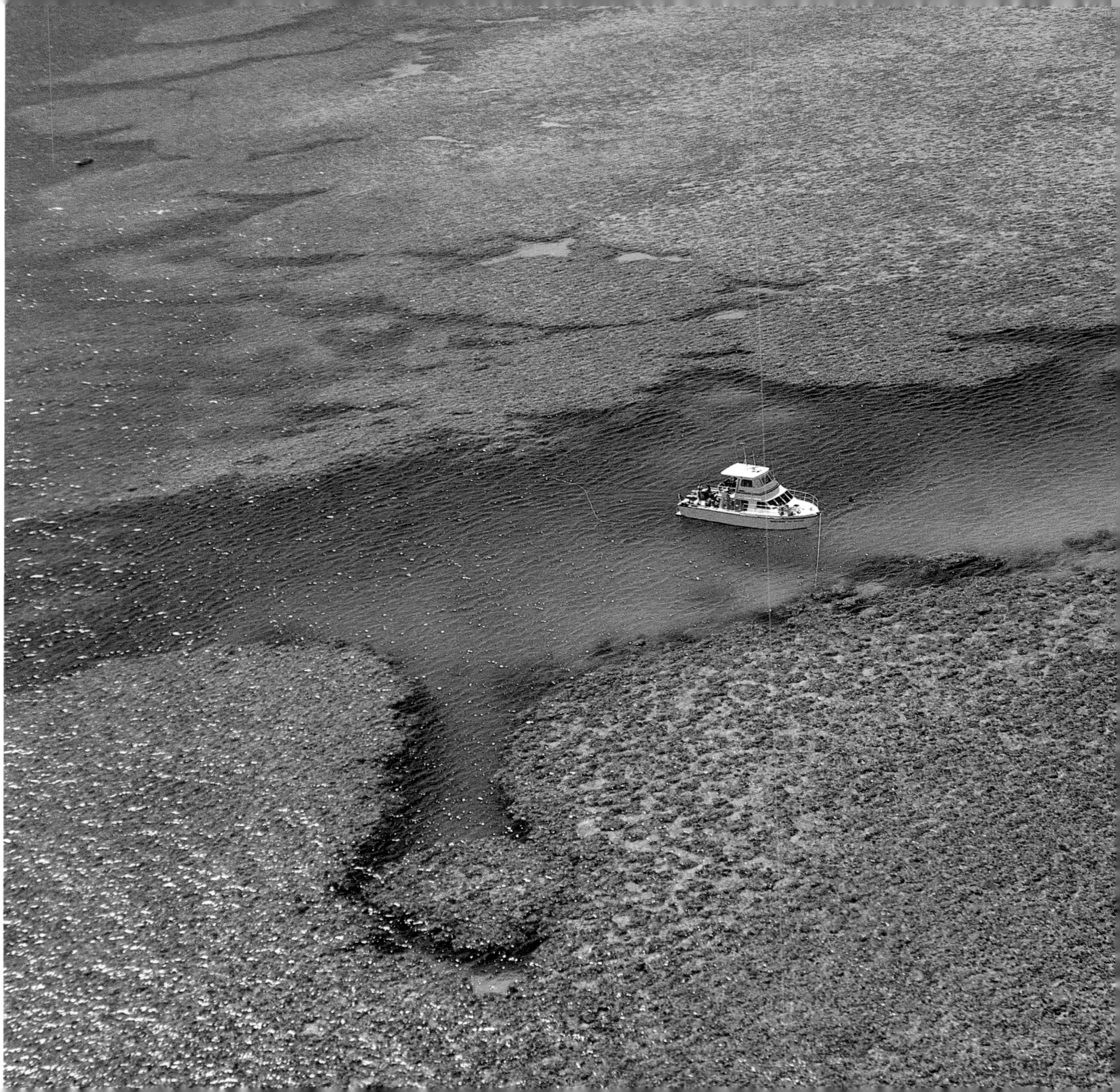

CONTENTS

FOREWORD

Dear Reader,

As my friends know only too well, the writing, photography and production of this book has been a project that has occupied most of my life for the past two and a half years.

When I first started researching and writing this book, I wondered why a detailed guide to the Great Barrier Reef, Australia's most spectacular region, did not already exist.

I soon realised that no traditional publisher could possibly have justified both the time and resources necessary to compile it. I then took the bold step of deciding to publish this book myself.

This would have been impossible, however, without the financial assistance of the companies listed opposite who recognised the need for such a comprehensive guide to The Eighth Wonder of the World.

To their credit, none of the sponsors directly associated with the Great Barrier Reef region ever asked for (or received) any control over the editorial content.

If you look carefully at the photograph on this page (shot over Bait Reef) you will see a unique reef formation. The reason I selected the image for this page was simple - all the sponsors of this book have my heart-felt thanks for their support.

They proved to me that if you are passionate about an idea and can demonstrate its value, a surprising number of people will help you fulfil your goals.

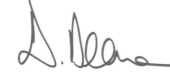

David Heenan

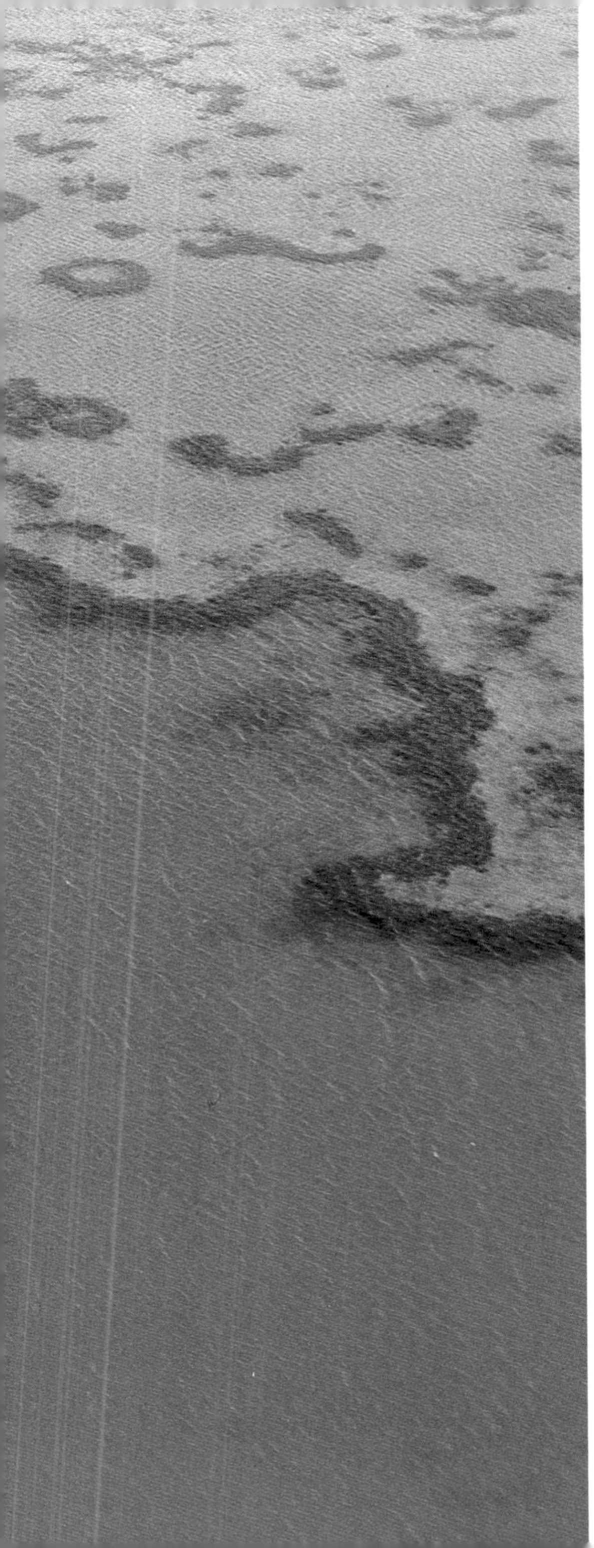

SPECIAL ACKNOWLEDGEMENTS

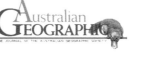

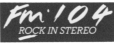

Australian Geographic — The Journal of the Australian Geographic Society

Holden

Ampol — The Australian Company

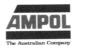

FM 104 Rock in Stereo

Orpheus Island

The Courier-Mail · The Sunday Mail

Bank of Queensland — You can count on a Queenslander.

Australian Resorts

Lindeman Island

Haulmark

Q.H. & M. Birt Pty. Ltd.

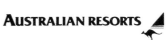

Pivot — Pivot Group Limited

Jennings — Way Ahead

Queensland Tourist & Travel Corporation

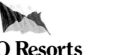

P&O Resorts

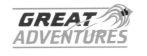

Great Adventures

Ken Done

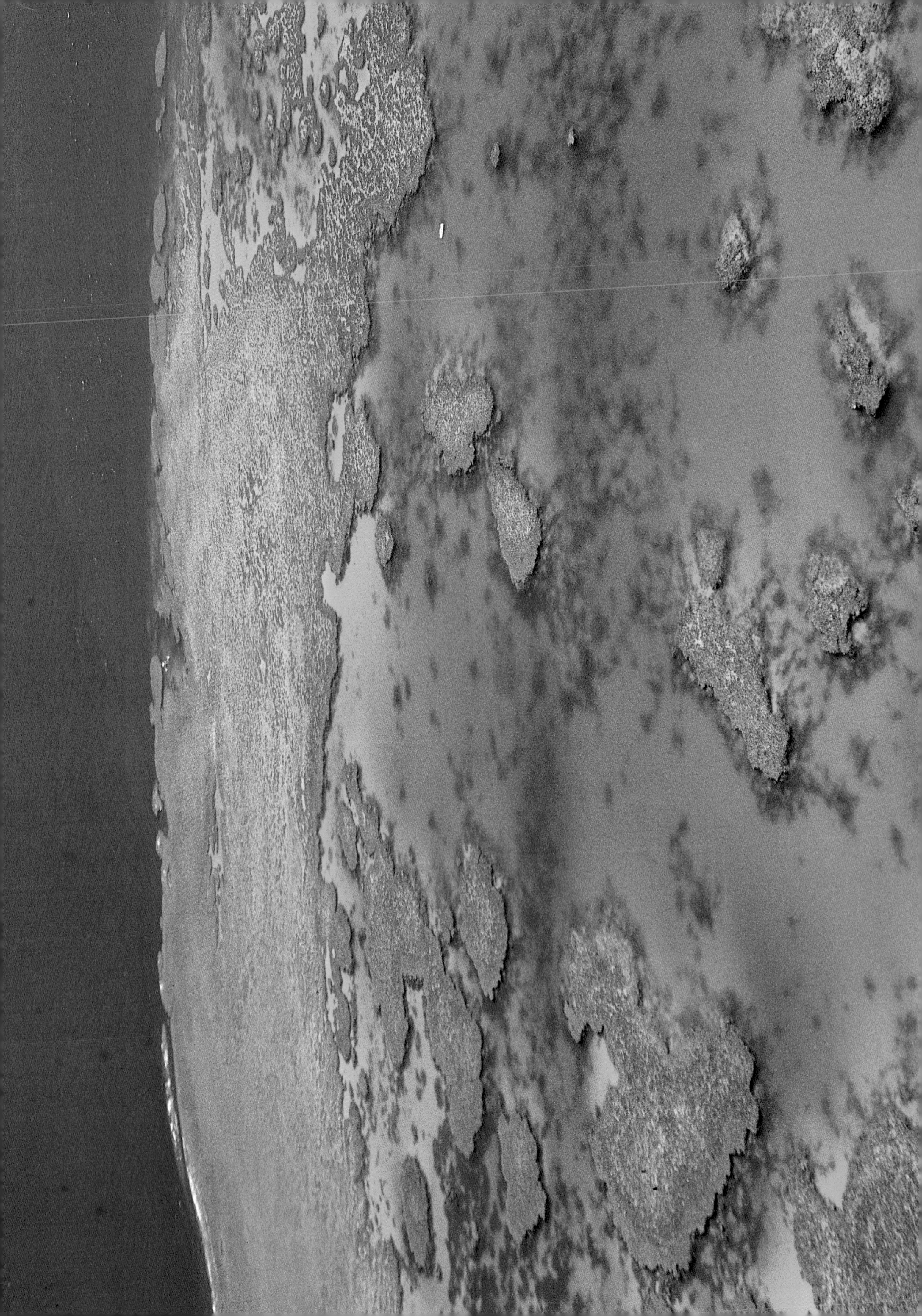

THE EIGHTH WONDER OF THE WORLD

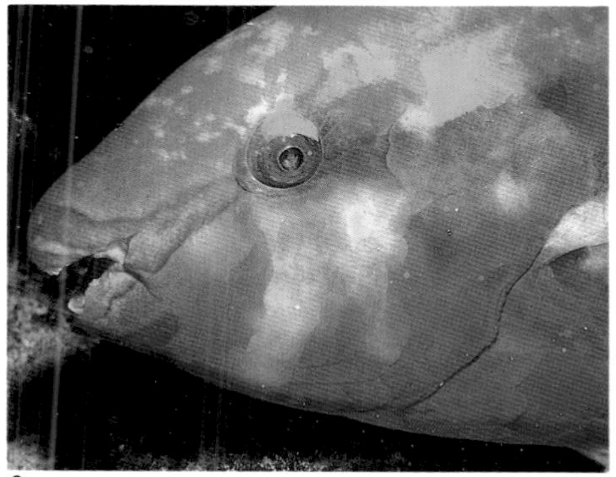

2

3

Few destinations on this planet are able to offer what the Great Barrier Reef can promise. It is an area of extraordinary beauty whether you see it from sea, land or air.

Those who have never visited the Reef will find an amazing underwater world filled with such colour and variety that words often seem totally inadequate to describe it.

The Great Barrier Reef is actually made up of almost 3,000 individual coral reefs - the largest single reef system in the world.

This huge patchwork of reefs begins in the Torres Strait, which separates New Guinea and Australia, and runs down the north-eastern coast of Australia for 2,500 kilometres.

Scattered throughout this intricate maze of submerged reefs are beautiful coral cays and a large number of continental islands, most of which are surrounded by their own fringing reefs.

Although yachtsmen can easily visit many islands, most people prefer the comforts of home on dry land while they explore the splendours of the Reef.

People, in fact, have a choice of eighteen Great Barrier Reef islands where they can holiday at resorts and also enjoy one of the world's greatest natural wonders.

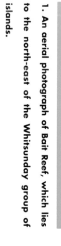

4

1. An aerial photograph of Bait Reef, which lies to the north-east of the Whitsunday group of islands.

2. A Parrot fish. Only mature males have bright, gaudy colours such as those displayed by this stunning specimen.

3. A delicate Harp Gorgonia coral. These beautiful animals have a hard but flexible skeleton, and strain microscopic plankton from the water.

4. Well-known underwater photographer Valerie Taylor with a school of Juvenile Stripey Snapper.

1

1

1. **A Hatchling Green turtle makes a dash down a beach to the open sea. Many are preyed upon by sea-birds before they reach the safety of the sea.**

2. **The magnificent spectacle of a breaching Humpback whale. These creatures can weigh as much as 40 tonnes.**

This volume is written as a comprehensive guide for those people wishing to visit the Reef and one or more of these eighteen islands.

An area as large as the United Kingdom.

The region known as the Great Barrier Reef is vast, covering an area of approximately 350,000 square kilometres. This makes it greater in size than either Victoria or the United Kingdom, and half the size of Texas.

It harbours an incredible array of marine life. There are over 400 kinds of colourful hard and soft corals to be found in the region and more than 1,500 species of fish.

There is also an astonishing number of other sea creatures and plants which are part of a complex ecosystem that has evolved over millions of years.

The Reef is home to about 4,000 types of molluscs including clams and snails. There are thousands of different sponges (the "vacuum cleaners" of the sea), worms, crustaceans (like crabs and shrimps), and echinoderms (such as starfish, sea urchins, and sea cucumbers).

The Great Barrier Reef is the breeding ground, too, for some of the world's endangered animal species. Each year, Humpback whales journey 5,000 kilometres to the Great Barrier Reef all the way from the Antarctic to mate.

They return the following year to the warm, shallow waters of the Reef to give birth to their calves - which have no protective layer of blubber to insulate them against the freezing polar waters.

Humpback whales can grow to 15 metres in length and can weigh as much as 40 tonnes. Few people who see these magnificent creatures "breaching" or leaping almost clear of the water can ever forget the spectacle.

With whales now fully protected in Australian waters, Humpbacks are being sighted by visitors to the Reef (between the months of July and October) with increasing frequency.

The Reef is also one of the most important habitats for sea turtles. Of the planet's seven species of sea turtles, three breed on the Reef.

Dugongs, rare marine mammals which feed on sea grasses, inhabit the waters of the Reef as well. The only sounds that these shy creatures make have been described as bird-like chirps.

Surveys indicate that more dugongs live in the Great Barrier Reef region than any other area in the world.

The cays and islands within the Great Barrier Reef region are also inhabited or visited by over 240 species of birds. Over 35 of these species are sea-birds.

Birds are attracted to the Reef for two simple reasons. There is a plentiful supply of food, and there are many islands ideal for nesting.

Some islands attract noisy colonies of tens of thousands of birds.

These birds often have to cope with natural disasters, however. Some birds prey on the eggs and chicks of others, and whole colonies of birds on low cays can be destroyed by storms and cyclones.

Created by billions of coral polyps.

The Great Barrier Reef is the largest structure ever created on earth by living organisms. What is even more astonishing is that some of these organisms are so small that they are barely visible to the human eye.

The principal engineers of this vast labyrinth of reefs are tiny animals called coral polyps. In hard corals, each polyp builds an external, cup-like skeleton of calcium carbonate.

As a founder polyp constantly divides a coral colony is formed. Its growth is helped by the presence of diminutive single-celled plants in the cell tissue of polyps.

Called zooxanthellae, these minuscule plants make use of the carbon dioxide provided by coral. They then give back essential elements which boost the growth of coral. Tiny algae, also found within the skeletons of corals, aid growth in the same way.

Different corals grow at different rates. Staghorn corals can grow as much as 20 to 30 centimetres a year. Other corals can grow as little as three millimetres in the same period.

Coral colonies come in many different sizes and shapes. These are reflected in names like Mushroom, Plate and Brain corals. Staghorn corals have branches that look like the miniature antlers of deer.

The many beautiful colours of live corals are produced by pigments in the outer layers of coral tissue, and by the minute zooxanthellae plant cells and other algae found in their skeletons. Together, the pigments and algae can give corals brilliant colours such as red, green and yellow.

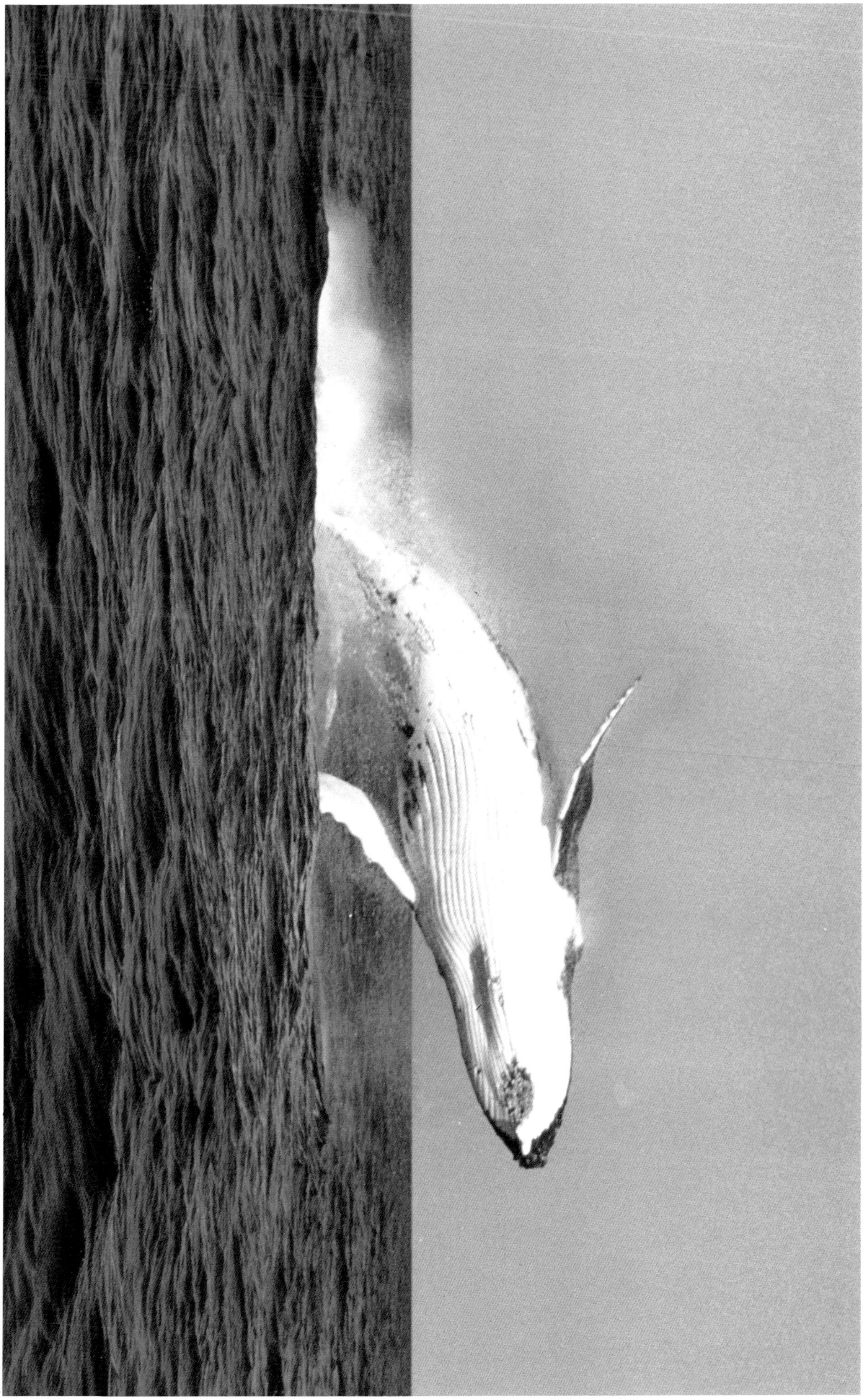

2

1

2

3

4

The reason coral loses it colour when removed from the water is simple. Once coral is removed from its natural environment, the sensitive polyps die along with the tissue that holds the colour pigmentation.

Stressed corals - such as those exposed to too much light, high temperatures or fresh-water - can also eject their zooxanthellae. All that eventually remains of dead hard corals are their white limestone skeletons.

Corals feed on microscopic animals floating in the water around them. They catch these minute animals by using tentacles which are armed with barbed darts of stinging cells (fortunately, the stinging darts of most corals have little effect on humans because our skin is too thick for them to penetrate).

The stinging cells paralyse their victims and allow the coral's tentacles to pass immobolised prey to its mouth. Once broken down, the nutrients from this food are then shared by the whole colony.

Coral polyps normally feed at night-time. During the day, most coral polyps retract into their hard protective skeleton, away from foraging fish.

As hard corals die, they are cemented together by their own limestone. As this process is repeated, a reef many metres thick is gradually built up with living corals on its surface providing shelter and food for countless fish, starfish, molluscs and other animals.

How coral polyps reproduce.

Most coral polyps reproduce by spawning annually. Those people who have witnessed this event agree that it is quite spectacular since most corals spawn en masse.

Many corals are hermaphrodites which means that a single polyp produces both sperm and eggs. The eggs released by polyps vary in colour from bright pinks and reds to blues and greens. Released en masse, the event is like a technicoloured snowstorm.

The corals spawn in a synchronised fashion over several nights following a full moon in October or November.

Once sperm and eggs unite, tiny rounded larvae called planulae are formed. These swim or drift on the surface of the water, usually for a few days, and then find a suitable place to settle. Here the planulae change into polyps and form new colonies of their own.

To build a large reef this process has taken place countless times over thousands of years.

Reefs can take many shapes but three are more common than others. These three are long narrow ribbon reefs, patch reefs which are usually round or oval, and fringing reefs around continental islands.

Reefs have actually grown on the Queensland coast at various intervals over the last two million years. As sea levels rose and fell by as much as 150 metres during this period, reefs died and later formed the foundations or platforms for new ones.

When the polar ice caps melted at the end of the last Ice Age - about 10,000 years ago - the sea rose yet again, flooding a wide coastal strip of the mainland. The "modern" reefs we can see today have

5

6

7

grown in the shallows waters of this continental shelf in the past 8,000 years - a relatively short time in geological terms.

Secrets that may benefit mankind.

Apart from hard reef-building corals there are also many soft, fleshy corals that have no hard skeleton.

Because of their limestone skeletons, hard corals are safe from all but a few predators such as Parrot fish which use strong, beak-like teeth to devour coral tissue and skeletons.

Although they may appear to be more vulnerable, soft corals have special defences of their own. Some have tiny needles made of limestone to protect their polyps.

Soft corals also secrete chemicals called terpenes, substances which are responsible for the sweet smelling perfumes of many plants and trees on land - but the terpenes produced by soft corals make coral tissue extremely unappetising to fish.

Some terpenes are toxic. Soft corals, however, do have a number of predators who seem immune to these toxic substances like the Egg Cowrie and the Crown of Thorn starfish.

Soft corals can move across hard corals, killing them by releasing terpenes and then growing over them. Fortunately, a balance is maintained between the two relatives because soft corals are damaged more easily by storms and are shorter lived than hard corals.

In recent times, scientists have been collecting and analysing chemical compounds such as those released by soft corals in the hope that they may have important medicinal qualities.

The Reef may provide many benefits to mankind. Scientists, for instance, are now investigating the mucus produced by corals. This substance shields corals from the detrimental effects of ultra-violet rays and scientists believe it could lead to the development of a much better sun screen to protect humans.

The discovery of this UV blocking agent is also of interest to commercial manufacturers of products like plastics and paints.

There are many other substances on the Reef that may prove of great value. NASA scientists are currently studying the humble Brittle starfish because its tiny mouth is apparently made of a substance harder than titanium.

1 & 2. Bundles of eggs and sperm being released by coral polyps.

3. A large colony of Plate coral releases thousands of egg and sperm bundles creating a colourful "snow storm".

4. Polyps extended from their hard skeletons.

5. A soft coral commonly known as "Teddy Bear" coral.

6. A Nudibranch (Nembrotha purpureolineata) displays its amazing colours. These shell-less snails are molluscs which feed mainly on sponges.

7. A Flatworm, brilliantly coloured in purple and orange, glides around yellow Cup coral and sponges.

A brightly coloured Nudibranch (*Chromodoris magnifica*) in search of food.

A beautifully spotted Coral Cod.

1

2

3

4

Underwater partnerhips.

A complete food chain exists on the Reef where larger fish devour smaller ones, and so on. However, just as algae and zooxanthellae co-exist with corals, other animals and plants on the Reef have developed similar relationships of mutual benefit.

Grabham's Cleaner Shrimps are one interesting example. They live together at places called cleaning stations.

By waving their antennae, the shrimps attract fish to a station - which is not unlike a local car wash!

When fish move into one such area they hover patiently while the shrimps thoroughly remove any parasites and foreign bodies from its skin. The shrimps are fed and the fish leave the stations clean.

Small Cleaner Wrasse fish also provide a similar service, even cleaning the teeth of larger fish.

Clams are another creature that live in happy partnership with others. Clams - which can weigh up to 260 kilograms - obtain much of their food by filtering plankton from the water around them but like corals they also shelter photosynthetic algae. The algae live in the beautifully coloured "mantles" of clams and provide nutrients to their host.

Other unusual relationships exist on the Reef. Anemones, close relatives of the corals, have stinging tentacles which paralyse any intruders. One exception is the Clown fish.

These small and colourful fish are immune to the anemone's sting. This immunity allows a Clown fish to cheekily retreat to the waving tentacles of an anemone whenever it feels threatened.

The fish life on the Reef is prolific. Workers from the Australian Museum once recorded 860 different species on a single reef.

The smallest species of reef fish are Gobies which weigh less than a gram. The largest species - like sharks and Black Marlin - can weigh well over 1,000 kilograms. In between are other fish of many sizes - although the number of species decreases rapidly as they get larger. Most fish on the Reef weigh under two kilograms and the vast majority are under half a kilogram.

Many of the smaller fish are patterned and vividly coloured. The bright colours of a few, but not all, warn predators that they are poisonous to eat.

Some fish have very unusual features. One fascinating species that night divers sometimes see are Flashlight fish. They have a light organ under their eyes which contain luminous bacteria.

These fish, which have the ability to turn the light organs down into dark recesses, use the light for recognising other members of their school and for seeing food.

Together, reef fish present a kaleidoscope of colours that is breath-taking. Fortunately, all visitors to the Reef can enjoy the myriad of fish and other marine life.

Although snorkellers and divers can move freely amongst the Reef's many inhabitants, there are also Underwater Observatories, semi-submersible craft and glass bottom boats operating on the Reef which allow all visitors to experience its splendours (all such facilities and excursions to the most accessible reefs are covered in the chapters that follow).

Two types of islands within the region.

Two different kinds of islands are found within the Great Barrier Reef region - continental islands and cays.

Continental islands were once mountain peaks on the coastline of Australia. When sea levels rose after the last Ice Age, islands were formed and extensive coral reefs have developed around many of them.

Lizard Island, a continental island towards the northern end of the Reef, even has its own large lagoon with acres of coral.

Fringing reefs can have almost as many species of corals as outer reefs. Fringing reefs are more vulnerable, however, to man's activities and sedimentation has had an adverse effect on some.

An area with a great variety of fringing reefs is the Whitsunday Group of islands which lies about 900 kilometres north of Brisbane. Here there are narrow fringes around rocky shores, protected bays that are filled with reef, and wide reef flats.

The vegetation and wildlife on the continental islands is usually very similar to that on the mainland nearby. Most have areas of lush rainforest but some - like Bedarra, Dunk and Hinchinbrook Islands - have considerably more than others.

Of the eighteen resort islands within the Great Barrier Reef region, 15 are continental islands. The majority of these have fringing reefs and are also reasonably close to spectacular outer reefs and cays.

Three resorts are located on cays. These are islands that have actually developed on reefs over thousands of years.

Cays are created as coral debris

5

1. This Hawkfish is holding onto coral with its fins to resist the tidal flow of water.

2. A Three Spot Angelfish.

3. A Blue-girdled Angelfish.

4. A Fairy Basslet.

5. Flashlight fish have a small luminous organ under each eye which enables them to see food at night.

accumulates at the sheltered or western side of the reef that it sits on (the prevailing winds on the Reef come from the north-east and south-east).

Slowly a sand-bank forms. As birds start to visit it, they leave droppings with seeds from other vegetated cays. Other seeds are washed or blown ashore.

The first plants to grow are grasses and herbs that are very tolerant to salt. Then small trees and shrubs start to take hold. These act as windbreaks, protecting the inner part of the island.

This growth gives forest species like the luxuriant, large-leaved Pisonia tree the chance to establish themselves in the centre of the cay.

Cays are much smaller and lower than continental islands - most are not much more than four metres above sea level. Cays, particularly those in the very early stages of development, can shift and change their shape quite significantly, especially when exposed to cyclonic conditions.

A World Heritage Site.

The Great Barrier Reef region stretching from Lady Elliot Island in the south to Cape York, the northern tip of Australia, was declared a World Heritage Site on October 26, 1981.

The protection of the region is the responsibility of the Federally funded Great Barrier Reef Marine Park Authority which started its operations in 1976. The Authority has its headquarters in Townsville as well as a multi-million dollar Aquarium of immense size where you can learn much about the Reef and see many of its inhabitants.

To protect the Reef but still allow the wise use and enjoyment of it, the Authority introduced three major categories of zones.

In Scientific or Preservation Zones the only human activity allowed is strictly controlled scientific research.

In Marine National Park Zones three major uses are permitted - scientific, educational and recreational.

General Use Zones allow commercial and recreational fishing.

Activities prohibited within the Park include oil exploration, mining, spearfishing with Scuba gear, and the taking of certain specimens of fish or shell species.

The day-to-day management of the Marine Park is entrusted to Queensland's Department of Environment and Conservation (previously known as the National Parks and Wildlife Service). Their rangers patrol the Marine Park aboard both aircraft and boats.

With the data gathered by these rangers and scientists engaged in marine research, the Authority is constantly monitoring, interpreting and sharing valuable information about the Reef and its marine life.

With this information and the proper management of human activity in the Marine Park, the Authority hopes to preserve the Reef and its rich resources for future generations.

Visiting the Reef.

A trip or holiday to the Reef should be an experience you will remember with pleasure for the rest of your life. Here are a few basic tips, however, to make it as enjoyable as possible.

The best time of the year to visit the Great Barrier Reef is normally from April onwards. The months of January, February and March are known as the wet season in Tropical Queensland.

This is, in fact, the cyclone season. Although you would have to be very unlucky to experience a major cyclone you could, nevertheless, experience very heavy downpours of rain - some that last for days on end. With so much moisture in the air and the summer heat at its peak, the humidity at this time of the year can also be extremely uncomfortable for those unaccustomed to it.

The very best months to visit the region are generally acknowledged to be August, September and October - when the days are usually very warm and sunny but dry.

Even in the middle of winter, however, the days can be completely cloudless and comfortably warm - with the nights cool and balmy.

So whether you visit the Reef in summer or winter you should be prepared for a strong sun that can easily burn unprotected skin - an effective sunscreen cream is therefore essential. A pair of good quality sunglasses and a hat of some sort are investments you will not regret as well.

Most visitors to the Great Barrier Reef will remember to take a camera - but you should also consider taking along a pair of binoculars to enjoy a closer look at wildlife.

Most of the islands with accommodation also have an excellent network of walking trails maintained by the Department of Environment and Conservation. If you plan to go on walks, it is sensible to purchase and pack a water canister. You can become very thirsty on a hot day in the tropics after just a little physical exertion.

Also take an old pair of sneakers for reef walking - coral can be extremely sharp. When reef walking, it is commonsense to only handle those creatures you have some knowledge of. Some inhabitants of the Reef, although small or beautiful (like living Cone shells), have first class defence mechanisms. Many are extremely fragile, too.

If you do handle a marine animal be sure to put it back into the water as soon as possible so that it does not dry out and perish.

Care should also be taken wherever birds are nesting. Nests can easily be trampled underfoot. If you approach a bird too closely it may leave its nest - exposing its eggs and chicks to predators like Gulls.

The extraordinary beauty of the Great Barrier Reef has attracted visitors from all over the world. Protected from mining and other destructive activities, it is still one of the greatest, unspoiled areas on earth.

Charles Darwin, the famous naturalist, visited the Great Barrier Reef in the 19th century. "Travellers tell us of the vast dimensions of the pyramids and other great ruins, but utterly insignificant are the greatest of these, when compared to these mountains of stone," he wrote, referring to the mighty reefs of coral that are so rich in marine life.

The rest of this book from Chapter Three onwards is designed to give you all the information you need to plan and enjoy your trip to this amazing destination.

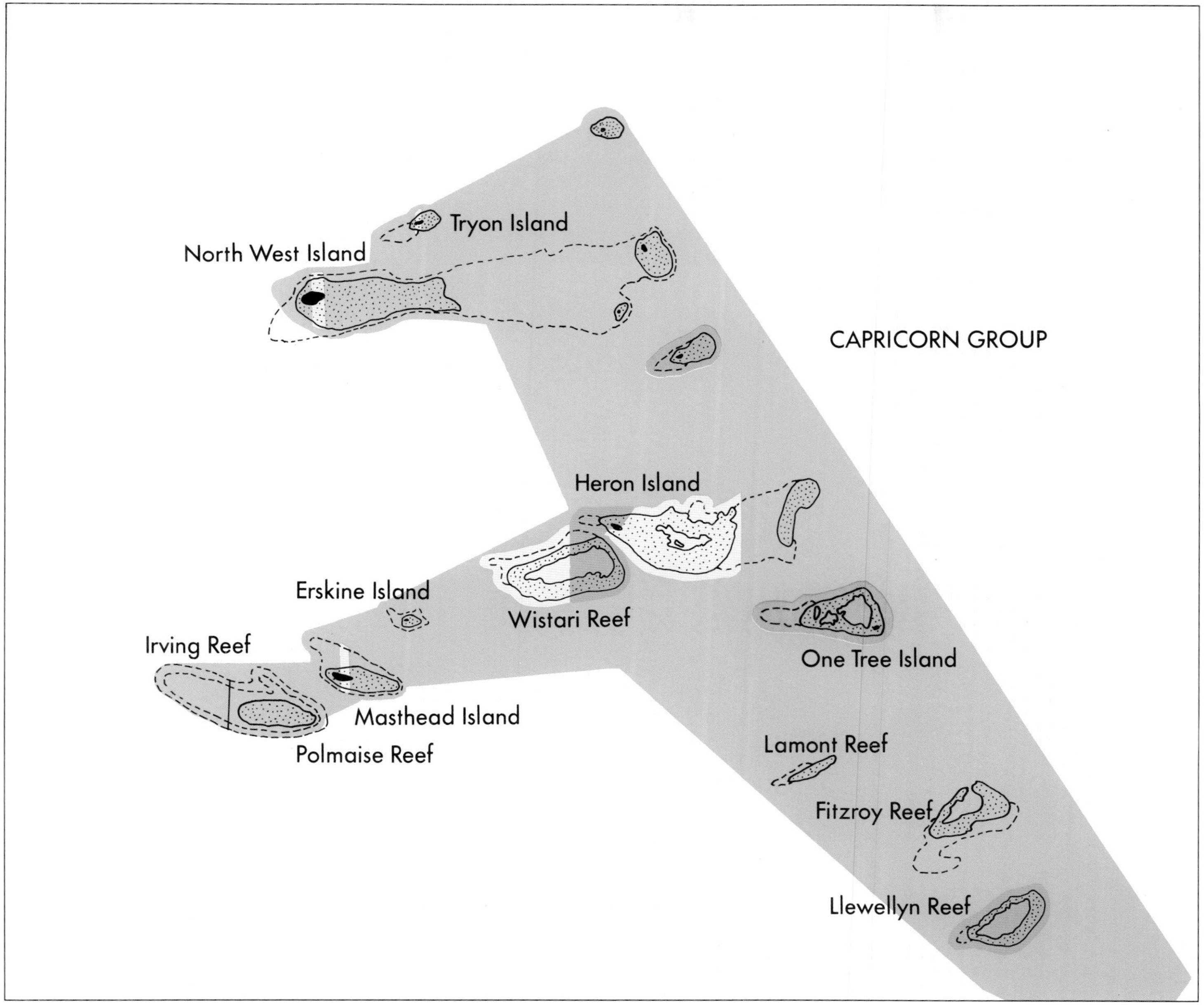

1

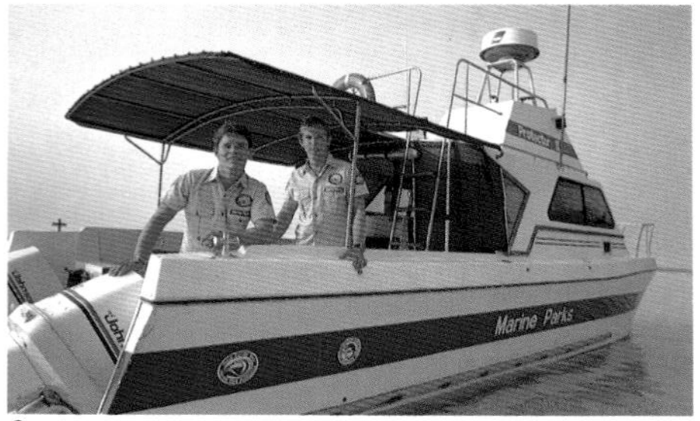

2

1. The region where Heron Island is located is an example of how the Great Barrier Reef Marine Park is protected and zoned for different uses. The area in dark blue is a General Use zone; in the area marked yellow, recreational activities are permitted but no commercial fishing is allowed; the area in orange is a Scientific Research zone; and the area in green is a Preservation zone.

2. Marine Park Rangers on patrol.

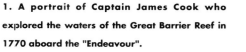

MAN AND THE REEF

2

3

Long before Europeans ventured into the waters of Australia, coastal and island tribes of aborigines had an intimate knowledge of the Great Barrier Reef.

Indeed, since aborigines arrived in Australia more than 40,000 years ago, hundreds of generations would have witnessed the slow formation of the Reef for it is a mere 10,000 years old - a short time in geological terms.

Unfortunately, we know little about the aborigines who visited the islands and reefs because any archaeological evidence found to date has been scant. Most of the information known about these early inhabitants was gathered during the first documented voyages made by Europeans.

From their observations and the archaeological evidence that does exist it is known that both Murray and Darnley Islands, which lie at the northern tip of the Reef, had quite large native populations. The people who lived on these two islands were the Miriam people of the Torres Strait.

These islanders had large dugout canoes up to 20 metres long which held up to 50 men. Equipped with outriggers and sails, they travelled hundreds of kilometres along the Reef.

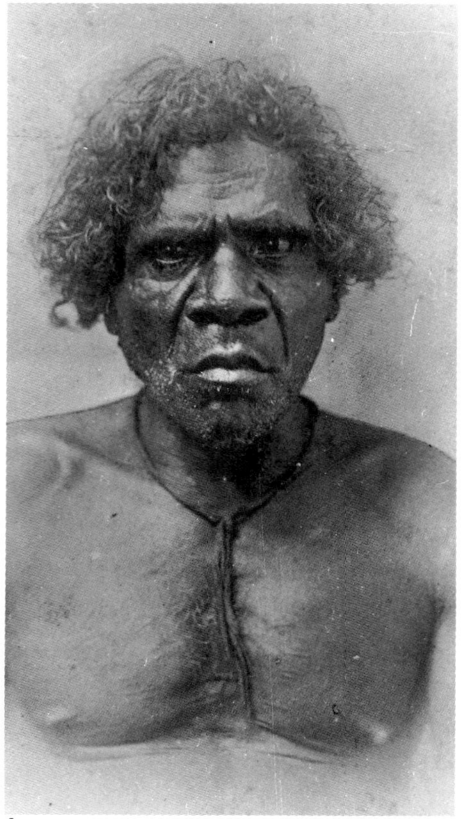

4

1. A portrait of Captain James Cook who explored the waters of the Great Barrier Reef in 1770 aboard the "Endeavour".

2. The corvette H.M.S. "Fly" which helped survey the Great Barrier Reef in the 1840's under the command of Captain Francis Blackwood.

3. Aborigines dance at a jamboree on Palm Island around 1925.

4. One of the last aborigines to live on Great Keppel Island.

1

1

2

1. A group of aborigines on Palm Island, an Aboriginal Reserve, in 1935. About 2,800 aborigines live on the island today.

2. The breastplate of what is believed to be the last tribal leader of the aborigines who once inhabited the Whitsunday Group of islands.

Aborigines living at Cape York had smaller versions of these outrigger canoes. Four hundred kilometres south at Princess Charlotte Bay the aborigines had dugout canoes but these only had one outrigger.

Aborigines also lived on Hinchinbrook, Dunk, Great Palm, Whitsunday and Great Keppel Islands. These aborigines had bark canoes stitched together with vines rather than dugout canoes. Despite their fragile appearance these canoes were used in all but the roughest of weather.

Canoes enabled aborigines to travel to smaller islands in search of food, to the mainland for religious ceremonies, or for attacking enemies.

They were also used for hunting dugongs, turtles, rays and sharks. These were speared with long harpoons.

There has been much speculation about who were the first men from further afield to explore the Great Barrier Reef and the coastal areas along it. There is evidence that the Chinese and Malays as well as the Dutch, Portuguese and Spanish all sailed through these waters long before James Cook.

An old map of the world that was produced in the late sixteenth or early seventeenth century confirms this.

Drawn by an Italian priest named Father Ricci, who was a missionary in China, it clearly shows the north-eastern coastline of Australia from Cape York down to where Townsville is situated.

An inscription on this ancient map even mentions that a Castilian ship was wrecked on this coast.

Apparently an ancient manuscript also exists in China that proves the Chinese had visited both the northern and eastern coasts of Australia over two thousand years ago.

In Japan, history books contain references to voyages made from that country down the eastern coast of Australia in the early fifteenth century. Indeed, an expedition supposedly sailed as far as Tasmania.

Navigated by James Cook in 1770.

The earliest fully documented voyage through the treacherous waters of the Great Barrier Reef was made by that great seaman, Captain James Cook, in 1770.

Cook left Botany Bay on May 6 of that year aboard the "Endeavour" to explore Australia's uncharted northern waters. Little did he know the dangers that lay in store.

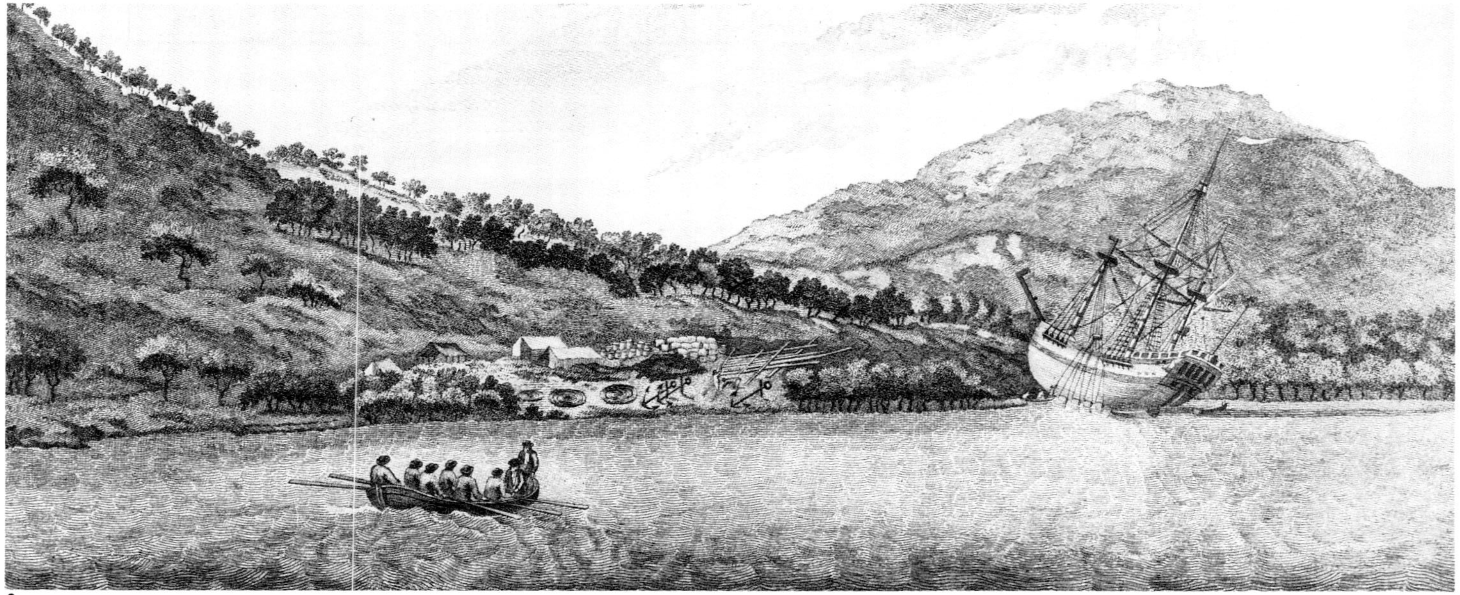
3

4

In fact, it is quite remarkable that Cook and his crew survived all of the many coral reefs that lay in wait as they sailed up "Australia's Grand Canal" - although, as we know, they came very close to being wrecked on more than one occasion.

As Cook sailed north and encountered various islands along the Great Barrier Reef he named many of them, including the Whitsunday Group, Dunk Island and Lizard Island.

Cook and scientists aboard the "Endeavour" were also faithful in keeping journals which provide an invaluable record of the aborigines, flora and fauna that they saw at the time.

It is perhaps ironic that the 'Endeavour" sailed over 1,000 kilometres inside the Reef before it almost claimed the ship and its crew. On the other hand, Cook was ignorant of the fact that the passage between the Reef and the mainland narrows more and more - like a funnel - as one sails north.

On Trinity Sunday, 1770, the "Endeavour" entered Trinity Bay - the place where the city of Cairns now stands. Cook continued north, constantly checking the water level by "heaving the lead".

What Cook did not know was that the character of the Reef changes dramatically in this area. So numerous are the individual reefs at the northern end of Trinity Bay that it is impossible to sail in a straight line without running into walls of coral.

On the day following Trinity Sunday, disaster struck. At 10:00 p.m. the "Endeavour" ran aground on a small coral reef not far from Cape Tribulation. All hands turned out to lighten the ship, throwing iron and stone ballast, and other heavy items overboard - including six ten-pounder guns (which were recovered in 1969).

The pumps were manned continuously and a sail was hauled under the hull to cover the hole and lessen the leak. The efforts of all aboard were fortunately rewarded and four days later the ship limped into the mouth of the Endeavour River.

The ship remained here for two months while it underwent repairs. During this time the men replenished their supplies of fresh water, caught fish and turtles, and shot either a wallaby or kangaroo.

They also came into close contact with aborigines who were described as being of "small stature, and quite naked and black". At first they seemed "very inoffensive and

3. The ship "Endeavour" being careened at the mouth of the Endeavour River after striking a reef near Cape Tribulation. The vessel took two months to repair.

4. A statue of James Cook that was erected in Cooktown near to the site where the ship "Endeavour" was beached.

1

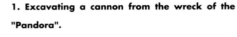

tractable". Later, however, the natives set fire to the grass around the camp in an attempt to capture some of the stores that were ashore. This happened on several occasions until they were shot at and one was wounded.

The "Endeavour" eventually set sail again on August 3, 1770, but more trouble lay ahead. For days the "Endeavour" was trapped in a maze of dangerous reefs and Cook landed on Lizard Island to climb a mountain peak in order to see a way out. Fortunately, a channel was finally found and the ship took to deeper water.

Although all aboard must have sighed with relief another terrifying nightmare awaited them. Several nights later the crew heard the thunder of waves breaking over a nearby reef and discovered that the ship was drifting towards it "surprisingly fast".

2

1. Excavating a cannon from the wreck of the "Pandora".

2. The cannon being cleaned and treated by conservators of the Queensland Museum.

The wind had dropped away to nothing and there was no possibility of anchoring because the water was too deep. In a desperate effort to avoid certain destruction, the ship's pinnace and yawl were launched in an attempt to tow the "Endeavour" to safety.

They were a mere 80 metres or so from "the jaws of destruction" when a light breeze sprang up and a small opening in the reef not much longer than the ship itself was sighted.

As they moved closer to it, however, they realised that water was gushing out of it "like a Mill stream" because of the ebb tide. This carried the "Endeavour" away from immediate danger. The crew waited for the tide to turn yet again and then virtually surfed through the narrow and dangerous passage.

3

The opening that carried them to safety was named "Providential Channel". Cook's relief in extricating the "Endeavour" and crew from this near disaster is very clear from an expressive entry in his journals. "It is but a few days ago that I rejoiced at having got without the Reef but that joy was nothing compared to what I now felt at being safe at anchor within it."

Cook subsequently sailed to Cape York, the northern most tip of Australia, and then returned to England. His reports and charts led to the colonization of Australia.

Other brave navigators like Captain Philip King and Captain Blackwood later charted the Reef in more detail but over a thousand ships were still wrecked up and down the reef before 1900.

One well-known vessel that was shipwrecked in 1791 was the H.M.S. "Pandora", the 24-gun Royal Navy frigate that had the mission of recapturing the "Bounty" and its mutinous crew.

4

3. A French Wanded Bottle recovered from the Pandora.

4. Halves of hour glasses found at the wreck site. The right one has yet to be cleaned.

The "Pandora" was enroute to England with 140 aboard including 14 prisoners from the "Bounty" when it slammed into one of the northern reefs. Thirty one crew and four of the mutineers drowned. The survivors managed to make it to Timor.

The remains of the "Pandora" were discovered in 1977 and the Marine Archaeology Department of the Queensland Museum began excavation of the wreck in 1983.

The wreck is still in a good state of preservation and has provided much information about life in the Royal Navy during the eighteenth century.

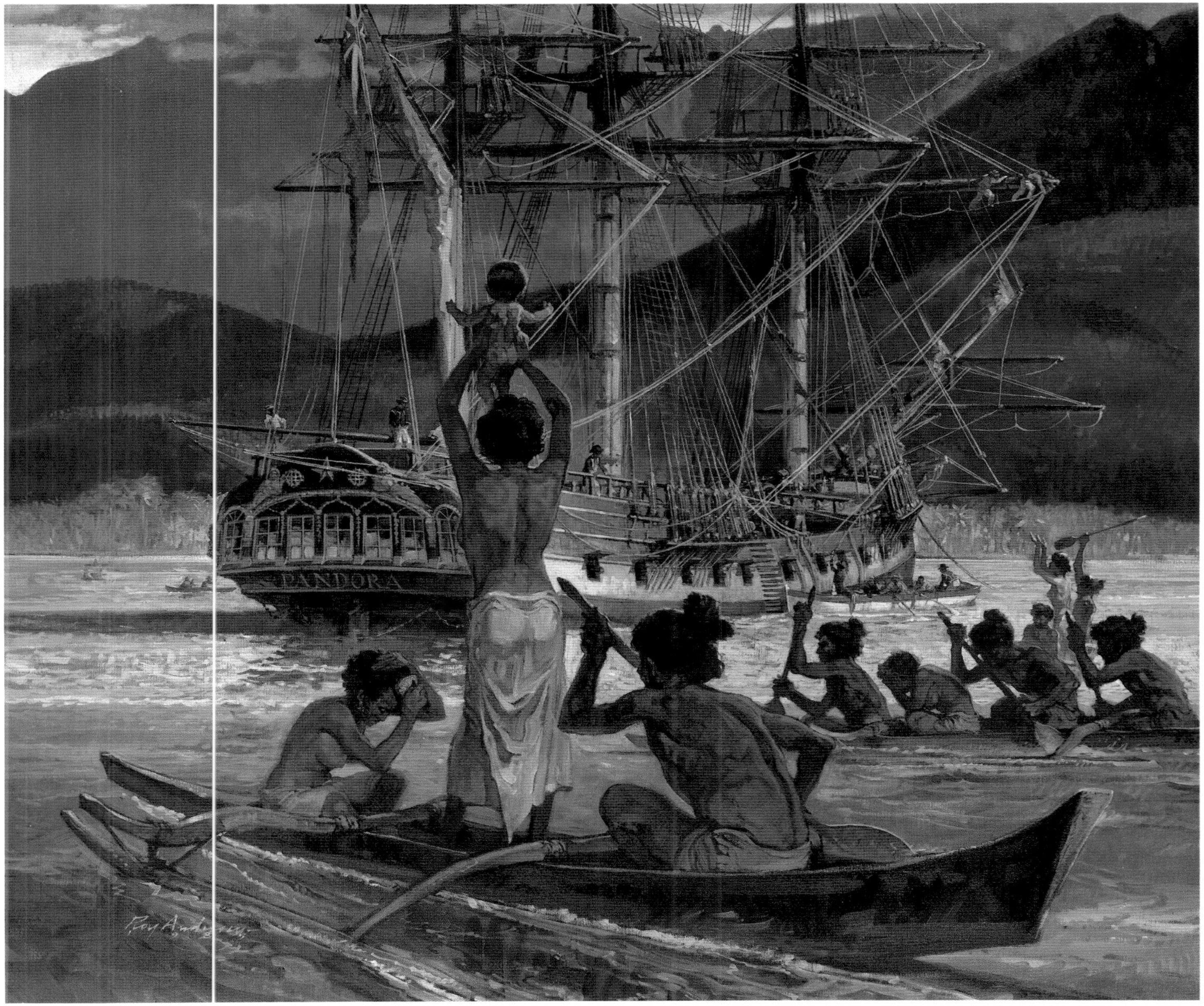

5

6

5. The "Pandora", a man-of-war that was sent to Tahiti to capture the mutineers from the "Bounty". The "Pandora" was wrecked on the Great Barrier Reef on its return trip to England.

6. This silver and gold pocket watch probably belonged to Hamilton, the ship's surgeon.

Another victim of the Reef was the S.S. "Gothenburg". This 120' iron steamer - which was also rigged as a three-masted schooner - was carrying general cargo and 2,600 ounces of gold bullion from the Pine Creek goldfields south of Darwin.

Aboard were many miners with money belts bulging with gold, and various dignitaries including Mr. Thomas Reynolds, the ex-Premier of South Australia, Mr. Justice Wearing of the South Australian Supreme Court and Mr. Whiteby, the Crown Prosecutor. These latter two gentlemen had just conducted the first Circuit Court ever held in the Northern Territory, which was then part of South Australia.

The "Gothenburg" struck Old Reef about 60 kilometres north of Bowen on February 24, 1875, at about 6:40 p.m. At first, nobody was too concerned for the captain felt the ship would drift off the reef on the morning high tide. Many passengers even retired to their bunks but during the night a fierce gale arose and rising seas turned the ship almost broadside on to the reef.

Scenes of terror followed with over 100 people being washed away and drowned as they attempted to man the lifeboats.

One successful prospector who had about 300 ounces of gold around his waist and in the pockets of his coat was one of the first to jump for a lifeboat. Although he was warned by several other passengers to discard his heavy hoard to ensure that his jump was successful, he refused. Holding onto his gold the prospector took the risk, only to fall short by less than a metre. The man disappeared like a stone.

Only a handful of people from the "Gothenburg" survived. Some escaped, making it to a deserted island where they lived on bird's eggs until they were rescued.

The wreck of the "Gothenburg" was not discovered until 1971. It was found by a party of skin divers aboard a launch skippered by Bert Rubiolo, a canefarmer. The party claimed the salvage rights, and apparently recovered all the gold bullion.

The search for treasure laden wrecks.

During the early days of white settlement in the Torres Strait all sorts of items were recovered from old wrecks including Spanish coins, Milan blades, cannon and copper ingots.

There have also been many stories about wrecks that have foundered with untold wealth aboard.

Back in the 1920's there was much excitement in Townsville when a stranger arrived in town with a spectacular story. He claimed that a wrecked galleon filled with treasure was lying on a lonely beach on the eastern side of Cape York. This ship had apparently come to grief two centuries earlier whilst making its way to the Philippines from Peru, loaded with gold for the Royal Treasury of Spain.

Armed with old and yellowed charts made by one of the crew members who had originally escaped the wreck, the man convinced some of Townsville's residents to form a syndicate. With capital of £1,000 an expedition was organised to search for this long lost treasure ship. Months went by but not a single gold bar was found.

Although large numbers of crew members and passengers perished along with the vessels which were wrecked on the Reef, many escaped a watery grave. Some survived, however, in rather arduous circumstances as a Mrs. Fraser was once able to testify.

She was aboard the brig "Stirling Castle" when it smashed into what is now known as Swain Reef on May 21, 1836. Mrs. Fraser, the captain's wife, managed to reach land along with some other survivors. The others were apparently all murdered by aborigines but Mrs. Fraser lived in captivity for several years.

Her life was a misery, living and working like a slave. Sometimes the blacks compelled her to climb trees for wild honey, burning her with firesticks to force her higher.

Mrs. Fraser was eventually rescued by a convict who had lived with aborigines himself.

He took her to Brisbane where she boarded a ship for England, and ended up marrying the captain of this same vessel.

There are a good number of other documented cases of white women living with aborigines. In more than one case they were obviously shipwrecked as infants or children and had subsequently been reared by aborigines.

There were also many cases of convicts living with aborigines, although this was usually by choice since most had escaped. They learned the language of aborigines or islanders in the Torres Strait, adopted their customs, took part in headhunting expeditions and even indulged in cannibalism.

One man that adapted all too well to native life was a barbarous white man known simply as Wini. The belief is that he was a convict who had escaped from Norfolk Island. There have also been suggestions that he was a Frenchman.

Wini lived on Badu, an island in the Torres Strait. When he arrived on the island he did so with two others in a small open boat. Upon arriving the three men were immediately confronted by a crowd of hostile natives armed with knives and clubs.

Realising that his chances of survival were not too high, Wini decided there was only one way to save his own skin. Without further ado he slaughtered both his companions, beheaded them and then presented the heads to those natives he felt had most influence. His gory tactics worked. Wini was acclaimed as a great warrior and accepted into their society. He soon earned a deadly reputation.

Wini learned their language and then moved quickly to establish his position, picking fights and killing any native he saw as a threat. Before too long he was the most important person in the tribe.

Wini's reputation was fearsome. He murdered the crews of shipwrecked boats and looted their cargo. He also employed treacherous means to massacre a complete tribe on a nearby island and led headhunting expeditions to others.

Finally, a police schooner was despatched to take appropriate action against Wini and the savage islanders. It was immediately attacked but the police soon won the upper hand and Wini was shot dead.

1

2

Adventurers lured by Bêche-de-mer.

A very colourful part of the Great Barrier Reef's history is related to the Bêche-de-mer industry. Bêche-de-mer or sea cucumbers - which live in the shallow waters of a reef - have been considered a delicacy in the East for hundreds of years.

It is known that the Chinese and Malays fished the northern waters of Australia for Bêche-de-mer long before Australia was settled by Europeans but the first white man to put the industry on a commercial footing was James Aickin.

He started to collect Bêche-de-mer near Lady Elliot Island - the southern most island of the Great Barrier Reef - in 1804 and it was not long before many others were out to make their fortunes in the same way.

Once it was collected from the sea-bed, Bêche-de-mer was dried and smoked. It was then shipped to China where, in the 19th century, it fetched between £80 and £140 a ton. Since tons of Bêche-de-mer could be gathered on the reefs at low tide in those early days it was a lucrative enterprise.

Bêche-de-mer fishermen faced many dangers, however, in their quest for riches. The schooners and crew were often attacked and slaughtered by marauding aborigines.

Some of the crews aboard schooners were made up of South Sea islanders who had been kidnapped and then sold as slave labour for between £10 and £15 a head. The despicable practice of "black-birding" actually continued well into the 1870's.

Although some were forced to work on schooners most of the victims were destined to work in the canefields of south Queensland.

Bêche-de-mer divers did not have easy lives. Sometimes they were attacked by sharks and also Gropers, giant Cod that were often over two metres in length. Unlike sharks that would normally circle a victim before attacking, Gropers would make a single, sudden headlong attack.

Many a story abounds about an unwary Bêche-de-mer or pearling diver being trapped by a giant clam. In actual fact, such stories are no more than myths - there is no documented case of a diver's life being claimed in this way.

If you were once thrilled by such tales, do not be disappointed. There are plenty of other stories about the Great Barrier Reef awaiting you in the pages of this book and others that are both true and exciting.

1. Bêche-de-mer luggers moored at Cooktown, North Queensland, in 1906. (From an early postcard.)

2. Native divers prepare to dive for pearls on the Reef in 1914.

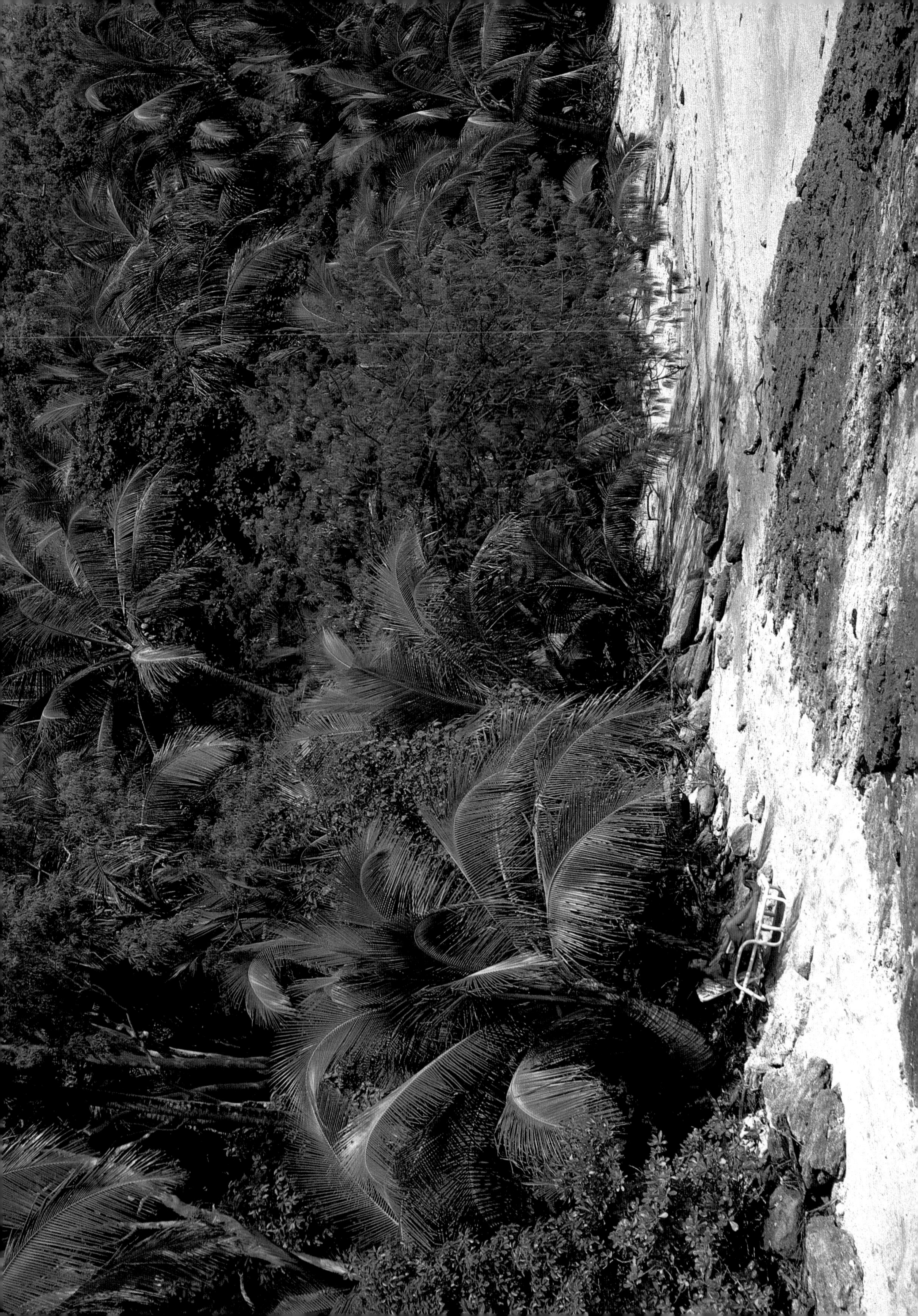

BEDARRA ISLAND

2

3

1. Casurina Beach on the western side of the island. Some of the small villas at Hideaway Resort overlook this beautiful beach.
2. These large boulders, called Gull Rocks, lie at one end of Melaleuca Bay.
3. Bedarra Island is covered with lush rainforest more dense than most other islands within the Great Barrier Reef region.
4. Noel Wood, the hermit who has lived on Bedarra for over 50 years, at the entrance to his home.

To enjoy total seclusion and wild but beautiful surroundings you may think that it is necessary to forgo other pleasures like fine cuisine and attentive service.

As a privileged few have discovered, however, this is not so if you stay on Bedarra, a small island that lies about 160 kilometres north of Townsville and 120 kilometres south of Cairns.

This green oasis is just six kilometres from Tully on the mainland and is very close to Dunk Island, another much larger resort island. The island is triangular in shape, with each of its three sides about one and a half kilometres long.

Bedarra belongs to what is known as the Family Islands, a small group of islands named originally by Captain James Cook in 1770.

In the summer the temperature on Bedarra ranges between 23°C and 31°C. In the winter, the temperature is somewhere between 17°C and 26°C.

The island has had a series of names in its history. The oldest, however, is undoubtedly "Biagurra", a name given to it by aborigines long ago.

4

1

The island received its present name of Bedarra from Edmund J. Banfield, the famous beachcomber and writer who lived on nearby Dunk Island from 1897 to 1923 (see Chapter Six).

Along with Dunk and Hinchinbrook, two resort islands in the same vicinity, Bedarra is the most tropical of the continental islands that you can stay on within the Great Barrier Reef region. All three are covered by rainforest more lush and dense than islands either to the south or north.

Despite its small size, Bedarra has a number of beautiful sandy beaches.

You can also visit an outer reef, 22 nautical miles away from Bedarra Island, with relative ease.

On the island there are two small, intimate and luxurious resorts - both operated by Australian Airlines - which cater for no more than 32 people each. Since no daytrippers are permitted on this private island, seclusion is assured.

These facts have made Bedarra both a very desirable and exclusive island. The select few that are fortunate enough to visit the island will not be disappointed.

Some of the people who have visited Bedarra in the past include The Duchess of York, Peter Allen, Dolly Parton, Tony Randall of "The Odd Couple", Art Garfunkel, and Sir James Ramsay, Governor of Queensland.

One person who has enjoyed Bedarra Island much longer than anybody else is Noel Wood, an artist. He discovered the charm and beauty of the island long before any tourist and has led a hermit-like existence on one corner of the island for over 50 years.

The beauty of the island has also appealed to film-makers. In 1969, scenes for the movie "Age of Consent", starring James Mason, were shot on Bedarra Island.

Biagurra, "place of perennial water".

As Captain James Cook headed north aboard the ship "Endeavour" in 1770 he encountered "a parcel of Small Islands" spread out over 14 kilometres which he subsequently named the Family Islands.

According to his journal dated June 8, 1770, "while we did this we saw on one of the nearest Islands a Number of the Natives collected together, who seem'd to look very attentively upon the ship; they were quite naked, and of a very Dark Colour, with short hair".

Whether they were on Bedarra or one of the other islands close by is not clear but we do know that aborigines lived or hunted on the Family Islands. All of the dozen islands, some quite tiny, have aboriginal names.

Bedarra is a corruption of the name given to it by aboriginals, Biagurra, meaning "place of perennial water". Bedarra, in fact, has six perennial springs of fresh-water.

Its first official name on marine charts was Richards Island. When Lieutenant Richards surveyed the area in 1886 aboard the "Paluma" he named all the individual islands within the Family Group after the different officers aboard his ship, including himself.

Early maps produced by the Lands Department have it marked as Allison Island, an incorrectly spelt version of the first leasee's name, Captain Henry Allason. Allason was a champion English rower who read "Confessions of a Beachcomber", one of the books written by E.J. Banfield on Dunk Island. This book prompted Allason to leave England to seek out his own tropical island.

The price of paradise at the turn of the century was not high. Allason paid the Queensland Lands Department the princely sum of £20 for both Bedarra and the neighbouring island of Timana.

Allason and his wife settled on the most western point of Bedarra Island, near the sandspit, in 1913. He soon became quite well-known in the Cardwell area for his long distance swims between the local islands.

A year later when World War I broke out Allason was called up by the British Army and went to fight the Kaiser in Europe. Unfortunately, he was gassed in France and spent the remainder of his life in Nice, attempting to regain his health.

During the 1920's Ivan Menzies, an actor who performed with the Gilbert and Sullivan Opera Company, sought out Allason in Nice. Menzies persuaded Allason to sell Bedarra Island and bought it for the not insignificant sum (in those days) of £500 sterling.

Menzies had a plan to build a home on the island for underprivileged English orphan boys which would provide them with a good start in life. His improbable scheme never came to fruition, nor did he ever visit the island himself.

Menzies sold his title in 1932 to a London syndicate headed by a chemist and keen big game hunter named Harris. He was the only member of the syndicate to ever step ashore on Bedarra.

Harris shipped out nine tons of provisions including trunks of trinkets and glass beads to trade with the local "cannibals" that he expected to encounter. Harris duly arrived on Bedarra but soon chose to live on Dunk Island, which was not quite as isolated.

A Modern Day Robinson Crusoe.

Countless people around the world have, at some time or another, dreamed of escaping the rat-race. Many of those have undoubtedly dreamed of living on some tropical island.

Of the millions of wishful candidates only a few, however, have fulfilled this dream. Noel Wood is one such man.

Except for a few brief interludes Noel Wood, an artist, has led a hermit-like existence on Bedarra for some 50 years. In the early 1930's, Noel lived in Adelaide making more than a reasonable living from painting portraits and landscapes.

In 1935 he picked up a copy of the "Queenslander Annual" which contained an article "It Can Be Done" which described the life of a man living on an island within the Whitsunday Group.

This inspired Noel so much that he decided "to get to a place with a warm climate where one could live for approximately nothing and solve one's problems in paint and colour". After holding a successful exhibition in 1935, Noel bought a Model T Ford and headed north to search for his own Garden of Eden.

His journey north was an adventure in itself. After reaching Brisbane he set off for

Noel Wood on his private beach at Doorila Bay.

Rockhampton. If the road is considered imperfect today, imagine the challenge that faced Noel in 1935. There were only dirt roads in those days and Noel was forced to negotiate more than one stream or river because there were so few bridges.

He eventually made it to Rockhampton, the first person that year to do so by road, only to discover that all the desirable islands in that area were not available. So Noel headed for Townsville. Here he learned about Jack Harris and Bedarra Island from Spencer Hopkins who had once owned Dunk Island.

Noel Wood subsequently visited Harris who was now living in a hut on Dunk Island. He agreed to show Noel a corner of Bedarra Island that he was prepared to sell. They sailed across to the island in rough seas with Nuggett Rivett, a character who spent 20 years on Dunk Island running an oyster lease, building boats and raising ducks.

The weather conditions meant that Noel only had half an hour on Bedarra Island in which to make a decision. The unspoiled beauty of the island quickly captivated Noel and he secured 15 acres on the spot for about £45. The agreement was signed on top of an old chest of Nestle's condensed milk cans - some of the provisions that Harris had shipped out from England but never used.

Noel returned in July, 1936, and soon began clearing land close to Doorila Bay for a homesite and garden. The going was tough but the colourful tropical garden and many acres that Noel now has under cultivation is proof of his hard labours.

"This theory," he says, "that an island environment is a good place in which to paint or to write is a fallacy. There is far too much work to be done. In other words you have to do all your own building, plumbing, and gardening, and look after your boats yourself. There's no-one to call on for help."

Noel is a vegetarian through necessity rather than persuasion. He lives from a multitude of trees and plants including Taro, a nutritious starch vegetable.

Avocados and cashews are on the menu, too, along with winged beans. Noel often plucks some of the mauve flowers off the bean plant for they are quite edible. He wastes nothing.

Noel's home is at the centre of his beautiful tropical garden. To a first-time visitor, it is almost invisible since most of the walls and roof are camouflaged by a profusion of vines and plants.

His main living quarters are simple yet impressive, especially when you remember that he built them himself. He lives mainly in one building some 13 metres long by seven metres. It is constructed mostly out of stone and teak salvaged long ago from a shipwreck, and has a thatched roof.

Noel's home has a stone fireplace most people would envy. His kitchen sink - which has water piped from a fresh spring - is located at one end of his home and looks directly out onto his garden. There are no panes of glass to come between Noel and Nature.

Although Noel has spent a disproportionate amount of his time merely surviving he has still managed to paint. Indeed, his paintings can be found in art galleries and private collections both in Australia and overseas.

Whilst Noel has spent most of the last five decades on Bedarra Island he has also spent a year in Hollywood working as an art director on films, several years in Ireland and one in Europe.

Noel has few luxuries at his island abode. One that he does enjoy occasionally is a "Bedarra Martini". For your interest, this is one part vodka, one part vermouth, with freshly squeezed lime juice and ice.

Surprisingly, Noel never feels lonely by himself. Once the daily work is finished outdoors, he loves to read and has an extensive library. Noel's only complaint is that bookworms have steadily worked their way through it, too.

Most of his books are about different countries of the world or are of a philosophical nature. Although the son of an Anglican parson, Noel is a Zen-Buddhist. In chatting to him, he never elaborated too much further on this point but there are some revealing words taped to the wall of Noel's cosy home. They read: "Love where you are, Love whom you are with, Love what you are doing".

Noel's life is certainly unconventional by most people's standards. Yet as a person he is immensely practical, disarming with his frankness and friendliness, is well informed and alert despite his isolation and contempt for newspapers, and he has a wonderful sense of humour.

In throwing away the trappings of the twentieth century, Noel seems to have found a happiness and contentment that few of his fellow creatures can claim.

Of course, Noel is someone who has

2

1. The luxuriant and colourful garden planted by Noel Wood decades ago now hides his house almost totally from view.

2. A canvas yet to be completed by Noel Wood. His paintings can be found in galleries and private collections around the world.

not only had dreams. He has also worked very hard to make them come true.

A rare nesting site for the Grey Swiftlet.

Bedarra Island has an amazing variety of plant and animal life.

It is one of the few recorded nesting places for the migratory Grey Swiftlet. This very fast flying bird is a smaller species of the better known Welcome Swallow.

The Grey Swiftlet is usually no longer than 115 millimetres. Its wings and most of its body is dark black-brown in colour. Its tail is both dark and forked. A band across its rump, however, is very pale grey and its underbody is grey-brown.

The future of the Grey Swiftlet on Bedarra seems assured, especially since it nests in overhangs of rock and caves along the more rugged and inaccessible coastline of the island.

Grey Swiftlets nest together by the hundreds. The space in the caves can be so limited that their nests are often joined together, bound by hardened saliva.

In a darkened cave, the Grey Swiftlet emits a sharp clicking sound. The echoes from these help the tiny bird to orientate itself. In the open air the Swiftlet utters a shrill cheep as it dives adeptly for insects.

Another migratory visitor between the months of September and March is the Torres Strait or Nutmeg Pigeon. These birds are pure white in colour with slate-black tail and flight feathers, and yellow bills. They feed on the fruits of rainforest trees.

At night you may also hear the "chopping" call of the Large-tailed Nightjar, a loud sound which this bird will happily repeat for hours on end.

As you walk along the track that bisects the island you will often encounter the bright red-headed Brush Turkey and dark brown Jungle Fowl or "Keerowan", as the aborigines refer to it. Even if you do not spot these birds you can usually hear them rustling around noisily in the undergrowth. Both birds build large mounds of fallen leaves in which they lay their eggs. The eggs then incubate from the heat of the packed, decomposing organic material surrounding them.

A delightful little bird that you will see on Bedarra and many other Great Barrier Reef islands is the Yellow-breasted Sunbird. This tiny bird has a long curved bill to feast on the nectar of flowers, an olive-green back and bright yellow underparts. "Sired by a sunbeam, born of a flower, gaiety its badge," is how E.J.Banfield described this small, colourful creature which builds nests in the jungle and often under the eaves of a resort building.

As you explore the island you will also come across many different trees and plants. These include large Pinda trees with fluted buttresses, tall Quandong trees with scarlet leaves, the *Eugenia cormiflora* which adorns its dark trunk with scores of white blossoms, Paperbark trees which produce yellow blossoms and a nectar which reduces many a bird to an inebriated condition, native orchids, vines and luxuriant ferns of many kinds.

A plant of interest that is sometimes found crawling over rocks on the island is the Derris creeper. Aborigines used to crush the leaves of this plant, known to them as "Pagarra" or "wild dynamite", and throw them on the surface of water to catch fish. A chemical in the leaves of the creeper would stun the fish, making them easy to catch and collect. Since the effect of the Derris leaves is only a temporary soporific to fish, it would in no way endanger the fishermen when eaten.

Sandy beaches and dense jungle.

One of the most enjoyable pastimes for visitors on Bedarra is exploring its foreshores. If you are staying at Hideaway Resort on the north-western corner of Bedarra you will find a beautiful sandy beach to the south of the jetty.

This beach is called Casurina Beach and is the one most preferred for swimming and sun-baking. Catamarans and windsurfers are also available here for guests.

The jetty, incidentally, is a good spot to do a bit of fishing. Tackle and bait are provided free and guests have caught sizeable Coral Trout, Cod and Sweetlip.

East of the jetty is another beach called Calophyllem Beach. This looks towards Dunk Island. This beach received its name from the big trees *Calophyllum inophyllum* which have large fig-like leaves and a white flower. Throughout Polynesia this is known as the Tamanu tree.

At the most northern of Calophyllem Beach you will encounter a small stretch of mangroves. These are very distinctive because of their long, tangled roots.

Scientists have established that mangroves are a vital source of nutrients in the beginning of a very important cycle in the marine ecosystem. Many small fish and crustaceans feed and breed around mangroves.

At the end of Calophyllem Beach you round a small rocky headland and enter Melaleuca Bay. A feature of this area are the huge boulders called Gull Rocks that lie just off-shore. This is an unspoiled and very beautiful spot, and ideal if you wish to have a picnic lunch one day during your visit.

It is not easy to walk any further than this, even at low tide. If you do so, you will also intrude on the private domain of Noel Wood, Bedarra's long-time resident. (Visitors to Bedarra are asked to respect his privacy and not arrive unannounced.)

The other walk that all guests should enjoy is the one that leads from Hideaway Resort to the Bedarra Bay Resort. This takes you from one end of the island to the other. It is perhaps one and a half kilometres long and takes you to a height some 100 metres above sea level but it is well worth doing, despite the effort required in places.

Minutes from the resort you are in another world, that of the rainforest. A canopy of foliage almost blocks out the sun completely and you are surrounded by dense green jungle. There is much to see - and smell, since the rainforest has its own distinctive odour - including ferns, palms and small creatures like goannas and Scrubfowl if you are observant.

Naturally, guests staying at the Bedarra Bay Resort can walk in the other direction to explore the northern side of the island. At the southern end of the island you can explore Hernandia Bay and Wedgerock Bay which faces south and is a little more rugged in its beauty.

Another way to see more of the island

1

is in a dinghy with an outboard motor. Both resorts have these and you are free to circumnavigate the island, weather permitting. This mode of transport allows you to see some of the spectacular cliffs on the south-western side of the island and visit places like Melaleuca Bay with ease.

Guests staying on Bedarra also have the opportunity of exploring a coral cay and its reef. To do so, you have two options.

You can be taken to nearby Dunk Island to board a large motor powered catamaran there. The trip aboard this fast vessel takes 50 minutes and the destination is Beaver Cay. Here you can snorkel or view coral and marine life from a glass bottom boat or semi-submersible craft.

If you are interested in fishing, there is a 42′ game-fishing boat available for charter.

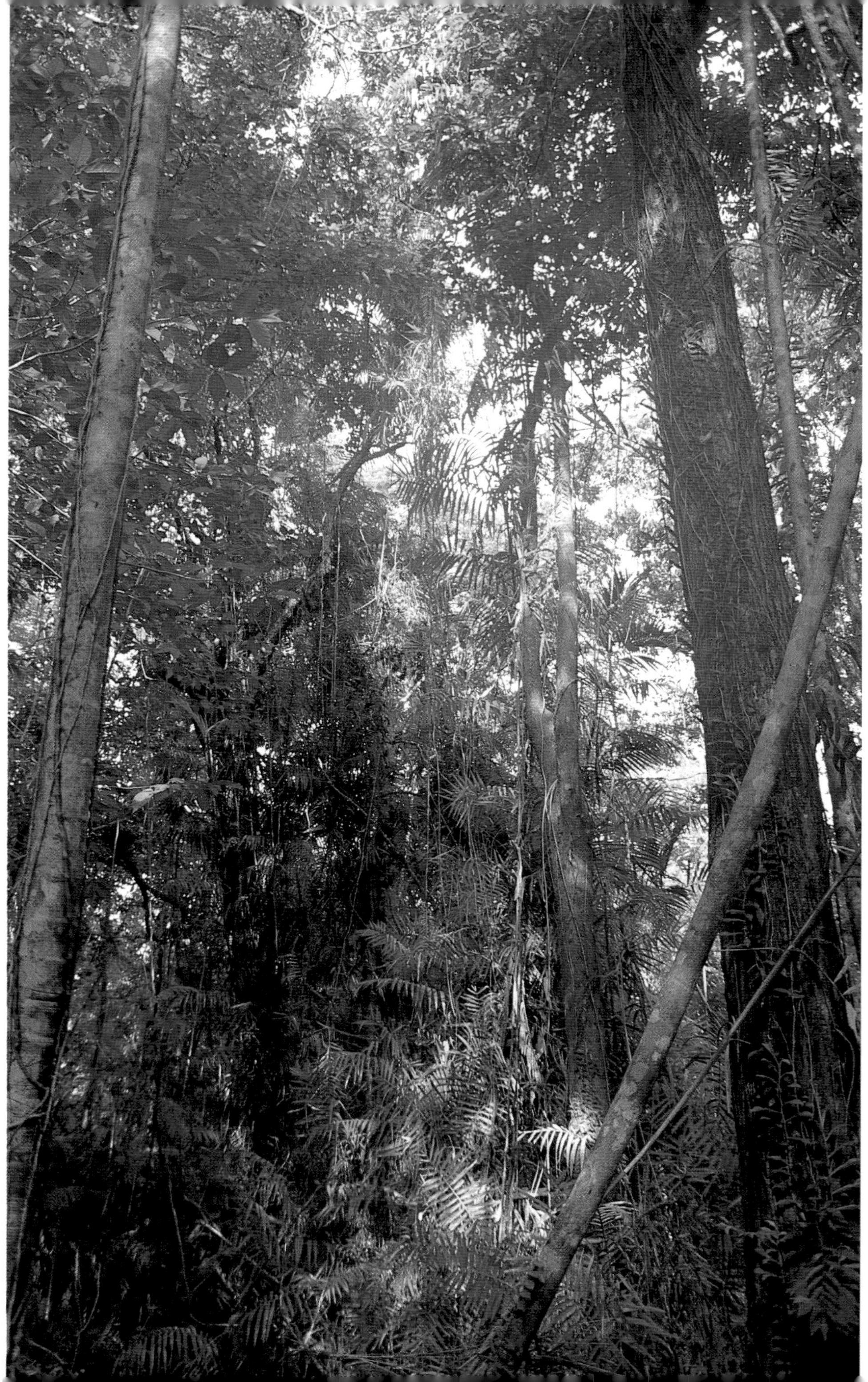
2

3

1. The island is one of the few known nesting sites for the Grey Swiftlet.

2. Light seeps through the canopy of lush rainforest on Bedarra Island.

3. Mangroves at the northern end of Calophyllem Beach.

1

2

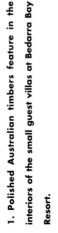

3

1. Polished Australian timbers feature in the interiors of the small guest villas at Bedarra Bay Resort.

2. Villas at Bedarra Bay Resort nestle in rainforest and have striking views.

3. A bird's-eye view of Bedarra Bay Resort.

Guests on Bedarra will often charter this boat and go first to Beaver Cay to snorkel, trolling for fish on the way (and on the return trip).

After visiting Beaver Cay the boat will then move on to Taylor Reef for bottom fishing and catches of fish like Red Emperor and Coral Trout.

Two small and exclusive resorts.

Bedarra Island actually has two resorts on it. Both are operated by a subsidiary of Australian Airlines and are of a very high standard. Each has its own style and mood but accommodates no more than 32 guests.

One is situated at the north-western corner of the island and is called Bedarra Hideaway. The second resort, Bedarra Bay, is at the other end of the island. The original Hideaway Resort was completely demolished and rebuilt in 1987, and the Bedarra Bay Resort was built and opened in the same year.

The Bedarra Bay Resort is situated on the site of an old homestead known as The Plantation. This graceful home, built for John Busst in 1940, had striking views to the north over Hernandia Beach and Noel Wood's Doorila Bay.

The mud-brick house had a long front verandah with green lawns running down to sandy Hernandia Beach, beautiful gardens and an orchid garden established by a later owner. The late Prime Minister Harold Holt and Dame Zara were regular visitors to the home while John Busst lived there.

In this idyllic area, sixteen small private villas now nestle into lush, tropical rainforest. They are built in weatherboard and painted green so they blend in with the surroundings. Each has a small garden around it.

The interiors are luxurious in an understated way. Polished Australian timbers have been used extensively in the interior of the open split-level villas. Sleeping quarters with an ensuite bathroom are on the mezzanine level, and a living area and private verandah are on the lower level. All the villas are air-conditioned and have ceiling fans, radios and even hair dryers.

The main lodge, which directly overlooks Hernandia Beach, houses a lounge, bar, restaurant and terrace alongside a freshwater swimming pool.

Hernandia Beach is sandy and with the small number of guests staying at the resort, it is never overcrowded. Hernandia Bay, which is also known as Bedarra Bay, is

4

5

4. **Beyond the beautifully landscaped gardens of the resort is Hernandia Beach. Both face Doorila Bay, the home of Noel Wood, visible in the background.**

5. **The resort's restaurant and pool area.**

a protected bay ideal for windsurfing or sailing catamarans.

You also have the option of wandering over to Wedgerock Bay to enjoy another beach which faces south. This is just a couple of minutes walk from the main resort complex.

This beautiful bay was one of the places where footage was shot for the movie "Age of Consent", starring James Mason. This movie was produced in 1969 and tells the story of Brad, an Australian painter who returns to Australia, disenchanted with life in New York.

Involved in the story is a rich spinster, a devious gold-digger and thief, a gin-soaked harridan and her sexy young grand-daughter Cora, played by Helen Mirren. Cora models for Brad, the lead character played by James Mason, and they eventually fall in love.

One of the pleasures of staying at either of the small resorts on Bedarra is the club-like feel that both have. With so few guests, it only seems natural to befriend your fellow visitors over a drink or two and become better acquainted.

A rather uncommon feature of both the Bedarra Bay and Hideaway resorts is the fact that they have an open bar. This simply means that all drinks are included within the tariff including the fine vintage wines, cocktails, liqueurs, ports and even Moet et Chandon champagne. There is no limit to what you can consume.

There is also no barman. You simply help yourself as if you were at home. A complete cocktail guide is provided for those who wish to experiment with new drinks, and most guests soon do.

Another pleasure to be enjoyed at either resort is the fine food. The menus change daily and the chefs at each resort take great pride in both presentation and pleasing your tastebuds. The menus at both resorts are always different and reflect the style of each chef.

Whereas most resorts offer a smorgasbord luncheon both resorts on Bedarra have special luncheon menus. Usually the dishes on these are small but tasty portions that will still enable you to enjoy the wonderful meal served in the evening.

The luncheon menu offered to guests at Bedarra Bay on one occasion was as follows. As an appetiser there was a choice of Prawn Ravioli with Sorrel Sauce or Chilled Pear and Vodka Soup.

Guests then had a choice of three

1

2

3

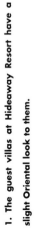

1. The guest villas at Hideaway Resort have a slight Oriental look to them.

2. The Shoji screen panels in the bedroom area slide back to reveal a miniature indoor garden and sunken bath.

3. Sandy Casurina Beach on the western side of the island is right on the doorstep of Hideaway Resort.

4. The entrance to Hideaway's stylish restaurant, bar and lounge.

dishes - Rock Oysters topped with Crabmeat, Cheese and Hollandaise Sauce; Shortcrust Pastry Tartlettes filled with Zucchini and Bacon on a Chive Cream Sauce; and Prime Eye Fillet sauteed in Sour Cream, Stroganoff Style.

Dessert was Orange Sorbet flavoured with Grand Marnier.

In the evening, the gastronomic delights continue. One menu offered guests Cream of Cauliflower Soup with Toasted Almond or a Light Melange of Local Avocados and Herbed Seafood as a starter.

There was then a choice of four main dishes - Sirloin Steak served with Onion Sauce; Fresh Fish Fillet topped with Scallop Sauce and served between crisp skins of Puff Pastry; Pork Fillet stuffed with Spinach, garlic sauteed and served with Mushroom Sauce; or Breasts of Chicken fried in Butter and Brandy Cream and Peppercorn Sauce. Dessert was Crême Caramel au Cointreau.

Guests at Bedarra Hideaway can expect a range of ever changing menus that are just as mouth-watering. One dinner menu offered guests Duck Salad served on a Parsleyed Buckwheat Blini or Cauliflower Soup with Smoked Cheese Croutons as the first course, Boned and Rolled Loin of Lamb filled with Proscuitto and Salami or Red Emperor Fillets topped with poached Oysters in a Sauterne Beurre Blanc as the main course, and Fresh Poached Peaches with a Rhubarb Sorbet and Raspberry Sauce for dessert.

At either resort there is a selection of about 15 good quality Australian red wines and around the same number of white wines to accompany your meal. All, of course, are included within the tariff.

Hideaway Resort at the north-western corner of the island also has sixteen villas and caters to exactly the same number of people as Bedarra Bay. The look and style, however, is a little different.

The villas at Hideaway have a slight Japanese touch and, according to the architect who designed both resorts, "a feeling of Gaugin in the colours".

They have high raked ceilings, walls painted in a very pale grey with black trim. There is black lacquered furniture, wooden floors, shoji screen panels in the bedroom which slide back to reveal an indoor garden, and a sunken bath in the bathroom. All have a queen-size and single bed, are air-conditioned and have ceiling fans.

4

Although the villas are screened by dense rainforest they are virtually metres away from the beachfront. Some overlook Casurina Beach, others sit next to the beach on the northern side of the sand spit looking out towards Timana Island.

There is a bar, restaurant and lounge in the main resort building which reflects the same subtle oriental theme that the villas have. The result is certainly stylish and sophisticated. There is also a very pleasant terrace overlooking the freshwater swimming pool where one can sip drinks, chat or read.

The resort is situated in beautiful, tropical gardens. During the new landscaping the colour purple was chosen to add brilliant splashes of colour amongst the verdant green undergrowth. Among the plants there are Cordylines, Bromeliads, Crotons, Hibiscus, Bougainvilleas, and sweet-smelling Jasmine. The result is a visual treat that you could never tire of.

Like Bedarra Bay, Hideaway has a floodlit tennis court as well for those who wish to work off the extra calories they may collect at meal-times.

Which resort you select is entirely up to you. Both are of an equally high standard and if you stay at one you can still easily explore the area where the other is located. Both offer a private, peaceful existence and either will satisfy any guest who seeks, appreciates and can afford the finer things in life.

Some guests choose to spend some of their holiday at Bedarra Bay and the rest at Hideaway.

Guests are free to lunch at either.

How to get to Bedarra Island.

To reach Bedarra Island you would normally fly from either Townsville or Cairns to nearby Dunk Island which has its own airstrip. Each of these flights are about 45 minutes in duration.

You would then transfer to a launch for a 30 minute boat ride to Bedarra Island. If you are travelling by road, you would drive to Mission Beach and take a water taxi or small hovercraft to Dunk Island and then transfer to Bedarra's launch.

The telephone number of Bedarra Hideaway Resort is (070) 688 168. Their telex and facsimile numbers are 46151 and (070) 688552 respectively.

The phone number for Bedarra Bay Resort is (070) 688 233. Their telex and facsimile numbers are 46150 and (070) 688215 respectively.

Reservations for both resorts, however, must be made through Australian Airlines or a travel agent. Bookings cannot be made direct with either resort on Bedarra.

For fifty years Noel Wood has lived in seclusion and happiness on this bewitching little island. If that is not recommendation enough, one only has to look at the pages of the Visitor's Book at either of the resorts.

You'll find past entries such as these. "If heaven is half as good as this I'm going to start mending my ways." "My fourth visit." "On the seventh day He created Bedarra." "On a scale of 10 Bedarra just has to be a 12."

BRAMPTON ISLAND

2

3

Brampton Island has a rather colourful history. Last century, convicts who escaped from a French penal colony in New Caledonia rested on the island before landing on the Australian mainland.

Pearling luggers also anchored here and during the early 1900's horses were bred on the island for the Indian Army.

Brampton is one of the islands within the Cumberland group which lies at the southern end of the Whitsundays. It is about 32 kilometres from the North Queensland port of Mackay, often called the "Sugar Capital of Australia".

Like some of the other islands in the Cumberland group it was named after a town in the Lake District of England. Other islands in the area include St. Bees, Keswick and Carlisle. The latter is joined to Brampton at low tide.

The island was classified as a National Park in 1936. It has lush rainforest in parts, eucalypt forests, a hilly terrain with a peak that reaches 230 metres above sea level, deserted bays with shimmering turquoise water and a large fringing reef which is good for snorkelling.

4

1. The clear blue waters of Oyster Bay - the inlet to the north of this is Dinghy Bay.

2. The grave of Captain John Williams, Master of the "Ching Tu", who was buried on Brampton Island in 1902.

3. Brampton's own train - it runs between the resort and the island's deep-water jetty which are about a kilometre apart.

4. A motor launch lies anchored in beautiful Oyster Bay.

1

Brampton also has a thriving population of animal and bird-life, and there are well maintained walking tracks to enable you to easily explore the island.

In summer the temperature on the island hovers between 22°C and 29°C and in winter it ranges between 13°C and 22°C.

A resort was established on Brampton as early as 1933. The island's resort is now owned and operated by Australian Airlines. Over the past four years they have spent $17 million totally up-grading and developing the resort.

Nevertheless, the atmosphere is relaxed, informal and less sophisticated than some of the other Great Barrier Reef resorts - a feature that repeatedly brings many people back to the island.

Once a stepping stone for escaped French convicts.

Archaeological evidence suggests that Brampton Island was once used by aborigines for foraging and hunting expeditions but never served as a permanent settlement.

A midden or mound of discarded shellfish and bones at Western Bay is evidence of their visits.

James Cook was responsible for naming the Cumberland group of islands, of which Brampton is one, after the Duke of Cumberland, brother of King George III, during his historic voyage north on the "Endeavour" in 1770.

The individual islands, however, were not named until 1879. The person who named them was Staff Commander Bedwell of the Royal Navy who was surveying the area at that time. He named Brampton and other islands in the group after towns in the Lake District of England.

Last century, before Thursday Island became established as a base for pearling luggers, these craft and Bêche-de-mer fishermen sailed through nearby Whitsunday Passage as they headed north after the cyclone season had ended.

Because Brampton Island offered a safe anchorage and had good camping sites and water, it became a favourite stop-over for them.

On one occasion Monty Wellesly, a well-known Bêche-de-mer fisherman, arrived at Brampton alone aboard his lugger "Puki" with an axe wound to his left shoulder and an open head wound inflicted by a club. He had been attacked by his native crew. Wellesly used a Winchester rifle to shoot seven of them before the remainder hurriedly retreated aboard "Puki's" dory.

Fortunately, there was another boat at Brampton when Wellesly arrived and he was subsequently taken to Mackay Hospital to recover.

In the late 1800's Brampton Island was also the final stepping stone to the mainland for the occasional group of convicts who had escaped from the French penal settlement of Ile Nou in New Caledonia. They had been banished to this distant French colony for crimes ranging from murder to counterfeiting.

When these convicts made their escape they braved a long and dangerous sea voyage in small open boats suffering both starvation and exposure in the hope of enjoying freedom in the sparsely populated British Colony.

Not all of the convicts were French. One man who escaped in 1890 was Tom Folden, an Englishman who later settled in the Mackay district. The story goes that he escaped from Ile Nou with four other men including a former naval officer who had misappropriated French Navy funds.

With provisions purchased from an American whaling ship and a small boat they sailed over 1,600 kilometres and then encountered the Great Barrier Reef. Here a strong current and waves drove them onto a reef, overturning their boat and throwing them into the sea.

Three of the men survived and they managed to right the overturned boat on the lee side of the reef. They then continued their journey without sails or oars. Using only planks to propel them they eventually landed on Carlisle Island and then Brampton where they found fresh water and shellfish.

During the 19th century the island provided a brief sanctuary for at least two other people. A Chinese man, George Thomasin, eloped from Sydney with Tamaela, a pretty Malay woman, aboard his lugger. Tamaela's husband, however, did not take kindly to the idea and he hotly pursued the lovers aboard his own lugger "Jefka".

The couple reached Brampton Island but Tamaela's husband found George's lugger, set it alight and began searching for them. George and Tamaela managed to escape in a dinghy, first to nearby St. Bees Island and then to the mainland.

Before the turn of the century, coconut palms were planted on Brampton Island by the Agricultural Department of the Queensland Government. Since they are now so much part of the landscape, it may come as a surprise to many to learn that the coconut is not indigenous to the Queensland coast. The coconuts planted on Brampton were actually imported from Indonesia. As the palms grew they were then used to stock other islands in the district.

The coconuts were first planted on the island to provide food and drink for shipwrecked sailors. The Queensland Government also planted sisal on Carlisle, Brampton's neighbouring island. Rope was once produced from sisal hemp.

In 1902, Captain John Williams was buried on Brampton Island. He was the Master of the "Ching Tu", a vessel which belonged to the Australian Oriental Line and traded between Sydney and Hong Kong.

Before he died of pneumonia Captain Williams expressed the wish of being buried on an island rather than at sea so his shipmates laid him to rest under a large fig tree on Brampton Island. They marked his grave with a marble headstone on the return voyage from Hong Kong and this can still be seen within the grounds of the island's resort.

Like so many islands in and around the Whitsundays, Brampton Island was originally settled as a pastoral property. The island was first leased from the Crown by William Vereker Binden in 1913 but he died just 12 months later.

Prior to that (in 1907) Joseph and Sarah Bussutin had moved to the area with their five children. Joseph suffered from malaria and doctors had advised him that an island climate could help his condition. At first, they settled on St. Bees Island, 18 kilometres from Brampton.

Channel Reef separates Brampton and Carlisle Islands.

In 1916 the Bassutins also took up the lease on Brampton that W.V. Binden had held until his death. The intention of the Bassutins was to breed Chinchilla rabbits on the island but the climate proved too harsh for this delicate species and they all perished.

In 1922, the Bassutins used Brampton Island (and Carlisle) to raise mounts for cavalry units of the Indian Army. The mechanisation of armies finally put an end to this venture. Some descendants of these horses, however, are still roaming wild on Carlisle Island.

Meanwhile, the Bassutins were also taking in paying guests at their homestead on St. Bees. These people were probably the first paying guests to stay on any of the Whitsunday Islands. One Christmas, one of Joseph Bassutin's sons took some guests across to Brampton. The fact that they loved its beaches and beauty so much helped persuade the Bassutins to transfer their growing tourist trade from St. Bees to Brampton.

In 1932, Arthur and "Pidge", the sons of Joseph Bassutin, started building a small resort on Brampton. The facilities were very primitive by today's standards but that didn't bother the visitors who were enchanted by the island. The first tourists arrived aboard the old ship "Canberra" which provided a passenger service along the eastern coast of Australia.

Each cabin had a name like "Anglers Abode", "Beauties Boudoir" and "Cobblers Corner". The Bassutins also named many of the island's bays although their choice of names for these were somewhat less colourful.

In 1933, one could travel by steamer from Sydney on three week's holiday - which included 11 days on Brampton Island - for just over £27 ($55).

In the same year, Brampton Island was the first Barrier Reef island to install a radio transmitter. Unfortunately, the resort lost their radio operator a couple of years later so carrier pigeons were used to carry messages between the island and mainland. These proved to be a highly efficient means of communication and they were used up until wartime.

For recreation the guests in the 1930's used to go reef fishing, turtle hunting (long before the days that they became a protected species), ray harpooning, shell collecting and swimming. Sometimes they were even taken to the Proserpine River over on the mainland where they could go crocodile shooting.

During World War II, the resort was closed. In 1941, Flight Lieutenant Macarthur arrived on Brampton to set up a camp to train Malays in the art of infiltrating Japanese lines. The camp was eventually set up on Carlisle Island for secrecy and because its more rugged terrain was a better training ground. When the war ended, Brampton's resort was re-opened but not before the guest accommodation was completely rebuilt.

A resort developed by "Captain Tom".

After the Bassutins retired in 1959 the island changed hands, and again in 1963 when the lease was purchased for £100,000 ($200,000) by Roylens.

This was a family company founded by Tom Maclean, often known simply as "Captain Tom".

Years before he purchased the lease of Brampton Island, Tom Maclean offered tourists the opportunity of seeing the Whitsunday Islands aboard "Shangri-La", a vessel that had once been the personal launch of General Macarthur.

He then bought a number of ex-navy Fairmile launches which had originally been deployed along the coast of New Guinea during World War II. Tom Maclean refitted them and pioneered cruising in the Whitsundays and on the Great Barrier Reef.

When Tom Maclean took over the management of the island he constructed a deep-water jetty and added a new dining room and kitchen. Meals had previously been served in a hall that was used for recreation.

After the meals were over, all the chairs and tables would be stacked away and everyone participated in the fun and games that followed. There were games like deck quoits, indoor bowls and also dancing - including waltzes, polkas, and Boston two-steps - to music from records or a pianola.

When the deep-water jetty was built in 1966 the only suitable location was quite some distance from the resort so Tom Maclean had a small railway line built between the two. A small diesel locomotive that had been used in a Lithgow coal mine was purchased and miniature passenger coaches and cargo trucks were built in Mackay. They are still in use today.

The first plane to service Brampton was a Grumman Mallard, a 12 passenger twin-engined amphibious flying boat operated by TAA who were eager to get into North Queensland's flourishing tourist industry. Local conditions made its use short-lived, however, and so an airstrip was built on the island. This was officially opened on March 21, 1965.

At that time the cost of accommodation on Brampton Island was £4 ($8) a day, the launch fare was £3 ($6) return and the airfare was £2/13/- ($5) each way.

A colourful character who worked on the island for over 20 years was Hazel Naylor. She was the official hostess who greeted and helped to entertain guests.

On Saturday nights, while the adults were dining, she would often take the children along to the jetty for the popular pastime of feeding the stingrays there. The party would be accompanied by Yvonne, a pet emu, two boxer dogs and Cooking Fat, the island's only cat.

When the children were not busily feeding the stingrays their eyes were often turned upwards since Hazel believed strongly in UFO's.

In 1966, Prince Charles visited the island. Hazel, who had not been informed of the impending visit, came up to His Highness and said: "Now I know the face, don't tell me, it will come to me!"

An embarrassed Tom Maclean whispered in her ear and told her that it was no less than Prince Charles. "Now I know," said Hazel. "I've seen you on a stamp."

The prince, who is not without a sense of humour, replied: "That's my mother. I haven't made it yet."

A couple who helped make the resort famous was Bob and Dolly Dyer who were well-known to most Australians in the 1960's.

1

2

They had a very popular quiz program on national television, "The BP Pick-a-Box", and one of the prizes offered was a holiday on Brampton Island. The island was a favourite of the Dyers and they actually had a villa on it for many years.

During a Royal Visit to Australia in 1970, Tom Maclean received an M.B.E. from Queen Elizabeth aboard the "Britannia" in Brisbane, for his services to tourism.

As the years passed by, Tom Maclean eventually realised that a family concern would find it very difficult to compete with the resorts operated by large companies. So in April, 1985, he reluctantly sold the Brampton Island resort to TAA, now Australian Airlines. Despite the fact that he is well past retirement age, Tom Maclean is still enthusiastically involved in Roylen Cruises.

Over 11 kilometres of walking tracks.

Brampton is an easy and wonderful island to explore by foot. There are good tracks and you constantly round bends to discover something new and beautiful.

Many species of birds inhabit or visit the island and the terrain and vegetation is never constant.

On the eastern side of the island there are open areas of grassland. On the edge of these grassland areas are gullies where tall Hoop pines grow.

On the sheltered and often steep slopes of Brampton Island you will find forests of eucalypts including Moreton Bay Ash, Ironbarks and Bloodwood as well as other trees and shrubs such as Cocky Apple, Maiden's Blush and Cupania.

Eucalypt blossoms are a food source for Honeyeaters, Rainbow Lorikeets as well as the fruit bats which reside near Turtle Bay.

You will also come across dense, lush rainforest with vines, ferns and colourful butterflies in the more protected valleys and gullies where the soil is damper.

On walks there is a variety of animal life to be seen, too - such as grey kangaroos, goannas, skinks and harmless green tree snakes - if you tread quietly and look carefully.

There is a single walking track that will take you right around Brampton Island. Three tracks branch off this one to take you to other places of beauty and interest.

The resort lies at the northern tip of Brampton Island. If you decide to head off in a clockwise fashion around the island or wish

1. The "Roylen Star" anchored off the resort's main beach in 1957.

2. Tom Maclean of Roylens pioneered cruising in the Whitsundays and operated the resort on Brampton Island for over 20 years.

1

2

3

1. In rainforest near the top of Brampton Peak a spider builds an intricate web.

2. The red and yellow flower of the Red Head Cotton bush.

3. Oak Bay and Turtle Bay (in the background). Both are less than half an hour's walk from the resort.

to get to the top of Brampton Peak, walk to the end of the resort's golf course but not quite as far as the airstrip. Here you will find the beginning of the main trail.

Within minutes of starting out on the main walking trail you will reach a branch which forks right to Brampton Peak. The round trip to the peak and back will take you about two hours. The track at times is reasonably steep in places but the effort is well rewarded. The panoramic views at certain vantage points are spectacular.

As you get nearer to the top of Brampton Peak you will walk through dense rainforest dotted with Umbrella trees and countless Maidenhair ferns. You should also see many butterflies in the summer and the odd Scrubfowl.

The view from the look-out near the top of Brampton Peak is almost beyond words. At the look-out the ground plummets away in front of you and far below you can see the resort as well as the narrow channel that separates Brampton from Carlisle Island. With good eyesight you can even make out people snorkelling in the channel and walking along the beautiful beach that the resort enjoys.

On Carlisle Island you get a clear view of the steep forested slopes of Skiddaw Peak which is another 150 metres higher than Brampton Peak. This peak is apparently the remnant magma plug of the volcano which originally created the twin islands.

In that era, some 10,000 years ago, it would have been possible to walk between the mainland and what is now Brampton Island for the sea then was significantly lower. The fringing reefs around both Brampton and Carlisle Islands have developed within the last 5,000 years.

From Brampton Peak, which is 230 metres high, you are given a bird's-eye view of the brilliant turquoise waters and fringing reefs of these islands. To the west you can see the mainland on the horizon and to the east you can see other uninhabited islands within the Cumberland group.

If you have not taken the fork to Brampton Peak but have stayed on the main track your first destination will be Turtle Bay. This is just a kilometre or two from the resort and has a lovely sandy beach. There is a barbeque here as well for those who want to enjoy lunch away from it all.

Further on you will encounter a fork to the left which will take you to Oak Bay,

4

5

6

4. Pretty Oyster Bay is located in the south-eastern corner of Brampton Island.

5. The brightly coloured berries of the Pittosporum tree.

6. Sulphur-crested Cockatoos are a common sight on the wooded slopes above Dinghy Bay and Oyster Bay.

fringed by Casuarina trees, and Echo Point. The beach at Oak Bay is rocky and Echo Point is a small, exposed headland on the most westerly side of the island. Echo Point is, in fact, situated on a small peninsular. The walk to Echo Point and back to the resort would take you about two hours.

A third fork about 200 metres on from the one leading to Echo Point takes you down to Dinghy Bay. From the main track this takes no more than five minutes to reach.

If you are still on the main island circuit the track starts to climb along wooded slopes which occasionally afford you picturesque views of Relief Point, the south-western tip of Brampton, as well as Dinghy Bay and Oyster Bay which lie side by side.

As you walk along the main trail in this area you are likely to see large flocks of wild Cockatoos. You will also find that the very distinctive Black-boy plant is common on the slopes which the path traverses here.

You will eventually reach a vantage point on a ridge high above Oyster Bay which gives you breath-taking views to the east, west and south. It is also the half way point on the island circuit.

The view looking west over Dinghy Bay and Oyster Bay is idyllic and would be worthy of any post-card. Yachts often moor in the shallow waters of either of the bays as well as craft with keen fishermen aboard.

The beaches at Dinghy and Oyster Bay are secluded, beautiful and sandy. Unfortunately, they are virtually impossible to reach except by boat - although you can reach one small beach within Dinghy Bay (but not the main one) by taking a short diversion off the track that leads to Echo Point.

To the south one looks towards a grassy headland of considerable size. In all truth, however, there is nothing of special interest in this direction. Being exposed to southerly winds the landscape tends to be somewhat sparse in vegetation.

To the west you overlook Western Bay and Clump Point, an area where mangroves thrive. The path winds down towards this Point but not before it passes a long sandy beach. At the end of this beach there is another barbeque site for those who would like to spend lunch at this end of the island.

At this point the track heads inland and you do not emerge from dense forest until close to the deepwater jetty about a kilometre from the resort. The time it will take you to

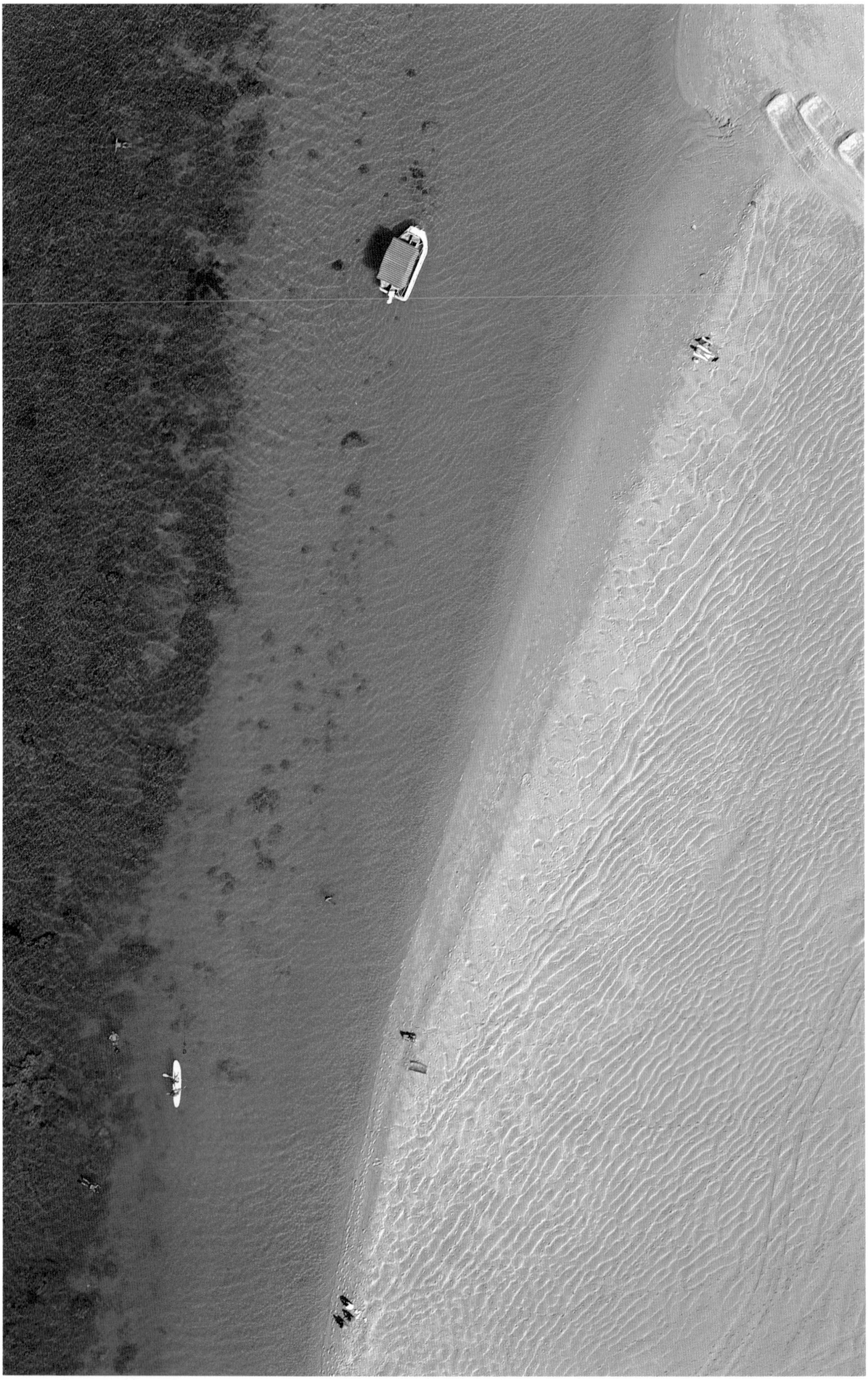

1

complete the circuit around the island without stopping too long anywhere along the way will be about two and a half hours.

A coral reef between Brampton and Carlisle Islands.

At low tide it is also possible to explore Carlisle Island because the shallow channel between this island and Brampton is exposed in parts. There are no trails, however, on Carlisle Island and the terrain is rough. The easiest walking is along the foreshores of Carlisle.

The channel between the two islands is a place that many people spend hours exploring. There is a coral reef here and it is excellent for snorkelling and reef-walking at low tide. There are both hard and colourful soft corals to be found as well as many species of fish common to the Great Barrier Reef.

The channel is undoubtedly the most accessible place for snorkelling. Other good places to snorkel are Oyster and Dinghy Bays on the eastern side of Brampton Island but these delightful spots can only really be reached by boat.

If you are a diver you will find plenty to explore around Brampton Island and at an outer reef. If you wish to learn to dive this can be arranged.

Each week there are usually three cruises to an outer reef aboard a large motor powered catamaran. The destination is Credlin Reef where there is a permanent pontoon. This is a wonderful place to go diving and snorkelling. You can also travel inside a semi-submersible craft and see the wonders of the Great Barrier Reef without getting your feet wet.

Another way to appreciate the scope and beauty of the Reef is from the air. Seair Pacific have regular seaplane flights from Brampton Island to Bushy Atoll, about 80 kilometres from the island. This three hour excursion enables you to explore the Atoll above and below water for two hours.

This excursion cannot be too highly recommended. Since the seaplanes are not large only a small group of people can visit the Atoll each time, and the Seair Pacific pilots are great guides who explain and inform you about different aspects of the Reef. Scenic flights over the Whitsunday Islands are available, too.

Three times a week there is a boat cruise that takes you through the beautiful Whitsundays and gives you a chance to land at Hamilton Island (see Chapter 10) for about two hours.

You can also go on half day fishing trips twice a week. These are around Brampton, Carlisle and Pelican Islands and give you the chance to catch fish like Sweetlip, Red Emperor, Red Cod, and Parrot Fish. On your return you will find the chef only too willing to cook your catch for dinner.

Apart from all the snorkelling, diving and fishing you will probably just like to swim and laze in the sun, too. What you will find for this is a lovely sandy beach on the doorstep of the resort itself. The water does, however, recede a considerable distance at low tide but the resort has both a salt-water and fresh-water pool for those who like to swim at any time.

The sandy flats are also very pleasant to roam at low tide and sometimes you can even walk across to Pelican Island, a tiny island off Brampton.

The sandy flats provide entertainment for guests, too. A competition is often held to see how far any golfing guests can hit a golf ball. The record is 310 metres.

A relaxed, friendly resort.

The resort on Brampton Island provides accommodation for 260 guests. About 95% of the guests are Australians and the remainder are from overseas. Brampton is popular for honeymooners, sometimes accounting for 30% of the guests, but families would account for more of the resort's accommodation than couples.

Regardless of these numbers and figures, anyone could visit Brampton Island and enjoy themselves immensely. Guests mingle happily together and there is a very friendly, relaxed atmosphere that is not always found to quite the same degree on all of the islands.

Millions of dollars has been spent recently in up-grading and building new suites for guests. There is now only one grade of accommodation and all suites are known as Blue Lagoon Units.

Some look directly over the main or eastern beach, others are built in a delightful garden setting near the golf course and overlook Carlisle Island.

All suites have private bathrooms, fridges, and radios. They are air-conditioned and have ceiling fans, too.

The tariff for accommodation includes breakfast, lunch and dinner. Activities guests can enjoy without extra charge include windsurfing, catamarans, surf skis, water

2

1. A spectacular bird's-eye view of snorkellers viewing coral in the channel between Brampton and Carlisle Islands.

2. Colourful Staghorn coral exposed at low tide in Channel Reef.

1

2

3

1. **Blue Lagoon Units at Brampton's resort. All accommodation is of the same standard.**

2. **A tame Emu wanders amongst guests outside the resort's Coffee Shop.**

3. **The resort's lounge, bar and restaurant at sunset.**

4. **A couple relax on the sandy spit at the very northern tip of the island. The small island in the background is Pelican Island which is just a few hundred metres off-shore from the resort.**

trikes, golf (the resort's course has nine holes), tennis (there are three courts, two with lights for night-time playing), archery, carpet bowls, volleyball, and cricket. Coral viewing in glass bottom boats and snorkelling gear is included as well.

The only activities which are extra are water-skiing, water tobogganing, pool and billiards, the fishing trips and cruises.

The meals served at the resort are excellent. At breakfast and lunch you help yourself to a wonderful selection of both cold and hot food and the meals in the evening are a la carte.

The evening menu changes daily. You would normally be offered a soup, an entree and then a choice of three main dishes and desserts.

Here is the menu that guests enjoyed on one occasion. Cream of Pumpkin Soup followed by Scallops Mornay as an entree. Then a choice of Coral Trout Bowen, grilled and topped with a Mango and Sherry Sauce; Chicken Indienne, Boneless Chicken stuffed and baked with a Mild Curry Filling; and Fillet Steak Dianne, Prime Beef accompanied by a Garlic Brandy Sauce.

Guests could then indulge in either Peach and Passionfruit Pie or assorted ice-creams, a cheese board, coffee and dinner mints.

On Saturday nights there is a towering seafood smorgasbord - and the tables are almost buckling under the piles of Moreton Bay Bugs, Mud Crabs and huge Prawns. About once every fortnight there is also a Carvery night and an evening when there is a large smorgasbord of Asian food.

The restaurant's wine list features a small but good selection of Australian reds and whites. There are also a number of local champagnes and several imported French champagnes.

Before and after the evening meal there is usually entertainment of some kind. Pre-dinner drinks in the Entertainment Lounge is usually accompanied by a little light music and from 9:30 p.m. there can be anything from a "Gypsy Mediterranean" or "Rock 'n'Roll" musical night to a fancy dress competition or country dancing. You can then expend more energy if you wish at the Disco in the Late Night Bar.

If you feel thirsty or hungry between mealtimes there is a Coffee Shop at the resort which sells everything from milk-shakes to sandwiches, pies and cakes.

4

The resort also has a boutique that sells a very good range of swimwear and casual clothes (especially for women), toiletries, souvenirs, film, magazines, newspapers, paperbacks, postcards and stamps. There is a daily postal service between the island and the mainland, and a Westpac Agency for withdrawals and deposits.

Although there are no phones in the rooms of guests, there are pay-phones, telex and fax facilities should you need them. Guests may also be reassured by the fact that there are two registered nursing sisters normally on the staff of the resort.

Parents will be pleased to learn that there is a program of special activities for children during school holiday periods. These include nature walks, treasure hunts, costume making, cricket and other games.

The children even have dinner together and watch videos while their parents relax alone. Outside of school holiday times, baby-sitting facilities are available for a reasonable hourly charge.

How to get to Brampton Island.

No camping is permitted on Brampton Island but boats and yachts are free to visit the island. Yachtsmen are welcome to visit and dine at the resort. There is no mooring charge.

Private aircraft may also land at Brampton without charge. There is sheltered parking and a fuelling facility for visiting aircraft.

If you wish to contact the resort their address is simply Brampton Island, via Mackay, Queensland, 4740. Their phone and facsimile numbers are (079) 514499 and (079) 391744.

To get to Brampton Island you may either fly or travel by boat from Mackay. The flight time between Mackay and Brampton is not much more than 10 minutes aboard a Twin Otter. The boat trip aboard the "Spirit of Roylen" or "Sunbird" takes 40 minutes.

In his autobiography Tom Maclean claims that the Cumberland and Whitsunday Islands are "more attractive to man than any other in the world" because of their natural beauty and proximity to the Great Barrier Reef. It is certainly true that Brampton is one of the prettiest islands within the whole Great Barrier Reef region.

In past decades the Bassutins and Tom Maclean did their utmost to ensure that Brampton was also one of the most relaxing and friendly to visit. Visitors today will be pleased to know that the tradition of hospitality they established on "The Coconut Isle" has not disappeared.

DAYDREAM ISLAND

2

3

1. Sunlover's Beach, at the north-western corner of Daydream Island. Clear water and healthy outcrops of coral off-shore ensure excellent snorkelling.

2. The main jetty, a pleasant place to daydream as the sun slips behind the mainland.

3. Daydream before its resort was closed for redevelopment.

4. A legacy left by Bernard Elsey, a former owner of the island, is a rare collection of man-sized wood carvings. Originally from the Philippines, each one was carved from a single tree.

1

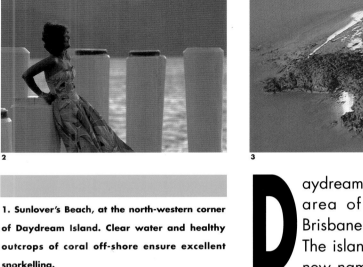

Daydream Island is a small island within the Whitsundays, an area of great beauty about 900 kilometres north of Brisbane.

The island's original name was West Molle - it was given a new name in the 1930's by Paddy Lee Murray who set out from Sydney on a world cruise and got only as far as the Whitsundays. He fell in love with West Molle Island, purchased it and renamed it after his yacht "Daydream".

The island is just over one kilometre long, half a kilometre wide and covers an area of 27 acres. Although it is not large, Daydream has a number of beautiful natural features, including three beaches - one fringed by outcrops of coral and colourful fish life.

There is also a small but dense jungle of tropical vegetation inhabited by Cockatoos, colourful Lorikeets and tiny Sunbirds - Australia's hummingbirds.

Daydream is the closest island to Shute Harbour - this is only five kilometres away - so it happens to be a popular destination for daytrippers as well as guests.

Both will soon enjoy new facilities. A new resort of international

4

1

1. The cover of an old brochure advertising Daydream Island.

2. The yacht "Daydream" after which the island is named. Photographed around 1935.

3. Paddy Murray (on the right), owner of the yacht "Daydream", and the author Henry G. Lamond hamming it up for the camera.

4. Passengers from the S.S. "Katoomba" visit Daydream Island, circa 1935.

5. The original reception lounge on the island.

standard will open on the northern tip of Daydream at the end of 1990. New facilities for daytrippers will also be available at the southern end of the island.

Once visited by aborigines.

A tribe of aborigines once lived within the Whitsunday group of islands. Henry Lamond, who owned the island up until 1933, made the acquaintance of Percy, one of the last aborigines to live in the area.

Percy told Henry Lamond that long before Europeans arrived, the tribe used to go from island to island in search of food.

These aborigines - who had the most fearsome reputation - moved between the different islands using bark canoes. They visited Daydream Island "for the raiding of nests and the countless thousands of Torres Strait pigeons during the summer months". These birds congregated on the island in large flocks, apparently attracted by the wild figs growing on it.

The aborigines also captured turtles in nearby Long Island Sound.

Daydream, once known as West Molle Island, was one of six Whitsunday islands owned by Henry Lamond. He was a well-known author who left outback Queensland to settle in the Whitsundays.

His son Bill, who spent his childhood on South Molle between 1927 and 1937, remembers visiting Daydream with his father. They shot pigeons on the island when food supplies were limited, especially during the Depression years.

Henry Lamond owned Daydream - or West Molle as it was known as then - up until 1933. He sold it to Paddy Lee Murray, a retired major.

Paddy had left Sydney aboard a yacht - accompanied by his wife Connie, a deckhand called Chilla and an Airedale dog named Toby - intending to cruise around the world.

The Murrays, however, liked the Whitsundays so much that they persuaded Henry Lamond to sell them West Molle Island. They bought it for £200 ($400) - paying a deposit of £100 and agreeing to pay off the balance at the rate of ten shillings ($1) a week.

Having bought the island the Murrays renamed it after their yacht "Daydream". A year later they went into partnership with another couple, and built a small resort.

Back in the 1930's the accommodation they provided for guests was simple. There were a number of small shacks built of timber with galvanised iron walls and roofs. The shacks had iron shutters in place of windows and the floors were made from crushed coral.

The dining room was built in the same fashion but was large enough to house one long table with fixed benches and a few smaller tables. Basic as these facilities may sound by today's standards, they were considered palatial at the time.

The first groups of guests arrived on cruise ships like the "Canberra", Ormiston", "Manundah" and "Kanimbla" which used to anchor off-shore for a day or two. There was no wharf or jetty in those days. Crew rowed the guests close to shore in longboats and the passengers then waded to the beach.

Just after the war guests also arrived by seaplanes or flying boats, as they were known as in those days.

The first guests paid £1 ($2) a day to stay on Daydream. This was for full board. Drinking water, milk, cream and home-made butter came from South Molle Island.

The island has had a number of different owners since those early times. In 1941, it was bought by Captain "Skip" Moody for £2,000 ($4,000). "Skip" Moody was a famous barn-storming pilot who once had the nerve to fly a Moth, nick-named "Puss in the Boots", under Brisbane's Victoria Bridge.

Someone who knew Daydream very well in the 1940's was Annie Lewis, a cook who worked for three different owners of the island. She lived in a cottage where the Airlie Beach Hotel now stands and commuted to the island by a motor powered dinghy.

If the Molle Channel was too rough to cross, Annie would simply hug the coastline and then light a fire on the mainland beach opposite to Daydream. This would be a signal for someone to go across to her by launch and tow her to the island.

During World War II, the resort on Daydream was closed but there was a caretaker on the island. On one occasion, when fuel was presumably in very short supply, Annie actually rowed all the way from Airlie Beach to Daydream to deliver stores to the caretaker. Lewis Street at Airlie Beach is named after this hardy woman.

In 1947 Daydream was acquired by Reg Ansett, around the same time that he bought Hayman Island. To help establish his new resort there he actually closed Daydream's resort in 1953. He then dismantled the buildings and moved all

2

3

4

5

1

2

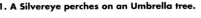

1. A Silvereye perches on an Umbrella tree.

2. A short distance from the island's resort is a small pocket of rainforest where ferns and vines flourish under a canopy of tall trees.

3

4

3. One of the wild Sulphur-crested Cockatoos that reside on the island.

4. A Yellow-breasted Sunbird sips nectar from the flowers of an Umbrella tree.

equipment from Daydream to Hayman.

The resort was re-established in 1967 by Gold Coast entrepreneur Bernard Elsey. Just two years later Cyclone Ada virtually flattened the entire resort but it was rebuilt within just 12 months.

Daydream was subsequently bought by Queensland businessman Jim Kennedy but is now owned by the Pivot Group and Jennings Industries who are spending over $70 million to build a new resort on the island.

A small tropical jungle.

Since Daydream is a small island it is relatively easy to explore by foot. A most enjoyable walk is the track which leads from the south of the island to Sunlover's Beach at the north-western side of the island.

The walk takes little more than 15 minutes but the track winds through a small tropical jungle where Cockatoos shriek and colourful butterflies flitter through dense, green undergrowth.

When you reach Sunlover's Beach you will find a small coral beach which is both beautiful and secluded. Indeed, most visitors would agree that this is the prettiest place on the island. Sunlover's Beach is a wonderful place to have a picnic, to sunbake and snorkel. There are some excellent outcrops of coral directly off the beach, the water is usually extremely clear and there are dozens of multi-coloured fish to be seen.

You can actually snorkel for about 100 metres along the shore-line from Sunlover's Beach until you reach a small point at the northern end of the island. Around this point are some coral rock pools which are worth exploring as well.

This area is also a place favoured by those who like to try their hand at fishing from one of the dinghies you may hire. Good catches are made off the jetties, too. The fish most commonly caught are Coral Trout, Cod, Red Throated Sweetlip and Parrot fish.

A track from Sunlover's Beach will take you to the very northern end of Daydream Island where the new resort is being built. It is aptly named Northpoint and there is another coral beach here. The best time to swim here is at high tide - at low tide the water is very shallow.

Around Northpoint you will often see a Sea Eagle hovering high in the sky, keeping an eye out for prey. A pair of these powerful looking sea-birds nest on the northern end of the island each year.

The eastern side of the island is somewhat bare and rocky but there are still some things of interest to be seen. Along the shore-line you will come across large numbers of cuttle fish bones and more than one visitor has found the odd oyster to enjoy. You will enjoy marvellous views of North and South Molle Islands and a constant parade of yachts sailing by.

One yacht that you may see from time to time is Gretel. Launched in 1962, this famous 12 metre sloop was the first Australian Challenger to actually win a race in the America's Cup. Now Gretel cruises the Whitsundays - and guests staying on Daydream Island can spend a day aboard her. This cruise includes lunch and a two or three hour stop in the Langford Reef area so you can go snorkelling.

5

Boat trips to the Reef and other islands.

There are a number of other boat trips that guests staying on Daydream can enjoy. Another takes you to Hamilton Island, another resort island within the Whitsundays (described in Chapter 10).

There is also a half day cruise to South Molle Island, the closest island to Daydream. This cruise gives you two and a half hours to explore South Molle.

A third cruise which is well worth considering is to Hook Island and Nara Inlet. This trip allows you to visit the famous Underwater Observatory at Hook Island where you can see a large variety of coral and tropical marine life in its natural environment. Nara Inlet is a very beautiful fjord-like inlet on the western side of Hook Island.

6

7

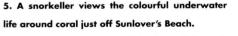

5. A snorkeller views the colourful underwater life around coral just off Sunlover's Beach.

6. Sunlover's Beach, a small but beautiful beach just a minute or two's walk from the Daydream's new resort.

7. Whitehaven Beach on the eastern side of uninhabited Whitsunday Island, a magnificent destination about 15 minutes away by a Seair Pacific seaplane.

The other cruise which will be of great interest is one aboard a large high speed motor catamaran that takes you to Hardy Reef which has 7,500 acres of coral. Here you have three hours to snorkel, dive or view the Reef from a Coral Sub.

Another way to see the Reef is by seaplane. The flights give you an amazing bird's-eye view of the Reef and you also touch down to view the Reef's magical underwater world.

The seaplane flights are offered by Seair Pacific and you can fly to either Bait or Hardy Reef. At Bait Reef you can view coral from a semi-submersible craft and snorkel. One and a half hours is spent at Bait Reef.

At Hardy Reef you can snorkel, see coral from a glass bottom boat and go reefwalking. A full two hours is spent out at Hardy Reef.

If you would like to explore the underwater world of the Reef by diving, contact the Dive Shop on Daydream Island. If you have never dived before, you can have an introductory dive or do a complete PADI Open Water Diver Course.

The introductory dive includes tuition, all gear and one dive accompanied by an instructor. The dive site is the fringing reef near Sunlover's Beach.

The week long PADI course includes all tuition, gear, boat trips and four dives - two on some of the beautiful fringing reefs found around many of the Whitsunday islands and two on an outer reef.

Experienced scuba divers have a choice of several dive sites around Daydream itself - Sunlover's Beach, Northpoint and a wreck lying off-shore from the old jetty.

For the best dives, however, they board "The Whitsunday Diver", a superbly equipped 46′ boat which operates out of Shute Harbour. This picks up divers from Daydream and heads off to Manta Ray Bay, a superb diving site on the northern side of Hook Island (see Chapter 14), or one of the outer reefs (usually Bait Reef).

A new resort at the northern tip of Daydream.

Around Christmas, 1990, a new resort will open at the northern tip of Daydream Island. Over $70 million is currently being spent on the new facilities.

These include 301 guest rooms and suites in beautifully landscaped gardens with a lagoon, waterfalls and large swimming pool. There will also be several bars, two restaurants, convention centre, a health club, library and music room, games room and child-minding centre.

A small marina alongside the resort is being constructed as well to allow people on boats who are cruising in the Whitsundays to visit Daydream Island.

An elevated board-walk on the eastern side of the island, half a kilometre long, will link the resort area to the southern end of the island.

Here there will be a tavern, bistro, bakery, shops, tennis courts and pool for people who wish to visit the island for a day from Shute Harbour and other islands. Guests staying at the resort at the northern end will also have the use of these facilities.

Three grades of accommodation will be available at the main resort. All

2

accommodation, however, will be air-conditioned, and have private balconies, bathrooms with baths and showers, mini-bars, and colour TV's.

There will be 286 rooms of 3-star standard, ideal for couples and families (many units will have interconnecting doors for family use). These rooms will be set in lush, landscaped gardens and most will overlook a large pool.

A lot of care has gone into the planning of the resort. Several of these rooms have even been specially designed for people who are physically disabled.

There will also be 13 suites of slightly larger size with expansive views over Dangerous Passage, the stretch of water between Daydream and South Molle Island.

In addition, there will be two luxury villas - each with three bedrooms and their own lounge, dining room and kitchen.

The island's new resort will have two restaurants - one large and one smaller, more intimate restaurant. Both will have terraces so guests can dine indoors or outdoors.

The smaller a la carte restaurant will be on the third level of the new resort complex - offering guests magnificent views towards nearby North Molle Island.

Lively night-time entertainment has always been a feature of Daydream - and the new resort will continue that tradition.

How to get to Daydream Island.

To reach Daydream Island you can fly to nearby Hamilton Island direct from most major Australian cities and then transfer by launch to Daydream.

Alternatively, you can fly to Proserpine, transfer by coach to Shute Harbour and then transfer by boat to the island.

If you arrive at Shute Harbour by car there is security parking available. Simply contact the Shell Service Station on (079) 46 9438 or Shute Harbour Car Security on (079) 46 9166. The postal address of Daydream Resort is P.M.B. 22, Mackay. Qld. 4740. The telephone and facsimile numbers of the resort are (079) 469200 and (079) 469216 respectively.

Daydream was one of the first islands to attract visitors to the Whitsundays. With the addition of the new resort, this tiny but pretty island is likely to maintain its appeal for yet another generation of honeymooners and holiday-makers wishing to visit the Great Barrier Reef.

1. The sun rises over the beautiful stretch of coral beach on the south-western corner of Daydream Island.

2. A model of the new resort and marina being built at Northpoint. It will be open at the end of 1990.

DUNK ISLAND

2

3

Dunk Island, which is on the same latitude as Fiji, is undoubtedly one of Australia's best-known islands.

Many people in Australia and overseas learned about it decades ago through articles and books written by Edward Banfield, who lived a secluded life on the island between 1897 and 1923. He wrote four books about his life on the island, the first and perhaps most famous being "Confessions of a Beachcomber".

Of all the continental islands within the Great Barrier region Dunk Island is one of the most tropical in terms of vegetation.

A large area of the island is covered in dense jungle but there are also eucalypt forests, grassy areas and mangrove flats. The landscape includes hills and valleys, cliffs and precipices, rocky promontories, sandy beaches and small coves.

Dunk Island lies about 160 kilometres north of Townsville and 120 kilometres south of Cairns. It is six kilometres long and about two kilometres wide at its broadest point.

The summer temperatures on the island range between 23°C and 31°C, and the winter temperatures are between 17°C and 26°C.

4

1. A boat cruises past Purtaboi Island, a small island which lies directly off-shore from the resort on Dunk Island.

2. The stunning Ulysses butterfly which can be seen on Dunk Island during the months of June and July.

3. Brammo Bay - the island's resort lies hidden by the palm trees fringing the beach.

4. Lush rainforest covers large areas of the island.

1

Most of Dunk Island is now classified as a National Park and visitors can explore much of its beautiful rainforest on excellent tracks maintained by the National Parks and Wildlife Service.

Over 90 different species of birds have been recorded on the island. Another winged resident is the brilliant blue Papilio Ulysses butterfly, which has been adopted as a symbol for Dunk Island.

Aborigines once lived on Dunk Island. The tribe was known as the Djiru and their name for the island was Coonanglebah.

The island received its present name from James Cook. He named it after George Montagu Dunk, Earl of Halifax and First Lord of the Admiralty.

In 1969 the movie "The Age of Consent", starring James Mason, was filmed here as well as on nearby Bedarra Island.

Today, the island is a popular destination for visitors. The resort on the island has been long established and caters for up to 400 guests. About two thirds of the guests are Australians with the rest coming from overseas, mostly the United States. Apart from water sports the resort has a golf course, tennis courts and horse riding.

A member of the Family Islands.

Dunk Island is one of a dozen islands within a group named the Family Islands. Dunk is by far the largest. All the others are uninhabited except for Bedarra, another very small resort island nearby (see Chapter Three), and tiny Timana Island where a talented weaver resides.

James Cook encountered the islands and named the group as he threaded his way northwards in 1770. According to his Journals he passed through them on June 8 of that year. He noted that "we saw on one of the nearest Islands a Number of the Natives collected together, who seem'd to look very attentively upon the Ship; they were quite naked, and of a very Dark Colour, with short hair".

Cook passed Dunk on the eastern or seaward side. It is obvious that Cook considered it to be the most appealing island within the Family Group because it was the only individual one that he named. Cook named it after his patron, George Montagu Dunk, Earl of Halifax, Earl of Sandwich and First Lord of the Admiralty.

Born a Montagu, this canny nobleman exchanged his illustrious name for that of his wife's rather undistinguished one. He chose to do so for the very simple reason that inheritance of her father's rather impressive fortune depended on it.

Lord Montagu Dunk also invented the humble sandwich. He was such a passionate gambler that he created the sandwich to ensure that as little time as possible would be wasted on meals.

The next visit to Dunk of any note was in May, 1848, by the warship HMS "Rattlesnake", under the command of Captain Owen Stanley. The "Rattlesnake" was, in fact, the escort for the "Tam O' Shanter" which carried the well-known explorer Edmund Kennedy. Kennedy was deposited on the mainland opposite to Dunk Island to begin what became a fateful overland expedition.

John MacGillivray, the naturalist aboard the "Rattlesnake", spent 10 days on Dunk Island. As his party explored the northern part of the island trouble erupted.

Two of the young "gentlemen" in MacGillivray's party went on a hunting trip and approached a native camp a little too closely. When the aborigines tried to resist their advance the two white men fired shots at them. The aborigines fled but did not forget the incident.

From that point onwards the natives of Dunk Island developed a treacherous reputation. The island natives were a very independent people who had virtually no contact with mainland tribes. They enjoyed a plentiful supply of sea-food and clearly regarded the arrival of white men in their domain as a most unwelcome intrusion.

One well documented incident occurred in 1877. On January 18, the men aboard a schooner called either the "Thomas Hardy" or "Thomas Harris" sailed from Cairns to Dunk Island. The purpose of the trip was to collect wood for their Bêche-de-mer boilers.

When they arrived at Dunk Island the schooner moored about half a mile off-shore and two of the crew members - Humphrey Coughland and Alexander MacIntosh - were put in charge of a hut on the island.

The following morning Harris, the skipper of the schooner, was aroused by a loud cry. Harris immediately went up on deck where he found a member of his crew dying from a wound in the head.

An article in an early edition of the "Australasian Encyclopaedia" vividly describes the dramatic events that followed. "Looking up, he saw a blackfellow stalking the mate. When he shouted a warning, the native then attacked the captain with the half-axe he was carrying".

Harris was wounded but he managed to retreat to the safety of his cabin where he kept his revolver. Harris, however, had difficulty loading the weapon because of the severe wound that he had suffered.

"In the meantime other blacks had arrived and were trying to break the cabin door with their half-axes. The captain managed at length to load the revolver, and he fired a shot through the skylight. Hearing the shot, John Shaw - a seaman - broke his way through the lazarette door.

Blacks were cutting and hacking at everything they could reach, and the steward who got in their way was half-scalped before he could crawl away to join the captain and the others in the cabin.

The captain now had two men to lead against half a dozen blacks. They made the charge and two blacks were killed in the first encounter. After a further struggle the rest of the blacks were killed or driven into the water.

Harris then found the bodies of two seamen hacked to pieces. Coughland and MacIntosh were both found murdered in their hut on Dunk Island..."

Another bloody incident occurred on Dunk Island the following year. This took place some time after a steamer called the "Merchant", carrying a cargo of cedar, left Port Hinchinbrook to head south. This ship - which had just been repaired after running aground on a shoal - then had the misfortune to find itself at sea when a bad cyclone hit the Queensland coast. The "Merchant" was totally wrecked on this occasion and the crew were never seen again.

The wreckage of the doomed vessel,

however, was found over a very wide area. The enterprising crew of one salvage boat subsequently arrived at Dunk Island searching for the remains of the "Merchant's" valuable cargo. They scoured the island's beaches until they encountered some of the local and hostile natives. The crew suffered wounds and bruises but were lucky enough to escape.

Some of the cedar from the "Merchant" actually lay on Dunk's beaches for almost 20 years until E.J. Banfield took up residence on the island. He salvaged at least one log and used the timber in building a punt as well as different items of furniture.

E.J. Banfield, a journalist turned beachcomber.

Living on a tropical island has long been considered a romantic dream. What person has not read the exploits of the shipwrecked Robinson Crusoe without feeling somewhat envious of his unencumbered life?

Whilst Robinson Crusoe was a fictitious character, however, Edmund J. Banfield was not. And whilst the former was eventually rescued and returned to "civilization", the latter loved Dunk Island so much that he lived on it happily until his death.

Edmund J. Banfield was born in Liverpool in 1852. He left England for Australia in 1854, along with his two sisters and a brother, under the care of his mother. His father, Jabez W. Banfield, had already migrated to this country ahead of the family.

After joining several rushes to the goldfields Jabez Banfield helped found a newspaper in Maryborough, Victoria. In 1857, Banfield senior took his family to

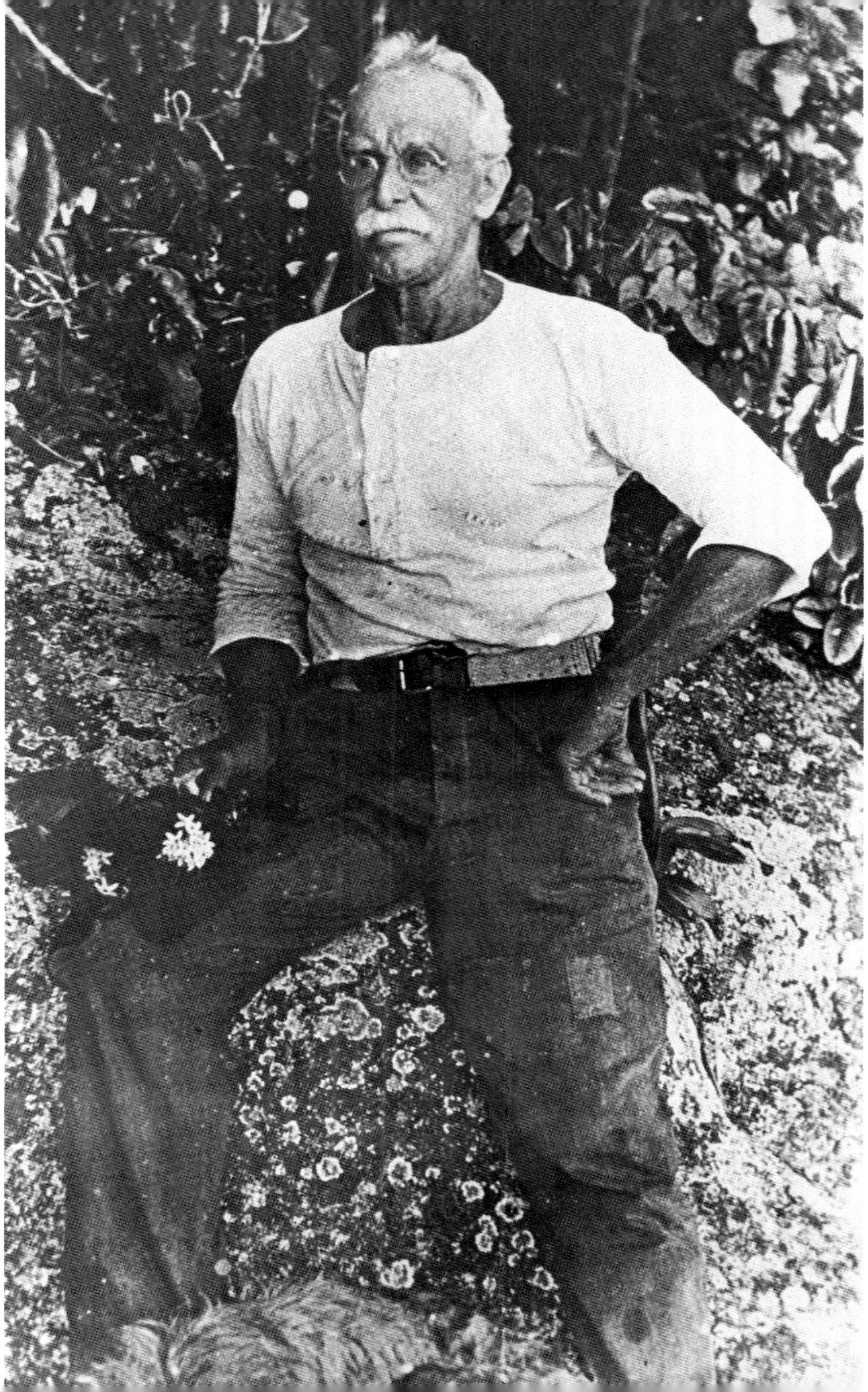

Ararat where he ran another newspaper. It was here that his son Edmund also began a career in journalism.

Edmund Banfield worked later in Sydney as a journalist and then, in 1882, took the rather adventuresome step of moving to far-off Townsville. He worked with the "Townsville Daily Bulletin" for 15 years, until he became desperately ill through overwork and exhaustion.

In September, 1896, Banfield camped on the beach of Dunk Island with his wife Bertha and a few friends. Banfield, who had previously absorbed the writings of Thoreau, the American philosopher who advocated a life close to nature, was immediately captivated by the thought of living on this beautiful island.

Banfield subsequently managed to lease a small area of Dunk Island for a period of 30 years at an annual rental of two shillings and sixpence an acre, and later secured a larger freehold block.

When the Banfields arrived on Dunk to take up permanent residence in 1897 they were greeted by Tom, an aborigine who they had become acquainted with on their first visit. Tom helped the Banfields unload their many provisions and worked for them on and off for many years. Unfortunately, the attractions of rum and opium prompted Tom to travel regularly to the mainland. On one visit he died after being speared by his half-brother during a drunken fight.

After their arrival the Banfields lived in tents for only a short time since Edmund had had the foresight to ship a prefabricated hut to the island. This was made out of cedar and "so contrived with nicely adjusting parts

1

1. The grave of Edmund J. Banfield and his wife Bertha.

2. The Banfield's first home on the island.

3. The Beachcomber sits at the stern of his boat, the "Yan-O-Lee", with a visitor to the island.

4. Edmund Banfield shares the verandah of his home with an unknown guest.

5. The second, larger residence built by the Banfields. Unfortunately the house no longer exists.

and bolts, and all its members numbered, that a mere amateur could put it together." On Banfield's own admission it also had the advantage of being easily dismantled if life happened to become unendurable on Dunk Island.

Despite the many different hardships of becoming almost completely self-sufficient Banfield found Dunk a joyful place to live. "Scent and silence," he wrote, "is the phrase which expresses the individuality of our island and better 'scented silence' than all the noisy odours of the town."

For six years this small hut sheltered the Banfields, and the occasional bat, until a larger bungalow was built. Over four acres was also cleared as a plantation for fruit and vegetables including bananas, oranges, papaws, pineapples, custard apples, melons, sweet potatoes, maize, strawberries, herbs and even coffee.

The sea provided food, too. There were oysters for the taking, crabs from the mangrove flats and an abundant supply of fresh fish. In addition, the Banfields had a few poultry as well as cows and goats which provided milk and fresh meat. They also arranged for a coastal steamer that passed the island weekly to drop off any supplies needed from the outside world and any mail for them.

Although there were many back-breaking chores to be done each day, Banfield still had time to contemplate and study nature. Indeed, he acquired a remarkable knowledge of the teeming wild-life on Dunk Island and meticulously recorded it.

To finance the few supplies they needed from the outside world, Banfield wrote articles about life on Dunk Island for newspapers and journals under the whimsical pen-name of Rob Krusoe. Ten years after arriving on Dunk Island his first book "Confessions of a Beachcomber" was also published.

This volume was followed by "My Tropic Isle", "Tropic Days" and "Last Leaves from Dunk". In colourful prose, Banfield shared the secrets of nature that he had uncovered, wrote about the legends and often macabre customs of the local aborigines, and told many engrossing stories of his own experiences as well as those of visitors.

One local aboriginal legend he recorded tells the story of how the Southern Cross constellation originated. Long ago two aboriginal fishermen speared a huge shovel-nosed shark whilst they were fishing off Dunk Island in their canoe. The speared shark, named Dooey-dooey, dived - capsizing the canoe and throwing the two men into the water.

Dooey-dooey then dragged the canoe through the water by the harpoon rope. The two men tried in vain to catch the canoe, swimming in pursuit from Dunk Island as far as Magnetic Island and then out to the Great Barrier Reef and over the horizon of the South Pacific, all to no avail. They can still be seen - Dooey-dooey and the canoe (forming the cross) and the two men following behind (the two stars alpha and beta Centauri).

In "Confessions of a Beachcomber" Banfield also tells how the local aborigines would capture a large turtle. They would first catch a "sucker" fish, which has the ability of pressing a disc with ridges on the upper part of its body against a smooth surface and then forming a vacuum in between. This would be fastened to a light line until a turtle was sighted from a canoe.

The "sucker" fish would then be thrown in the turtle's direction to which it would inevitably attach itself. The aborigines would then play the turtle until it was exhausted. Sometimes this would take an hour or more and the patient natives would on occasions be towed seven or eight kilometres out to sea before it tired. The turtle would then be harpooned, hauled alongside, and towed ashore - no mean task in a fragile bark canoe.

Turtles can still be seen in the waters around Dunk Island and, sometimes, a dugong. This harmless creature, commonly known as a "sea cow", looks like a cross between a hippopotamus and a seal. This "strange, paradoxical mammal", as Banfield described it, grazes on sea grass.

Banfield's books were read around Australia and overseas and they brought him fame and mail from right around the globe. Letters came from children, one writing that Dunk would undoubtedly be "a fine place to play Indians!". Others came from professors and even from a group of prisoners in an American penitentiary. Banfield also received letters from would-be Crusoes and some even arrived unannounced.

Mention should be made as well of Bertha Banfield, his "merry little wife". She was always a cheerful and uncomplaining companion for Edmund throughout the many lonely years they spent together on Dunk Island.

2

3

4

5

Since she had no children the only other company Bertha had was Essie, an Irishwoman, who was an "assistant" to the Banfields from 1904. Essie had previously worked for them when they had lived in Townsville.

Unfortunately, Essie was visiting Townsville when Edmund Banfield died of appendicitis on June 2, 1923. Bertha was alone on Dunk Island with her husband's body for three days until she was able to attract the attention of a passing steamer, the "Innisfail".

An 18-year old steward on the steamer saw her waving a sheet on the beach. At first this was interpreted as a greeting. Then she collapsed on the beach and those on board realised there was something amiss. A party was then despatched ashore where they heard of Banfield's death.

After making a coffin, the crew of the steamer laid Banfield to rest in his own garden with Captain Robertson reading the burial service.

A stone cairn still marks the spot (which is just a short distance from the resort on Dunk Island). It bears the following inscription: "If a man does not keep pace with his companions, perhaps it is because he hears a different drummer. Let him step to the music he hears."

Bertha remained on Dunk Island with Essie for another year. Then, perhaps to make up for the many years she had spent in isolation on the island, she travelled and lived in Queensland, New South Wales and Victoria.

Bertha outlived her husband by 10 years. When she died in 1933, her ashes were deposited beneath the cairn that marked the final resting place of Edmund Banfield.

Interest in Edmund Banfield still remains high. His books have been reprinted and the Royal Queensland Theatre Company recently produced a play about his life. Well-known Australian actor Ray Barrett, who now lives on an island himself, played the part of the Beachcomber.

A tropical paradise teeming with life.

During his life on the island, Banfield recorded dozens of species of birds on Dunk Island. In fact, over a hundred different species have been sighted on Dunk and nearby Purtaboi since records have been kept.

For those people interested the impressive list includes the Pelican, Australian Little Grebe, Little Pied Cormorant, Pied Cormorant, White-faced Heron, Reef Heron, Mangrove Heron, Nankeen Night Heron, White Ibis, Straw-necked Ibis, Brown Goshawk, Whistling Kite, Black Kite, Brahminy Kite, Wedge-tailed Eagle, White-breasted Sea Eagle, Osprey, Beach Stone-Curlew, Red-Capped Dotterel, plus five varieties of both terns and pigeons.

Other varieties are the Silver Gull, Sulphur-crested Cockatoo, Rainbow Lorikeet, Peregrine Falcon, Scrub-Fowl, Brush Turkey, Rednecked Rail, Grey Plover, Whimbril, Eastern Curlew, Masked Plover, Common Sandpiper, Grey-tailed Tattler, Dusky Honeyeater, Spice Finch, Shining Starling, Yellow Oriole, Spangled Drongo, Yellow Figbird, Southern Figbird, Masked Wood-swallow, White-breasted Wood-swallow, Pied Currawong, Rainbow Bird, Dollar Bird, Shining Bronze Cuckoo, Laughing Kookaburra, Blue-winged Kookaburra, Pheasant Coucal, Channel-billed Cuckoo, Koel and Barn Owl.

Four species of the striking Kingfisher family have been sighted - the Azure Kingfisher, Forest Kingfisher, Mangrove Kingfisher and Sacred Kingfisher.

Other species - many with fanciful names - include the White-tailed Nightjar, Welcome Swallow, Tree Martin, Grey Swiftlet, Noisy Pitta, Magpie-Lark, Brown Songlark, Australian Pipit, Varied Triller, White-winged Triller, Little Cuckoo-skrike, Black-faced Cuckoo-shrike, Large-billed Warbler, Grey Fantail, Rufous Fantail and six species of the Flycatcher.

To complete this extensive list there is the Rufous Shrike-thrush, Bower Shrike-thrush, Mistletoe Bird, Yellow-breasted Sunbird and the Grey-breasted Silvereye.

Even if you're not normally an avid birdwatcher still consider packing a pair of binoculars for this purpose should you decide to visit Dunk Island. Most people develop an instant interest in the bird-life they suddenly find around them because of the many unusual varieties, colours and calls of these feathered inhabitants.

If you are interested in the bird-life you can also join a special birdwatch tour organised by the resort. This is usually conducted once a week at 6:00 a.m. and you return in time for breakfast.

One of the delights of Dunk Island are the walks that you can enjoy. A short but very enjoyable walk is the one to Muggy-muggy Bay. This secluded cove lies north of Brammo Bay where the resort is situated and takes not much longer than 15 minutes to reach. The track runs parallel to the water and along the way you'll see a rich variety of vegetation including Paperbark and Umbrella trees, and many Maidenhair and Birds Nest ferns.

Another walk which is well worth the effort is the one to the top of Dunk's highest peak, Mt. Kootaloo, which is 271 metres above sea level. Almost at the outset of the walk you pass the grave of Edmund Banfield. Shortly afterwards you cross a small ravine via a swing bridge and then the track becomes like a tunnel through dense, verdant rainforest.

The round trip to Mt. Kootaloo takes around two hours. Once again you travel through lush rainforest of towering trees forming a green canopy overhead with countless palms, ferns and small plants at ground level.

Although there are no kangaroos, wallabies or koalas on the island you will not be disappointed by the bird-life to be heard and seen.

During the months of June and July you should also see many butterflies flitting gaily through the rainforest including the spectacular Ulysses which is vibrant blue in colour. This has a wingspan of around four inches or 10 centimetres. It is not only one of the largest butterflies in Australia but probably the most beautiful, too.

One of the small creatures you may encounter on your walks is the Echidna. They were known to the aborigines that once inhabited Dunk as "Coom-bee-yan" and were regarded by them as a delicacy.

1

This shy creature is, in fact, a spiny ant-eater. Banfield described it as "an animal which possesses some of the features of the hedgehog of Old England, and resembles in others that distinctly Australian paradox, the platypus". Occasionally an albino Echidna is found on Dunk. Apparently, these are unique to the island.

As you near the highest point of Mt. Kootaloo you will get a spectacular view of Brammo Bay and the mainland in the distance. At the top of Mt. Kootaloo its slopes are so heavily wooded that you cannot enjoy 360° views but you can see some other members of the Family group of islands.

At the summit of Mt. Kootaloo are the remains of a radar station. During World War II this played a vital role in monitoring the Battle of the Coral Sea.

2

3

1. The buttressed trunk of a tall rainforest tree.

2. A swing bridge near the resort crosses a small ravine. The path, through dense rainforest, leads to Mt. Kootaloo.

3. Large palms flourish in the warm, damp conditions of the rainforest.

1

2

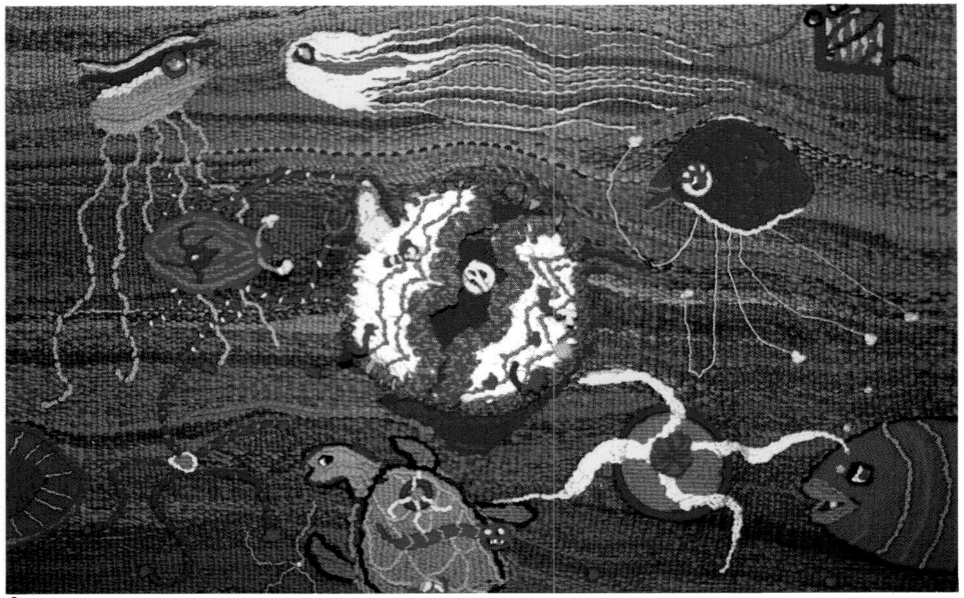
3

1. A small colony of artists can be found on the western side of Dunk Island. This is the potter's studio.

2. Bruce Arthur, the founder of this community, weaves tapestries with wool he has dyed himself.

3. A completed tapestry by Bruce Arthur.

If you walk in a south-easterly direction from the resort you will find yourself not in dense rainforest but in open fields. Here Dunk Island has its own herd of 80 Fresian and Jersey cows which provide guests at the resort with fresh milk every day.

Beyond the dairy farm on Dunk Island there is also a small colony of artists. This was founded in 1974 by Bruce Arthur, a weaver and former professional wrestler, who first began his artistic life on nearby Timana Island.

Bruce's work has brought him national acclaim and his tapestries hang in the foyers of grand hotels and theatres. A lot of Bruce's tapestries have been commissioned by well-known Australian artists such as Clifton Pugh and Fred Williams. They visit or send Bruce detailed designs and he then weaves them using wool specially dyed by him.

Artists come and go from Bruce Arthur's haven, learning the craft of weaving. The small community also includes a resident potter.

Visitors staying on Dunk Island can visit the small colony and see the artists at work two mornings a week, usually on Tuesdays and Fridays. Both tapestries and pottery made by Bruce Arthur and the other artists can be purchased.

The walk to Bruce Arthur's will take you about half an hour. Twenty minutes further on you will find Coconut Beach, a long sandy beach fringed by trees.

A feature of this beach are the beautiful *Callophylum* trees, more commonly known as Cyclone trees. These grow as high as 20 metres, have very low lying foliage and can be very old.

A circular trail will actually take you to Coconut Beach and back via Mt. Kootaloo if you wish. If you choose this longer route rather than simply backtracking you should allow about five hours for the round trip.

Another destination worth visiting is Purtaboi, the small rocky island close to Dunk Island and lying directly off-shore from the resort at Brammo Bay.

Edmund Banfield described it as "dainty and unique - its hill crowned with low-growing trees and shrubs, a ruddy precipice, groups of Pandanus palms, beach lined with Casuarinas, (with) banks of snow-white coral debris..."

From August through until December you will also see *Dendrobium discolour* or Golden Rock Orchid in flower on Purtaboi.

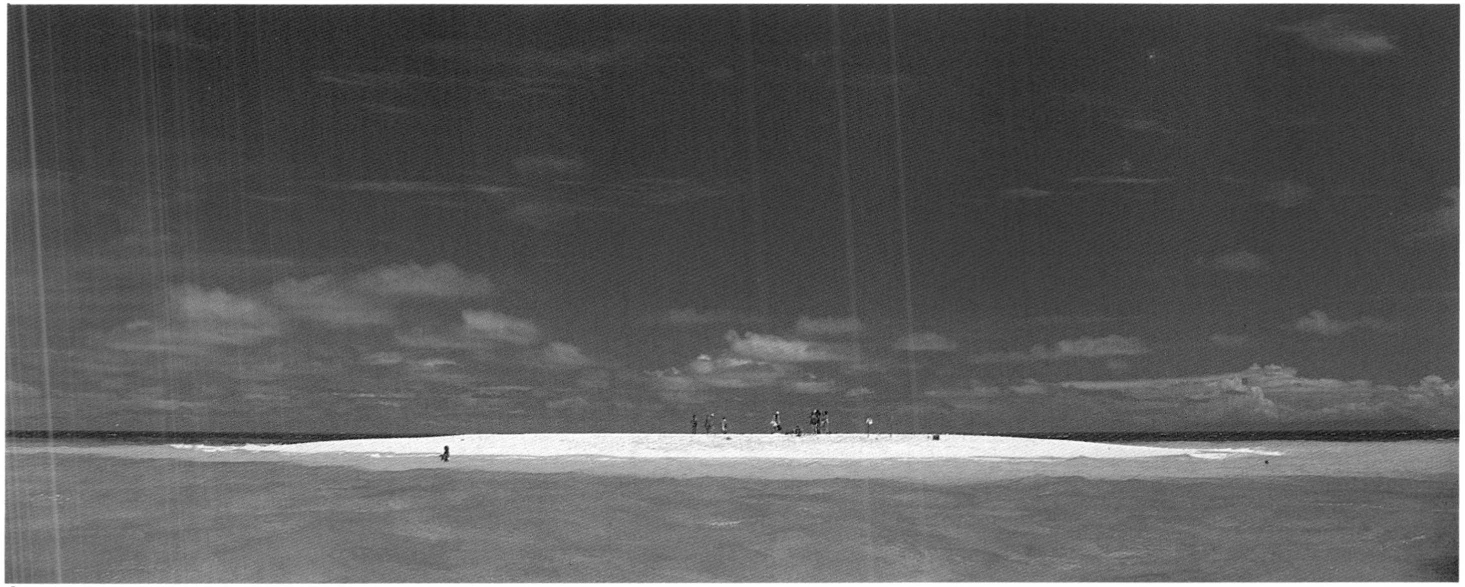

4

5

4. Guests from Dunk Island visit Beaver Cay and snorkel around it.

5. Although small, the cay is a convenient landing place for many sea-birds.

This little island was very close to where the survey ship "Rattlesnake" anchored in May, 1848, and actually served as a station for Captain Stanley when he determined various astronomical positions.

Purtaboi is a bird sanctuary and many birds nest on this little island so care must be taken not to disturb them. Banfield was the first to record that hosts of sea-birds nested on Purtaboi as well as Torres Strait or Nutmeg Pigeons, Doves, Honey-eaters, Reef Herons, Cormorants and Large-billed Shore Plovers.

Apart from birdwatching you can also enjoy both swimming and snorkelling. Purtaboi has a small but beautiful sandy beach and if you like picnics, it's a wonderful spot to have one.

To get to Purtaboi simply hire a dinghy with outboard at the Watersports shed.

Visit the Reef by boat.

From Dunk Island it is also easy to visit an outer reef. Good weather permitting, a fast motor catamaran whisks visitors out to Beaver Cay each day. Here you can snorkel or view its coral gardens and marine life from a glass bottom boat or semi-submersible craft.

You have plenty of time to laze around on Beaver Cay itself, a small area of sand not much more than 20 or 30 metres long. This sand has slowly built up on the surrounding reef over hundreds of years from broken particles of coral.

The boat trip out to the Reef aboard "Quickcat" takes about 50 minutes. Once there, you spend a couple of hours at Beaver Cay and the reef around it.

If you are an experienced, certified scuba diver there is a special dive package. This includes the cruise out to the Reef aboard "Quickcat", hire of all scuba gear and one guided dive.

If you have never dived before but would like to enjoy the experience there is a one day diving course available which includes instruction, cruise to the Reef, all gear and one dive.

Underwater cameras can be hired as well.

Dunk Island is also a great place to visit if you enjoy fishing. A game-fishing boat operates from the island and you only have to spend a little time at the bar at night to discover that fishing in the Great Barrier Reef region can be an unforgettable experience.

There are Spanish Mackerel, Sailfish and Barracuda to do battle with and if you

Brammo Bay with the mainland in the distance.

go bottom fishing you can expect to haul up fish like Coral Trout, Sweetlip and Trevally.

Each year, during the month of September, Dunk Island plays host to a game-fishing tournament. Known as the Dunk Island Billfish Classic, it attracts more than 50 game-boats and game fishermen from Australia and overseas, all hoping to land record Marlin and Sailfish.

Naturally, demand for accommodation in this period is heavy so if you wish to join in on the action you should book well ahead. Entry forms and details for the tournament can be obtained from most travel agents or through the resort itself. The resort can arrange charter boats for this event as well.

People also have success fishing off the jetty at Dunk Island, and many take out a runabout to see what they can catch. Hand-lines and bait are available from the Water Sports centre, free of charge.

The dinghies are also a wonderful way to explore some of the secluded bays and beaches of the island. With a picnic hamper from the resort, you are assured a wonderful day.

Another pleasant way to spend your time afloat is sailing aboard the "Neptunius", a magnificent 52' yacht. It's a great way to see and explore some of the uninhabited islands of the Family Group.

You can see the area by helicopter, too. There are local scenic flights and there is a day's trip by helicopter to Orpheus Island (see Chapter Nineteen).

A 30 minute flight takes you over more than a dozen tropical islands including Hinchinbrook, the world's largest National Park Island (see Chapter Thirteen), and you then land on Orpheus where you visit the island's Marine Research Station and Giant Clam Farm. You can then snorkel or view the beautiful soft and hard corals of this island's fringing reef from a glass bottom boat. Lunch is aboard a luxury cruiser.

A steady flow of visitors since the 1930's.

Tourists started to come to Dunk Island as far back as 1934. Banfield's old bungalow provided the accommodation for those first visitors. The "resort" was owned by Spencer Hopkins of Townsville and managed by the George Morris family.

Noel Wood, who has lived on nearby Bedarra Island for some 50 years, occasionally helped out at the resort and remembers those early days. Dinner was often braized turtle accompanied by a bottle of claret (ten pence a bottle).

Draught beer from Cairns and different brands of bottled beer from Melbourne were served - including Melbourne Bitter, Abbotts and Fosters. There were no refrigerators back then, of course, and the beer was stored in concrete boxes with ice. The labels inevitably floated off in the water from the melting ice and the barman simply slapped the nearest label onto the nearest bottle. None of the customers seemed to notice or complain, Noel remembers with good humour. Much has changed since those early days.

The island and resort passed through different hands but since 1978 the resort has been fully owned by Australian Airlines and they have continually up-graded the facilities. A lot of attention has gone into the design of new additions. The main resort complex that was built about six years ago won a number of national awards.

One stunning feature of the complex is the Cascade Pool where water pours down like a waterfall from one swimming pool into a second and then a third.

If you would like to swim in the sea you will find at least four beautiful and safe beaches around the island. As with many islands, the water around Dunk can be quite shallow for a few hours at low tide but you'll always have plenty of time during the day to enjoy the clean, blue waters of the Coral Sea.

One beach is right on the doorstep of the resort at Brammo Bay, the second is close on the other side of the sandy Spit and is called Pallon Beach. There is a small secluded beach 15 minutes walk from the resort at Muggy-muggy and, further afield, there is Coconut Beach (both described earlier in this chapter).

The resort - which accommodates up to 400 guests - is set in tropical gardens with a profusion of brilliant Bougainvillea, Hibiscus, Frangipani, purple Bauhinia and many other beautiful and colourful plants. The gardens are kept in their beautiful state by a horticulturalist and eight gardeners.

The standard of the facilities is excellent and there is a range of accommodation for all budgets. According to the resort's Tariff Sheet there are three forms of accommodation. However, there are really five types of accommodation but only three tariff levels.

At the top of the range there are luxury Beachfront Units which have only recently been built.

At the mid-priced level you have a choice of Garden or Beachfront Cabanas. The Garden Cabanas are newer and a little more spacious whereas the Beachfront Cabanas are a little older but are right at the water's edge.

The same is true for the slightly smaller Banfield Garden Units and Banfield Beachfront Units which both fall within the lowest tariff level.

All forms of accommodation have private bathrooms, air-conditioning, ceiling fans and mini-bars are available on request.

All meals are included in the tariff. These are served in the Beachcomber Restaurant which overlook beautiful Brammo Bay.

Breakfast and lunch are served buffet style and in the evenings there is a menu that changes daily. The menu on one occasion offered guests Tomato and Chive Soup and then a choice of two entrees - Brace of Quail served with Cashews and Wild Plum Sauce or Fruit and Cream Cheese Balls.

There were three delicious main courses to choose from - Fish poached lightly in Champagne and Lemon Thyme, and served with a Smoked Salmon Sauce; Breast of Chicken pan fried and served with a Creamy Prawn and Mushroom Sauce; and Buffalo Fillets marinated and sealed, sliced into medallions and served with a rich Game Sauce.

For dessert there was a selection of Tropical Fruit Salad, Cream Caramel or Chocolate and Brazil Nut Pate. Guests could then enjoy cheese and biscuits, and coffee or tea.

If you love seafood then you will certainly look forward to Friday nights. In the

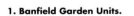

1

2

3

4

5

1. Banfield Garden Units.

2. The interior of the resort's new, luxury Beachfront Units.

3. Banfield Beachfront Cabanas.

4. The exterior of the new Beachfront Units. Brammo Bay lies directly beyond the palm trees on the right.

5. The resort's Cascade Pool.

evening a wonderful seafood banquet is served in the Beachcomber Restaurant. Guests are treated to a mammoth smorgasbord of lobster, prawns, mud crabs, reef fish and oysters.

On Tuesday, Wednesday, Thursday and Saturday evenings you also have the option of dining in Banfields Restaurant. If you choose to dine in this intimate a la carte restaurant, you will not be disappointed although it attracts an additional charge.

The menu changes regularly but you can expect mouth-watering starters such as Scallops poached with White Wine and Ginger Sauce and Oysters served with a Spicy Tomato Coulis, main courses like Fillet of Buffalo served in a Port Wine Sauce and Chilli Lobster, and desserts like Crêpes Suzette and Pecan Pie.

The wine list for both the Beachcomber Restaurant and Banfields is identical. It offers a good selection of about 17 Australian white wines and 13 reds.

At night, after the evening meal, there is always some form of entertainment. There is a resident band and guest artists play occasionally. There is also a late night bar and disco three nights a week.

An evening child-minding service is available for those with children. There is even a special dinner at 5:30 p.m. every night for children over the age of three. During the day children have their own activities centre staffed by two or three adults.

Guests staying at the resort have many activities to choose from during the day. Apart from swimming, windsurfing and catamaran sailing you will find a 6-hole golf course, clay target shooting, an archery range, horse-riding, aerobics, softball, badminton and tennis courts. There are also air-conditioned squash courts. There is even a cricket match on Sundays when Dunk's Dozen, made up of resort staff, play a team of guests.

The use of all sports facilities and most equipment is free. Only horse riding, clay target shooting and activities which involve the use of fuel - such as water-skiing and paraflying - are extra.

Horse-riding is a delightful way to see some of the island.

You are always accompanied by an experienced stockman and quiet horses are available for those who have never tried this form of transport before! Free pony rides are also available for children.

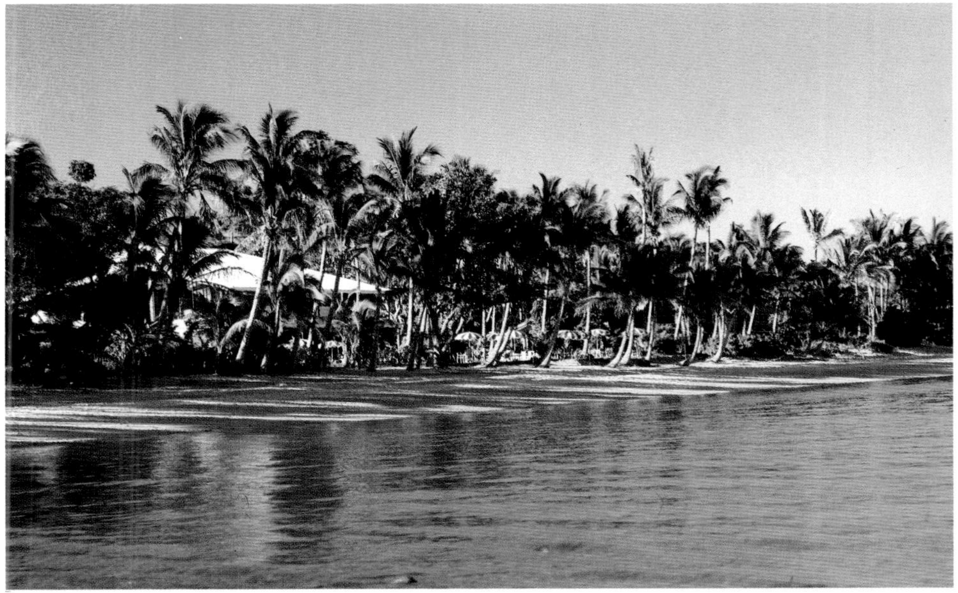
6

7

8

9

10

If all this activity sounds too much you can always retire to one of the resort's three bars. There is also a boutique with a wide range of items including casual wear, swimwear, toiletries, books, magazines, newspapers, postcards and stamps (there is a daily postal service) and a 24-hour film processing service. The resort even has a hairdressing salon.

For those guests who can't wait for mealtimes there is the Jetty Cafe as well, which serves hot and cold snacks, ice-creams and cool drinks. Morning and afternoon tea is also served in the Main Lounge and at the Pool Bar.

The management really have thought of everything to make your stay as enjoyable and relaxing as possible. Along with the natural beauty of Dunk Island and a tropical lushness that few other islands can match it's hardly surprising that it is one of the most popular destinations within the Great Barrier Reef region.

How to get to Dunk Island.

To visit Dunk Island you have several options. There are daily flights between Townsville and the island, and flights from Cairns every day. Flights from both Townsville and Cairns to Dunk take about 40 minutes.

If you are travelling by road on the mainland you can travel across to Dunk Island by boat. There is a regular ferry service operated by Lawrence Kavanagh Cruises from the Clump Point jetty and water taxis also run regularly from South Mission Beach and Wongaling Beach.

There is a hovercraft operating between Dunk Island and Mission Beach, too.

Should you wish to contact the resort a Dunk Island their address is P.M.B. 28, Townsville, Queensland 4810, and their phone number is (070) 688199. The resort's telex and facsimile numbers are AA148851 and (070) 688528 respectively.

At the end of Brammo Bay there is a small camping site. Camping permits must be obtained prior to arrival, however, from the National Parks and Wildlife Service. These can be obtained from their Cardwell office. The phone number of the N.P.W.S. at Cardwell is (070) 668601.

Dunk Island's original name was "Coonanglebah" which means Isle of Peace and Plenty. Banfield found it to be so, and few visitors to this tropical island today would feel inclined to disagree.

6. A view of Dunk Island's resort from Brammo Bay.

7. The "Neptunius", a yacht which takes resort guests on day cruises through the Family Islands.

8. Horse-riding is a popular way to explore Dunk Island.

9. Clay target shooting is another activity resort guests can enjoy.

10. Dunk Island has its own 6-hole golf course.

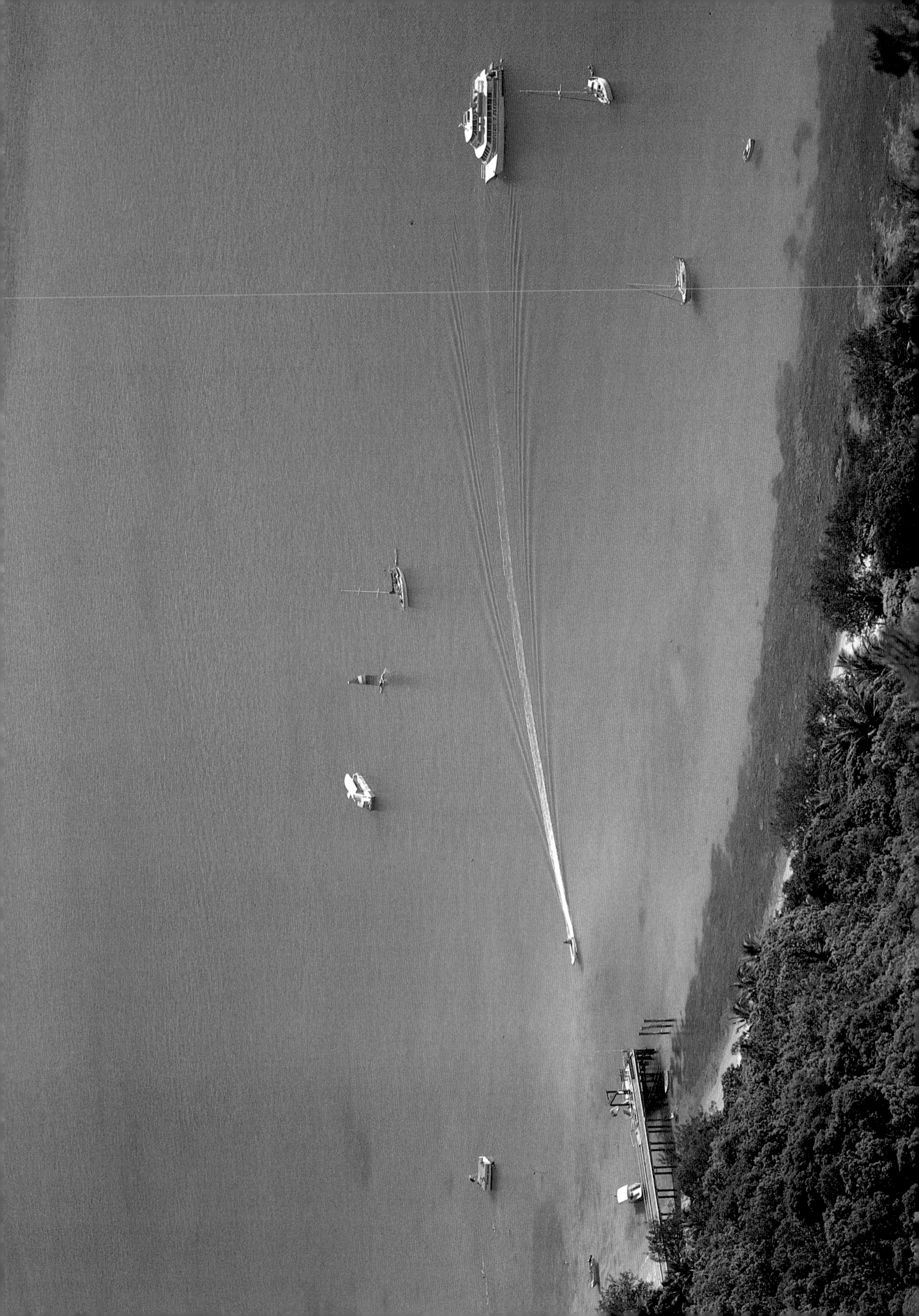

FITZROY ISLAND

2

3

4

5

1. A panoramic view of Welcome Bay where the island's resort is situated.

2 - 5. People arrive at Fitzroy Island. Some cruise out from Cairns for the day on boats operated by Great Adventures, others stay at the resort.

6. Nudey Beach, a pretty coral beach on the south-western corner of the island.

1

Like so many of the Great Barrier Reef islands, Fitzroy was named by James Cook on his historic journey of exploration up the eastern coast of Australia in 1770.

Fitzroy is a large continental island that lies just 24 kilometres east of Cairns. It is the third most northerly resort island within the Great Barrier Reef region.

The vegetation on Fitzroy Island is very similar to that on the mainland nearby - there is both eucalypt forest and areas of lush tropical rainforest.

In the rainforest some of Australia's largest and most colourful butterflies can be found.

At least 35 different species of birds can also be observed on Fitzroy Island.

Aborigines once hunted for food on Fitzroy. They held feasts on the island, too - with cannibalism a regular feature.

Late last century large numbers of Chinese migrants to North Queensland were quarantined on Fitzroy Island. It was also the scene of a serious revolt.

During World War II an RAAF unit was stationed on the island.

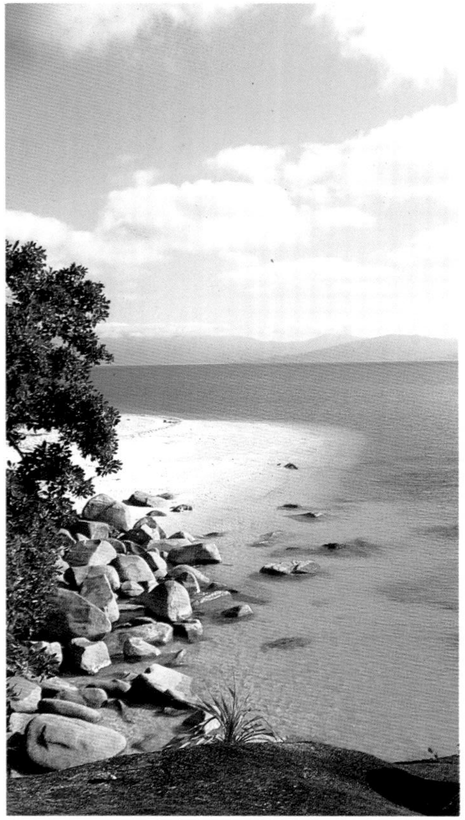
6

1

1. An aboriginal church on Fitzroy Island built partly with coral (burnt to make lime). This photograph appeared in the "Queenslander" in 1909. The church no longer exists nor do aborigines still live on the island.

2. A yacht lies alongside the jetty in Welcome Bay at sunset. Being close to Cairns, the island attracts visiting yachts and cruisers.

Today, it has a modern resort which is also one of the most affordable. The key attractions are the beautiful bushwalks, the coral beaches, and its close proximity to the coral gardens of the outer reefs.

The scene of a Chinese revolt in 1877.

James Cook named Fitzroy Island as he passed by it on Sunday, June 10, 1770, aboard the "Endeavour"

Cook named it in honour of the Third Duke of Grafton who was the Secretary of State in England in the year 1765, 1st Lord of the Treasury in 1766 and Lord Privy Seal in 1771. This gentleman was a very influential man - his forebear also happened to be the illegitimate son of King Charles II and Barbara Villiers, the Duchess of Cleveland.

The first recorded visit by a European was made by Captain King in 1819. King visited Fitzroy aboard the 56' Royal Navy cutter "Mermaid" during the second of four voyages that he undertook to help chart the waters around Australia.

To take refuge from a gale, King anchored in what is now known as Welcome Bay. He took the opportunity to refill the ship's barrels with fresh water from the same spring which now supplies the resort.

The expedition found no aborigines inhabiting the island but Allen Cunningham, the botanist aboard the "Mermaid", found well-worn tracks and conclusive evidence that Fitzroy was often the venue for cannibal feasts.

Two groups of aborigines lived nearby on the mainland. Both groups were very different. One was known as the Rainforest Blacks and the other simply as the Forest Blacks.

The Rainforest Blacks were a more tolerant, "civilised" race whereas the Forest Blacks were taller, more aggressive and treated their women with little respect. Both groups, however, indulged in cannibalism as an enjoyable and convenient food source.

This was perhaps prompted by the fact that aborigines, contrary to popular belief, were not conservationists. In their search for food they regularly poisoned fish holes. They also trapped birds and turtles, and then gathered so many of their eggs that many species were driven almost to extinction in the local area.

The source of water that King found on Fitzroy Island was a traditional water hole of these aborigines. This supply of fresh water and a safe anchorage prompted many ships to call in regularly at Fitzroy last century including the "Fly", "Beagle" and "Rattlesnake" - all vessels of historic note.

When the "Rattlesnake" anchored, Thomas Huxley (who later became a world famous biologist) went ashore with several other scientists to examine and collect anything of botanical and zoological interest. One completely new species they discovered was the flying fox or fruit eating bat.

Whilst the "Rattlesnake" was anchored at Fitzroy they were suddenly joined by the "Will o' Wisp", a Sandlewood cutter. Hearing that the crew had been attacked by hostile aborigines, Huxley went aboard with medical supplies.

Captain Roach, the Master of the ship, reported that his crew had been overwhelmed and savagely wounded by aborigines boarding the "Will o' Wisp" from canoes. The injured seamen were saved by the mate. He fought the marauding natives back with a sword and then turned the ship's gun on them.

In 1873 an interesting maritime incident took place in the waters around Fitzroy. In January, H.M. "Basilisk" was patrolling the area under the command of Captain Moresby.

The "Basilisk" was an impressive vessel for the times. She was a paddle steamer of 1,071 tons and had a crew of 180 officers and men.

One reason they were patrolling these waters was to apprehend the white skippers of Bêche-de-mer and pearling boats who kidnapped Torres Strait islanders or aborigines and forced them to work aboard their vessels for little or no remuneration.

Early in the month, Moresby boarded four pearling boats - the "Challenge", "Crishna", "Melanie" and "Woodbine". A fifth boat escaped by outrunning the "Basilisk", much to the chagrin of Moresby.

Moresby immediately set up a court on Fitzroy Island and put the officers of the four captured vessels on trial. He charged them with contravening an Imperial Act aimed at preventing "Criminal Outrages on Natives of the Islands in the Pacific Ocean".

Judge Moresby found the defendants guilty, confiscated their boats and "set free the eighty native slaves" aboard them - although not before they had cleaned the bottom of the "Basilisk".

Just over four years later, Fitzroy Island was the site of another serious incident.

2

1

2

3

1. Colourful Bougainvillea in flower around the resort.

2. A female Cairns Birdwing butterfly emerges from her chrysalis.

3. A male Cairns Birdwing butterfly. Birdwings are not only exceptionally beautiful but are also Australia's largest butterflies.

During the 19th century, thousands of Chinese migrated to Northern Queensland in search of gold.

When it was discovered that some of the Chinese were suffering from smallpox it was decided to isolate and quarantine the migrants on Fitzroy Island. This decision was apparently made for political reasons as well as health reasons because the success of Chinese migrants was the cause of great jealousy amongst European settlers.

In April, 1877, almost 3,000 Chinese were confined on Fitzroy Island. With virtually no food or shelter, the conditions were so intolerable that the Chinese finally rioted and "the hills resounded with the report of firearms". A number of Chinese were killed during the quelling of the riot and were buried on the island.

An island rich in plant-life.

Fitzroy Island supports many different species of trees and plants. Many of these provided valuable food and materials for both the aborigines and early settlers.

The timber from the Sheoak trees found down by the beaches was once used to make the yokes that went around the necks of bullocks.

The oil from the seed of the *Pangamia Pennata* or Indian Beech was used as a lubricant, soap and medicine.

The nuts from the Native Nutmeg tree which is found within the rainforest were used as a spice in cooking.

The bark and seeds of the *Barringtonia Calyptrata* tree contain natural chemicals that were used by the aborigines to poison and capture fish.

The Tamarind tree can also be found on Fitzroy although it is not a native tree. In all likelihood seeds were brought here and planted by the Chinese who were quarantined on the island in the 1870's. Its fruit is used in cooking and is a rich source of Vitamin C.

The timber from the Turpentine tree - found in the eucalypt forest - is both borer and fire resistant so it is often used in boat building and the construction of jetties.

Some of the trees on the island are also extremely old. One such species is the Zamia Palm. There is one particular specimen on the island which is estimated by some to be nearly 1,000 years old.

There are many other species of trees and plants of interest on Fitzroy Island. On your walks around the island you will see

4

5

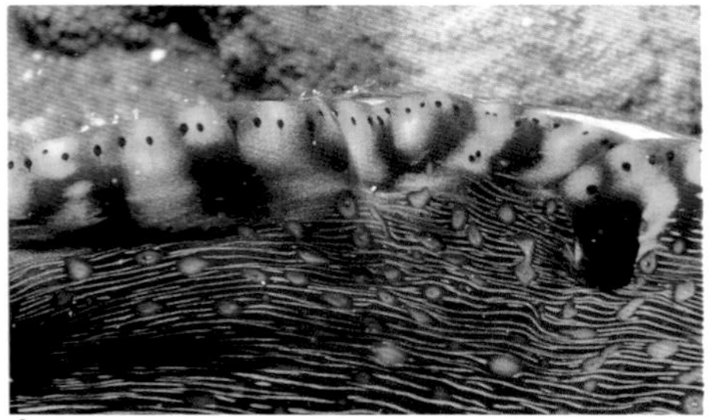
6

4. **A brilliant Blue Triangle butterfly sips nectar from a flower.**

5. **This man holds a young clam. It was bred in the tanks of the clam farm which has been established at Welcome Bay.**

6. **The vividly coloured "mantle" of a Giant Clam.**

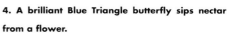

towering Date Palms and a huge variety of other ferns as well as several different types of native Orchids.

The list of other plants and trees could probably fill a small book but another one worthy of mention is the Euodia tree. It provides the basic source of food for the entrancing black and turquoise Ulysses Butterfly.

Apart from this magnificent specimen you can see a number of other stunning butterflies on Fitzroy Island like the Lesser Wanderer (black, orange and white), the Orchard Butterfly (which has bright red and blue spots on dark brown and white wings), and the Giant Birdwing (which is green, black and gold). The best time to catch a glimpse of these exotic creatures is between the months of January and March.

An important site through World War II.

A walk well worth doing is a circular one that takes you to the northern tip of Fitzroy Island, then up to the highest point of the island, and then down through dense rainforest behind the resort. Along the way you will see many things of interest and enjoy views that are quite spectacular.

The round trip will take you about one and a half hours to two hours depending on how often you may stop.

For the first few minutes after heading off from the resort the walking track runs parallel to the beach at Welcome Bay. This is a lovely beach, part coral and part sand.

This is the beach closest to the resort so if the coral does bother you or your feet, it's best to head for the northerly end because this is sandier.

Within a few minutes of starting out on your walk you cannot fail to notice an area on your right enclosed by high wire fences. Behind these you will be intrigued to see rows of large tanks. This establishment is, in fact, a clam farm.

This is a commercial venture in its infancy. Under current legislation, clams are protected in Australia and cannot be marketed or consumed here. All clams bred at this farm are therefore exported - particularly to replenish areas in the Pacific where clams are now almost extinct.

The clams are bred in tanks and are left in these until they are one year old. They are then transferred into the sea just off Fitzroy Island.

The young clams are first placed in

1

1. **The lighthouse on Fitzroy Island. Its rotating lights are actually powerful locomotive lights which have a range of 22 nautical miles.**

2. **Nudey Beach, which is less than 20 minutes walk from the resort, is probably the most beautiful beach on the island. The path to it winds through lush rainforest.**

trays with protective screens because they are irresistible delicacies to predators. Up until the age of three, Maori Wrasse, Parrot fish, stingrays, and octopus all have the muscular strength or jaws to force their shells open.

The clam farm is not yet open to the public who visit Fitzroy Island but it will be at some point in the future.

Continue along the track and it will soon take you up a very steep incline which eventually leads you to the lighthouse on Fitzroy Island. The first lighthouse was established on the island during wartime in 1943 to guide allied shipping through the treacherous Grafton Passage. There was also a Naval Signal Station and R.A.A.F. Radar Station operational here at the same time.

In addition, there was a Coastal Artillery Gun Emplacement to help repel any possible enemy attack from the north. This was no idle threat since Sydney Harbour had already experienced a submarine attack by the Japanese, and they had bombed Darwin on numerous occasions.

In the 1950's a more permanent lighthouse was established on Fitzroy Island. The present tower, faced with white ceramic tiles, was built in 1973 to rehouse a powerful light system that has a visible range of 22 nautical miles in clear weather.

The light source at the top of the lighthouse is provided by three banks of five lights that constantly rotate. Each of these 15 lights are actually powerful locomotive lights.

Today, the Fitzroy Island lighthouse is one of the few remaining manned lighthouses in Queensland. Weather information is relayed from the lighthouse three times a day and this is subsequently relayed all around Australia.

The circular track will then take you along the western side of Fitzroy Island and finally up to the top of the island. Here you can climb up and sit on a rocky pinnacle that gives you an expansive 360° view.

You can see the mainland very clearly including the aboriginal reserve directly opposite the island. It is also very easy to see half a dozen long, beautiful and deserted beaches stretching along the coastline.

Out to sea you can see a small sandy cay, Sudbury Cay, and glimpses of another larger cay in the distance, Green Island (this is another resort island and is covered in Chapter Nine). You can also see yachts and shipping for miles and miles around.

As you walk up to and descend from the peak of Fitzroy Island you will observe another striking feature of the landscape. A large number of huge boulders dot the landscape high above sea level. It is almost as if some giant has decided to have a game of marbles on the island and then left the game unfinished.

On your way back to the resort you will descend into an area of lush, green rainforest. Stand quietly in one place and you will be surprised by the life, smells and sounds not really noticed by the impatient bush-walker. In this dark, dank environment you will see ferns, colourful fungi, butterflies flitting about, birds, vast and intricate spider webs, lizards rustling about in the undergrowth, and much more.

Because of the dense vegetation on Fitzroy it is impossible to explore the south-eastern sector of the island by foot. The only easily accessible spot south of the resort is Nudey Beach - and this is a short, undemanding walk which will take about twenty minutes each way.

Once again, you pass through lush rainforest. You then come to a beautiful, secluded, coral beach that is most picturesque.

Its name is Nudey Beach and it is a favourite spot for visitors who love to bask in the sun. You are not obliged to divest yourself of all clothing as the name might suggest - although a few do.

The Nudey Beach area is great for swimming and snorkelling, too, so resort guests will often take along a picnic lunch and spend the whole day here. It is probably the prettiest place that you can reach easily on the island and should definitely be on your itinerary.

There is one other walk that you can take and that is to the Secret Garden. This walk leads you into the heart of the island and through rainforest all the way. The path takes you up into a secluded gully that abounds with luxuriant vegetation. There are dozens of Bird's Nest ferns clinging to surrounding rock faces and you may also come across some of the native orchids that grow on Fitzroy Island.

A dazzling underwater world for divers and snorkellers.

The best area for snorkelling is around Nudey Beach and also off Little Fitzroy Island which is a tiny island at the northern tip of Fitzroy Island itself. Peter Boundy's Dive Shop, which is located in the resort complex, runs regular boat trips around to Little Fitzroy for snorkelling.

2

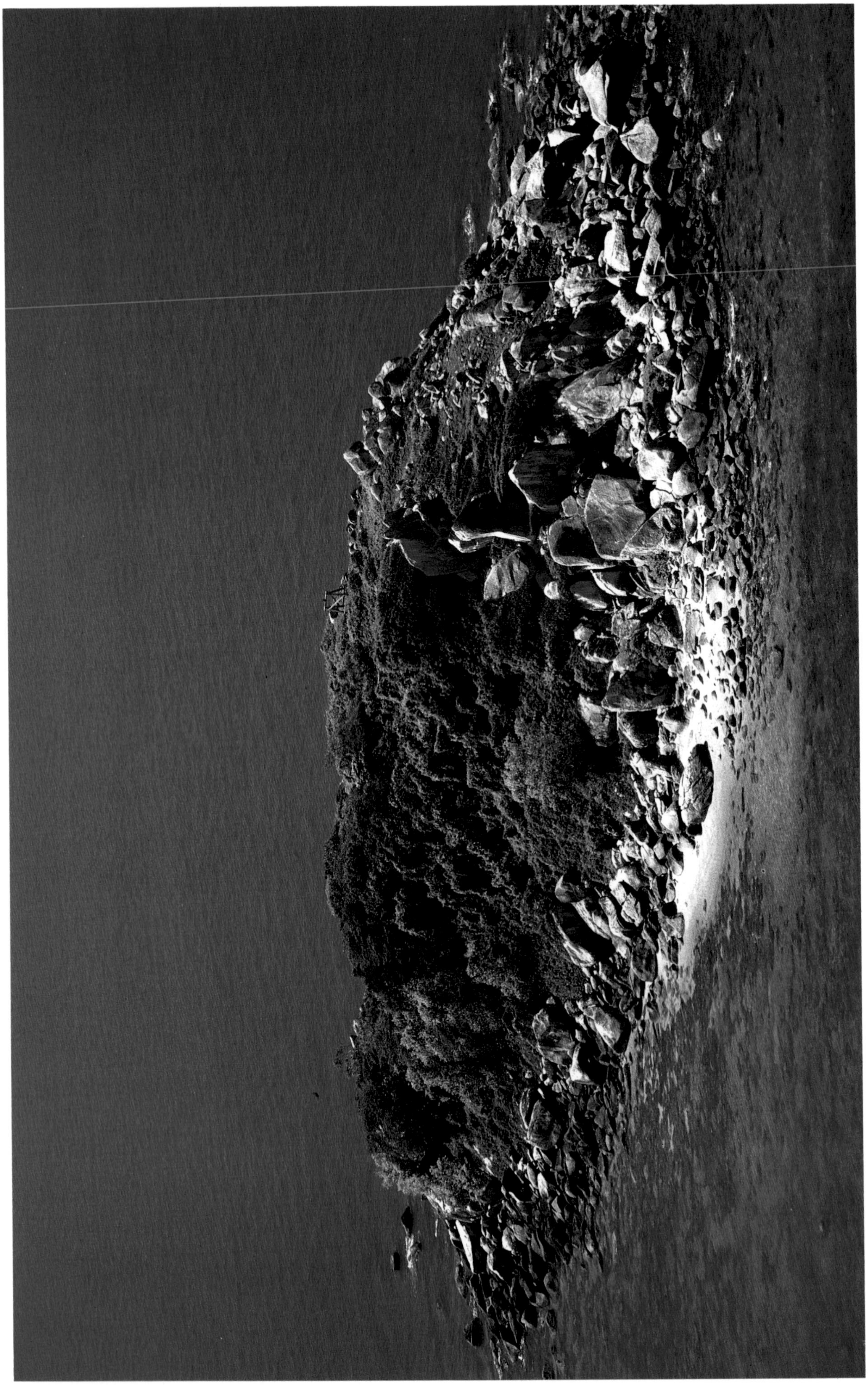

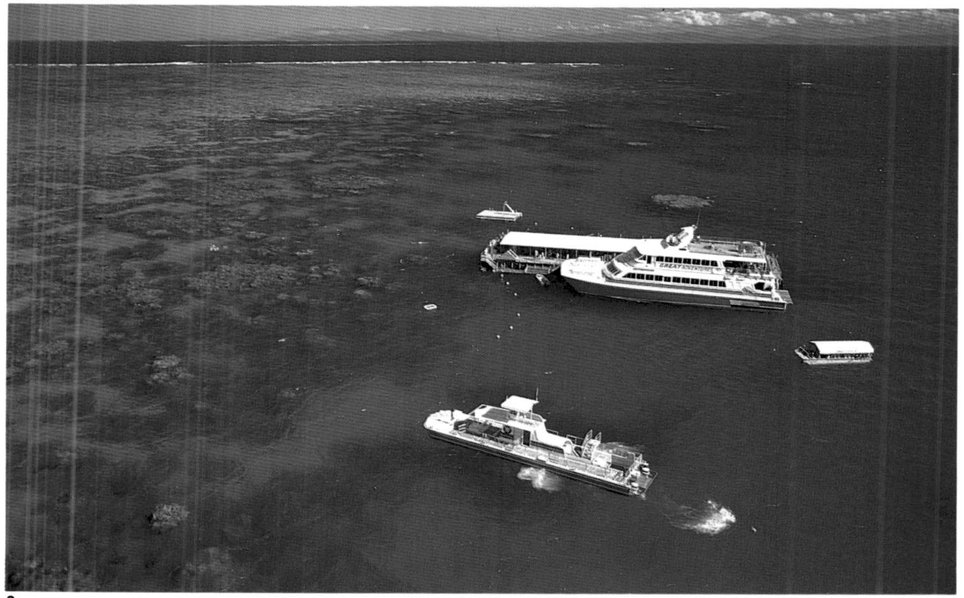

2

They have also pin-pointed 15 excellent dive sites around Fitzroy Island to which they take scuba divers. There is lots to see - including Manta rays and turtles, brightly coloured Parrot fish, Clown Trigger fish, Maori Wrasse, Mackerel, large clams, spectacular Fan and Gorgonia corals, and anemones.

All diving and snorkelling gear, as well as underwater cameras, may be hired from the Dive Shop. Peter Boundy's Dive Shop also offers a half-day introductory dive which includes instruction and all gear, or you can do a four or five day dive course during your stay to qualify you for either a NAUI or PADI certificate.

People wishing to do either of these courses should contact the Dive Shop at least four or five days before their arrival on the island. The phone number of the Dive Shop is (070) 510294.

Snorkellers and divers will enjoy a visit to Moore Reef, too. This is about 45 minutes by boat from Fitzroy Island. Three and a half hours are spent out at Moore Reef before finally returning.

There is a large floating platform at Moore Reef and visitors can lunch here, snorkel, dive and view the wonders of this outer reef from a semi-submersible craft. A smorgasbord lunch is included.

It should not be forgotten that there is also a semi-submersible craft at Fitzroy Island, from which you can view the marine life of the island's fringing reef.

Back at Welcome Bay there are many other watersports to be enjoyed. Catamarans, surf-skis, windsurfers and canoes can all

3

be hired.

A very affordable tropical island.

Fitzroy is currently one of the most inexpensive resort islands you can visit within the Great Barrier Reef region. The island appeals to both families and singles including many back-packers because there is accommodation to suit every budget.

Most of the resort's buildings are modern, well designed and set in landscaped gardens.

On the foreshore overlooking Welcome Bay there are 10 attractive and comfortable villa units. These have two bedrooms. One has a double bed, the other has two single beds. The small villas have their own patios, bathrooms, colour TV's, ceiling fans and mini-bars.

4

1. Little Fitzroy lies off the very northern tip of Fitzroy Island. It is a popular place for snorkelling.

2. From Fitzroy Island you can also visit Moore Reef to snorkel or dive.

3. The Reef's extensive coral and marine life can also be viewed aboard a glass bottom boat.

4. A brightly coloured Rabbit fish.

1

2

3

4

5

1. One of the resort's small villas that overlook Welcome Bay.

2. The comfortable interior of a villa unit.

3. The resort's pool and spa.

4. The main resort complex which houses a shop, bar and cafe.

5. One of the large Beach Houses which provide budget accommodation.

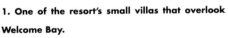

Accommodation is also available in one of several large Beach Houses. These offer hostel style rooms, each with two double bunks (accommodating four people). There are private lockers in each room and linen is provided.

Showers and toilets for guests staying in the Beach Houses are located in a central block, and there is a separate recreation room and cooking facilities. In addition, you have your own small refrigerated compartment for food that you may bring or buy from Fitzroy's own mini-market.

The Beach Houses are mainly occupied by under 35's, many being backpackers from overseas but it is also great budget accommodation for families and these will in no way feel left out.

If you wish to camp you will also find well maintained sites with clean toilet and fresh water shower facilities. The camping grounds have their own barbeque facilities as well.

Camping permits must be obtained at the Great Adventures Visitors Centre at Wharf Street in Cairns before travelling to Fitzroy Island. It is also advisable to book tent sites at least two weeks in advance, especially around school holiday time.

Regardless of the accommodation you choose you are welcome at the main resort restaurant which is open each evening. Visiting yachtsmen are welcome, too.

The restaurant's menu changes regularly but you can expect a choice of around five entrees such as Avocado topped with Fresh Seafoods and served with the Chef's Special Sauce, or Slivers of Veal, sauteed with a selection of Fresh Herbs and combined with a Salad and dressing of a Hot Mustard Vinaigrette.

For your main course you could expect an appetising choice of around eight dishes such as Barramundi, oven baked with Lemon and Butter, or King Prawns flambeed with Brandy and presented with a Spicy Honey Chilli Sauce.

The selection of main courses also includes a Roast of the Day.

To follow there is generally a choice of mouth-watering desserts such as Apple and Cinnamon Pie, or Pears marinated in Mint Liqueur and dipped in Dark Chocolate.

The restaurant and adjoining Mango Bar, incidentally, serve a wonderful selection of exotic cocktails. Ask for the list and experiment - you'll enjoy the experience!

6

At lunchtime the Flare Grill right by the swimming pool is open and this usually offers a Roast of the Day, T-bone Steak, Ham Steak and Pineapple, and grilled Reef Fish.

If you simply want a light snack, there is a snack bar close to the pool, too. This also offers a full cooked breakfast.

The bar adjoining the Flare Grill is a popular venue at night and during the summer months there is usually live entertainment here on weekends.

How to get to Fitzroy Island.

To reach Fitzroy Island you travel by high speed catamaran from Cairns.

If you are passing through Cairns and do not have much time, you can visit Fitzroy Island on a day cruise. The departure time for all visitors wishing to go to Fitzroy Island is

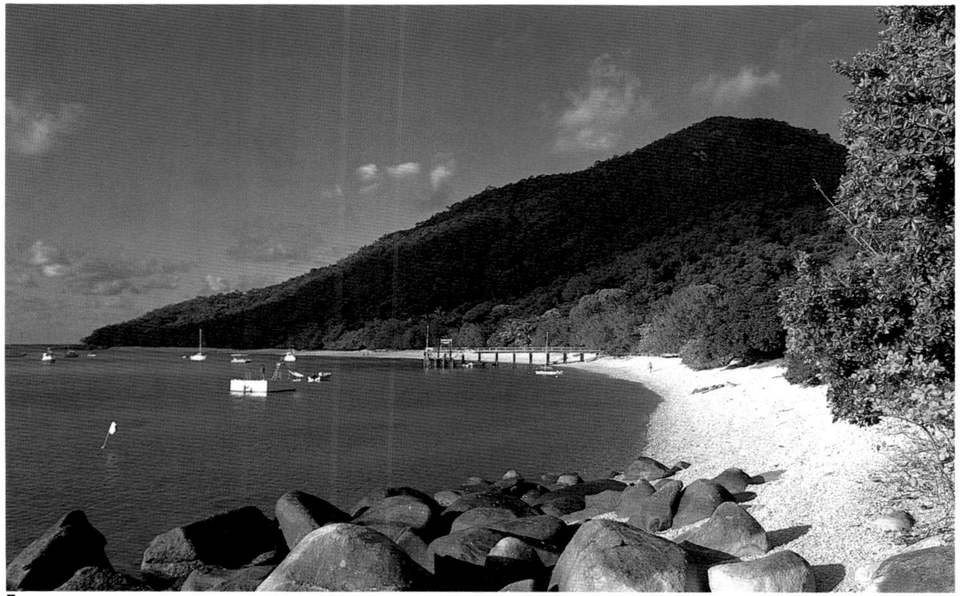

7

8:30 a.m. daily, and boats return to Cairns at both 3:15 p.m. and 5:15 p.m.

Reservations or more information about Fitzroy Island may be obtained through the Great Adventures booking office in Cairns. Their phone number is (070) 515644.

The phone number of the resort itself is (070) 519588. Their facsimile number is (070) 521335. Should you wish to write, mail should be addressed to Fitzroy Island Resort, Great Adventures Pty. Ltd., P.O. Box 2120, Cairns, Queensland 4870.

In summary, the natural beauty of this tropical island and the low cost of staying on it makes Fitzroy a very attractive holiday destination for many Australians and overseas visitors.

To find out just how much people have enjoyed it in the past you need go no further than the Visitor's Book. Here, in conclusion, are a few comments from it.

Fitzroy Island is "The Original Garden of Eden, only with a bar". "We will return." "Happy staff, always smiling." An "idyllic escape from the southern winter".

8

6. Where else can a yachtsman hang his washing?

7. The long coral beach at Welcome Bay.

8. A couple relax on the beach at Welcome Bay.

GREAT KEPPEL ISLAND

2

3

1. Long Beach, at the south-western corner of Great Keppel Island, is a favourite beach for both yachtsmen and resort guests. At the end of the beach is Little Monkey Point.

2. A family prepare for a day of relaxation on Fisherman's Beach.

3. Two Swedish girls acquire a suntan on the Spit at the southern end of Putney Beach.

4. Leeks Beach - two kilometres of sandy beach and not a single soul on it.

Great Keppel is an island renowned for its beautiful beaches. In fact, of all the resort islands within the Great Barrier Reef region, it would have some of the best beaches.

Great Keppel Island lies close to the Tropic of Capricorn.

It is approximately 520 kilometres north of Brisbane and 48 kilometres east of Rockhampton, one of Queensland's major provincial cities.

Most of the island is National Park.

The average temperature on Great Keppel is 22°C in winter and 28°C in summer.

Great Keppel has an interesting history. Like its neighbouring island, North Keppel, it was once inhabited by aborigines. There is also an historic homestead on the island.

If you enjoy snorkelling or diving there are some excellent outcrops of coral around Great Keppel and nearby islands to enjoy.

Visitors are also a short helicopter ride or boat trip away from beautiful North West Island, a coral cay right on the Reef itself.

Visitors to the island have a wide choice of accommodation as well.

4

1

1

1. An old homestead now unoccupied but preserved with memorabilia of its former residents, Ralph and Lizzie Leeke.

2. A photograph of Keppel Islanders taken in 1897.

3. Children in front of an aboriginal hut in 1898.

4. One of the last aborigines to live on Great Keppel Island.

5. A group of Keppel Island aborigines visit Emu Park near Rockhampton in 1887 to celebrate the Jubilee Reign of Queen Victoria.

Unlike most other Great Barrier Reef islands, Great Keppel has more than one resort that you can stay at. Collectively, they offer both mid-priced and budget accommodation.

An island originally known as Wapparaburra.

Both Great and North Keppel Islands were named by Captain Cook on May 28, 1770, after Rear Admiral Augustus Keppel.

Admiral Keppel was born in 1725 and entered the Royal Navy at the tender age of 10. He received his first command, aboard "The Centurion", at the age of 19. He was appointed First Lord of the Admiralty in 1782, and became Viscount Keppel in the same year.

Long before Captain Cook named Great Keppel Island, however, it was known by its aboriginal inhabitants as Wappara-burra or "resting place".

Archaeologists have established that aborigines have been visiting Great Keppel for at least 700 years (and nearby North Keppel for some 4,000 years).

In 1884, it was reported that 54 aborigines lived on Great Keppel Island. From all accounts some of these also lived on North Keppel from time to time.

The Keppel Islanders had little contact with aborigines on the mainland. There were differences in their language and even in their physical characteristics. Nor did they have the same tools and weapons. They did not use boomerangs, for example.

Most of the Keppel Islanders' food came from the sea. They netted fish and collected shellfish like oysters, mussels and cockles. They also harpooned large fish, turtles and dugong. This food was all cooked in an open fireplace.

Their seafood diet was supplemented by wild oranges, grapes, cherries, figs, and the flowers and shoots from the hibiscus tree. They made damper, too, by pounding and baking the fruit of the grey mangrove.

The word "mortgage" was never in the Keppel Islanders' vocabulary. Their houses were constructed by simply bending saplings over into an arch, thatching them with bark, and then piling stones and earth up around the side. Archaeologists have found the remains of one of these houses on a hill overlooking the sea near Wreck Beach.

Captain Cook may have named Great Keppel Island but he never actually landed on it. The first European to do so was McGillivray, a naturalist aboard the HMS "Rattlesnake" which helped survey the Reef. McGillivray went ashore at the spot now known as Leeke's Creek, in 1847. McGill-ivray noted that he saw some aboriginal women and children at the time.

Thirty years later a dramatic maritime incident took place close to Great Keppel Island that is worth recounting. On February 1, 1877, a coastal steamer called the "Blue Bell" was steaming into Keppel Bay on the mainland opposite when those on board suddenly felt the ship slowly rising up from the sea.

At first, the terrified crew and passen-gers thought that they had encountered some monstrous sea creature. In the following minutes, however, it became apparent that the steamer was wedged in a rock that was rising slowly from the ocean.

Fearing for their lives, some of the frightened people jumped overboard but fortunately no lives were lost.

After rising about eight metres the rock came to a standstill, leaving the ship high and dry. The "Blue Bell" was subsequently abandoned and she eventually broke up.

The only explanation for this bizarre incident was that the rock rose as the result of an earthquake under the sea-bed.

Leeke's Creek, mentioned earlier, gained its name from Ralph and Lizzie Leeke who grazed sheep on the island from the 1920's through to the 1940's.

Today, you can still see and visit the historic house in which they lived. It is a classic Australian homestead made out of weatherboard with a corrugated iron roof. It has just one small living room, bedroom, bathroom and kitchen.

In the days that the Leekes lived there it was lit by a pressurised gas-light system. The homestead also featured possum skins as bed and floor coverings.

The house is still furnished and has much memorabilia relating to the Leeke family. On one wall there are photographs and fascinating details of the Leeke family tree which goes back as far as the Norman Conquest. Ralph's grandfather was Sir Henry John Leeke, an Admiral who was stationed in colonial India.

Ralph Leeke spent quite a lot of time away from the island because he was a professional fisherman. When he was at home Ralph loved to go oystering at the mouth of Leeke's Creek, usually returning with a whole kerosene tin full of them. On one such occasion he returned with a fine Parrot

2

3

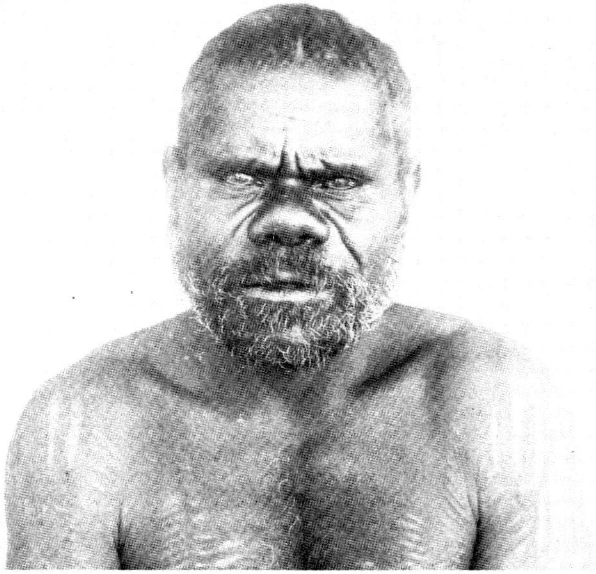
4

Keppel Island Aborigines
Celebrating the
Queens Jubille Record Reign
Emu Park
Queensland
5

1

2

fish. The talented Ralph caught it using the laces of his sand-shoes as a line.

Lizzie, his wife, was obviously a very colourful character.

Bill Leeke, Ralph's nephew, often visited them both as a child. In 1979 he revisited Great Keppel Island and vividly recalled one occasion when Aunt Lizzie, a weather-beaten and robust woman, set out to muster the sheep. She tramped across the rough terrain wearing a black woollen bathing costume, sand-shoes, a big hat and - since it was raining - a sugar bag that served as a cape.

Seventeen sandy beaches.

Great Keppel is a large, continental island that is about seven kilometres from east to west and five kilometres from north to south. It covers 3,500 acres and rises to 165 metres (542 feet).

Although not all of them are easily accessible to the normal visitor, the island boasts 17 squeaky clean beaches. Some are surf beaches.

All in all, Great Keppel has 28 kilometres of beaches. Some are long wide stretches of fine white sand, others are in small secluded coves.

There are three or four superb beaches within easy walking distance of the resort areas which are all situated within minutes of each other on the western side of the island.

Directly adjacent to the resort area is Fisherman's Beach and Putney Beach. Both are long sweeping beaches which are so beautiful and safe that many people will never bother going further afield.

There are at least two other beaches worth visiting, however. The first is Shelving Beach which is in a tiny secluded cove just 15 minutes south of the main resort.

The other is Long Beach. This is situated beyond the airstrip on the southern side of the island. It is a magnificent wide beach that is about two kilometres long and a wonderful place to take a picnic lunch. The scenery is superb with views towards Monkey Point and two small uninhabited islands - Halfway Island and Humpy Island. To complete the idyllic picture there are usually two or three dozen yachts anchored in the clear turquoise water off Long Beach.

When winds are a little gusty on the beaches closest to the resorts, you will find Long Beach totally protected with the water there like a millpond. Long Beach is a leisurely half hour walk from the resort area - and should not be missed.

If you enjoy bushwalks, there are plenty of places to go. Leeke's historic homestead is just an hour's walk away. To enjoy panoramic views in all directions you can also climb to the top of Mount Wyndham. This walk will take you about one and a half hours each way.

If you are feeling particularly energetic there are two longer walks. One is to the Lighthouse on the far eastern side of Great Keppel and takes about two and a half hours. Another trail that forks off to the left from this one, about two and a half kilometres from the resorts, will take you to pretty Butterfish Bay on the northern side of the island.

You should not attempt to circum-navigate Great Keppel on foot - unless you

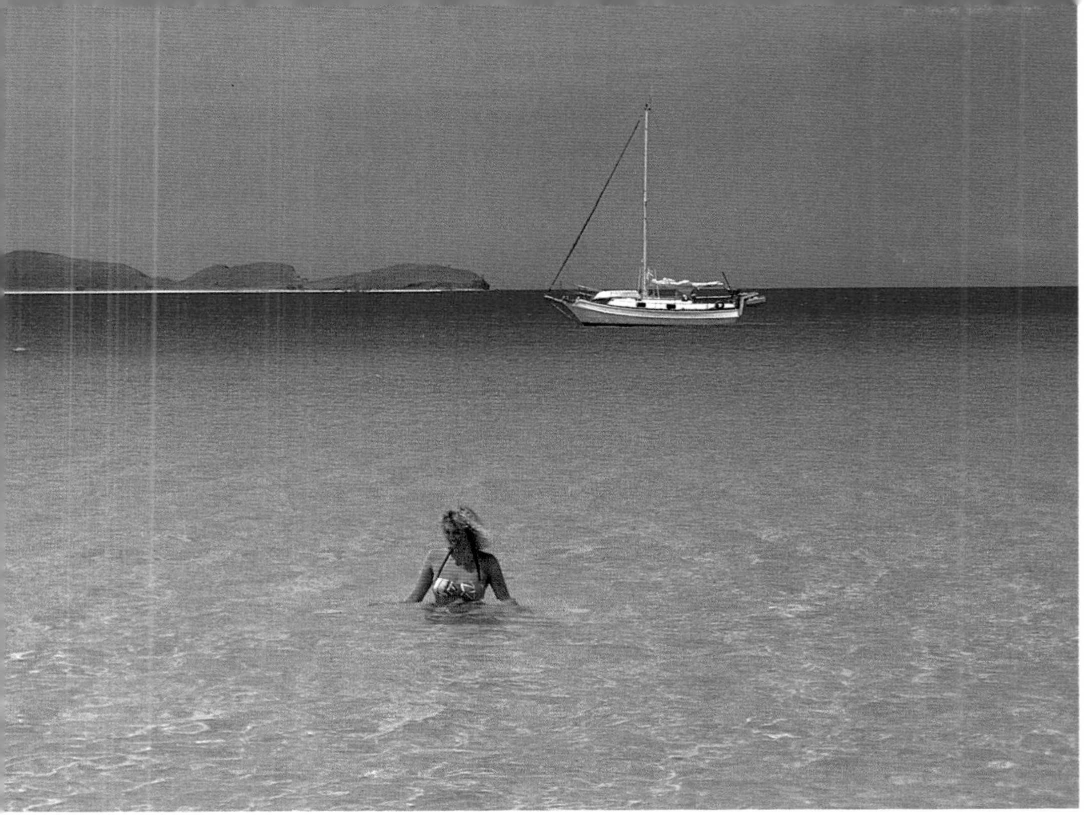

3

you take a tent!

You simply cannot walk around it in a single day. Nor are there established tracks that completely circumnavigate the island.

An exciting underwater world awaiting snorkellers and divers.

There are a number of places to snorkel around Great Keppel Island. The best location is Clam Bay although that entails a rather long trek from the resort area. The next best spot to snorkel is at the northern end of Long Beach and that is quite accessible. The closest spots are around Shelving Beach and Monkey Point but the coral here is not as prolific.

If you don't snorkel you can always see a magnificent garden of coral and profuse marine life by visiting the Underwater Observatory at nearby Middle Island. This large observatory took two years to build and complete, and was opened in 1980. The construction is robust, to say the least. The windows alone are 23 centimetres or nine inches thick!

From the observatory you will see a huge variety of colourful fish ranging from Angelfish and Butterfly Fish to brightly marked Bat Fish and Spotted Rock Cod. You will also see stingrays and clams with their beautifully coloured mantles.

A courtesy craft leaves the main resort beach, Fisherman's Beach, for the Observatory at regular intervals throughout the day.

If you are a scuba diver - or would like to learn - you will find that there is even more to see and enjoy underwater around Great Keppel and nearby islands.

If you wish to dive, contact Capricorn Reef Diving at Putney Beach. They handle all dive charter operations on the island with fully qualified instructors ready to show you the wonders of the local coral reefs and those out at North West Island, a coral cay.

Capricorn Reef Diving offers daily introductory scuba dives for the novice which include an hour's lecture on the basics of diving, a session in the water off Putney Beach to familiarize you with your equipment, and a dive closely supervised by an experienced instructor on a coral reef.

Capricorn Reef Diving also conduct a full five day P.A.D.I. Open Water Certification Course. The only items you need to take along if you wish to do this course are a medical certificate and passport photograph. The course commences every Monday at

1. An aerial view of Little Peninsula and Butterfish Bay on the northern side of Great Keppel Island. The house that can be seen is occupied by fishermen.

2. The clear blue waters of Long Beach with Humpy Island in the background.

3. Deserted Wreck Beach on the western side of the island. There is a small automated lighthouse on the far point.

1

2

3

1. North West Island, the largest coral cay on the Great Barrier Reef, can be reached from Great Keppel by helicopter or boat.

2. A turtle in North West's lagoon. The island is a nesting site for both Green and Loggerhead turtles.

3. The aerial view of North West Island and its fringing reef which you enjoy as you fly in by helicopter.

9:00 a.m.

Advanced, Divemaster, Assistant Instructor and Master Scuba Diving courses are available, as well as speciality courses including underwater photography and night diving.

There are at least nine dive sites that Capricorn Reef Diving take people to regularly - and if you want to snorkel further afield you should also contact them because some of these sites are just as wonderful for snorkelling.

Olive Point near the Underwater Observatory at nearby Middle Island is commonly used for snorkelling and introductory dives. You will see predominantly Staghorn coral here, large patches of colourful anemones and Clown fish.

At Miall Island there are two dive spots. At Miall Cove there is a gently sloping wall of Staghorn, Brain, Plate and numerous soft corals. The other site is Hole in the Wall with diverse marine life around scattered bommies.

Another popular place for diving is Barren Island. It has some spectacular dives at different sites with coral plateaux, caves, crevasses and assorted bommies with healthy coral and abundant marine life.

A dive for experienced divers only is The Child, a stone's throw away from Barren Island. It has five caves, one of which extends 40 metres into the island with a series of three blowholes. In the front of the cave entrance there is a rock and coral wall descending to 33 metres. Two large Moray eels also live in the cave and divers can always expect to see large fish such as giant Queensland Gropers, Giant Turrum, Spotted Eagle Rays and Spanish Mackerel.

The small islands just south of Great Keppel, Halfway Island and Humpy Island offer some spectacular sights, too.

If you wish to contact Capricorn Reef Diving before your visit to Great Keppel their phone number is (079) 39 4217.

All diving gear is available for rental or purchase from the dive shop, and at least two charter trips leave each day.

Visit the Barrier Reef's largest coral cay.

When you stay on Great Keppel you have the opportunity to visit North West Island as well. This is a coral cay of extraordinary beauty which is thriving with life both on land and in the waters around it.

4

5

6

7

8

Quite frankly, this is one experience that should not be missed. One of the reasons is that you can view the Great Barrier Reef from the air because you can make the trip to North West Island by helicopter.

The forty minute flight each way is nothing short of spectacular. It starts with a bird's-eye view of Great Keppel and its legendary beaches.

The flight then takes you low over smaller islands, craggy outcrops of rock and ribbons of reef clearly visible under shallow water.

Finally, you approach North West Island - at the heart of the Great Barrier Reef itself. The sight is breath-taking. "Whoever thought water could come in so many hues of blue?" is probably a question that you will ask yourself repeatedly.

As you fly closer you will see waves breaking over the island's outer reef, then see North West's tranquil lagoon. By now you will also have discovered the patch of lush green undergrowth at the centre of the lagoon - not much larger than a couple of city blocks - surrounded by an endless circle of white coral beach.

Once you have landed on North West Island there is plenty to do and see. Try not to devote too much time to lying on the beach and working on your sun-tan, although you could hardly find a more idyllic place to do so. Now is your chance to study the Great Barrier Reef, one of the natural Wonders of the World, at close quarters.

Being a coral cay, North West is literally a part of the Great Barrier Reef itself. The island is composed of coral debris and sand, derived from the surrounding reef.

North West Island actually covers an area of 91 hectares which makes it the largest coral cay on the Great Barrier Reef. There are many different species of plants on the island.

It is also the largest breeding site on the Great Barrier Reef for two species of birds, the White Capped Noddy and the Wedge Tailed Shearwater.

The noisy Wedge Tailed Shearwaters or Mutton Birds nest on North West Island between October and May.

The White Capped Noddies nest between October and March.

The Noddies feed on fish during the day and return to the island at night. Their droppings form a valuable fertiliser, known as

4. After walking out over the reef flats at low tide this fisherman stands at the very outer edge of the island's reef.

5. The highly manoeuvrable Greater Frigatebird. It feeds on flying fish, squid and preys on the nests of other sea-birds such as Terns and Boobies.

6. A Grey-tailed Tattler searching for food.

7. A Moray Eel in a shallow pool on the reef flats.

8. A giant clam with its colourful "mantle".

guano.

Between 1894 and 1900 North West Island was worked for the guano. Over 100 people are reported to have lived on the island during that time. A grave of a baby girl, the daughter of a Captain of a guano ship, can still be seen on the north-western side of the island.

Perhaps the most interesting way to spend your time at North West Island is to walk out over the reef flats at low tide, wearing old sand-shoes to protect your feet from the sharp coral.

Here you will discover a multitude of marine life including colourful Staghorn and soft corals, clams, sea anemones, Blue Linkia starfish, Cowrie shells, Bêche-de-Mer or sea cucumbers, and small but harmless Epaulette Sharks. (Please remember, however, that North West is a National Park and that you are not permitted to harm or collect anything, including shells, from the island.)

Depending on the weather conditions, you can then accompany your friendly pilot and guide and go snorkelling off the edge of the outer reef. The coral and marine life in evidence here is both diverse and abundant.

If you are a scuba diver, arrangements can be made so you can dive off the reef at North West Island.

In all likelihood you will also see turtles in the lagoon during a summer visit to North West Island. The island is actually the most important nesting site for Green Turtles on the southern Barrier Reef and small numbers of Loggerhead Turtles nest here, too.

The helicopter service to North West from Great Keppel is operated by Paradise Charter Services. Bookings must be made in advance at the main resort or by phoning Paradise Charter Services on (079) 391454. A maximum of three passengers can be taken on each flight so an early booking is recommended.

Incidentally, they also make helicopter trips to "Koorana", a crocodile breeding farm on the mainland. You will receive a personal tour of the farm by John Lever, a world-wide authority who promises to dispel many myths about these endearing creatures.

There is also a boat service out to North West Island four times a week. The boat is "Capricorn Reef Seeker", a high speed 36 metre catamaran capable of carrying 360 passengers. The trip to the cay takes one and a half hours.

Once at North West, passengers have three hours to snorkel, dive or view coral from a glass bottom boat. Tides permitting, you may walk on the reef flats as well and explore the island itself.

If you wish to dive at North West Cay, contact the Capricorn Reef Dive Shop at Putney Beach.

Accommodation to suit all pockets.

If you wish to holiday on Great Keppel Island you have a number of different options.

You have the choice of staying at the main resort owned and operated by Australian Airlines, Wapparaburra Haven Cabins or Tent Village, a YMCA Youth Hostel or you can camp.

It is probably fair to say that all of these places tend to attract couples and singles under the age of 35 more so than families. However, it should be said that families are

1

just as welcome and will enjoy themselves wherever they choose to stay. Indeed, the main resort has special facilities and activities for young children that parents will be most thankful for. The beaches, too, could not be better and safer for children.

The main resort which is owned and operated by Australian Airlines accommodates up to 400 people. There are currently two grades of accommodation - Beachfront and Garden Units. The tariffs include all meals and most activities.

All rooms feature balconies, wardrobes, private bathrooms, a refrigerator, ceiling fans and have both tea and coffee making facilities.

By early 1990 the resort will also have 60 luxury Villa Units on the hill overlooking the golf course and Fisherman's Beach.

The list of activities at the resort is extensive and a daily newsletter keeps you informed of special events. There is certainly no excuse to be bored. The resort has catamarans, sailboards, aqua bikes, and paddle skis. You can also go para-sailing, or take a dinghy and simply go fishing.

On land there is a 6-hole golf course, tennis, squash and badminton courts, archery range and a cricket field. You can play netball and volleyball or go horse riding as well.

If you wish to go bushwalking, knapsacks and thermos flasks are available - and a picnic lunch can be easily arranged.

If you would like to go to a beach further away from the more accessible ones or even visit one of the smaller islands nearby you can ask to be dropped off by speedboat. The drop-off charge depends on the

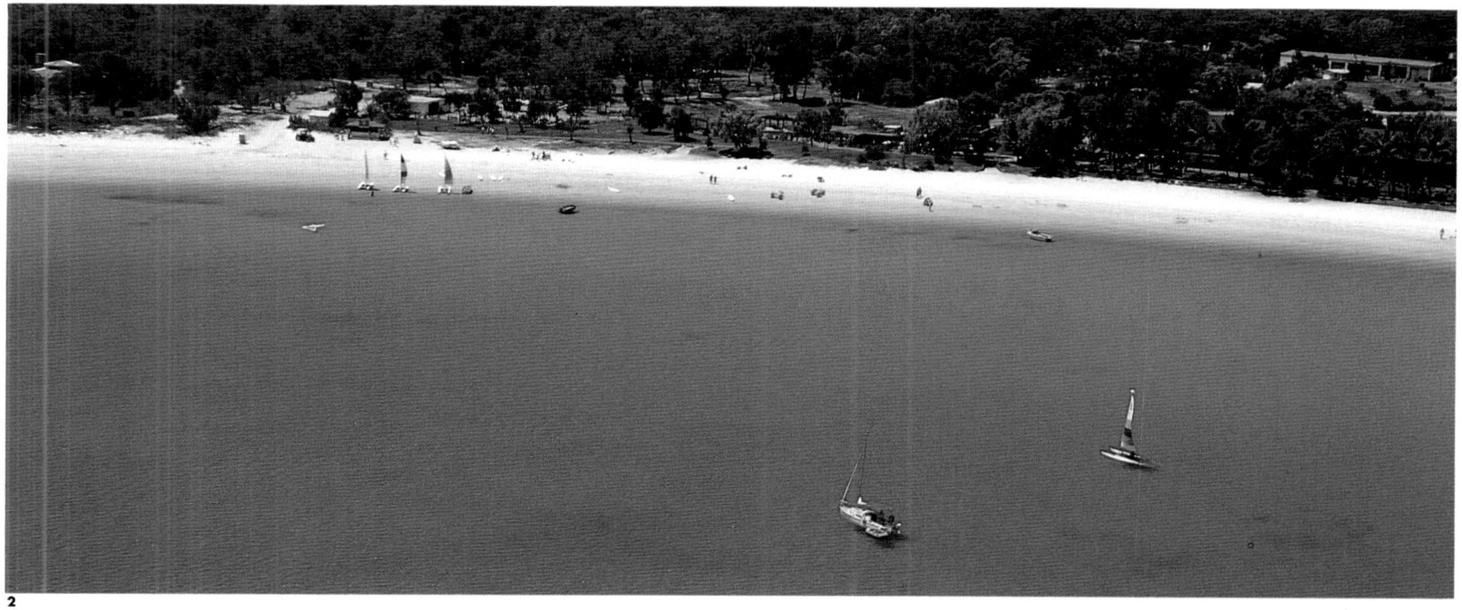

2

3

1. The helicopter which flies passengers to North West Island. The day's excursion is highly recommended.

2. Fisherman's Beach and the island's largest resort which is operated by Australian Airlines.

3. Five guests enjoy the thrill of riding the "Big Banana".

the destination but is very reasonable.

There are also daily cruises around Keppel Island for guests at the main resort and these are free. In fact, all standard activities are free of charge at the resort except for coral viewing by glass bottom boat, dinghies with outboards, para-sailing, snorkelling trips to Middle Island, cruises, tobogganing and water-skiing.

Yacht cruises are available, too. The yacht "Binda" sails regularly to either Halfway or Humpy Islands, just south of Great Keppel. It's a very pleasant way to spend a morning and both of these small islands are great locations for snorkelling.

There are half day and full day boat trips on another vessel for those who like fishing. Lunch is included and rods and bait are provided.

Parents will be pleased to note that babysitting facilities are available for a small charge and during the school holidays the resort runs a Kids Klub for three to 11 year olds. This operates from 9:30 a.m. each day and keeps the children occupied with sports, games and activities ranging from cricket to body painting. Participation in the Kids Klub is free except for some special activities.

There is also a separate club for 12 to 16 year olds.

Both clubs have their own dinner times and the entertainment continues afterwards with more games and videos.

All meals for other guests are served in the Admiral Keppel Restaurant. Breakfast is buffet style and lunch is a smorgasbord of hot and cold dishes.

In the evening, dinner is a la carte and the menu changes each day. A soup of the day is normally served, along with an entree, a choice of three main dishes, and a selection of desserts or cheeses.

The cuisine may not be of gourmet standard but it is certainly good, tasty fare. The first two courses on a typical evening's menu could well be Pea and Ham Soup, followed by Kilpatrick Oysters.

You could then choose between three dishes such as Pepper Steak Tropicana, Beef Tenderloin smothered in a Spicy Cream sauce with Pineapple; Chicken Keppelitis, tender Breast of Chicken sauteed with Tomatoes and Mushrooms, served on a bed of rice; and Baked Coral Trout.

You might then be tempted with something like Chocolate Mousse or Pineapple Crumble for dessert.

1

2

1. These comfortable cabins at Wapparaburra Haven accommodate up to six adults.

2. Tent City at Wapparaburra Haven has permanently erected tents, each with electric lighting, in landscaped gardens.

3. Guests at Wapparaburra Haven have direct access to a beautiful sandy beach called Putney Beach.

4. A girl soaks up the sun on Putney Beach.

Friday night is Island Night with a vast seafood smorgasbord and Pig on the Spit. It is a banquet fit for a king.

After dinner, the fun on Great Keppel continues for those who still have energy left to keep going. Following the evening meal there is always some form of entertainment in the Sand Bar adjoining the restaurant. It might be a live band, a talent quest, a limbo competition on Island Night, a newly released movie - whatever it is, it is usually enjoyed immensely by all.

Then you can head off to the Wreck Bar and the disco there. Good music, live bands - it's just the place to truly get wrecked!

The Wreck Bar, incidentally, is open to guests from Wapparaburra Haven and the YMCA. So if you choose to stay at either of these places you can still enjoy some great night-life.

The main resort also has a daytime cafe open to all with hot and cold takeaway food, drinks and ice-creams; a separate shop with an excellent range of clothing, souvenirs, toiletries, newspapers, magazines, stamps and post-box; plus a hairdressing salon.

Wapparaburra Haven offers two types of accommodation. They have small, modern cabins that sleep up to six adults. These cabins have a compact living area and kitchenette.

The cabins are located in an area that has been beautifully landscaped with trees and ferns, and are just minutes away from either Putney or Fisherman's Beach.

For a budget holiday they represent extremely good value.

All cooking utensils, crockery and linen are supplied - all you need to bring are towels. Guests share a modern amenities block for showers and toilets.

A shop situated near the entrance of Wapparaburra stocks a large range of groceries, meat, dairy foods, and fresh bread as well as hamburgers and sandwiches. It also has a small but good range of swimwear, coral jewellery, souvenirs and items like camera film.

In addition, there is a very attractive and homely BYO restaurant that you may dine at. The menu is very reasonable in price and offers appetising entrees like Prawn Cocktails and Long Beach Scallops prepared in a lemon and orange marinade and served with a seafood sauce.

The main courses vary from steaks and locally caught Reef Fish cooked in Coconut

3

4

and grilled in butter to Port Curtis Prawns sauteed in Garlic and Spring Onions, and served with a rich creamy sauce. Desserts include Pecan Pie, Cheese Cake and Fruit salad.

Takeaway meals are available, too.

Wapparaburra also offers accommodation in their Tent City. Tents are available with or without bedding. There is electric lighting in each tent but guests must bring their own towels. There is also a large, communal kitchen. All the tents are in very pleasant landscaped surroundings.

Wapparaburra has a camp-site as well if you wish to bring your own tents, bedding, cooking utensils, etc. Here the basic facility is space, although you do have use of a shared amenities block.

Windsurfers, catamarans, surf skis and dinghies with outboards are available for hire at the Beach Shed on Putney Beach. Fishermen can purchase bait and tackle.

These boats may also be hired if you decide to stay at the YMCA. This hostel is very, very basic indeed. In the author's opinion the facilities at Wapparaburra are of a much higher standard and in far more pleasant surroundings.

Should you wish to stay at the YMCA Hostel you must book and pay at the Rockhampton Youth Hostel prior to arrival or make a mail booking through the Youth Hostel Association in Brisbane.

How to get to Great Keppel Island.

The telephone number of the main resort operated by Australian Airlines is (079) 391744. Their facsimile number is (079) 391775.

Wapparaburra Haven's telephone number is (079) 391907.

To get to Great Keppel you really have two choices. You can fly from Rockhampton aboard an Australian Airlines aircraft. This flight takes approximately 15 minutes and connects with normal domestic flights on the mainland. (Private aircraft are also permitted to land on the Great Keppel airstrip.)

Alternatively, you can catch one of the boats operated by Great Keppel Island Tourist Services from Rosslyn Bay each day. They also offer a coach connection with both Yeppoon and Rockhampton. Their phone number is (079) 33 6744 or (079) 27 2948.

Should you wish to drive to Rosslyn Bay, undercover accommodation for your car is available at Kempsea Car Park. Their telephone number is (079) 336670. A courtesy bus service operates between the car park and the departure point for the boats going to the island.

With its marvellous beaches, choice of mid-priced and budget accommodation, and range of daytime and night-time activities, Great Keppel is a great destination, particularly for the under 35's - although anyone older and with families will still enjoy themselves immensely.

The advertising theme of the resort operated by Australian Airlines has long been "Get Wrecked on Great Keppel".

Regardless of where they get wrecked on the island, few people seem to regret the experience.

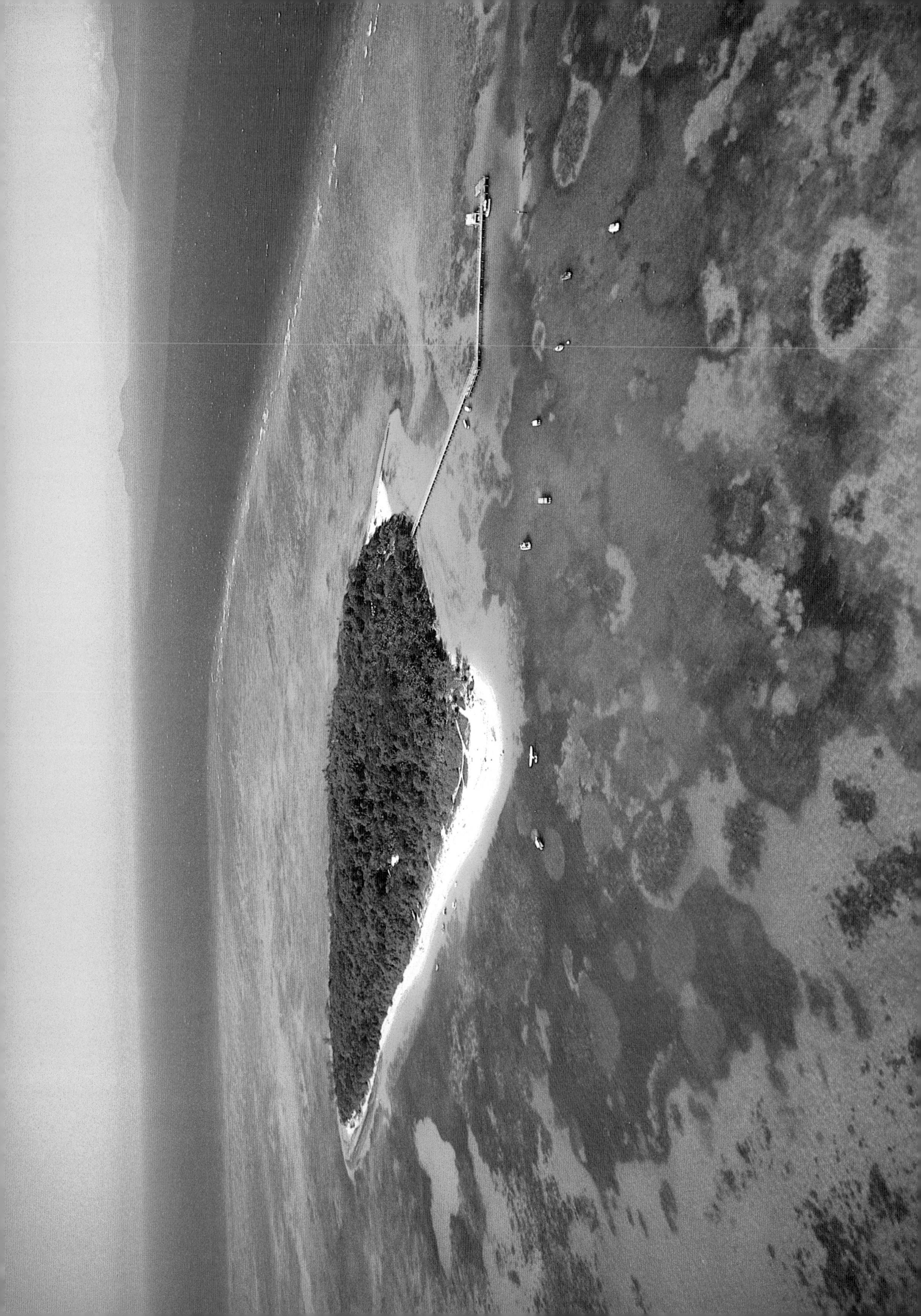

GREEN ISLAND

2

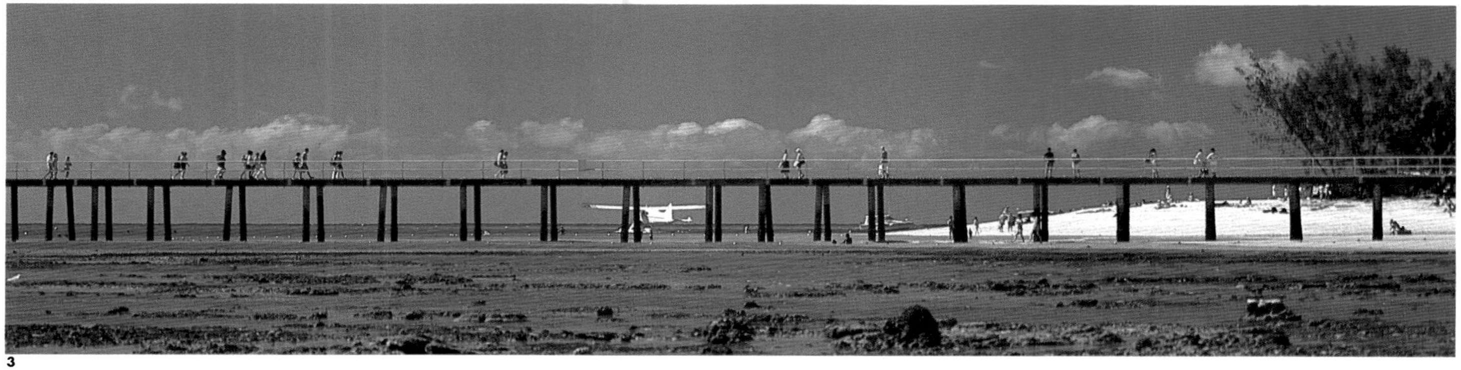
3

Green Island is a small coral cay that lies 27 kilometres off Cairns.

It was one of the first Great Barrier Reef islands to see regular visitors. Pleasure cruises went to Green Island as early as 1890.

Since then many thousands of people have visited the island as day-trippers. There is also a small resort that caters for up to 100 guests.

The island is just 260 metres wide and 660 metres long. It occupies a mere 12 hectares but has 500 hectares of reef surrounding it.

The reef surrounding Green Island is now a Marine Park and two thirds of the island is National Park.

Green Island was named by James Cook in 1770 on June 10.

In the 1800's at least two ships were wrecked on the island's reef. Five Bêche-de-mer fishermen were also slain by aborigines on Green Island.

For years Green Island has been a popular destination for day visitors who come to the island because of a major attraction, the Underwater Observatory.

4

1. Green Island from the air - its famous Underwater Observatory is clearly visible at the end of the jetty. Neighbouring Fitzroy Island and the mainland can be seen on the horizon.

2. Some of the colourful and interesting marine life on display in aquariums at Marineland Melanesia, another attraction on the island.

3. Visitors arriving at Green Island. In the foreground are the reef flats which are exposed around the island at low tide. The resort's main beach can also be seen.

4. A Reef Heron, one of the island's many feathered inhabitants. They feed mainly on small fish up to 15 centimetres long.

1

Another feature of the island is Marineland Melanesia which contains aquariums with a very wide range of tropical fish and creatures common to the Great Barrier Reef, captive crocodiles of enormous size from the north of Australia, and an extensive collection of primitive art.

There is also a theatre on the island which has the exclusive rights to screen films shot by Noel Monkman, the first film-maker to capture the underwater life of the Great Barrier Reef.

The temperature on Green Island in the summer ranges between 21°C and 29°C. During the winter it is somewhere between 16°C and 24°C.

Named after James Cook's Astronomer.

Lieutenant James Cook passed Green Island in 1770 as he sailed up the eastern coast of Australia on his first world voyage aboard the "Endeavour" ship. Although he described it as a "low green woody island" Cook actually named it after one of the ship's scientists.

Charles Green was both Chief Observer and Astronomer in Charge for the expedition. When Cook visited Hawaii in 1769 it was Green who was responsible for the heavenly observations of the "Transit of Venus".

Green's cabin aboard the "Endeavour" was somewhat cramped if the headroom was anything to go by. It was no more than five feet four inches - less than two metres.

The conditions of Green's appointment included a bonus of 200 guineas on the successful return of the expedition to England. Unfortunately, the astronomer died on January 29, 1771, on the journey back to his homeland, shortly after the "Endeavour" left Java.

In 1858, a man by the name of S.V. Main was attracted to Green Island because of the numerous Bêche-de-mer or sea cucumbers on the reef surrounding the island. These creatures were a delicacy in the East and were considered a great source of profit locally.

Main arrived on Green Island accompanied by five South Sea islanders in his employment. The Bêche-de-mer station that he established consisted of palm thatched huts, storehouses and a tarpaulin covered smokehouse.

Main and his men appeared to enjoy a comfortable and carefree existence on the island. They obtained seeds from the Sydney Botanical Gardens and grew guava, grapes, corn, pumpkin, turnip and cabbage. They also had a ready supply of birds and fresh fish. Stingray liver oil was used for cooking.

As a business venture, however, the Bêche-de-mer station did not prove profitable so Main eventually abandoned the island. The buildings were still intact when he left which is rather surprising for a cyclone had hit the island whilst they were still on it. The cyclone must have been very severe for according to Main the island was almost totally engulfed by the sea at the time.

During the 1800's many ships came to grief in the area as they attempted to navigate their way north. One such ship was the "Antagonist" which was wrecked on Green Island's reef on May 14, 1863. She was carrying horses to India.

The scene of two early massacres.

On March 8, 1872, three more Bêche-de-mer fishermen arrived at Green Island aboard their cutter "Goodwill". Their names were Dan Kelly, Bill White and Bill Rose.

They brought three Palm Island aborigines with them to dive for the Bêche-de-mer. Two of the aborigines were accompanied by women.

It was decided that Kelly and the three aboriginal men would spend each day out on the reef aboard "Goodwill" collecting the sea cucumbers. White and Rose would remain on the island with the two women cutting wood, smoking the previous day's catch, and cooking.

After dinner each evening, Kelly rowed the three aboriginal men out to the cutter where they had to spend the night alone. Their women and the three white men camped on the island. The three aboriginal men were then rowed ashore just in time for breakfast.

The aborigines tolerated this arrangement for four days. After breakfast on April 12, Kelly went down to launch the dinghy again. His task, however, was interrupted by a loud groan from the camp.

Kelly turned and saw Rose trying to escape from Billy, one of the blacks. Billy was wielding a bloody axe and Rose had blood pouring from a nasty head wound.

As they both disappeared into one of the huts, White staggered down towards the beach and into the water with a second aborigine named Dicky close behind, chopping at him with a tomahawk.

Kelly managed to push the dinghy out into the water and headed for the cutter. Within minutes all three aborigines were in pursuit, swimming after him. He used an oar to fend them off but they were so determined that he rejected the idea of seeking refuge on the cutter. Instead, he rowed a long 16 kilometres to Oyster Cay where there was another Bêche-de-mer station run by a fellow called Philip Garland.

By the time they returned to Green Island aboard Garland's ketch "Telegraph" night had closed in and there was no sign of either the blacks or "Goodwill".

When they ventured ashore with a light they found the savagely mutilated bodies of both Rose and White lying on the beach. The camp itself had been ransacked and plundered.

They buried the bodies next morning and then sailed to the mainland to report the tragic incident. Robert A. Johnstone, the local police sub-inspector at Cardwell, and a party of native police subsequently searched the coast around Trinity Bay.

They did so aboard the police boat which was an old, open whaleboat that had been used by the Captain of the "Maria", to escape this ship after it had been wrecked in the vicinity. The whaleboat leaked so badly that one crewman was required to bail continually.

When Johnstone and his men actually landed at Trinity Bay they were attacked by some of the local blacks but managed to fight them off. They then found remnants of a burnt boat and clothing which had belonged to the crew of Kelly's cutter "Goodwill".

It was quite obvious that the five Palm Island natives responsible for the atrocity on

1

2

Green Island had been killed themselves by the local aborigines.

Johnstone, incidentally, combined his occupation of police Sub-Inspector with that of both naturalist and explorer. His reminiscences were later published and are still regarded as a valuable record of early life in North Queensland.

Several months after the tragic events on Green Island, Kelly returned to Green Island on July 10 aboard the "Eliza" with four companions and ten aborigines. Believe it or not, history virtually repeated itself.

By now there was another camp on Green Island and a man by the name of James Mercer was in the process of establishing a new Bêche-de-mer station. With him was Charles Reeves, John Finlay, a Kanaka, three aboriginal boys and a woman.

On the night of July 10, Kelly was standing watch at his own station and noticed a few strange movements around his black boys' camp. Kelly armed himself with a gun. A short time later he noticed a boat drifting along the edge of the reef.

Kelly was alerting his companions when the blacks in his camp told him that the natives at Mercer's camp had killed all the white men there. They had done this because the whites had refused to give them bread that night.

Kelly and his companions manned their own whaleboat and overtook the other boat. In it were the four aborigines from Mercer's camp. They dived into the water, however, and escaped in the darkness.

When Kelly and his mates went to Mercer's camp they found the bodies of Mercer, Reeves, Finlay and the Kanaka, as well as two blood stained axes.

Several years after these massacres another Bêche-de-mer fisherman took up residence on Green Island. His name was George "Yorkie" Lawson, and this colourful character owned the cutter "True Love".

It seems, however, that Yorkie's true love was actually a drop or two of liquor. Whenever he and his Jamaican companion "John the Baptist" sailed into Cairns with their catch most of what they earned ended up in the hands of publicans. This practice was aided by the fact that Yorkie distrusted banks completely.

While Yorkie was living on Green Island a schooner called the "Epolu" was wrecked on its reef on Sunday, April 25, 1886. She was carrying stores aboard for a

1. A family of aborigines, the only full-time residents on Green Island in 1920.

2. Bob Hayles, who operated one of the first boats to cruise the Great Barrier Reef, on Green Island in 1920.

1

2

1. A party of gentlemen who cruised the Reef and its islands with Bob Hayles in 1921.

2. Bob Hayles' boat "The Mandalay" about to leave on a Great Barrier Reef cruise from Townsville in 1921.

3

4

3. A group of aborigines from a Mission on the mainland picnic on Green Island in 1948.

4. The dining room of the island's resort in 1941.

5. Visitors to Green Island in 1932 view coral through boxes which had glass bottoms.

copra plantation in the South Seas.

Luckily, the crew survived. They drifted around Trinity Bay for a few days, reluctant to land for fear of being attacked by the local natives, and were then rescued by the S.S. "Bulimba" which belonged to the British India Steam Navigation Company.

While the crew were being taken to Townsville, Yorkie made sure that he was a major beneficiary of the spoil gathered from the wreck. He was careful, though, to hide it well and Revenue officers searched the island fruitlessly for contraband on more than one occasion.

The only items officially recovered from the wreck of the "Upolu" was the ship's cat and a pig. The wreck went up in flames. It is believed that another man and woman living on the island at the time also went out to plunder the wreck, found a plentiful supply of spirits, got drunk and accidentally blew up both the wreck and themselves.

Yorkie also used unorthodox methods to catch fish. He would use dynamite. Unfortunately, he blew one arm off whilst on one fishing expedition but despite this setback Yorkie remained both an excellent swimmer and diver.

He also had a hook screwed onto the stump which helped make up for his handicap. On a later visit to Cairns, however, someone noticed that he had dispensed with the hook and asked why. "I'll never use it again," he replied and explained why.

The previous week he had thrown an anchor over the side of his boat and the hook had caught in a link, dragging him to the bottom. He only escaped by turning around and around, thus unscrewing the hook.

When his Bêche-de-mer days came to an end Yorkie was appointed caretaker of Green Island by the Government and received the sum of £20 a year. He supplemented this income by breeding poultry and catching fish.

Yorkie died peacefully on Green Island, on April 14, 1907, at the age of sixty eight.

The world's first Underwater Observatory.

Organised cruises to Green Island began as far back as 1890 aboard a local coaster, the "Zeus". In 1928, a regular fortnightly service between Cairns and Green Island was operated by Charlie Hayles.

Charlie Hayles actually developed the world's first glass bottom boat in 1937 which enabled visitors to see the wonders of the reef more easily. The following year Hayles was granted a lease for a tourist resort on the island.

By 1941 guests could stay in one of six cottages or three small cabins. There were also seven permanent tents that had corrugated roofing over the canvas, and a dining-room.

The tariff for staying on the island was £2/17/6 ($6) a week. This included all meals, prepared on a wood stove by Mrs. Shepherd, an old cook who had previously worked on various sheep stations.

Derek Scott, who worked at the small resort and later became a skipper for Hayles, remembers that Torres Strait islanders from

5

1

1. The Underwater Observatory at Green Island which thousands of people visit each year.

2. The stunning beach that can be enjoyed on an excursion to Michaelmas Cay.

Trochus and Bêche-de-mer schooners would often come ashore and dance for the guests.

As interest in the Great Barrier Reef grew, Green Island was perfectly located to study it. In 1939, a photographic laboratory was even established on the island so that the diverse marine life of the reef could be captured on camera.

In 1954, the world's first Underwater Observatory was opened at Green Island. It was designed and built by Vince Vlasoff and Lloyd Grigg on the foreshores of Cairns Harbour. It took a year to build. After being floated out to Green Island it was sunk, bolted to steel pins driven into the reef, and also anchored by chains.

In cyclonic weather the Observatory can be partially flooded with 50 tonnes of water to withstand abnormal pressure from winds and turbulent seas.

The Observatory which is located at the end of a long jetty at Green Island has 22 observation windows made of glass over 30 millimetres thick. After winding down 30 steps to the bottom of the Observatory's chamber you are about five metres under the water's surface.

Through the Observatory's windows you can see a spectacular garden of both hard and soft corals.

Many of the corals have names that quite accurately describe their appearance - such as Staghorn, Mushroom, Golden Leaf, Lace and Plate. You will also see giant clams, anemones and over 50 species of fish that inhabit the Great Barrier Reef. Hopefully, you will even see one or two of the huge turtles that inhabit the Reef.

Many people have visited the Underwater Observatory including Queen Elizabeth II, Prince Phillip and Princess Anne. The royal party called in on the Observatory during their 1970 tour of Australia.

At the Observatory you can also see full-size replicas of a cannon and anchor from Cook's ship, the "Endeavour", which was wrecked further north on the Reef.

When Cook ran aground he dumped six cannon overboard along with many other items in an attempt to lighten his ship and thus escape the treacherous coral reef. The ship was refloated at high tide with the loss of an anchor and subsequently repaired (see Chapter Two for the full story).

One of the designers and builders of the Observatory, Vince Vlasoff, actually helped recover the cannon with his vessel

2

"Tropic Seas", after they were located in 1969 by an American expedition from the Academy of Natural Sciences in Philadelphia. The anchor was located by an Australian expedition on Christmas Day of 1971, buried underneath one metre of coral. Vlasoff also assisted in its recovery and the historic anchor now lies on display at the Science Museum in Melbourne.

On display at the Observatory is also an impressive collection of beautiful shells of many colours and sizes gathered from the Great Barrier Reef.

The Observatory is open every day of the year between 8:30 a.m. and 4:30 p.m. Night viewing is sometimes arranged for guests staying on the island.

If you want to get an even closer look at the many colourful fish and corals you can snorkel near the Observatory along a marked underwater trail. This is the best area to snorkel around Green Island because it was protected with great effort when much of the live coral around the island was destroyed by the Crown of Thorns starfish during the 1960's.

An island created by microscopic organisms.

Green Island is a cay which means that its existence is due totally to the efforts of countless coral polyps that initially created the reef on which it stands.

Thousands of years ago, broken fragments of coral washed up onto the leeward side of this reef and a sandbank eventually formed. As birds used it as a resting place they deposited seeds and organic humus which allowed plants like coarse grasses that were capable of withstanding high levels of salt water to take hold.

Grasses and creepers trapped fresh-water from rain and this allowed the growth of other plants from seeds that were transported by currents, wind and birds. Finally, large trees began to forest the cay. Today, over 40 species of shrubs and trees can be found on Green Island.

As you walk along tracks through the dense vegetation you'll come across enormous Fig trees draped with Jasmine, *Pandanus tectoris* or Screw Pines, a tall tree with brilliant red leaves called *Terminalia melanocarpa*, Grey Boxwood and Northern Yellow Boxwood trees, Beach Almonds and Drooping Sheoaks.

The coconut palms are not natives. These were planted in 1889 by Ebenezer Cowley, who was Director of the Kamerunga State Nursery near Cairns.

People who stay on Green Island can also visit nearby Michaelmas Cay which is not as fully developed as the former. It has only reached the stage of sustaining grasses and creepers. There are no trees at all.

The trip to Michaelmas Cay is well worthwhile. It is about 15 kilometres by boat from Green Island (and about 40 kilometres north-east of Cairns), and just half an hour away by a large motor powered catamaran. The snorkelling is good and thousands of sea-birds can be observed nesting on this tiny island during the summer months.

The colony of ground-nesting sea-birds is, in fact, one of the largest to be found on

1

2

the Great Barrier Reef. At the peak of nesting there can be over 30,000 birds on the cay. Six species of birds nest on Michaelmas, the most common being Sooty Terns and Crested Terns.

The female Sooty Tern lays a single egg in the sand and both parents help incubate this. A week after it has hatched, the chick joins others in a wandering group called a creche.

You will often encounter these creches on the beach. The birds seem quite impervious to the presence of human beings and you can approach them within a metre or so if you are careful. It is not uncommon to be met with the baleful stare of up to 40 young birds or more clustered closely together.

During the day the parents catch small fish, squid and crustaceans by making shallow dives into the sea. They then feed their chick by regurgitation. About 70 days after hatching, the young Sooty Terns can fly and leave the cay.

Other birds that you can see nesting on or simply visiting Michaelmas Cay include the Crested Tern, Roseate Tern, Ruddy Turnstone, Least Frigatebird, Reef Heron, and Brown Booby.

The cay is a National Park and bird sanctuary and visitors are not permitted access to all areas of it. This is for the protection of the nests. Birds that are disturbed fly off their nests and their eggs or chicks are either exposed to excess heat from the sun or preying gulls.

In 1926 geologists drilled a borehole on Michaelmas Cay to investigate the origin of the Great Barrier Reef. This indicated that the present reef growth has its foundations on a previously exposed reef now 17 metres below sea level.

While you are at Michaelmas Cay you can swim, snorkel and sunbake on the superb sandy beach.

You can also step aboard a glass bottom boat or a small semi-submersible craft to see all the colourful fish and different corals in the crystal clear waters that surround the island.

On your return to the large catamaran that takes you to Michaelmas keep an eye on the water. You will often see small stingrays darting around beneath the surface.

Another enjoyable trip that you can make is to Norman Reef which is about 45 minutes from Green Island.

3

1. Michaelmas Cay, a wonderful place to snorkel, swim and sunbake.
2. Young Sooty Terns on Michaelmas Cay.
3. Nesting Sooty Terns keep an eye out for Gulls which prey on chicks and eggs.

4

5

4. George Craig points out one of the artifacts in his collection at Marineland Melanesia.
5. There are number of huge crocodiles in captivity at Marineland Melanesia. One is even featured in the Guinness Book of Records.

An Aquarium and Theatre on Green Island.

Back at Green Island a visit to Marineland Melanesia should also be considered. This is open between 8:30 a.m. and 4:30 p.m. and is operated by a colourful character, George Craig, who has been on the island since 1971.

Prior to that he hunted crocodiles for 19 years around Darwin and in New Guinea. He migrated to Australia in his early twenties from England where he was a professional high diver and stuntman.

George Craig has established a very large sea-water Aquarium on Green Island with 19 tanks containing live corals, tropical fish, sea anemones and other forms of marine life. There is also information about all the residents in the tanks so you can identify many of the different and interesting species that inhabit the Great Barrier Reef.

In addition to the Aquarium there is also an impressive display of artifacts from New Guinea, Timor and Indonesia that George Craig collected over the many years he spent in that region. These artifacts are exhibited in two Long Houses from the Papuan Gulf and Sepik area of New Guinea. On display are also 11 skulls of crocodiles, most of which were shot by George himself.

Marineland Melanesia covers about one acre and within its grounds there are a number of huge crocodiles that George Craig has in captivity. One actually made the Guinness Book of Records. Its name is Oscar and it measures about six metres in length. Oscar was caught in New Guinea in 1967 and is estimated to be at least 70 years of age.

Another daunting specimen is Cassius. This fearsome looking crocodile also measures about six metres, has one foot missing, and is reputed to be the real "Sweetheart". This rogue crocodile attacked and terrorised many people aboard dinghies on the Finniss River, about a hundred kilometres south of Darwin.

"Sweetheart" supposedly lies stuffed in Darwin Museum but George Craig points out that this specimen is only some five metres long. Whether the specimen in Darwin Museum is really an impostor has not yet been clearly established but there is no doubt that Cassius is the largest salt-water crocodile ever caught in Australia.

Another attraction close to Marineland Melanesia is The Great Barrier Reef Theatre. This was originally built by Noel and Kitty Monkman who arrived on Green Island in 1929.

Noel Monkman was a diver who explored and photographed the Reef's fascinating life. He was, in fact, the first man in Australia to take a camera underwater and film the microscopic life of the seas.

Noel Monkman also wrote books and was amongst the first to alert the public about the need to protect the area. As an honorary ranger and fisheries inspector he also did much to prevent destruction of the fragile environment that he knew so well.

Two films shot by Noel Monkman can still be seen at the theatre by special request on one of the largest video screens in Australia. One is "Nests of the Sun", the other is "Invisible Wonders of the Great Barrier Reef".

Normally, however, the theatre shows two films shot more recently by well-known underwater photographer Val Taylor. One is entitled "The Mighty Coral Polyp" and the other is "Dive the Great Barrier Reef".

Directly adjoining the theatre is a small museum which documents the history of Green Island. It has many interesting photographs including some that show the extensive damage caused on Green Island when it was struck by Cyclone Winifred in February, 1986. Winds of 150 kilometres an hour battered the island.

Accommodation for 100 people.

Being so accessible to Cairns and having several attractions in addition to its own natural beauty, Green Island has long been a popular tourist destination. Many thousands of people visit Green Island each year - mostly for a day.

You can, however, stay on the island. There are two types of accommodation currently available, either Palm Units or Tropical Units. Together, these can hold about 100 guests but there are usually no more than 70 or so guests staying on the island overnight.

Children of all ages are welcome to stay on the island. (Parents should also be pleased to know that there are baby-sitting facilities available.

The Tropical Units are larger than the Palm Units and are ideal for families. Both forms of accommodation are very comfortable, being similar to a good motel room. All units were renovated between 1986 and 1987 and have their own bathrooms, air-conditioning, ceiling fans, mini-bar, fridge and television (but no radios).

With many day visitors, the mood of the island changes substantially. Before the first boat arrives mid-morning and the last boat departs at around 4:30 p.m., the few guests remaining on the island have it completely to themselves.

A leisurely walk around the island takes no more than 40 minutes and is most enjoyable in the morning, before it gets too hot, or in the late afternoon. The evenings, in particular, are a delight.

As the sun sets, you can enjoy a cocktail in the Sundowner Bar and then settle down to a very good meal in the restaurant served by friendly staff who seem to take pride in ensuring that everything is just right. Considering that this is not a plush, expensive resort the excellent service may even be unexpected but it is certainly pleasurable to experience. The mood in the restaurant amongst guests is casual and very relaxed.

In the evening there is either a seafood smorgasbord and carvery or a menu that offers a choice of two entrees, half a dozen main dishes and several desserts.

A typical menu (they are always changing) would be as follows. Soup of the Day followed by Avocado Royale or Seafood Crepes. For the main course you might then have a choice of Roast Rib Fillet Raifort, Steak Diable, Barramundi Amandine, Barramundi with Fine Herbs, a Seafood Platter or a Selection of Cold Meats. To accompany these main dishes you would also be able to choose from a selection of vegetables and salads.

You would then be tempted with desserts like Strawberry Cheesecake, Tropical Fresh Fruit Salad, Ice Cream and Topping, followed by a Cheeseboard.

The wine list offers a selection of good Australian wines and there are several champagnes available, both Australian and French. There is also a small selection of liqueurs and excellent ports.

After the evening meal, there is no organised entertainment. There will sometimes be a film, however, about the Reef which is both interesting and informative.

Lunch is normally barbeque-style in an outdoor garden setting. Room service is also available at lunchtime. A Snack Bar has everything from sandwiches to fish and chips, all very reasonably priced.

A shop at the resort stocks a wide range of casual clothing, souvenirs, coral jewellery, toiletries, magazines, paperbacks

1

2

3

and postcards. Green Island also has its own official Post Office and Commonwealth Banking facilities.

During the day, guests have use of windsurfers, surf skis and coral viewing boards. These are available at the main beach which is excellent for swimming and safe all year round. Other activities include archery, volleyball and table tennis.

There is also a qualified Diving Instructor who conducts a 5-day PADI course. Those interested should make further enquiries and bookings for this course before arrival on the island.

A one-day introductory dive course is available as well for those who have never dived before but would like to try it.

Divers can dive on reefs near Green Island where there is extremely good fish life and soft corals. They also have the option of diving at either Michaelmas or Norman Reefs.

How to get to Green Island.

Many well-known people apart from Queen Elizabeth have visited Green Island. Paul Hogan, Ray Martin, Bo Derek and the author Wilbur Smith are just a few of the many visitors who have stepped ashore.

Access to the island is by boat from Cairns.

For those who wish to contact the resort, their phone number is (070) 514644, their telex number is AA48332 and their facsimile number is (070) 513624. The resort's address is simply Green Island, Queensland, 4871.

Readers should be aware that major redevelopment is planned by the new owners of the resort area, Great Adventures Pty. Ltd.

By the end of 1990, a totally new resort should have opened on the location of the current one. When complete, the new resort will have 70 two-storey villas of very high standard available for accommodation. Another building will house a new restaurant, bar areas and shops.

Great Adventures will also be expanding the Underwater Observatory.

Despite the tragic events of last century, cyclones and the devastation caused by the Crown of Thorns starfish to much of its reef, Green Island is still one of the most popular destinations on the Great Barrier Reef. There is no reason to suggest that this will change.

1. The sandy spit and main beach adjoining the resort area.

2. Tropical Units at the island's resort.

3. Palm Units have either double or twin beds.

HAMILTON ISLAND

2

3

Hamilton Island is situated in the middle of the beautiful Whitsunday group of islands. It is over five kilometres in length, over four kilometres at its widest point and covers an area of some 1,350 acres.

Originally a pastoral lease, Hamilton Island has been transformed in part by the dreams of one man, Keith Williams, who has created the largest resort you can visit within the entire Great Barrier Reef region (and the South Pacific).

In fact, it is not so much a resort but a small, bustling town. The population of Hamilton Island at any one time is around 2,000 people. The island has its own harbour and marina crammed with millions of dollars worth of luxury boats.

There is a wide range of accommodation from Polynesian-style Bures to luxury penthouse suites and houses (several with their own butler service). There are eight restaurants, some offering snacks and light meals, others offering fine cuisine and silver service.

Hamilton Island has its own tavern, night club, delicatessen, bakery, supermarket, newsagency, school, church, Post Office, National Australia Bank, T.A.B., and shops with fashion from around the world.

4

1. The small but busy harbour at Hamilton Island. The island is a popular stop-over for yachts and motor boats cruising the Whitsundays.

2. Keith Williams, the person who planned and built the resort village on the island, aboard his multi-million dollar boat "Achilles II".

3. "Awesome", a high-speed power boat available for charter, is a fast and luxurious way to see the Whitsundays and Hardy Reef.

4. The small lighthouse at the entrance of Hamilton Harbour.

1

There is a Dolphin Pool and Fauna Park with kangaroos, emus, koalas, deer, parrots and other birds and animals.

Hamilton Island also has its own airport with direct flights by jet from Melbourne, Sydney, Brisbane and Cairns.

Even though the resort has only been open since 1984 a stream of guests including the rich and famous have visited Hamilton Island. Such guests have included the Aga Khan, Prince Albert of Monaco, the Queen of Denmark, the King and Queen of Nepal, tycoons like Rupert Murdoch, Alan Bond, Kerry Packer, Robert Holmes a Court, and celebrities such as the racing car driver Jackie Stewart, Elton John, Paul Hogan and John Denver.

George Harrison, one of the four ex-Beatles, has a magnificent five acre estate on the island.

Other well-known people like media personality Mike Willesee have also purchased condominiums or land on the island to build their own private hideaways in the midst of the glorious Whitsundays.

Visitors can enjoy a wide range of activities including tennis, squash, sailing, and scuba diving on the Reef which is one hour and 50 minutes away by high-speed catamaran and 25 minutes by helicopter.

The temperature on Hamilton Island during summer averages 28°C to 32°C. In the winter it ranges between 25°C and 28°C.

Keith Williams, a man with an impressive dream.

The evidence from journals of Captain Cook suggest that when he passed through the Whitsundays in 1770 on his historic voyage north, his ship the "Endeavour" passed within two kilometres of Hamilton Island. It remained unnamed, however, until the late 19th century.

Its name first appeared on charts following a survey of the area by Commander George Nares, Captain of the HMS "Salamander", in 1866. Why he named it Hamilton is still unclear.

The island was not inhabited until 1930. It was then used - like a number of islands within the Whitsunday Group - for grazing.

The first person to lease it for such purposes was a John McDonald, a doctor studying tropical medicine. The rent of the whole island at the time was £5 per annum.

Doctor McDonald stayed on the island until 1951. The pastoral lease then passed through several hands until October, 1975, when it was purchased by Hamilton Island Enterprises for the sum of $300,000. The person behind the decision to purchase the island was Keith Williams and it was used for several years for deer-farming.

This highly successful entrepreneur left school when he was just 13. His first job was as a bowser boy at a garage. When he was somewhat older Keith Williams' love of motorbikes led him into manufacturing parts for them, and in 1959 he also became the Australian Water Ski Champion. He started water ski shows in Surfers Paradise and in 1970 opened Sea World, which became and remains a major tourist attraction on the Gold Coast near Brisbane.

Keith Williams first saw Hamilton from a fishing dinghy hired from South Molle Island in the early 1950's. He next saw Hamilton Island when he cruised the Whitsundays aboard a motor yacht. At that time the only building on the island was a small homestead overlooking what is now Hamilton Harbour.

After his company purchased the island, several years passed by before Keith Williams unfolded his dreams for the island. This was to build a resort of true international standard and of a scale previously unheard of in Australia.

Keith Williams worked hard to make his dream a reality. Hamilton Island welcomed its first guests in December, 1984. The resort not only attracted people to Hamilton Island. It is true to say that it set new standards for other resorts within the Great Barrier Reef region to match and acted as a catalyst of major redevelopment on a number of other islands.

When Keith Williams is not personally overseeing new developments and improvements on the island he keeps a constant eye on much of the resort area from a large villa that overlooks both it and the turquoise waters of the Coral Sea.

When the King and Queen of Nepal visited the island in 1987, they stayed in this magnificent home. The large garage was converted into barracks at the time for eight Nepalese guards accompanying the royal couple.

Busy as he is overseeing the continual development of his own private kingdom, Keith Williams still finds time for personal interests. He has built up a rare collection of vintage motorbikes – the largest private collection in the world – and this is now housed in a small museum on the island. He also enjoys spending time relaxing and entertaining guests aboard "Achilles II", his luxurious $7 million motor yacht.

The same distance from the equator as Hawaii.

Hamilton Island lies right at the heart of the Whitsundays, a group of 74 islands which are about 900 kilometres north of Brisbane and around 500 kilometres south of Cairns. It is a yachting paradise and there are six other resort islands within the area (also covered in this book).

Hamilton Island is directly south of Whitsunday Island, the largest island within the whole group. Whitsunday Island is uninhabited, although during World War II it sheltered part of the American Fleet prior to the Battle of the Coral Sea in an expanse of water known as Cid Harbour. The British Navy also conducted trials with midget submarines in the area during 1944 and 1945.

Last century, illegal ships carrying island slaves to the cane fields of Queensland anchored there. Rumour has it that an ancient Spanish galleon also lies at the bottom of Cid Harbour.

Like this island and others in the Whitsundays, Hamilton is a continental island. Many thousands of years ago each island was the peak of a mountain range on a coastal plain that was then part of the Australian mainland. A substantial rise in the sea level since the last Ice Age flooded this plain and created the picturesque islands that now exist.

Over 150 species of birds have been

1

2

recorded in the Whitsundays and many can be found on and around Hamilton Island.

Larger animals like koalas and kangaroos are not found in their natural state on Hamilton Island or the other Whitsunday islands - although rock wallabies can be found on nearby Whitsunday Island. They may once have existed on Hamilton Island but were probably hunted out by the aboriginals who lived around these islands for thousands of years, island-hopping from one to another in canoes.

Hamilton is a hilly island, covered in dense eucalypt forest, towering Hoop pines and patches of rainforest.

The highest point on Hamilton Island is Passage Peak which rises to a height of 200 metres.

The route, if you wish to walk to the top of the peak, starts at the southern end of Catseye Beach which the main resort area overlooks. Once you walk past the last block of apartments you will encounter a dirt road that runs parallel to the water's edge. Walk along this and some fifteen minutes later you will find a sign and track leading to Passage Peak.

The climb to the top of Passage Peak from this point will take you about 30 minutes. The sight from the top is breath-taking.

There is a panoramic 360° view over many of the Whitsunday islands and on a clear day the scene before you seems endless.

Apart from seeing a dozen different islands or more you will see the sails of yachts scattered over the turquoise waters that surround each island. You will also see the wake of motor boats stretching far behind them.

To the west you will enjoy views over Whitsunday Passage - which Captain Cook sailed through in 1770. Beyond you can clearly see the islands of South Molle and Long, and to the south you will see others including Lindeman.

To the north and north-east, Whitsunday and Haslewood Islands are both clearly visible.

Around the islands mentioned you will also see smaller isles. At your feet, but far below, you will see the main resort on Hamilton and even catch a glimpse of the marina on the western side of the island. It hardly matters which direction you face, it is all postcard material.

1. A view of Catseye Beach and the resort from Passage Peak. The island lying directly behind Hamilton is Dent.

2. A small cocoon-like nest made by green ants. Aborigines use the contents to make a pungent drink called "bookgruin" or "ant cordial".

On the way up or down Passage Peak there is plenty to study in terms of trees, plants and birds. On occasion, you may catch a glimpse of a goanna - a large but harmless type of lizard.

Tucked amongst the twigs and branches of some trees you may also observe a cocoon-like construction about the size of a tennis ball, made of leaves sealed edge to edge. This is a nest made by the highly active green ant, a small insect that can inflict a nasty nip on the unwary person who brushes past its home.

Inside the nest is a supply of what the aboriginals call "bookgruin" or "green ant cordial". This pungent drink is made from the white larvae and adult ants inside, once they have been soaked in water.

If you are eager to explore more of the island by foot you will find a road at the back of the airport on the western side of Hamilton Island. This winds up to the top of another smaller peak overlooking the resort. Turn-offs take you to Palm Valley and Coral Cove, a small but pretty bay.

Continue on the main dirt road and you will eventually approach a small junction where one track leads up to Passage Peak and another takes you back to the resort. The complete circuit - including the ascent to Passage Peak but excluding the side-tracks to Palm Valley and Coral Cove - would take a good three hours.

One short journey worth taking by foot or vehicle from the resort is the one to the look-out on the hill at the northern end of Catseye Beach. This can be reached by the sealed road that leads to the Fauna Park on Hamilton Island.

1

From this wonderful vantage point, you can enjoy a panoramic view of Catseye Beach, Whitsunday Passage and Whitsunday Island which is directly opposite when you face due north. You can also enjoy interesting views over some of the luxurious private villas that have been built on Hamilton Island.

Visit the Reef by boat or helicopter.

Hamilton, like other islands within the Whitsunday group, has fringing coral reefs that have taken some 10,000 years to develop.

The best places to snorkel within easy reach are the northern end of Catseye Beach - where you can see Plate and Staghorn corals and many colourful varieties of fish - and the area stretching from the marina to North West Bay.

The reefs off Catseye Beach and Coral Cove (on the southern side of the island) are two locations where people dive regularly.

From Hamilton you can also go to two outer reefs - which are approximately 60 kilometres away - by high-speed catamaran, luxury speedboat or helicopter. Here you can snorkel, dive or view the never-ending wonders of the Great Barrier Reef from a semi-submersible submarine.

A trip to Hardy Reef by one of the helicopters in Hamilton Island's own fleet takes about 30 minutes and gives you a spectacular bird's-eye view of the Reef at the same time.

Three times a week, weather permitting, you can travel out to Hardy Reef by boat. Here there is a manned reef station with glass bottom boat, coral sub and resident diving instructor.

The average diving depth is between three and 12 metres. There is abundant fish-life, many used to being hand-fed, and colourful varieties of both soft and hard corals.

At Hardy Reef there are at least five different locations for divers including The Canyons, The Beach (an easy dive in a shallow lagoon), Pinnacles (a wall dive with crevasses filled with many soft corals, Feather stars and Fan corals), The Pontoon (one of the best stations for hand-feeding fish), and Shark Alley.

Twice a week, you can also visit Bait Reef. This reef has a spectacular terrain with shallow, protected lagoons and vertical walls dropping to 30 metres. There are narrow

2

canyons, beautiful coral gardens and masses of fish.

The various dives include The Stepping Stones, Anemoneville (where giant anemones abound), Gary's Lagoon (featuring good coral and large Maori Wrasse), Manta Ray Drop Off and Gorgonia Hill. Diving is between three and 30 metres.

If you wish to dive, contact the H20 Sportz Shop at the marina. Dive gear may be hired through H20 Sportz.

H20 Sportz also offer an introductory scuba dive course and the opportunity to gain a PADI Open Water Certificate which allows you to dive anywhere in the world. In addition, they offer special night dive courses for experienced divers.

The popular introductory dive includes pool instruction, all equipment and a dive out on the Reef closely accompanied by an instructor.

To gain Open Water Certification there is a five-day course. For the first three days there are four hours of theory and pool instruction. On the final two days you have two dive trips. Two dives are completed on each trip. This course normally starts on Monday of each week.

Another popular destination for diving and snorkelling is Manta Ray Bay which is at the northern tip of Hook Island. This is about 90 minutes by boat from Hamilton Island. The fringing reef here is one of the most beautiful to be found within the Whitsunday group of islands.

The floor of this sheltered bay is covered by coral and at the reef's edge there are bommies, caves and tunnels. The area is also teeming with colourful fish. The average diving depth is between three and 12 metres.

People who wish to enjoy the best dive locations in the region may cruise aboard the "Coral Cat" as well, a luxury 120' motor catamaran, which operates out of Hamilton Island.

This $3 million "floating hotel" takes divers to the best locations both at outer reefs and within the Whitsundays. Packages are available for five, six and seven days.

You don't even have to leave the island to enjoy another marine attraction. Alongside the main resort complex on Hamilton Island there is a Dolphin Pool. This is the home for two of these fascinating and intelligent creatures which seem to enjoy a special bond with humans.

3

4

1. Helicopters flying guests from Hamilton Island to Hardy Reef. Visitors can also go out aboard a high-speed motor catamaran.

2. Several people explore the colourful underwater life at Hardy Reef.

3. A brighly coloured Tube worm.

4. An Emperor Angelfish.

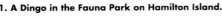

1

1. A Dingo in the Fauna Park on Hamilton Island.

2. A Park Ranger holds a cuddly Koala.

3. Dolphins being hand-fed in their special pool at the heart of the resort.

2

Each day you can see these delightful creatures being hand-fed at 9:00 a.m. and 5:00 p.m. They put on an effortless display of water acrobatics, much to the pleasure of all on-lookers.

About one and a half kilometres from the hub of the resort on Hamilton Island you will also find a Fauna Park covering an area of about 50 acres.

Here you can see some of Australia's best-known birds and animals. There are koalas, kangaroos, wallabies, wombats, dingoes and crocodiles.

There are also long-legged emus, too, and dozens of multi-coloured lorikeets that are hand-fed each day.

The Fauna Park is open to visitors daily between the hours of 10:00 a.m. and 5:30 p.m.

3

A playground of international standard.

In 1985 Hamilton Island received the Australian Tourism Award for the best resort in the country. Virtually since it first opened, the resort has attracted visitors from all over Australia and the world.

About 60% of guests who now visit Hamilton Island are Australians. The remaining 40% are from overseas.

The wonderful location of Hamilton Island, combined with the size and standard of the resort as well as the wide range of activities that it has to offer are undoubtedly the main reasons.

Another reason is that it is the only Barrier Reef island which you can fly directly to by jet from Melbourne, Sydney, Brisbane or Cairns. The island has its own airport - built jointly by Ansett and Keith Williams.

If you think the sound of aircraft may disturb your stay in the sun, do not be concerned. Firstly, the flight paths of planes are over the ocean. Secondly, the airport is located on the south-western side of the island with a hilly range between it and the main resort so most guests are unaware of the few daily incoming and out-going flights.

From the moment you step off an aircraft or boat you cannot help but be impressed by what meets the eye. As you ride by bus or taxi - yes, the island has its own taxi service - the first images you will see are probably those of Hamilton Harbour.

Along the shore-line there are buildings that reflect Queensland's colonial architecture. No more than two levels high, they have corrugated iron roofs, wide cool

4

5

verandahs and house a tavern, disco, as well as a whole range of stores and restaurants.

The main resort complex lies unseen on the other side of a hill just minutes away. Apart from a grand entrance foyer where you check in, you will find more restaurants, bars, a large entertainment centre, conference room, a range of boutiques, a hair and beauty salon, a same day photo service, plus the office where you can book some of the many activities the island offers.

Directly between the main resort complex and Catseye beach is one of the largest fresh water swimming pools in the Southern Hemisphere. It is nearly 100 metres long, 40 metres wide and holds almost two million litres of water.

It is hard to imagine anyone getting bored on Hamilton Island with the range of activities and excursions available. There are windsurfers, catamarans, paddleboards for hire and also the excitement of parasailing.

There are even internationally accredited instructors on hand to teach beginners or to coach more advanced skiers. The resort also has six floodlit tennis courts and two squash courts.

Throughout the year Hamilton Island plays host to several special events. On the long weekend of the Queen's Birthday in mid-July there is the Annual Outrigger Canoe Race. Teams from other resort islands and further afield race the full distance around Hamilton Island and Dent Island.

Following Easter each year, the island hosts a Race Week which is now firmly established on the yachting calendar as one of Australia's premier blue water classics. Over 150 yachts from Australia and overseas compete and enjoy the social life on the island.

At the heart of a boating paradise.

The Whitsundays is recognised as one of the finest yachting areas in the world. It has dozens of beautiful, uninhabited islands and other resort islands where yachtsmen are welcome, sheltered waters and many safe anchorages. It is also just 60 kilometres from several outer reefs.

With its protected harbour and facilities, boats are constantly arriving and departing from Hamilton Island. The scene at the harbour could easily be somewhere in the South of France. In the marina there are boats of every conceivable size. A game you can't help but indulge in is guessing the value

4. Each year, just after Easter, a fleet of over 100 yachts converge on Hamilton Island for Yacht Race Week for a series of hotly contested races.

5. "Apollo", a former winner of the Sydney to Hobart Yacht Race, is a regular contender. "Apollo" is now based at Shute Harbour and offers day cruises around the Whitsundays.

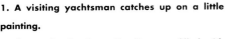

1

2

3

4

1. A visiting yachtsman catches up on a little painting.

2. The marina berths at Hamilton are filled with boats of all sizes visiting the Whitsundays.

3. "Corsaro", an Italian restaurant which overlooks the harbour.

4. Life around the marina is far from hectic.

of some of the stunning craft that you see berthed here. Some are worth millions each.

The harbour is deep, sheltered and has berths for 200 boats. Yachtsmen are always very welcome and they will find it is an ideal place to replenish supplies. The berths are serviced with electricity and water, and there are laundry facilities.

At the northern end of Hamilton Harbour two companies, Hamilton Boat Charters and Circa Marine, offer luxury yachts and motor cruisers for bareboat or crewed charter. Power boats are available for one day or more. Game-fishing boats can also be chartered on a half day, full day and share basis.

If you would like to try your hand at fishing around the island you can hire dinghies with outboards from the Bait and Tackle Shop next to the marina. This is an excellent way to explore some of the more secluded and inaccessible bays and coves.

Several cruises leave from the harbour throughout the week. One is aboard "Siska", a former winner of the Sydney to Hobart Yacht Race. Take this cruise and you will spend a full day sailing through the Whitsundays, visiting uninhabited islands and walking along deserted beaches. You will also have time to swim, snorkel and sunbake.

There are twilight cruises as well, and three times a week you can visit nearby Dent Island.

Dent Island has been the home of a colourful couple, Bill and Leen Wallace for over 30 years. Bill was an American serviceman who flew many missions across the Pacific during World War II.

When he first returned to Australia in 1951, Bill worked on cargo boats plying between Cairns and Thursday Island. He then headed for the Whitsunday area where, for a time, he dived for Trochus Shell which was used for buttons before the advent of plastics. Bill then skippered a boat on Long Island and lived on Hamilton Island in 1953 and 1954.

In 1955, Bill and Leen - an Australian girl he had met and married - secured a lease of about two acres on Dent Island which lies directly to the west of Hamilton. Bill made a living diving for coral. This was purchased as a momento of their Great Barrier Reef visit by guests from Lindeman and Hayman, two Whitsunday islands which had resorts in those early days. Leen also began to make beautiful jewellery from Pearl

5

6

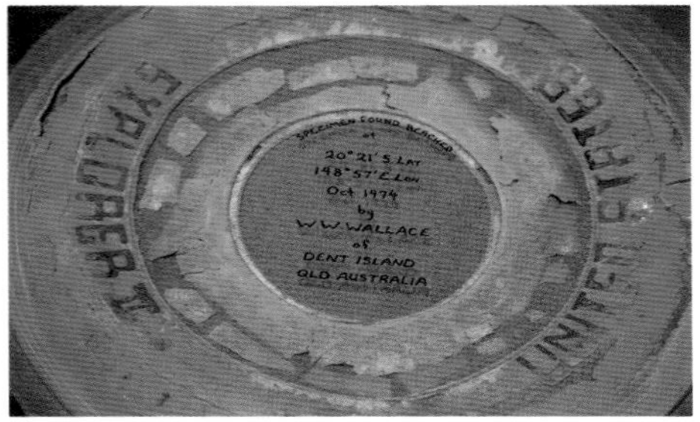

7

shell and Turtle shell (now imported).

Over the years they have created a true tropical oasis on their corner of Dent Island. They have planted dozens of palm trees and exotic plants, all of which have flourished and become a garden that is something of a showpiece.

In 1969, Bill also began the construction of a "Fale". Finished in 1972, this is styled after a native Samoan dwelling. Bill then brought over a Fijian artist to do the intricate carving that can be seen on the beams and elsewhere. This striking structure not only houses the jewellery and coral art that Bill and Leen have on sale but a large number of artifacts and items collected over the years.

Some are finds that Bill made whilst beachcombing. One such item is a large Indonesian figurine that he found almost completely buried by pumice stone on Whitsunday Island in 1958.

Another item of great interest that Bill once found was a small section from the American Explorer II satellite. This was launched from Cape Canaveral in 1958 but the second stage of the rocket carrying it failed to ignite and both rocket and satellite crashed to earth.

The section was discovered by Bill on the beach directly in front of his home in 1974. This remnant of the satellite obviously lay on the sea-bed for 16 years before being washed up. Bill has preserved this piece of space history by encasing it in perspex and putting it on display.

You will find your visit to Dent Island most enjoyable, especially since Bill and Leen are very hospitable hosts.

You will soon be able to play golf on Dent Island, too, since Keith Williams recently secured a portion of the island and is now constructing an 18-hole international standard golf course there for guests staying on Hamilton.

Another excursion that should not be missed is the cruise to Whitehaven Beach, located on the eastern side of Whitsunday Island. This is a half-day excursion aboard a large, high-speed, revolutionary wave piercing catamaran. Its destination is one of the most beautiful spots not only in the Whitsundays but along the whole eastern coast of Australia.

Whitehaven Beach is aptly named. It may seem quite inappropriate, considering its tropical location, but "snow white" is the best

5. "Foot", a sculptor who works in a waterside studio alongside the marina.

6. Bill Wallace, who has lived on nearby Dent Island for over 30 years, holds an Indonesian figurine that was washed up on Whitsunday Island.

7. Another interesting find made by Bill - a small section of the satellite American Explorer II.

1

2

3

way to describe the sand on this magnificent beach.

The dazzling white sand along the full length of this beach is, in fact, composed of silicia so pure that it is suitable for glass-making. The origin of this exceptionally pure sand which is more than 99% silicia is something of a mystery to geologists.

The beauty of Whitehaven Beach, however, is undisputed. From here you can also enjoy a panoramic view of Haslewood Island which lies opposite and swim in the turquoise waters of the Coral Sea.

Another way to see some of the Whitsundays is aboard "Awesome", a spectacular high-speed power boat. This exotic 21.3 metre craft - which bears more than a passing resemblance to the "Martini-style" ocean racing boats - is capable of reaching 45 knots and is the epitome of luxury.

A three and a half hour cruise on "Awesome" takes you past Hayman Island, the eastern side of Hook Island including beautiful Butterfly Bay and gives you time ashore at Whitehaven Beach to swim, sunbake and snorkel.

"Awesome" goes to Hardy Reef once a week, too. It takes you to Hamilton Island's own private pontoon where you can snorkel, dive or view coral from a semi-submersible craft. On the way home you may also enjoy a brief stopover at Whitehaven Beach or Chance Bay.

A voyage to the Reef and through the Whitsundays that the very well-heeled may wish to consider is one of the two, three or five night cruises aboard the $7 million "Achilles II". Lesser mortals do not have homes that could compare with the plush interior and furnishings aboard this magnificent craft. Champagne and fine cuisine are all included in the cruise cost. If you wish to know what this costs before you decide to book, you cannot afford it.

If you prefer total privacy and do not wish to share the plush comforts of such a craft with anybody else you could consider chartering "Achilles I". While this craft is a mere 108′ long it, too, offers passengers a degree of comfort that only a few will ever experience.

A more affordable way to see the magnificent Whitsundays is by air. As well as the flights out to the Reef mentioned earlier in this chapter, you can enjoy a 15 minute Adventure Flight over many of the islands,

1. People visiting Hamilton Island or other resort islands within the Whitsundays also have the opportunity to visit this idyllic spot - Whitehaven Beach on uninhabited Whitsunday Island.

2. Two, three and five night cruises of the outer reefs and Whitsunday islands are available aboard "Achilles II", a 37 metre luxury vessel based at Hamilton Island.

3. Two of the high-speed motor catamarans that take passengers out to Hardy Reef to snorkel and dive.

The view from an apartment behind Catseye Beach at sunrise.

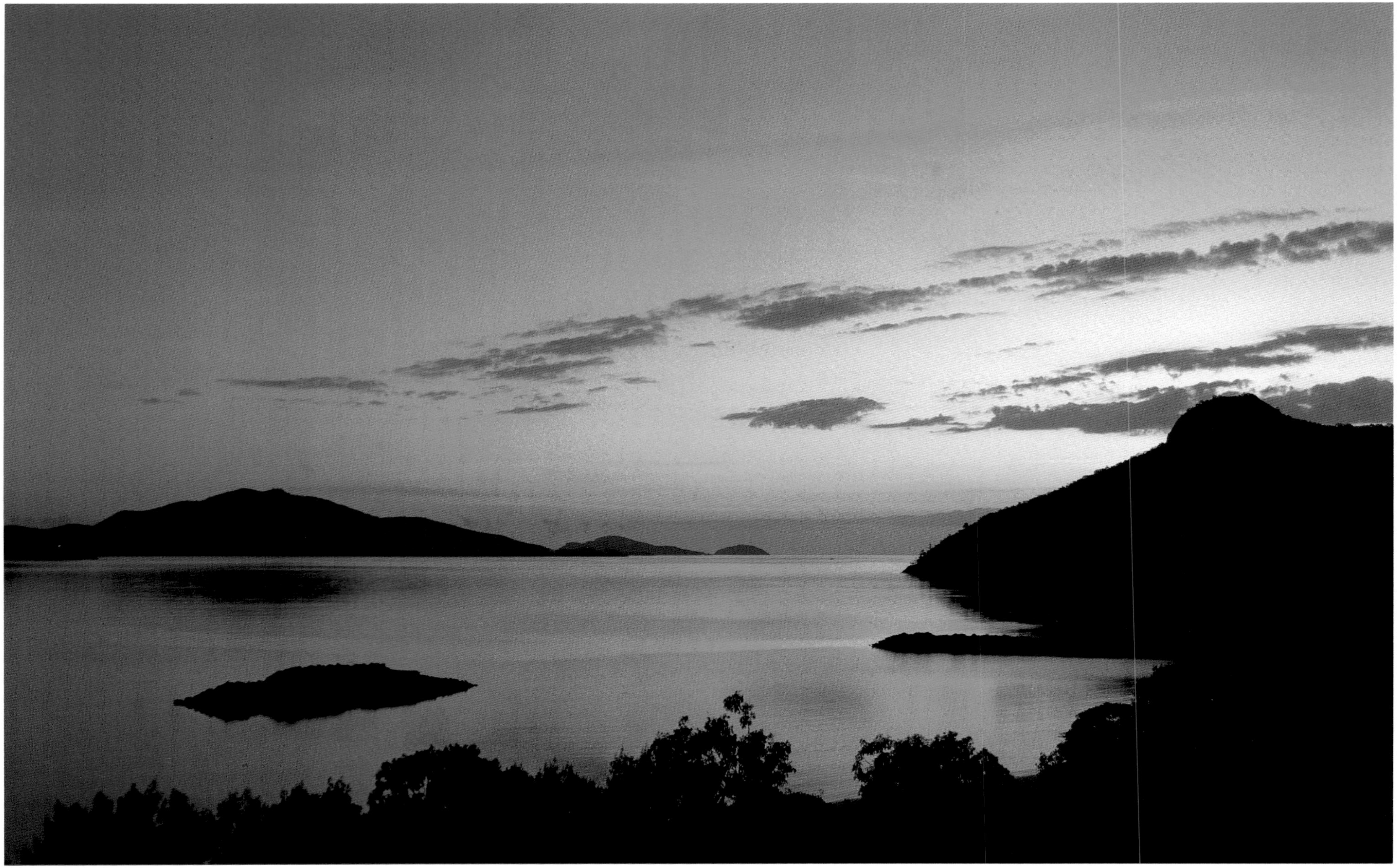

lagoons and beaches in the area.

Parents may wonder how they can enjoy some of the activities that the island has to offer when they bring their children to Hamilton Island. During the school holiday periods special activities are arranged for children between 9:00 a.m. and 5:00 p.m. to give their parents some welcome relief.

The supervised activities of the Kid's Club include everything from nature walks, sand modelling and painting to dance competitions, cooking, swimming and fishing. Baby-sitting and childminding facilities are available outside the hours that the Kid's Club operates.

Eight restaurants and cafes to choose from.

One of the most enjoyable aspects of staying on Hamilton Island is the range of restaurants, bars and cafes. No other resort island on the Great Barrier Reef can match Hamilton Island in this respect.

On the resort side of the island there are three restaurants and a coffee shop. One of the restaurants is the Dolphin Room, so named because it overlooks the Dolphin Pool. This a la carte restaurant offers an elegant setting and a varied menu. It recently received the Robert Timms Award for Excellence.

Guests are offered a range of appetisers and entrees like Scottish Smoked Salmon, and Oysters topped with Crab Meat, Ginger and overbaked with Sauce Bernaise. Pepper Steak, Beef Curry Madras and Duckling L'Orange are just several of the main courses, and there are desserts like Macadamia Nut Ice-cream and Strawberries Romanoff to follow.

Adjoining the Dolphin Room is a relaxing yet stylish cocktail bar and lounge called the James Cook Bar. It's a most enjoyable place to enjoy your favourite cocktail. In the evening live entertainment is usually provided by a resident pianist.

A wonderful place to dine, particularly at lunchtime, is The Beach Bar and Grill which directly overlooks Catseye Beach. This restaurant has a casual atmosphere and its speciality is steak although it has some seafood and pasta dishes.

The premiere restaurant on Hamilton Island would have to be The Outrigger Room. This restaurant is located at the very northern end of Catseye Beach and is open only in the evening.

In elegant surroundings you can enjoy an imaginative menu that has an emphasis on seafood. The menu offers entrees such as Fresh Oysters served on ice with a Red Wine and Peppercorn Vinaigrette or Moreton Bay Bugs served with Macadamia Nuts and Almonds, pan fried and served with a Sauce Maltese.

Then there are a dozen main courses to choose from - dishes like pan fried Coral Trout served with a Sauterne and Lime Mousseline Sauce, and Crayfish grilled and served with a Pernod, Ginger and Vegetable Sauce.

For dessert, you are faced with the excruciating choice of whether to have a four layered Ice-Cream Bombe served with a light Caramel Sauce, Crepes filled with Honey Ice-cream and surrounded by fruits flambeed with Galliano and Pear Brandy, or one of another half dozen dishes.

Around the water's edge at Hamilton Harbour there are more establishments where you can eat. Pirates Paradise which is located above the Mariners Inn Tavern offers a variety of grills, seafood, salads and fresh tropical fruits.

There is also a takeaway snack bar adjoining the restaurant. Next door to the Mariners Inn Tavern there is an Ice Cream Parlour as well with every imaginable flavour of ice-cream.

For those who love pasta there is the Ristorante Corsaro. This serves traditional Italian dishes, home-made pasta and genuine Italian gelato.

Adjoining the Ristorante Corsaro there is the Pink Pizza Parlour which is open 24 hours a day. This offers pizzas and snacks, including takeaway food.

Further along the waterfront there is a wonderful Chinese restaurant called Chung Shan Yuen which specialises in Cantonese cuisine. The decor is very smart and the food excellent.

Near the entrance to the marina you will find a Fish Market. Here you can buy fish and chips and a wonderful variety of fresh seafood that you can eat on the spot or take away.

Being a Fish Market you can naturally buy fresh seafood to cook yourself. A bakery, butcher, supermarket and delicatessen along the waterfront also cater to those who wish to prepare snacks or meals themselves.

Light meals can be enjoyed in the resort's Coffee Shop as well.

Throughout the week some of the restaurants such as The Dolphin Room, The Beach Bar and Grill, Corsaro's and the Mariners Inn Tavern feature live music. The Phoenix Room in the main resort complex often has live entertainment, too, with lavish floor shows featuring dance and music.

Throughout the week there is an Australiana Night, "Flames of Polynesia", and a Rock 'n Roll Night.

For those who like to disco there is Durty Nellies, a stylish and sophisticated nightspot open until 3:00 a.m. For those in a somewhat quieter mood, Durty Nellies also has a separate piano bar.

Studio apartments to villas with butler service.

At the moment, visitors can choose from seven different types of accommodation. The tariffs differ considerably depending on the type of accommodation so Hamilton Island not only attracts the rich and famous but families, honeymooners, and businessmen who make use of the conference facilities.

Altogether, Hamilton Island has just over 400 hotel rooms, apartments and penthouses. Together they can accommodate a total of 1,200 guests.

There are some common features to all forms of accommodation on Hamilton Island. Each has air-conditioning and ceiling fans, balconies, lounge chairs and coffee table, tea and coffee making facilities, fridge, mini-bar and even a hair-dryer.

The attractive free-standing Polynesian-style Bures are situated in gardens close to the main resort complex and have both a king size bed and a divan which converts into a single bed, ideal if you have a child. Essentially they are studio apartments in layout.

1

2

3

4

5

1. Polynesian-style Bures.

2. The interior of a Bure.

3. The hotel-style rooms in Allamanda Lodge.

4. The interior of a room in Bougainvillaea Lodge.

5. An aerial view of Catseye Beach and the resort on Hamilton Island.

Allamanda Lodge is a three level lodge just a stone's throw from the northern end of Catseye Beach. The lodge, which is named after the beautiful yellow flowering vine which adorns it, is directly adjacent to the main resort complex and overlooks the main beach.

This lodge has spacious studio apartments with a king size bed and a single bed. It also has two-bedroom apartments, ideal for families, which accommodate up to five people.

Bougainvillaea Lodge, named after the flowers of vivid colour that blossom around it, has rooms directly overlooking the main beach and views of Fitzallen Passage and Whitsunday Island. The hotel-style rooms all have balconies and two queen size beds.

Self-contained one-bedroom apartments are available in Whitsunday Towers East and West. These are very large, have their own kitchen, en-suite bathroom and are beautifully furnished.

Luxury self-contained apartments with two bedrooms are available in Poinciana, Hibiscus, Lagoon and Frangipani Lodges. Poinciana is set on a hill up behind the main resort complex whilst the others (like each of the Whitsunday Towers) are situated side by side along the beachfront. These apartments have a master bedroom with a king size bed and en-suite bathroom. The second bedroom has two single beds and its own bathroom.

There are also 15 plush penthouses, each occupying a full floor of the Yacht Harbour Towers which overlooks the marina and the Coral Sea. These superbly decorated apartments have a huge lounge and entertainment area, four bedrooms, each with its own bathroom. The master bedroom even has its own spa bath. With privacy in mind, the penthouses are fully protected by a security system which only allows their occupants to enter this oasis of luxury.

An alternative to the plush penthouses is the rental of a private villa. One such villa is "Illalangi". It sits on a hill which offers sweeping panoramic views over Whitsunday Island and Catseye Beach. This spectacular architecturally designed home features the finest furnishings and wonderful examples of contemporary art and sculpture.

"Illalangi" is air-conditioned throughout, has four double bedrooms, its own sauna, outdoor spa, swimming pool and huge timber decks with uninterrupted sea views. Complete privacy is assured - access is by

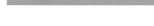

6

7

8

private road only - and guests may enjoy the services of a butler, chef and maid if they desire. In addition, guests have the use of a motor vehicle.

How to get to Hamilton Island.

The phone number of the resort on Hamilton Island is (079) 469144. Through this number you can also be connected to any of the facilities such as the boat charter company and the dive shop which you may wish to contact prior to your visit.

The address of the resort should you wish to write is P.M.B., Post Office, Hamilton Island, Queensland 4803. The resort's telex number is AA48516. Their facsimile number is (079) 469425.

Access to Hamilton Island is by boat or plane. The non-stop flight from Melbourne to Hamilton Island takes two hours and 40 minutes. From Sydney the flight time is two hours and from Brisbane it is just one hour and 10 minutes.

There are direct flights available as well, from Rockhampton, Ayers Rock, Cairns, Townsville and the Gold Coast.

Alternatively, you can board a boat at Shute Harbour, just 15 minutes from Airlie Beach by coach or car. Undercover parking is available at Shute Harbour if you wish to travel by car on the mainland. The companies offering this service are the Shell Service Station, (079) 469438, and Shute Harbour Car Security, (079) 469166.

Hamilton Island's large motor catamaran departs at 9:00 a.m. and 5:15 p.m. each day and the trip takes about 40 minutes. Whitsunday Water Taxis also go to Hamilton Island from Shute Harbour. Their phone number is (079) 469499.

"A world of its own" is a line that is used in promoting Hamilton Island - and it's true that no other island within the Great Barrier Reef region has a resort of the same scale. Other islands within the region offer greater seclusion and isolation than Hamilton Island. Yet this is precisely the appeal for the people who choose to stay and even live here.

If you enjoy the company of other people rather than wishing to escape them, like the idea of a sophisticated "village" environment with a wide choice of restaurants and holiday activities as well as the opportunity to enjoy the underwater wonders of the Reef, Hamilton Island will rate highly as a destination.

6. Harbour Yacht Towers has 15 penthouses, some of which can be rented.

7. "Illalangi", a private villa which may be rented, complete with butler.

8. The interior of one of the luxury penthouses in Harbour Yacht Towers.

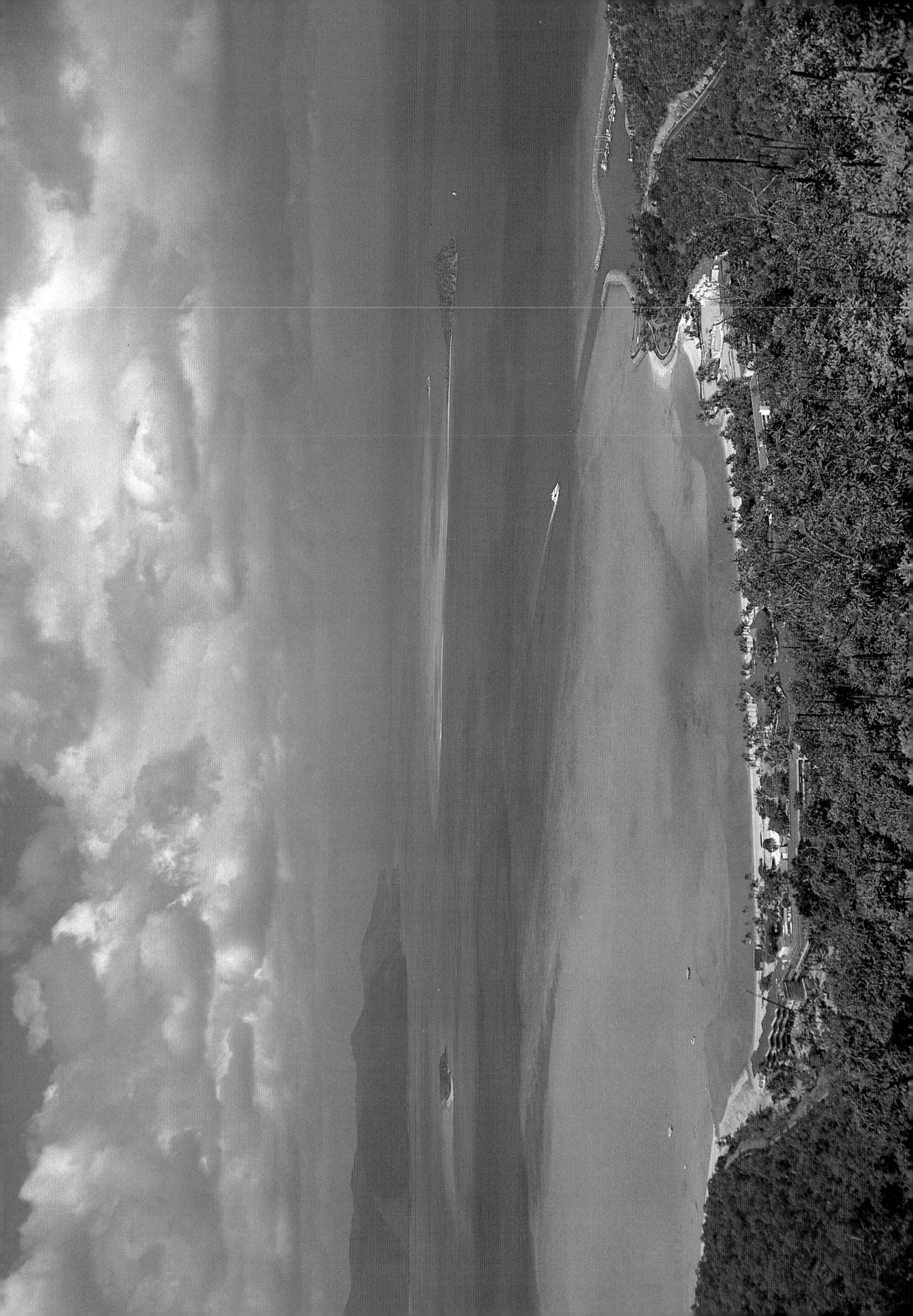

HAYMAN ISLAND

2

3

Hayman Island is the most northerly island in the Whitsunday Group. This spectacular group of islands lies about 480 kilometres south of Cairns and 900 kilometres north of Brisbane.

The island itself is 28 kilometres north-east of Shute Harbour, the gateway to the Whitsundays (tourism in this magical area has made Shute Harbour the second busiest port in Australia after Sydney Harbour).

In the summer months, the temperature on Hayman Island is normally somewhere between 23°C and 31°C. During the winter months, it ranges between 17°C and 26°C.

Hayman Island is just under five kilometres in length from north to south and just over one and a half kilometres from east to west.

The fact that the island is fairly mountainous means that visitors can enjoy some breathtaking views from several vantage points.

Hayman Island has been attracting visitors since the 1930's and the island's resort - which faces south and looks down the

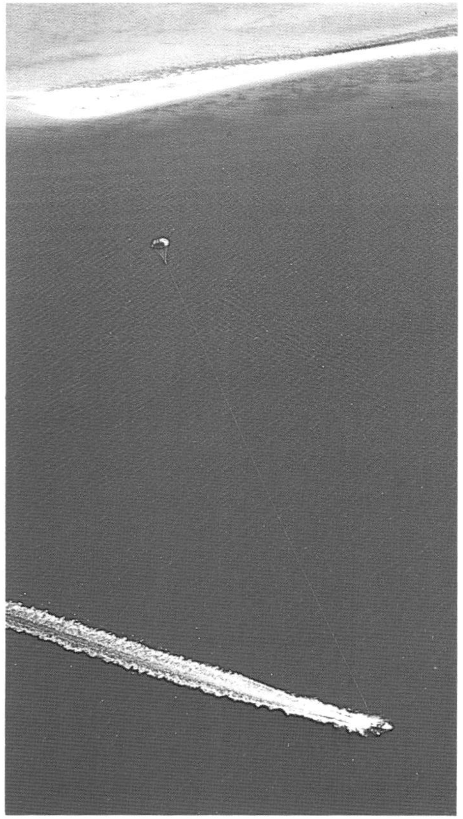
4

1. The view from Cook's Lookout, the highest point on Hayman Island, overlooking Whitsunday Passage. From left to right is part of Hook Island and several smaller islands - Black Island (also known as Bali Hai), Bird Island and Langford Island. Hayman's resort and marina is also visible.

2. A guest relaxes alongside the resort's huge salt-water swimming pool.

3. The sand-bar close to Langford Island - a place where visitors to Hayman will sometimes take a dinghy with outboard to swim and sunbake.

4. Parasailing near Langford Island.

1

1

1. An old brochure advertising The Royal Hayman Resort which opened in 1950.

2. Accommodation on Hayman in 1938.

3. The resort's dining room in 1938.

4. In 1951 most guests arrived by seaplane.

5. Hayman's school for children of staff, 1961.

beautiful Whitsunday Passage - has changed dramatically over the years. Today, a new and plush $300 million 5-star resort is attracting discerning, well-heeled visitors from all over the world.

Seven million dollars has been spent on landscaping alone and the resort itself houses many antiques and costly works of art. The wine cellar has over 50,000 bottles of wine, and many of the staff have been recruited from Europe's finest hotels.

One travel writer recently reported that "the new Hayman (resort) transcends most in the Pacific, Caribbean and Mediterranean".

The resort overlooks a sweeping crescent shaped beach and a blue lagoon with acres of coral gardens. Of the many islands in the Whitsundays, Hayman is also the closest to the outer reefs.

Once the holiday destination of Zane Grey.

Hayman Island was named in 1866 by Commander Nares of the "Salamandar" in honour of his navigator, Thomas Hayman, Master R.N. The "Salamandar" was a vessel that spent many years sailing the North Queensland coast provisioning and protecting the early settlements.

In the early 1900's, a sawmill was established on Hook Island, which is directly opposite Hayman Island. The mill was owned by Thomas Abell of Airlie Beach. The timber from this mill and another located on nearby Whitsunday Island supplied much of the timber used in buildings still standing in Bowen, Proserpine and Townsville.

As well as owning the mill on Hook Island, Thomas Abell also secured the lease of Hayman Island. One of his schemes was to graze cattle on Hayman but apparently this plan did not eventuate. In 1907 he sold the lease to the island and some Saanen goats that he had introduced to it, along with the milling rights, to Boyd Lee for the handsome sum of £30.

Boyd Lee was a local, legendary character. His exploits inspired the author Norman Caldwell to write two books - "Fangs of the Sea" and "Tritons of the Barrier Reef".

In 1931, Boyd sold the lease to Hayman Island after moving to Grassy Island. Boyd moved to Grassy Island because he considered it to be a more convenient base for fishing.

The lease to Hayman Island passed to Monty Embury, a school teacher from New South Wales. He organised expeditions to the island for scientists, zoologists and bird watchers. In 1933, a building was even erected to house a Biological Research Laboratory.

In 1935, however, Embury abandoned his venture and the lease to Hayman was sold to two brothers, Bob and Bert Hallam. They were both fishermen who had lived in the area all their lives (their father had cut timber on Whitsunday Island in the 1870's).

The Hallam brothers decided to establish a resort for fishermen on Hayman Island and soon attracted anglers from the south. They arrived by coastal steamer.

Zane Grey, the celebrated American novelist, film-maker and big game fisherman was an early visitor, too, and planted the first coconut palm on the island.

Zane Grey was also persuaded to use Hayman as the location for his movie "White Death". In August, 1936, a film crew spent two months shooting the film on the island. The story line was similar to "Jaws".

The making of the movie was undoubtedly a newsworthy event but a stranger occurrence in the area aroused the imagination of the public in the 1930's. Newspapers carried reports that fishermen, family groups and professional fishing crew had sighted a sea monster on various occasions off Hayman Island and the coastal town of Bowen.

This monster was described as "25 feet long, with a snake-like head, fins on each side, small eyes, an eel-like tail" and a twelve inch diameter body that was lime green in colour. Another report described the unknown creature as being "thirty feet long, (with a) head like a large turtle and body like a huge armoured hose..."

Like the Loch Ness monster, however, it proved to be elusive and was never captured. Nor was it photographed and no further sightings were made in later years.

In the late 1940's Reginald Ansett, one of the pioneers of the aviation industry in Australia, came up with the idea of establishing a winter resort to increase the profits of his airline. Reginald Ansett looked at many different islands along the Queensland coast but Hayman was the one that he fell in love with.

Reginald Ansett bought the lease from Bert Hallam in 1947 (Bert had bought out his brother Bob by now). The story goes that when Reginald Ansett asked Bert how much he wanted for the island he got the following answer. "Well, there are about a thousand

2

3

4

5

1

2

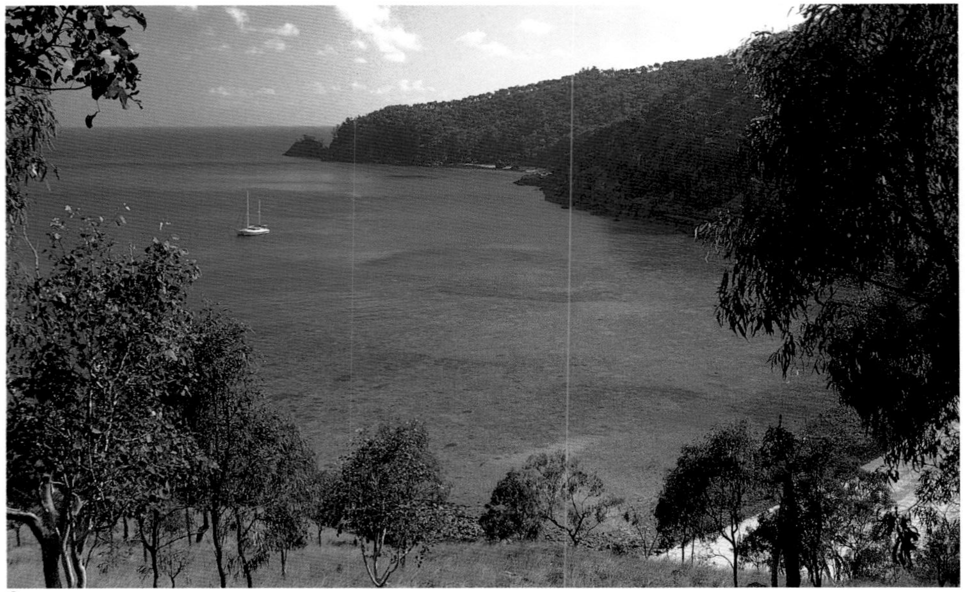

3

1. Arkhurst Island which lies off the south-western corner of Hayman Island. It is the home and nesting grounds for many sea-birds.

2. Several of the many majestic Hoop Pines that can be seen on the main walking trail leading to Blue Pearl Bay.

3. Beautiful Blue Pearl Bay, on the north-western corner of the island.

goats on the place. Say £10 each." And so the deal was struck for £10,000 ($20,000).

Reginald Ansett had great vision and built a magnificent new resort that would constantly draw visitors to Hayman for well over two decades. He invested what was then an enormous sum on redevelopment - £250,000.

The deadline to finish the new resort was hastily advanced when the news broke that King George VI planned to visit Australia. A trip to the Great Barrier Reef was to be included and arrangements were made for the royal party to stay on Hayman Island.

Ansett applied for a Royal Charter and permission was given to name the new hotel The Royal Hayman. Unfortunately, the regal visit to Australia was cancelled but the "Royal" remained part of the resort name.

The new resort took 600 men over two years to complete. The architecture and theme of the resort was very much Royal Hawaiian, with coral pink decor and black terrazzo floors. (When it was first opened it was also one of only two hotels in Queensland to boast a shower and toilet for every room!)

The Royal Hayman was opened officially on July 4, 1950, by Mr. A.W. (later Sir Arthur) Fadden, the Deputy Prime Minister of Australia. Reg Ansett, unfortunately, missed the official ceremony as he was unwell.

In the following years Hayman became a famous and popular destination around the world for those wishing to visit the Great Barrier Reef and the island saw many notable guests. For many years, visitors arrived at the island by seaplanes or "flying boats", as they were known as then.

Disaster struck the island, however, on January 17, 1970. Cyclone "Ada" battered the island with 150 mile an hour winds, uprooting trees and severely damaging or destroying most of its facilities. The resort was closed for six months before it re-opened.

In the mid-1980's it was decided to redevelop the resort once again and the result is impressive, to say the least.

Wild Cockatoos and Hoop Pines.

Many people would argue that Hayman now offers the best of both worlds. Whilst you can revel in the opulence and sophistication of the resort you can still enjoy the simple pleasures of walking and observing the beauty of nature on Hayman Island.

4

5

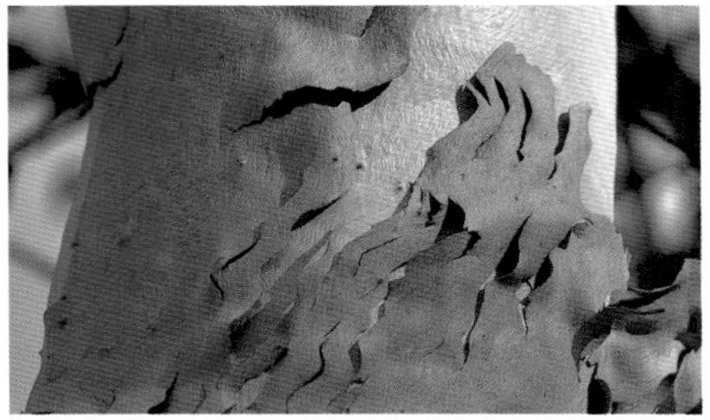

6

4. Dolphin Point, at the rugged northern tip of Hayman Island, is also regarded as one of the best diving sites in the Whitsundays.

5. One of the wild goats on the island. They are the off-spring of Saanen goats introduced to Hayman at the turn of the century.

6. The peeling bark on a eucalyptus tree. Eucalypts dominate the landscape on much of Hayman Island.

The island is unashamedly Australian in terms of vegetation and wildlife. Most of the trees you will see are eucalypts but you will also see many pine trees, too. These are the native pines which provided the timber for the sawmills in earlier days.

If you choose to walk clockwise around the island you will find that a track begins past the quarry close to the marina. This entails a climb to the top of a hill and from it you will clearly see the mainland and some of the other islands within the Whitsunday Group. The island closest to Hayman is Arkhurst Island where many birds nest.

As you wander along the track you are bound to hear and see a variety of birds. You will almost certainly see wild Cockatoos with yellow plumage on their heads and recognise the very distinctive laughter of Kookaburras.

Do not be surprised, either, if you occasionally see wild goats. Goats have been on the island ever since they were introduced at the turn of the century by Thomas Abell.

About thirty minutes after you set out you will come to a fork in the track. If you turn left the path will lead you down to Blue Pearl Bay. This is about ten minutes further on and well worth going to. It is exceptionally pretty and there is a very sandy and safe beach here.

Blue Pearl Bay is a perfect spot to take a picnic lunch (which may be ordered at the resort) and swim or snorkel. If this appeals to you remember to check the tides before you head off from the resort, however, because it is too shallow for swimming at low tide.

If you decide to walk to Blue Pearl Bay with children, keep a careful eye on them. For a few hundred metres there is quite a spectacular but steep drop down to the water just a few metres away from the track itself.

A feature along this track are the conifers that grow on the steep slopes that run 25 metres or so down to the water's edge. Compared to the hardy eucalypts they are very green in colour and very majestic in their height. Above them you may also see a Sea Eagle or two soaring high in the sky.

If you retrace your steps to the fork and go to the right you will slowly wind your way up to the top of a ridge until you come to yet another short detour which will take you to the Whitsunday Passage Lookout. This gives you a bird's-eye view of the marina and scenic views of Hook Island (which has the

1

1. **These distinctive plants, known as Black-boys, dot the landscape on the western side of Hayman island.**

2. **This beautiful beach is at Stanley Point on Hook Island which lies just over one kilometre south-east of Hayman. Guests staying at Hayman's resort can hire a dinghy with outboard to visit this lovely spot.**

highest peak of any of the Whitsunday islands) and the mainland.

Continue along the main track and you will encounter two more turn-offs. One will take you to Dolphin Point, the northerly tip of Hayman Island. This detour to the more rugged corner of the island will add at least another half hour or more each way if you decide to explore it.

The next turn-off will take you to Cook's Lookout which is even higher than the Whitsunday Passage Lookout. The views are even more spectacular from this vantage point (so if you wish to make only one detour from the main track this should definitely be your choice).

The colour of the water of Hayman's lagoon and Whitsunday Passage on a clear day is simply stunning in its range of hues. With the mountainous Hook Island in the background, small islands like Bird and Bali Hai immediately in the foreground, other larger islands like North and South Molle in the distance, and yachts dotted here and there, it is hard to imagine a more picturesque sight. Even if you are not an avid photographer you will berate yourself if you have forgotten your camera (or worse, run out of film).

You also get a wonderful view of the resort from Cook's Lookout with its beautifully landscaped gardens and pool, complete with its own "island" (the pool area actually covers five times the area of an Olympic pool).

Talking of water, if you are thirsty and have forgotten to take refreshments along with you, you will find a tank at Cook's Lookout. The fresh rainwater in it is a welcome bonus, especially on a hot day.

On this side of the island, the landscape is covered by the distinctive plants commonly known as Black-boys. These grow as high as two or three metres and have very long black stalks. From a distance these look remarkably like the spears that aborigines once carried, hence the grassy plant's name.

The track from Cook's Lookout - to the relief of some - is now completely downhill, meandering from one side of a ridge to the other. The landscape you will encounter on this side of the island is quite different from that on the western side, being somewhat more rugged and bare.

The last half hour of your walk will take you down near Groper's Point, the south-eastern corner of Hayman. From here you have a marvellous view over the channel and coral that separates Hayman from Hook Island. You can also see a couple of the magnificent beaches on Hook Island that you can visit easily with a dinghy and outboard.

The journey from the marina inland and then back to the resort will take you a leisurely three hours or thereabouts if you plan to stop only at Cook's Lookout. The walk is neither difficult nor strenuous for the average person.

Explore both the Reef and the beautiful Whitsundays.

Hayman is ideally located to explore both the Reef and the beauty of the Whitsunday Islands.

Although most of the resort islands in the Whitsundays are reasonably close to each other Hayman, nevertheless, is the closest to the outer reefs. One of these, Swain Reef, is just 28 kilometres away.

If you are a keen fisherman or diver you will certainly enjoy what Hayman has to offer in terms of boats and destinations. Yachts can also be chartered from Hayman Island and there are day cruises available, too, aboard several beautiful craft for those who simply want to sit back, relax and watch the world go by.

A highly recommended cruise is one to famous Whitehaven Beach, a stretch of pure white silica sand, on uninhabited Whitsunday Island. Here you can swim, sunbake and walk along one of the most beautiful beaches you will ever see.

You can also take a leisurely one hour cruise around Hayman itself, learning about its history and seeing different points of beauty and interest.

Another way to spend a day is relaxing aboard "Sea Biscuit", a magnificent 50' motor yacht named after a well-known American racehorse. This beautiful sailing boat will not only take you through the Whitsundays but anchor at secluded bays and beaches so you can swim, sunbake and snorkel.

Three times a week you can cruise to the Reef aboard "Capricorn" a large, high speed motor powered catamaran that is based at nearby South Molle Island. This will take you to Hardy Reef which has 7,500 acres of coral.

Out on the Great Barrier Reef you can snorkel (snorkelling gear is provided) or view many varieties of coral and colourful tropical fish from the semi-submersible "Coral Sub". This is a six hour excursion and a wonderful smorgasbord lunch is provided aboard.

2

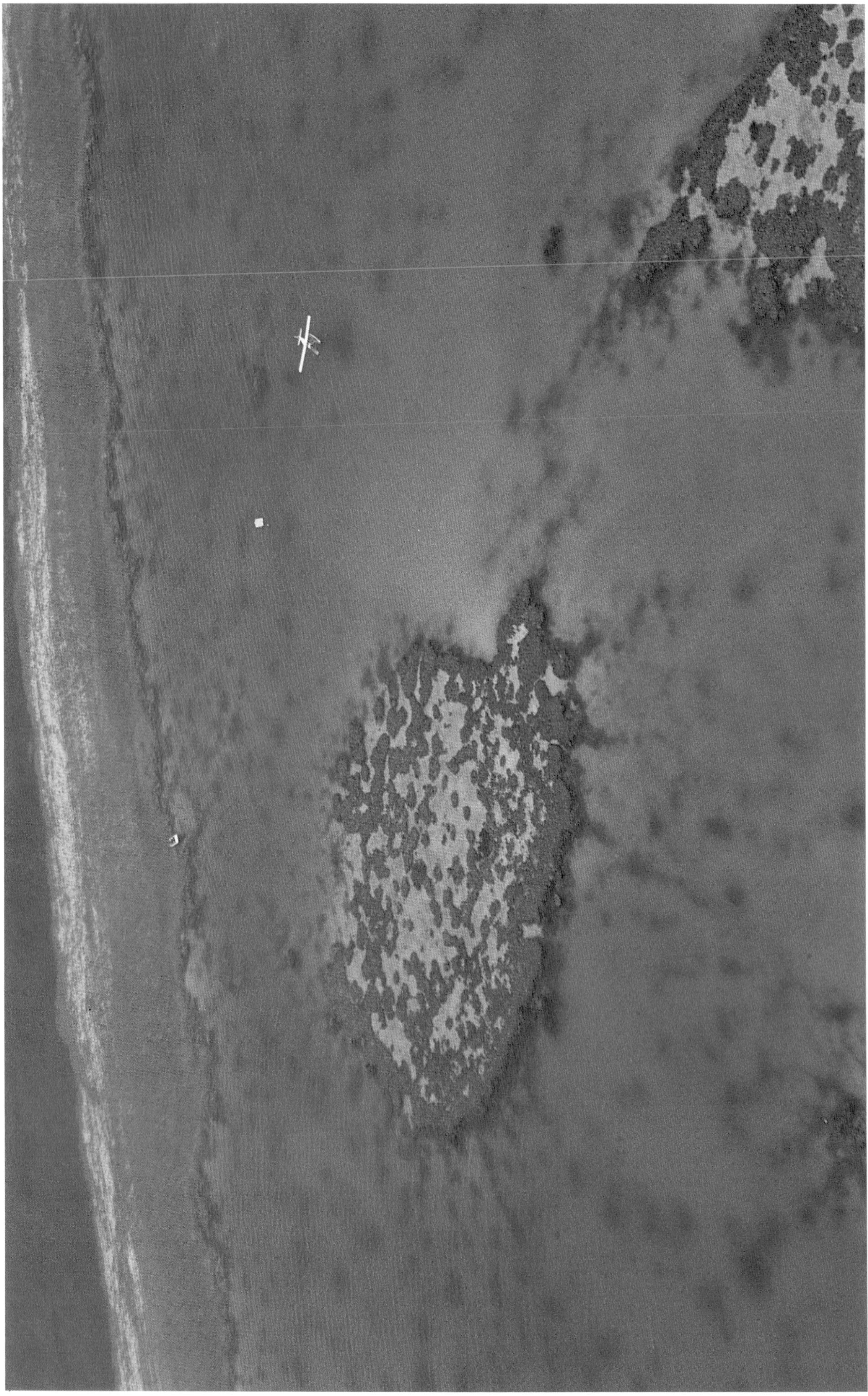

Another way to see the Reef is by helicopter. The view of the Reef from the air is spectacular and you can also snorkel, dive or view coral from a glass bottom boat or semi-submersible craft once the chopper lands on a large pontoon moored permanently at Hardy Reef.

Alternatively, you can fly out to the Reef by seaplane with Seair Pacific. Once again, you get a stunning bird's-eye view of the Great Barrier Reef from the air and then you can snorkel, and view coral from either a glass bottom boat or "sub". Snorkelling gear and sandshoes for reef walking are provided.

If you wish to dive or snorkel you can also cruise to one of the outer reefs aboard Hayman's own luxurious 18 metre "Reef Goddess". She travels at 20 knots and would undoubtedly be Australia's most sophisticated and luxurious day dive boat. The "Reef Goddess" is even equipped with video playback units so that footage taken during dives can be reviewed while you are having refreshments.

The destination for the "Reef Goddess" is Bait Reef where there are a number of great sites for snorkelling and diving. The site visited most often by the "Reef Goddess" is called The Stepping Stones. Here there are unusual formations of coral, giant sea anemones and many species of colourful fish. The visibility at Bait Reef is excellent, and usually better than that at Hardy Reef.

The "Reef Goddess" heads out to the Reef for both half and full days. Diving equipment is available for hire including Tekna Diver Propulsion Vehicles, underwater cameras and videos.

Another dive site that the "Reef Goddess" often takes divers to is Manta Ray Bay on the northern side of Hook Island. This is just 10 or 15 minutes away from Hayman Island and provides some of the best fringing reef and marine life within the Whitsunday group of islands.

If you have never dived before but would like to, you have two options. The first is the popular Introductory Scuba Course. This includes instruction on land and in a pool before a dive from the "Reef Goddess" out on the Reef closely accompanied by an instructor. It's a wonderful experience for those who want to explore the underwater world of the Reef.

You may also do a full PADI Open Water Dive Course whilst staying on Hayman which qualifies you to dive anywhere in the world. This course is spread out over five days. Advanced Open Water, underwater photography and night dive courses are available, too.

For those who love game fishing there is a 12-metre luxury game boat based at Hayman that is available for both private or group charter. If you are after Black Marlin or Sailfish, the best months to visit the island are September, October, November and December. Anglers regularly do battle with Black Marlin up to 400 lbs and Sailfish over 100 lbs.

During June, July, August and early September anglers can expect to encounter large Spanish Mackerel as well as Longtail and Yellow Fin Tuna.

The area is also excellent for handline fishing. The best spot around Hayman itself is Dolphin Point where you can find big Coral Trout, Sweet Lip, Red Emperor and Spanish Mackerel.

Fishing trips in the local area and around Hayman are organised regularly aboard the game fishing boat. Guests can also hire a dinghy with outboard and go fishing.

In addition, the dinghies can be used to explore Hayman, the northern side of Hook Island and several very small islands which are close by.

A resort of international standard.

The resort on Hayman Island is probably without equal on the Barrier Reef when it comes to both scale and opulence. The management wishes it to be recognised as one of the top five resorts in the world - and they are certainly striving very hard to meet that self-imposed challenge.

Their first objective was to build and furnish the resort so that it would make an undeniable statement in terms of both style and luxury. No expense has been spared to do this. At least $300 million has been spent on developing the resort.

The landscaping alone cost $7 million. Over 650,000 trees, shrubs and plants have been placed in the gardens in and around the new resort. One exquisite area is the Japanese garden adjoining the oriental restaurant.

The resort essentially has two wings. These have rooms and suites which can accommodate up to 480 guests. There are also five restaurants, bars, a library and boutiques.

The various areas which are public - like the foyers, restaurants and so forth - each

2

1. A Seair Pacific seaplane which has landed on the lagoon at Hardy Reef. Here passengers can go reef walking, view coral from a glass bottom boat and snorkel.

2. "Reef Goddess", the superbly equipped dive-boat, which operates from Hayman Island. Its destination is normally Bait Reef or Manta Ray Bay which are both superb locations for snorkelling and diving.

1

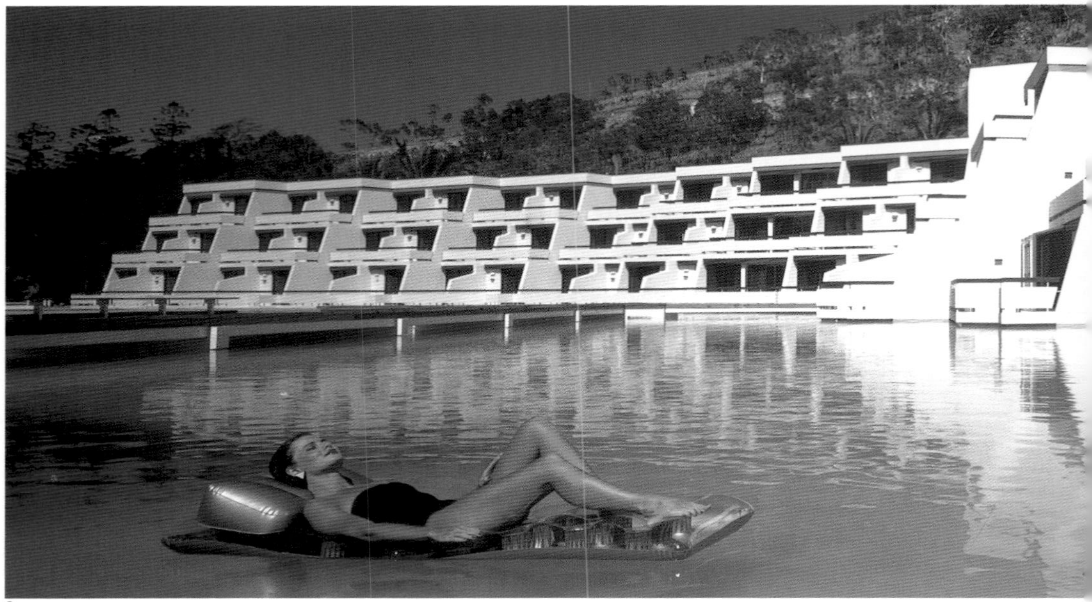

2

have their own decor and ambience. Needless to say, the change of style and moods has not been designed in a haphazard fashion. The decor changes subtly as you walk from one area of the resort to another.

Some reflect the best of contemporary design and furnishings whilst other areas have been carefully created to place the guest in the sumptuous surroundings of a celebrated and bygone age.

No expense has been spared on the furnishings throughout the resort. Much of the furniture was designed and manufactured specially for the resort whilst hundreds of thousands of dollars worth of antiques were purchased for some of the foyers, the panelled library (which contains over 4,000 books), the Club Lounge and the French restaurant La Fontaine.

These areas have a hand-made Tai Ping carpet that took six and a half months to weave. The foyer leading into La Fontaine has a 23 carat gold leaf dome and a 16th century chandelier.

Mention should also be made of the bathrooms provided for the patrons of La Fontaine. The powder room for the ladies is lined with a Mother of Pearl damask silk wallpaper from Paris - this cost a mere $42,000 - and even the taps and door hinges are plated with 24 carat gold. The gentlemen must make do with dark Portuguese marble and chrome fittings.

The resort has a wonderful collection of art. At least one and a half million dollars has been invested in procuring paintings by some of Australia's best known artists. Australian artists were also commissioned to create all the originals that can be found in the rooms of guests.

Special mention must be made of the acrylic sculpture that is a highlight of the hotel's main lobby. This magnificent piece was created by Arthur Flieschmann. Entitled "Dawn", it took nine years to create and was completed by the artist in 1932.

There are various types of accommodation on Hayman Island - Beachfront Rooms, Standard Rooms in either the Eastern or Western Wings, Garden Rooms, Suites and Penthouses.

As can be expected, the resort's rooms and one bedroom suites are very tastefully furnished and have beautiful marble bathrooms. They are all air-conditioned and have both televisions and telephones.

All rooms have VHS video players, as well. A range of video movies are available for hire from the Concierge Desk.

Eleven luxurious penthouse suites are also available. They vary in size - and no two are the same. Walk through the front door of your penthouse and, depending on your choice, it will reflect a North Queensland, Greek, Italian, Japanese, South Seas, Moroccan, Californian, English, French Provincial, Art Deco theme or one that is merely Contemporary.

A gourmet experience.

Guests should never have to complain of having a jaded palate whilst staying on Hayman. There are five restaurants to tempt guests.

The main food preparation area and

3

satellite kitchens which service these restaurants can only be described as vast and the reason is that everything consumed on the island is made on the island.

Eleven different types of bread are baked fresh each day, as well as pastries. Fresh pasta is made and even the beautiful chocolates for sale in the Viennese Coffee House are hand-made on the island.

Mention should also be made of the resort's wine cellar. This contains over 50,000 bottles of local and imported wines.

The premiere restaurant of Hayman's resort is undoubtedly La Fontaine, the French restaurant. This silver service restaurant would be on a par with the most stylish restaurants in Paris, New York or London. La Fontaine is the place to dress up (indeed, gentlemen are expected to wear ties and jackets), and enjoy the finest cuisine and wines.

Here are just some of the entrees you might expect: Iranian Caviar, Chicken Breast Salad with Truffles, Crayfish Salad with Ginger Mayonnaise and Clear Quail Soup with its own Poached Egg, garnished with Breast of Quail.

For the main course you can then choose from a wide selection of seafood, beef, lamb or poultry dishes such as Sweet Lip Fillets in a Caviar Cream Sauce, Poached Coral Trout, Panfried Veal Medallions served with fresh Pistachio Nuts, and Panfried Fillet of Pheasant with Chanterelles.

You can then indulge yourself with a selection of local and imported cheeses or desserts like Iced Passionfruit Souffle or an Oven-fresh Apple Tart with Calvados and Ice Cream. There is also a selection of Cakes and Pastries.

To add to the mood of the evening live music is usually a feature of the restaurant - with classical music being played by a harpist, pianist, cellist, violinist or guitarist.

La Fontaine is not the most inexpensive of restaurants but if you wish to spoil yourself you should not be disappointed. The service is impeccable, the surroundings exquisite and the cuisine world class. (La Fontaine is open only in the evening.)

After dinner you can retire to the superb Entertainment Centre, in the heart of the resort. In a beautiful cocktail lounge environment resort guests are treated to live dance music and cabaret shows.

Local and overseas artistes who have performed on Hayman to date include Nancy Wilson, Paul Williams, Rolf Harris,

1. Part of the new Hayman Resort complex. The vast salt-water pool covers an area five times the size of an Olympic pool.

2. The resort's pool at close quarters. Accommodation in the West Wing, which directly overlooks the pool, includes 84 Standard Rooms and six Suites.

3. The path leading to an open area called the Lanai. Here guests can enjoy breakfast, coffee and light snacks.

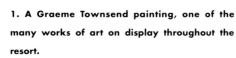

1

2

3

4

5

1. A Graeme Townsend painting, one of the many works of art on display throughout the resort.

2. "Dawn", a magnificent acrylic sculpture created by Arthur Flieschmann in 1932, adorns the main lobby.

3. The bedroom in of one of the resort's Suites.

4. The living area of a Suite within the West Wing.

5. La Fontaine, the resort's premiere restaurant.

Jackie Trent and Tony Hatch, and The Batchelors. In addition, Hayman has its own resident house band.

There are several other restaurants to choose from if La Fontaine does not appeal to you - La Trattoria, an Italian restaurant; Shima Teien, which offers Japanese, Chinese and Thai dishes; Planters, a restaurant with a Polynesian theme; The Beach Pavilion and the Viennese Coffee House.

La Trattoria has a casual atmosphere to it with rough plastered walls, terracotta-tiled floor and rustic tables. Open for both lunch and dinner, La Trattoria offers a wide selection of pasta, seafood and meat dishes. You can also order pizzas.

The Oriental Restaurant, Shima Teien, overlooks a beautiful and traditional Japanese Garden with over 40 varieties of azaleas and many other plants. Many of its details were fashioned after the gardens at Katsun Palace in Japan. The menu offers primarily Japanese dishes but there are also several Thai, Chinese and Indonesian dishes.

The Beach Pavilion has an a la carte barbeque menu and lighter snacks as well as a casual beachside bar.

Once a week a limited number of guests are offered the opportunity of enjoying a wonderful gastronomic experience aboard the sleek 35 metre "Sun Paradise" as it cruises the Whitsundays in the evening. The "Sun Paradise", which is a water jet powered craft capable of cruising at 20 knots, is the epitome of luxury.

As the sun sets, cocktails are served aboard. These are then followed by a set menu which on one occasion was Warm Quail Salad with Hazelnut dressing followed by Braised Coral Trout in Champagne and Sorrel or Grilled Tenderloin of Beef with Bearnaise Sauce. Dessert was Chilled Grand Marnier Souffle in a Tulip Basket with Fresh Fruits.

To complete this romantic evening aboard the "Sun Paradise" live musical entertainment is provided as well.

The Viennese Coffee House is open all day long for breakfast, lunch and dinner. It serves a wonderful breakfast and later in the day you can enjoy light meals such as open sandwiches and hamburgers.

If your schedule during the day is so busy that you simply retire to your room in exhaustion only to feel hungry a little later you need not starve. There is also 24 hour room service.

6

7

If enjoying all these culinary delights at any time unsettles your conscience or waistline, do not despair. Hayman have thoughtfully provided a modern, fully equipped gym for guests.

In addition, there are tennis courts, and down on the beach there are catamarans and windsurfers for hire. You can water-ski and experience the exhilaration of para-sailing too.

You may also go shopping for Hayman has several boutiques, a newsagency, same-day photo processing service and a hairdressing salon.

How to get to Hayman Island.

The postal address of the resort should you wish to contact it is simply Hayman Resort, North Queensland, 4801.

The telephone and facsimile numbers of the resort are (079) 469100 and (079) 469410 respectively. The resort's telex number is AA 48163.

The quickest and most convenient way to get to Hayman Island is to fly to nearby Hamilton Island. There are direct flights to Hamilton Island from Sydney, Cairns and Melbourne. Once you have landed on Hamilton Island you are then normally transferred to Hayman by the "Sun Goddess".

It is doubtful if any other island in the world has a craft like this to ferry guests to their destination. Like her sistership the "Sun Paradise", this spectacular 35 metre craft could hardly be more luxurious. If the three million dollar "Sun Goddess" is intended to give guests a hint of what awaits them on-shore 35 minutes away at Hayman then she succeeds.

Without doubt, the resort on Hayman is the most sophisticated and opulent to be found within the Great Barrier Reef region - with a level of accommodation and service equal to the most prestigious hotels in the world.

The only real danger for anyone staying on Hayman Island is that they may be tempted to stay within this oasis of luxury and not venture out to explore the natural beauty of the island.

One fact is certain, however. With its new 5-star resort, beautiful setting in the Whitsundays and proximity to the wonders of the Reef, Hayman Island is bound to attract those who both desire and can afford the very best in life.

6. The resort's Club Lounge.

7. Shima Teien, the resort's oriental restaurant, overlooks this exquisite Japanese garden.

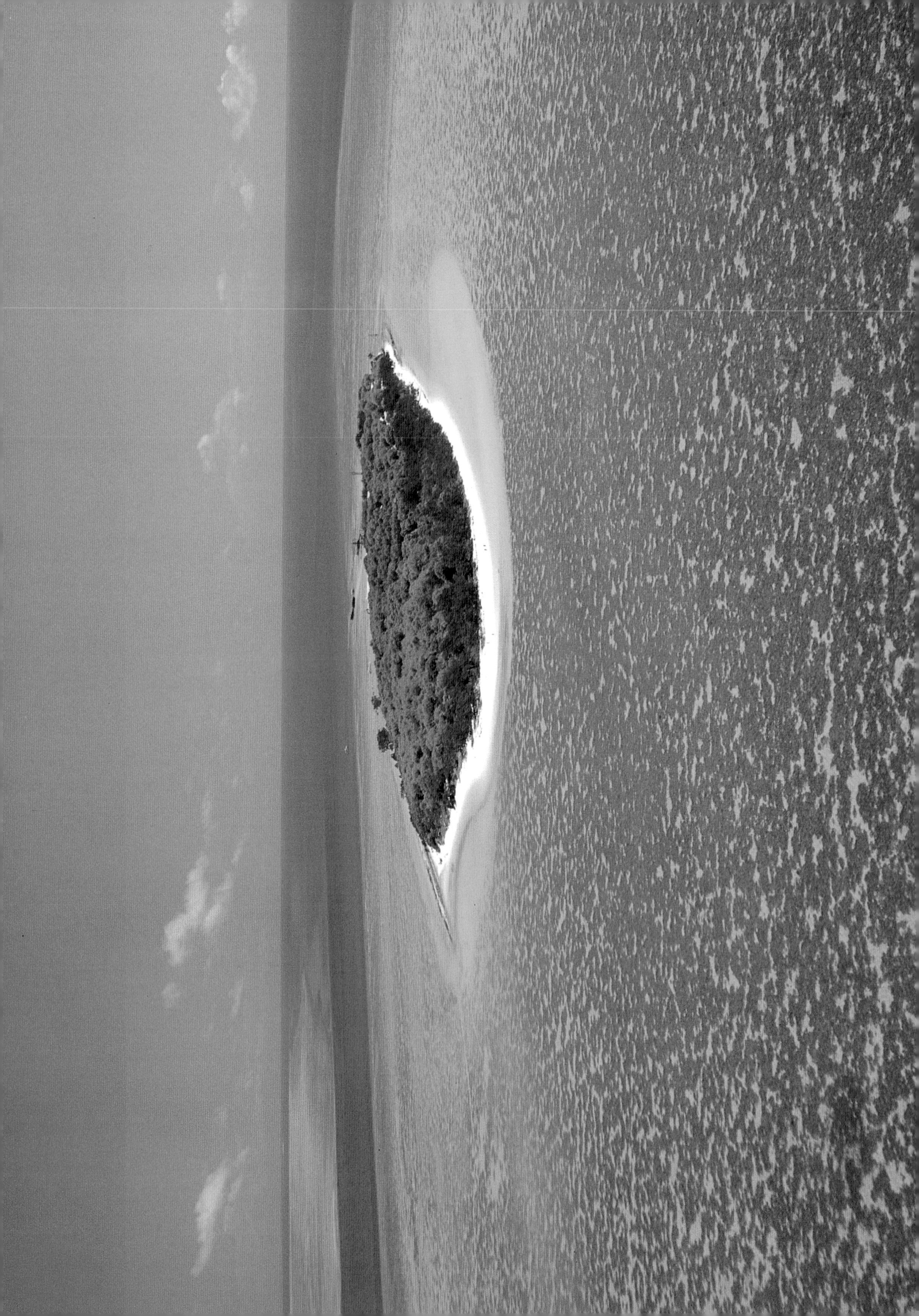

HERON ISLAND

2

3

1. Heron Island, a beautiful coral cay, is about 500 kilometres north of Brisbane.

2. A large but friendly Potato God.

3. One of the many Reef Herons after which the island was named.

4. Some of the best diving in the world can be experienced around Heron Island.

1

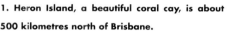

Approached from the air, Heron Island looks very much like a green jewel encircled by a thin band of pure white gold. Such is the beauty of this small coral cay that has lush vegetation, sandy white beaches, and which lies in the heart of a shimmering lagoon.

Heron is the epitome of a tropical island. It is only 42 acres in size, measures just 1.7 kilometres in circumference and is no more than five metres above sea level - yet it is hard to imagine any visitor leaving Heron Island disappointed because it has so many interesting and enjoyable features.

Heron Island is located on the Tropic of Capricorn about 500 kilometres north of Brisbane. It is one of the Capricorn Group of islands which lie about 70 kilometres off Gladstone, a busy seaboard city and port on the North Queensland coast.

A major attraction of Heron Island is the fact that the island is part of the Reef itself, being a coral cay. The Reef is literally on your doorstep. To see it, all you have to do is step out of your room and walk a few metres.

Heron Island is regarded as one of the best diving locations in the world.

4

It is an important sanctuary for bird-life as well. Each year thousands of birds visit Heron Island to breed.

Turtles also come here to mate and lay their eggs. Indeed, earlier this century turtles were so numerous in the area that a turtle soup factory was established on Heron Island.

In the summer, the temperature on the island hovers between 20°C and 28°C. In winter it ranges between 9°C and 21°C.

First visited by H.M.S. "Fly" in 1843.

The first recorded visit to Heron Island was made on January 12, 1843, by the 485 tonne corvette H.M.S. "Fly" which was under the command of Captain Francis Blackwood.

The mission of Captain Blackwood and his party was to survey all those channels that offered safe passage through the Great Barrier Reef. This task was considered of vital importance by the Admiralty at that time because so many ships had already been wrecked along the Reef.

To assist on this mission, the H.M.S. "Fly" was accompanied by the 161 tonne cutter "Bramble", under the command of Lieutenant Charles Yules.

It was Joseph Beete Jukes, a geologist aboard the H.M.S."Fly", who was responsible for naming the island. He did so after observing the many Reef Herons on it.

The survey party not only visited Heron Island but also other islands within the Capricorn Group including Wreck Island. They named it thus, after discovering the wreck of the 600 tonne vessel "America".

This ship was originally built in Quebec and was subsequently used to transport convicts. In 1831, she arrived in Hobart with 186 women bound for the penal colony in Tasmania. "America" then set out for Batavia in Java and it was on this voyage that she came to grief on the Reef.

Whilst Blackwood and his party were surveying the islands within the Capricorn Group, they saw many turtles. Jukes noted that "turtles were abundant. One night Lieutenant Shadwell, on one of the islands observing star altitudes, was actually obliged to place sentries around him to prevent turtles from running over his artificial horizon as it lay on the ground."

The next recorded visit was made to Heron Island by the Royal Australasian Ornithologists Union in October, 1910, although guano miners undoubtedly visited it before this. They obviously decided that there were richer spoils elsewhere.

Several other scientific expeditions were made to the Capricorn Group between 1910 and 1930, and the resources of the area were described as "virtually inexhaustible". It was glowing reports like these that no doubt prompted Mr. William H. Wilson to apply for a special lease on Heron Island for fishing purposes in 1923.

His application was refused but in 1925 Mr. L. Marsh applied for special leases over Heron and Fairfax Islands. His plan was to build turtle soup factories on both of these islands. When he was given the option of leasing only one or the other, he chose Heron.

Marsh was issued a ten year lease by the Lands Department, effective from July 1,

1

1923, for the annual rental of £10. The Australian Turtle Company was subsequently established.

The cost of the new factory, according to the company prospectus, was going to be £3,300. The first year's income was conservatively estimated to be £10,900. This was based on 2,500 turtles yielding 125,000 one pound tins of soup plus other by-products including 4,000 gallons of turtle oil.

The Australian Turtle Company, however, did not turn out to be a great commercial success. It was wound up voluntarily in 1927.

The lease was eventually taken over by Captain Christian Poulson.

Christian Poulson was a Dane who came to Australia at an early age. As an

2

adult he served as first mate aboard the steamship "Mamalla". This was in the early days of this century when coastal steamships were by far the quickest means of transport between the southern states and northern Queensland.

Poulson then settled in Gladstone and continued his seafaring life by operating launches out of this port.

When he took over the lease at Heron he used it as a commercial fishing base. He then decided to turn it into a resort with fishing as the main attraction.

Word spread quickly. At first, guests were accommodated in tents. As the island's popularity grew Poulson converted the old turtle factory into a dining room, kitchen, and power plant. He also built cabins along the seafront.

3

4

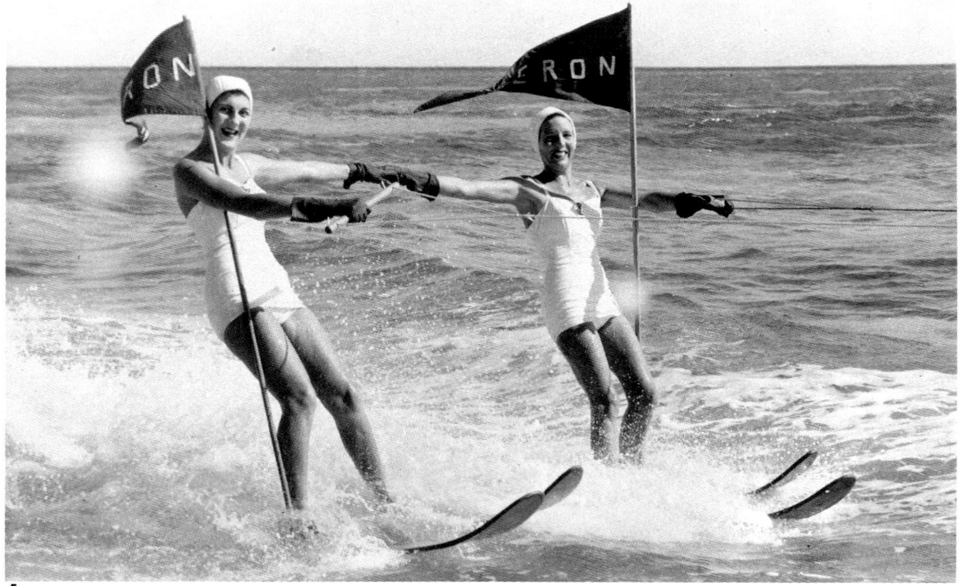

5

6

1. **A catch of turtles aboard a boat similar to those used on a commercial basis around Heron Island in the 1920's.**

2. **Captain Christian Poulson, who operated the first resort on the island, stands alongside a Giant Groper. Whether he personally caught this monster is not known.**

3. **A turtle race on the beach in 1938.**

4. **Anglers have enjoyed wonderful fishing at Heron for decades.**

5. **A water-skiing display in the 1950's.**

6. **"Miss Heron", one of the island's early speedboats.**

Some of the materials and equipment for the island came from the S.S. "Cooma" which ran aground on North Reef, about 25 kilometres north of Heron. The ship was bought for salvage by Poulson and Mr. Coleman, a Rockhampton hotelier.

Heron Island soon became a favourite destination for both businessmen and politicians from the south. Sir Leslie Wilson, State Governor of Queensland in the 1930's, was just one of the regular visitors to the island. The cost of staying on Heron Island in those days was between £5 and £8 a week.

By 1944 the resort had 40 cabins and the facilities even included a card room and tennis court. Poulson, however, was not a man to rest on his laurels. In those days, the boat trip from Gladstone to Heron took five hours. Needless to say, many guests suffered from seasickness. So Poulson decided to offer them alternative transport.

In 1947 he went into partnership with Captain S.C. Middlemiss, a pilot, and started a seaplane service from Brisbane to Heron and other island resorts further north. Their fleet consisted of three ex-RAAF Catalina seaplanes. The flight time from Brisbane to Heron was just over two hours.

Unfortunately, 1947 also proved to be a tragic year. On the evening of November 28, Poulson rowed out by dinghy to visit some friends aboard the launch "Irma". After telling them of some ideal angling spots he left the "Irma" to return to shore. He never arrived.

Poulson's overturned dinghy was later found by a Catalina drifting about 25 kilometres south of Heron Island. His body was never found.

In 1947, Poulson left behind him the most popular island resort on the Great Barrier Reef. Today, many would argue that it is still the best.

Two wrecks with a colourful history.

Many visitors to Heron are inquisitive about the large wreck at the mouth of the island's small harbour. It is the remains of a ship with an historic past.

She was named the "Protector" and was built in 1884 in England for £65,000. She was commissioned by the infant colony of South Australia who were afraid that they would be a target for Russian warships prowling the Pacific after the close of the

1

2

Crimea War.

After the Federation of Australian States in 1901, the "Protector" joined the Australian Navy and subsequently saw active service in China during the Boxer Rebellion, and in World War I. During World War II she was used for carrying supplies to New Guinea and it was on one such voyage that she was badly holed by a tug and subsequently abandoned on a beach near Gladstone.

She was saved from this ignominious end to her career by Captain Poulson, Heron Island's first tourist operator. He bought her for £100, had her refloated and positioned as a breakwater for visiting craft. Today, the "Protector's" hull is not only an interesting remnant of Australian history. She is also home to several species of birds that do not normally frequent the island itself.

Another ship of interest that was wrecked very close to Heron Island was the sailing ship "Deutschland". Back in the 1880's it was carrying a pipe organ purchased from Messrs. J. Porrit of Leicester, England, for the newly built St. Paul's Cathedral in Rockhampton.

After the ship ran aground on Polmaise Reef near Heron Island the wreck was bought by a syndicate headed by Captain Norris, a local seafarer. When the main hatch was opened they found 20 cases containing the organ components.

Much to their surprise, the salvagers found that the components were undamaged. All the cases were sitting on top of other cargo and, luckily, had not been submerged under water. The organ was subsequently despatched to Rockhampton and installed. It was replaced in 1966 by an electric organ, much to the regret of many local music lovers.

An island built on the Reef itself.

Heron Island, like any cay, was formed as coral debris accumulated at the sheltered or western side of the reef that it sits on (the prevailing winds come from the north-east and south-east) .

Slowly a sand bank formed. As birds started to visit it, they left droppings with seeds from other vegetated cays. Other seeds were washed or blown ashore.

The first plants to grow were grasses and herbs that were very tolerant to salt. Then small trees and shrubs like the low growing Octopus bush and Cardwell Cabbage shrub started to grow. These would have acted as windbreaks, protecting the inner part of the island.

This would have given forest species like the luxuriant, large-leaved Pisonia tree the opportunity to take hold in the centre of the cay, along with others like the Native Elm and Sandpiper Fig.

Today, about 50 different species of plants can be found on Heron Island. Some are native, some have been introduced.

There are some interesting facts about the Octopus bush which acts as a windbreak for less hardy species. The young, fleshy leaves of this bush can be eaten raw or boiled. Throughout the Pacific, islanders have long used these leaves to relieve itching and also to overcome the ill effects of eating toxic fish.

The soft wooded native Mulberry which grows to about five metres is also

3

found on Heron. In Samoa, the strong fibres from the inner bark of its trunk are used by the natives to make fishing nets.

A sanctuary for bird-life.

As a visitor to Heron Island you cannot help but develop an interest in bird-life. The reason is simple. There is an astonishing number of birds on the island.

At least 37 different species of birds have been observed on Heron Island. Some use it as a stop-over as they migrate, others are visitors from the mainland. For many, Heron is home.

One species that lives the year round on Heron Island is the Black Noddy Tern. This bird is predominantly sooty black in colour. Its legs, feet and bill are jet black. The top of its head is white.

4

It is hard to imagine, but approximately 100,000 Black Noddy Terns live on the island. As you walk along the paths that traverse the island during the breeding season (September to December), every tree seems to have a dozen or two Noddy Tern nests.

The birds are so numerous that you may even wonder at times if you are reliving a scene out of a Alfred Hitchcock movie, but there is never any need to feel alarmed. Noddy Terns are totally harmless and you soon become accustomed to their presence and trusting manner.

They are totally unfazed by the human beings they share the island with. Indeed, if you go for a walk at night you must exercise caution. You will often encounter Noddy Terns fast asleep in the middle of a track, blissfully unaware that they may be in dire danger of being kicked or trodden underfoot.

For food, Black Noddy Terns skim across the surface of the sea snatching up small fish from the schools of Hardy-heads that abound in the Capricorn region.

At low tide you will see Reef Herons, after which the island is named, out on the reef flats searching for small crustaceans, fish and molluscs. There are two colour varieties, white and grey.

Other birds that you will often see include the black Sooty Oystercatcher which has striking scarlet eyes and bill; the Banded Land-Rail, a hen-like bird which scrounges around the undergrowth for grubs and insects; the White Breasted Sea Eagle, which is often seen hovering high in the air looking for prey; the Silver Gull which likes to

5

1. The remains of the "Protector", a ship which served in China during the Boxer Rebellion and both World Wars.

2. A Brown Booby perches on the wreck. This bird dives for fish and squid and is very adept at pursuing its prey underwater.

3. The Black Noddy Tern. Thousands of these sea-birds live and nest on Heron Island.

4. White and Grey Reef Herons feed on small crustaceans, fish and molluscs.

5. The Banded Land Rail, a ground bird you will often see just metres away from your room.

congregate near the helicopter pad; and the Wedge Tailed Shearwater or Mutton Bird.

This curious bird tunnels into the ground to nest. Their tunnels are up to three metres in length with a small grass lined chamber at the end. Only a single egg is laid here and incubated.

Care should be taken when wandering off the beaten tracks on the island. It can be rather disconcerting to suddenly sink a foot or so into one such tunnel; it must be even more disconcerting for some unsuspecting Mutton Bird inside who has laboured long and hard to create this unusual nursery.

Another characteristic of the Mutton Birds is the eerie wailing sound they make whilst courting. More than one passing sailor or island visitor in the past has mistaken this sound for that of a lost, crying child.

Other superstitious mariners long ago heard the mournful concert of melancholy voices and believed the islands to be inhabited by spirits of the damned.

The Mutton Bird inhabits Heron Island between the months of October and May. During this time there may be as many as 17,000 on the island. The population of Mutton Birds in the whole of the Capricorn Group is thought to be about 3,000,000.

Reef Walking at Heron Island.

One of the most rewarding experiences for anyone visiting Heron Island is to walk across the reef flats at low tide and see some of the many different plants and animals that inhabit the Great Barrier Reef.

You can do this by yourself or you can join one of the reef walks regularly organised by the resort. These are highly recommended

1

2

because they are so interesting and informative.

The organised walk usually lasts for about one and a half hours and is a very casual affair. You simply follow one of the staff members who pauses occasionally to point out a turtle or small fish or stops to overturn a boulder to reveal and talk about some of the small creatures and plants that are hidden under these.

As you leave the beach you will enter the first of the three distinct areas on the reef flats, the inner sandy zone. Here, the areas of coral are quite patchy.

The most common creatures that you will encounter here are Bêche-de-mer or sea cucumbers. These rather odd looking animals - which are either black, very dark green or mustard coloured - actually play an important part in the formation of a cay like Heron.

Sea cucumbers scoop up sand into their mouths using short tentacles and filter it for organic matter. The fine sand they then excrete fills crevices more easily and helps build up a more solid reef.

Last century, sea cucumbers were greatly sought after. In China, they were considered a delicacy and there are some very colourful stories about the characters who fished the waters of the Great Barrier Reef for sea cucumbers in the hope of making their fortunes. (You can learn more about these adventurers in Chapter Two.)

As you wander through the shallow waters of the inner sandy zone you may also catch a glimpse of different fish including the Epaulette shark. These grow to about one metre long and are quite harmless. Epaulette sharks are light brown with distinctive dark markings on their shoulders, hence their name.

You should see more than one cobalt Blue Linkia starfish, too. These vividly coloured starfish can be up to 15 centimetres in diameter. If you turn one over carefully you will see its tiny mouth right in the centre. You will also see the hundreds of little sucker feet running down each arm which enable the starfish to move across the sandy bottom of the water in search of food.

As you walk further out you will enter the middle coral zone. Here the coral formations are much denser. You'll come across a variety of corals, including branching corals or Staghorns and soft corals.

You will see clams as well with their

3

exquisitely coloured "mantles", sea anemones and, occasionally, beautiful Cowrie shells.

Finally, you will come to the boulder zone which is close to the edge of the reef. Here, coral life is smaller because it is subjected to more wave action.

Under boulders you will find creatures like Brittle Starfish which have long spindly arms, Ringed Cowries which are off-white with a yellow ring around them, and timid Blue Swimmer crabs.

Abalone are also common. These slug-like creatures are green in colour and have a small shell on their backs. When disturbed or handled they often exude a bright purple dye as part of their defense mechanism.

You may see Pin Cushion starfish, too. They are dome-shaped and measure up to 15 centimetres across.

A scuba diver's paradise.

If you are an experienced scuba diver, or would like to learn to dive, your visit to Heron Island should linger long in your memory.

Paul Tzimoulis of America's "Skindiver Magazine" describes the island as "one of the few remaining places on earth where a diver can admire and appreciate the Reef ecology untouched and intact".

Over 70% of all Great Barrier Reef coral species are to be found in the area and 859 different species of fish have been recorded.

Valerie Taylor, well-known underwater photographer, once said that "Heron Island supports the richest and most diverse collection of tame tropical fish found anywhere in the world".

4

The water temperature for diving could hardly be better. Between July and August it averages 17°C and 26°C during the months of January and February. Visibility is also excellent - it ranges between 10 and 25 metres.

There are over a dozen different dives within minutes of the island. Because of the excellent visibility most of these sites can be enjoyed by snorkellers as well.

On the reef's edge, just a short distance from the harbour entrance, is the Heron Bommie.

Bommies are giant heads of coral that can vary between three and 30 metres in height. They are home to an amazing array of fish of all colours and sizes.

The Heron Bommie is no exception. You will see many different species including

5

1. Exploring the reef flats at low tide is a fascinating experience that no visitor to Heron Island should miss.

2. Guests from the resort learn about some of the many creatures that inhabit the reef.

3. A Bêche-de-mer or sea cucumber. Last century they were smoked and shipped to China where they were considered a great delicacy.

4. A brightly coloured starfish.

5. Virtually every boulder harbours marine life of some kind.

1

2

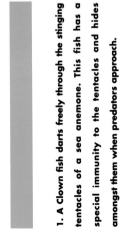

3

1. A Clown fish darts freely through the stinging tentacles of a sea anemone. This fish has a special immunity to the tentacles and hides amongst them when predators approach.

2. Although turtles look ungainly they can move with surprising speed underwater.

3. The silhouette of a Manta Ray gliding gracefully through the water. Although large, they are harmless, feeding on plankton and small fish.

Barramundi, Cod, Spangled Emperor, Coral Trout, Red Throated Sweetlip and Golden Trevally, to mention a few. After years of hand feeding, the fish are very tame.

At the Heron Bommie you should also get the chance to meet and feed two friendly Moray Eels, Harry and Fang.

About a hundred metres north-west of the Heron Bommie is Pam's Point. This was named after the daughter of one of Heron's early lessees.

The Staghorn coral here is home to thousands of beautifully coloured fish. There is also a large 10 metre Bommie with a magical cave alongside it with soft corals and sponges on the roof.

South-west of the harbour entrance are three other dive sites - the Coral Gardens, Staghorn Bank and the Canyons.

The Coral Gardens consist mainly of Staghorn coral growing down to about 12 metres. There is then a sandy bottom with Bommies of varying sizes scattered everywhere. A large strip of Staghorn coral also grows out from the reef edge into deeper water and a large school of yellow stripey Sea Perch always seem to congregate here.

Some 80 metres further along is The Staghorn Bank. This spot is normally used as a drop off point for drift dives back to the Coral Gardens. The area is completely carpeted with Staghorn coral and turtles are often seen resting here.

Another 80 metres away are The Canyons which have many holes and gutters which run down from the top of the reef.

On the northern side of the Heron Reef there are a number of superb diving locations.

The first of the sites, travelling from west to east, is Gorgonia Hole. A small wall runs parallel to the reef edge and is divided by a series of gutters, holes and swim-throughs.

This spot has a wonderful variety of coral from small delicate sea fans, sponges and crinoids to large Plate and Brain corals. In the many holes and crevices you will see coral fish like Sweetlip and Angel Fish. Other local residents include cray, crabs and octopus.

One hundred and fifty metres east of Gorgonia Hole is Plate Ledge. Drifts are often done between these two moorings and these offer some breathtaking sights. As the name suggests, there are numerous Plate corals at this dive site. Beautiful Gorgonia Fans are

4

also to be seen everywhere.

Further along is the Coral Grotto. The feature here is a large hole which interrupts a carpet of colourful Plate and Acropora corals. At this spot you will also clearly see the zone where the reef flat drops away to form the reef edge. Off this you will see some Bommies, too, all of which have many varieties of fish around them.

A hundred metres from the Coral is the Hole In The Wall. As you head towards it you'll be greeted by a convoy of Hussars fish demanding to be hand fed.

In addition, you will encounter a Bommie which has a large crevice that runs right down the middle of it. This is large enough to explore. A large but placid Eel called Olive and a Cod called Popeye can often be seen here.

In the cracks of the Bommie there are many different varieties of shrimps to be seen. On the east side of the Bommie is an overhang, and numerous delicate sponges cover the roof and walls. The actual Hole In The Wall is situated over the reef edge.

East again is a small bay known as Blue Pools. Here you will observe many fish swimming in and out of the coral. You'll both see and hear colourful Parrot fish, too, as they busily grind down coral rubble for food.

The next dive spot east is the North Bommie. This is a giant mushroom shaped coral head which is the home for Manta Rays and many different species of fish including Coral Trout and Butterfly Cod.

On the north side of Heron Reef there are another three main dives to enjoy - Coral Cascades, Tenements I and Tenements II. But

5

the choice of dive sites does not end there.

Less than one kilometre away from Heron Reef is Wistari Reef. Here there are two sites where you can dive as deep as 30 metres. If you wish you can also charter a boat to discover other nearby reefs.

Another fact of great interest to experienced divers is that each year, Heron Island has an Underwater Festival. In the future this will normally be scheduled for the month of October.

The Festival is a seven day event that gives you the opportunity to not only dive but learn about a range of topics including coral reef biology, diving medicine, underwater photography and cinematography from well-known experts in these fields.

At last count, attendance at this Festival cost no more than the normal package for

6

4. A colourful Beaked Coralfish.

5. A large but placid Moray eel that is accustomed to divers feeding and gently stroking it.

6. Scuba divers have at least 14 different sites to explore immediately around the island. All are just minutes away by boat.

staying on Heron Island. The only additional costs you should have are the usual ones for equipment and dive boat charges.

You must, however, complete a special Registration Form if you wish to participate in the special events of the Festival. So when you make your normal holiday reservation, mention to your travel agent that you wish to enrol for the Festival as well.

If you have never scuba dived before but would like to, Heron Island is a great place to learn. There are no long, uncomfortable boat trips to the different dive spots and when you are not underwater you still have the comforts of the resort and all the interesting features of the island to enjoy.

The dive tuition course is over seven days and leads to "C" card qualification as an Open Water diver. If you want to do the course, you must enrol for it prior to your arrival on the island. You should also note that this course always starts on Sunday so you need to arrive on the island no later than Saturday to participate.

The alternative is to take Heron's "One Day Scuba Experience". This allows you to dive on the reef, accompanied by an instructor, after a lesson that teaches you the basics of diving.

Heron Island also offers special packages for experienced divers which are combined with the normal accommodation packages. These dive packages include boat charges, airfills, tank, belt, weights and two dives a day. Like the dive tuition course, these packages need to be booked prior to your arrival.

All equipment including wetsuits can be hired on a daily basis. Snorkelling gear can also be hired.

As a snorkeller or diver you might be interested in underwater photography. If you do not have an underwater camera and would love to capture the beauty of the Reef yourself, head for the Dive Shop again. It has underwater cameras for hire and a film processing service.

If you are not a scuba diver and have no intention of ever becoming one you can still enjoy the underwater world around Heron Island. Simply step aboard the modern semi-submersible craft that usually operates twice a day.

This is very much like a small submarine except that it never goes completely underwater. It has large viewing windows below the water's surface and gives you the opportunity of seeing the diverse and colourful marine life on the reef without ever getting your feet wet.

Turtle Watching on Heron Island.

There are seven species of sea turtles to be found throughout the world. Six of these species can be seen in Australian waters and of these, two nest on the islands within the Capricorn Group.

The two species that breed within the area are Green and Loggerhead turtles. In fact, the Capricorn islands are one of the world's major breeding grounds for both these species.

The Green turtle is the most common. These can weigh anywhere between 91kg and 200kg. The total number that nest on Heron Island during any one summer can be as high as 1,200.

Over 50 female Green turtles usually

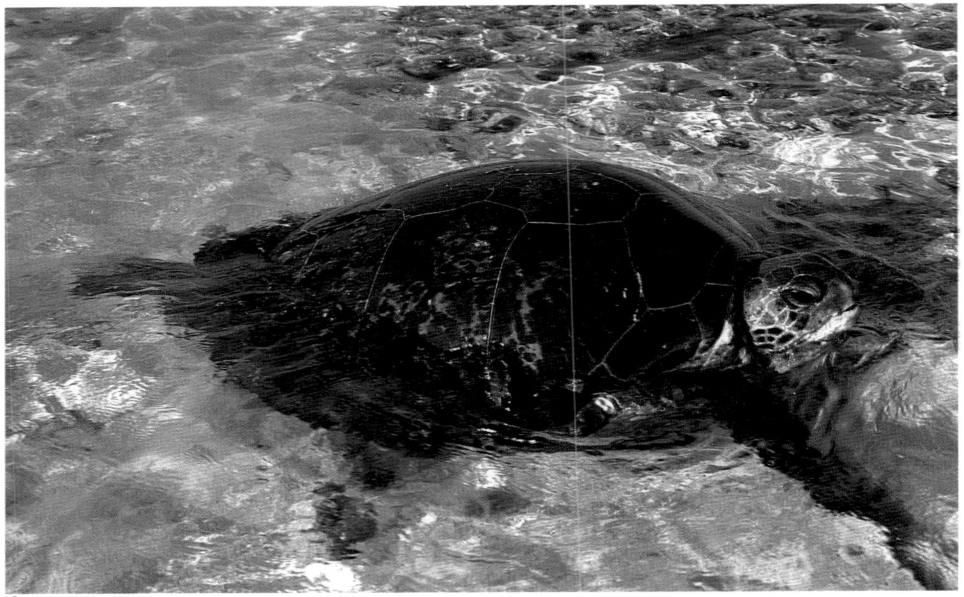

1

come ashore on Heron Island each night during the nesting season from late November through to January. (On nearby West Island, which is larger and uninhabited, as many as 400 come ashore nightly.)

The average Loggerhead turtle weighs about 100kg. No more than six would normally be seen on Heron on any one night and only 30 to 90 Loggerheads would nest on Heron each season.

Incidentally, only the female turtles visit the beaches of Heron or any other island. Male turtles rarely leave the water during their lifetime.

There are several other interesting facts about turtles. Turtles are usually over 50 years of age before they breed. Most female turtles also breed for only one season.

When the urge to lay eggs brings the female Green and Loggerhead turtles out of the ocean and onto Heron Island they will lay up to 120 eggs, each about the size of a table tennis ball. Green turtles will lay up to eight clutches of eggs every 13 nights. Loggerheads will lay up to six clutches at intervals of about 14 nights.

For years guests have observed the turtles that visit Heron Island. Follow a few simple rules and you can do so, too.

The best time to see turtles is an hour or two after a high tide at night-time. To find nesting turtles, walk along the beach at the high tide mark and look for turtle tracks. These will be about one metre wide. If you have a torch, take one along.

Turtle tracks can be easily seen without lights. Lights can also disturb turtles, so you should keep your torches off at this stage.

2

Simply follow the tracks carefully onto the dune until you locate the turtle. To avoid disturbing the timid turtle, be as quiet as you can and stay behind her until she starts to lay her eggs. Once the turtle is actually laying she is not normally disturbed by lights or noise. You can even gently touch her.

You can also dig the sand away from behind the turtle to see the eggs as they drop. Flashlight photographs can be taken at this stage without fear of disturbing the turtle.

Turtle eggs are incubated by the warmth of the sand. At Heron Island, they usually incubate for about nine weeks. The emergence of hatchling turtles from their nests and their precarious rush to the sea can be witnessed from mid-January until late March. They usually leave their nests at night which reduces their chances of being preyed upon by hungry birds.

3

If you come across turtles on Heron Island at close quarters please remember that they are now protected creatures and that it is an offence to either touch or collect their eggs.

A Marine Research Station established in 1951.

Much of the information known about turtles has been gathered by scientists working at the Research Station on Heron Island. This was established in 1951 and is now owned and operated by the University of Queensland.

This Research station is the oldest and largest one of its kind within the Great Barrier Reef region. It is also one of the principal coral reef research centres in the world.

Each year marine scientists and students from Australia and overseas visit Heron Island and conduct post-graduate and independent research programs into many different subjects.

The Station accommodates up to 90 people and has a wide range of sophisticated laboratory and field equipment.

The marine scientists who come to Heron Island study the general ecology of the reefs nearby. They are constantly learning more about how fish and corals live and capture food. They also observe and keep a close watch on the different bird species on Heron and surrounding islands.

The various research programs are not only giving new insight into the Reef and the diverse life it shelters. Scientists are gathering and testing toxins from different marine

4

1. Go reef walking and you could easily encounter a turtle like this one.

2. Mating turtles.

3. A marine biologist at the Heron Island Research Station holds a Blue Linkia starfish.

4. The National Parks and Wildlife Service have an Information Centre on the island and officers are always ready to answer questions about the local marine life and bird-life.

1

2

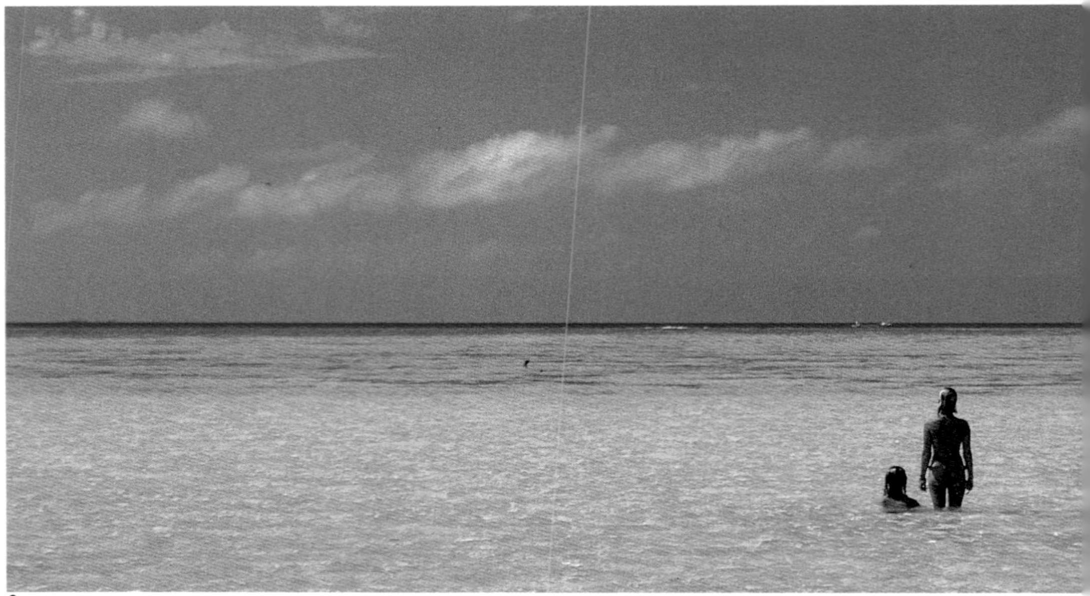
3

1 & 2. A fishing trip to one of the reefs a short distance from Heron Island usually yields a good catch.

3. Two girls cool off in the crystal clear waters of Heron's beautiful lagoon.

organisms in the hope that they may provide the key for the cure of cancer and other incurable diseases.

Visitors staying at the resort on Heron Island are welcome to visit the Research Station but only by prior arrangement. There are regular walks conducted that take you through the Station and this includes a visit to a permanent museum that houses items and information of great interest.

Another place well worth visiting on the island is the office of the Queensland National Parks and Wildlife Service. This is centrally located in the resort complex and has both displays and reference books that will satisfy your curiosity about the Reef and its many inhabitants. An officer is on duty at times throughout the day to answer any questions you might have about the marine life and bird-life in the region.

Many of the questions you have about the history and wildlife of the island will be answered during the walk regularly conducted by staff members of the resort. These guided walks are usually in the mornings, several times a week, and last for about an hour.

Fishing around Heron Island.

A most enjoyable way to spend half a day while you are staying on Heron Island is to go on a fishing trip to one of the nearby reefs (fishing is not permitted directly around Heron Island itself).

A maximum of 15 guests are taken aboard the resort's large Reef launch and the cheerful crew provide hand-lines, bait and refreshments.

It is a rare occasion when the fish are not biting. The most common fish caught are Coral Trout, Sweet Lip, Barramundi, Cod, and Red Throat Emperor.

Even if you do not personally catch a fish, it is still a great way to catch up on your sun-tan and to get to know a few new friends. (The charge for this trip is also very modest.)

If you wish to make up a small party of your own and go fishing you may charter the resort's fast "Shark Cat".

Another trip to be recommended is the one to nearby Wilson Island. This is a beautiful, uninhabited coral cay about one hour away by boat from Heron Island.

Wilson Island is small - you can actually walk around it in about 15 minutes - but there is plenty to see and enjoy.

Around the water's edge you can walk over coral rock with evidence of the coral skeletons it was formed from still clearly visible.

Like Heron, Wilson Island is also home to a great deal of bird-life. The Wedgetailed Shearwater, the Silver Gull, the Black Naped Tern and the Roseate Tern (an endangered species world-wide) all nest on the island in substantial numbers.

Two other birds fall within the "rare nesting" category on Wilson Island - the Crested Tern and the White Breasted Sea Eagle. In fact, Wilson Island is the only island within the Capricorn Group that has recorded a successful nesting of the latter.

Around the island during the summer you will almost certainly see turtles that have chosen Wilson Island to nest on.

Do not forget to take your mask and flippers with you. There is a beautiful small beach at the north-western tip of Wilson Island which is an ideal spot for snorkelling. The water is remarkably clear.

This beach is also a wonderful place just to swim and sun-bake, too. Civilisation seems to be a million miles away.

As you are reclining in the sun, the crew from the resort launch will be at the other end of this small island preparing a barbeque and a smorgasbord of food for lunch.

It is hard to think of a better way to spend a day.

Be sure to book early, however, after your arrival at Heron Island because the trip to Wilson Island is only offered twice a week and it is very popular.

4

5

A ship-shape resort run by P & O.

The resort on Heron Island is now fully owned and operated by P & O, the shipping line.

The standards, in all respects, are high.

The resort facilities have been recently refurbished and it now has 109 rooms, accommodating a maximum of 280 people. Usually, however, the resort would have no more than 200 or 230 guests at any one time. There are about 90 staff.

There are four grades of accommodation available.

For the budget minded, there are Lodges. These offer basic accommodation and do not have their own bathrooms. Guests in these Lodges share excellent facilities close by.

Next up the scale are Reef Suites.

4. Part of the resort complex (deserted because it is lunchtime!).

5. The area around the resort's swimming pool is a popular place to relax and have a cool drink.

1

2

3

4

5

1. A couple relax on the patio of their Point Suite.

2. Point Suites are spacious and located on the beachfront.

3. The comfortable interior of a Reef Suite.

4. Budget accommodation in Heron's Lodges.

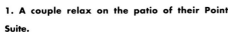

These are very comfortable, modern rooms - each with their own bathrooms and refrigerators.

Heron Suites are very similar to the Reef Suites but happen to be even more spacious and on the beachfront.

Finally, there are four Point Suites and one Beach House available. These are located on a small point directly overlooking the island's beautiful lagoon.

The rates for all accommodation include meals.

Lunch is usually a buffet of different hot and cold dishes, whilst dinner is a la carte with soup, a choice of two entrees and several main dishes and desserts. The menu changes daily and unless you are staying on the island for more than two weeks you will enjoy a different menu every evening.

Cream of Watercress Soup, followed by entrees of either Sliced Turkey Breast served on a Waldorf Salad or Mushrooms cooked with Paprika Pepper, Onion, White Wine and finished with Dairy Cream is a sample of how dinner may begin.

You might then have a choice of Fillet of Beef, coated with a Leek and Bacon Duxelle, wrapped with pastry and then baked; Pan Fried Pork Chops served with a Red Wine and French Mustard Sauce; or Poached Fillet of Red Throated Emperor topped with a Tomato and Basil Sauce.

The wine list features a selection of well-known Australian labels as well as several local and imported champagnes.

In the evening there is always entertainment of some kind. It is quite deliberately low key, without a lot of razzamatazz - and most guests seem to enjoy it this way.

Two evenings a week you can sip cocktails to light music played live. There is also an Australian Bush Dance night, a Casino night and a disco twice a week. On Sunday nights there is Heron's very own entertaining Quiz Show.

On one night there is a very informative slide show, too, on some aspect of the Reef - often presented by one of the marine biologists from the Research Station.

If you want to work off dinner there's another alternative. You can play tennis on lit courts in the evening - and during the day, of course.

The Resort Shop is the booking office for activities. As a store it also has an excellent selection of goods. You can

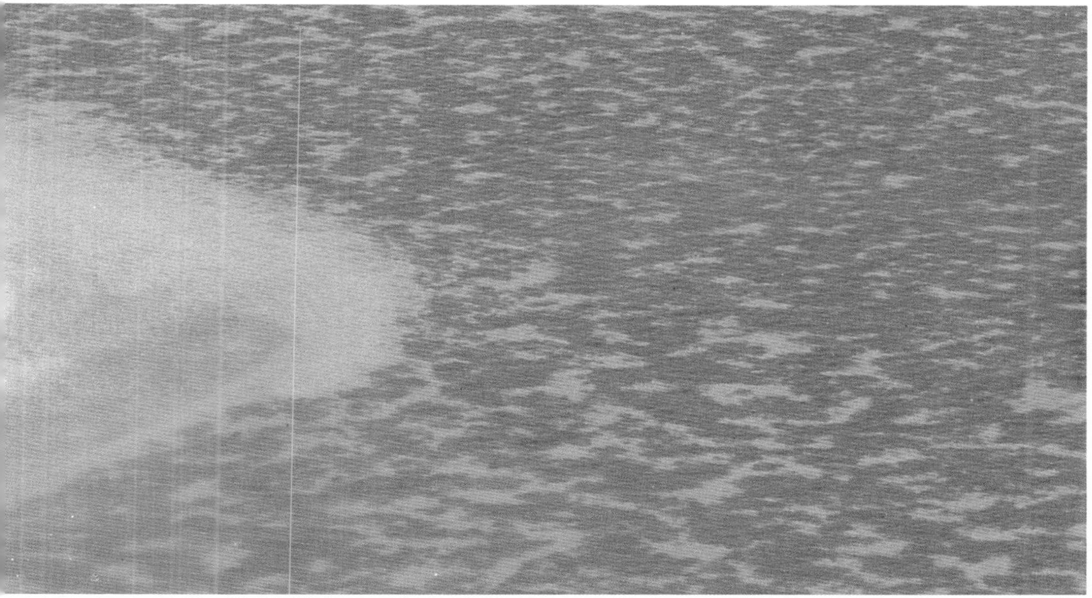

6

7

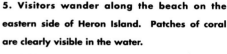

5. **Visitors wander along the beach on the eastern side of Heron Island. Patches of coral are clearly visible in the water.**

6. **Children enjoy the island as much as adults.**

7. **The sun sets over Heron Island.**

purchase everything from soft drinks, confectionery, ice-creams, paperbacks and magazines to camera film, toiletries, cigarettes and a good range of fashion swimwear, quality casual clothing and coral jewellery.

How to get to Heron Island.

Should you wish to contact the resort on Heron Island, their telephone number is (079) 78 1488. Their telex number is 49455 and facsimile is (079) 78 1457. Mail may be sent to Heron Island Resort, Via Gladstone, Queensland 4680.

In order to get to Heron Island you have two choices. You may arrive by either boat or helicopter.

A boat departs from the Marina, Gladstone, daily at 8:00 a.m. and 1:30 p.m. The trip, which is usually aboard a very modern and comfortable 33 metre motor powered catamaran, takes two hours.

Helicopters leave Gladstone airport daily - except on Christmas Day. The operators of the helicopters are Lloyds Aviation and their service connects with the flights of major domestic airlines. The trip to Heron Island by helicopter takes approximately 30 minutes.

The flight by helicopter is spectacular. Many guests, for this reason, choose to travel one way by helicopter and one way by launch.

It should be noted that local scenic flights by helicopter are available as well. These flights are a truly amazing way to see the Great Barrier Reef.

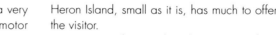

By now it should be very obvious that Heron Island, small as it is, has much to offer the visitor.

A gentleman by the name of R. Emerson Curtis visited Heron Island in the late 1940's. In an article, which was published in "Walkabout" magazine in February, 1948, he made these observations.

"Although one might walk completely around the shore of the island in fifteen to twenty minutes, there were always so many objects of interest, turtle tracks on the sand, birds in flight or nesting in the trees and beneath the trees, plants, flowers, seeds, shells, coral-rock, seaweed, as well as the ever-changing light and colour of the lagoon and the ocean and the sky above, that hours were spent each day just exploring the wonders of the little island..."

Little has changed.

HINCHINBROOK ISLAND

2

3

1. Hinchinbrook's vast mangrove forests are second in intensity only to those found in the Amazon Delta. Also visible is the chain of jagged peaks that bisect the island.
2. Fishermen photographed on Hinchinbrook in 1938 display a large ray they have caught.
3. Several people fish from the resort's jetty - fish often caught include Coral Trout, Cod, Bream and Mangrove Jack.
4. A special raised boardwalk allows you to explore a section of the island's mysterious mangrove forests.

1

No other island within The Great Barrier Reef region can match the magnitude, air of mystery and wilderness beauty of Hinchinbrook.

Hinchinbrook is actually the largest island national park in the world. It is 35 kilometres long and is 24 kilometres across at its widest point.

It has rugged mountains - including Queensland's third highest peak - dense jungle, spectacular waterfalls, luxuriant tracts of mangroves, secluded coves and sandy beaches.

Dolphins can sometimes be seen in Missionary Bay as well as dugongs, strange but harmless "sea cows".

Aborigines once lived on Hinchinbrook Island - and practised cannibalism.

Today, Hinchinbrook's natural beauty is still unspoiled. Nor is it overrun by tourists. There is only a small, low-key resort at Cape Richards at the northern tip of the island and this caters for no more than 50 people.

Yachtsmen drop in occasionally but the only other visitors are small groups of back-packers eager to explore this extraordinary

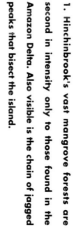

4

island - which lies about half way between Townsville and Cairns.

The nearest town to Hinchinbrook Island on the mainland is Cardwell, about 40 minutes away by launch. You can also fly to Hinchinbrook by seaplane from either Townsville or Cairns.

An island once inhabited by the Bandjin Tribe.

Hinchinbrook is rich in history. Long before the first Europeans discovered the island, aborigines made it their home. How long ago, nobody really knows.

Last century, however, Mr. M. Armstrong, an Inspector of Police, wrote about the Bandjin aborigines still living on the island in 1880. "The tribe wore no clothes in their original state, but those who are now allowed to come to Cardwell do so."

Both sexes had ornate scar patterns on their skin. The males had these markings on their backs, the females had them on their arms and shoulders.

Other reports reveal that ornamental necklaces made of red berries were worn by the aborigines and that the men smeared themselves with grease, red ochre and pipe clay when preparing to fight.

Cannibalism was practised by the Hinchinbrook aborigines with some whites being among the unhappy victims.

One notable exception was the Rev. Fuller who arrived in Cardwell during January, 1874. Against the strong advice of the local people, he decided that Hinchinbrook was the ideal place to establish a Mission to the Aboriginals. He moved to the island in March and camped at what is now known as Missionary Bay.

Contrary to all expectations the Rev. Fuller was still alive in July - due to the simple fact that the aborigines ignored him.

His Mission on the island, for the same reason, was a failure. He eventually moved to Bellenden Plains on the mainland where the natives were more numerous and, presumably, more approachable. Once again the aborigines chose to totally ignore the well-intentioned reverend.

Certain areas of Hinchinbrook Island were strictly taboo to the native inhabitants. One such place was the enormous granite cube on the peak of Mt. Diamantina known as "The Devil's Icebox". Aborigines believed that the gods transferred this massive block from nearby Dunk Island.

The sites of ancient aboriginal kitchen "middens" can still be seen on the island. These are large mounds of shells, stones and ashes adjoining old campsites. Study of these middens has revealed that Hinchinbrook's aborigines were very partial to various shell fish. Animal remains indicate that the Dugong or sea cow, turtle, and small marsupials formed part of their diet, too.

It is also known that the aborigines on Hinchinbrook Island had bark canoes and that they netted fish and caught them with hooks made from bone.

Various aboriginal artifacts have been found on the island including stone axes, knives, shields, spears and boomerangs.

Incorrectly identified by Captain Cook.

On his famous voyage of exploration in 1770, Captain Cook sailed along the eastern edge of the island naming its most prominent peak Hinchinbrook.

He gave it this name in June, 1770, after the family seat of his patron, George Montagu Dunk, First Lord of the Admiralty.

The truth is, however, that Cook did not realise that this impressive peak was on an island. He thought that the landscape he saw was nothing more than a rugged extension of the mainland.

His oversight can probably be forgiven, though, because the island is only cut off from the mainland by a fairly narrow passage that is a drowned river valley.

Captain Cook, being the extraordinary seaman that he was, did note correctly that Hinchinbrook's latitude was as close to the equator as Tahiti.

In more recent times Hinchinbrook Island provided shelter for the U.S. Fleet before it moved north to encounter the Japanese in the historic Battle of the Coral Sea during World War II.

Tales abound, too, of wartime aircraft that crashed on Hinchinbrook and met a watery grave in the seas around it. Both Australian and American aircraft returning to their Townsville base from action in the South Pacific apparently went down here on several occasions after running out of fuel.

One aircraft that definitely crashed on Hinchinbrook during World War II was an American B-24 bomber. The remains of this aircraft and its crew lie on Mount Straloch, at the southern end of the island.

An island teeming with wildlife.

Hinchinbrook is certainly not the island to visit if you are looking for the bright lights. If you love nature, and feeling very much a part of it, you will find Hinchinbrook a wonderful destination - and probably return to it again in the future.

It has a grandeur and primeval air that few people - young and old - feel untouched by. In the centre of the island a jagged chain of granite peaks form the backbone of the island. These include Mount Bowen, Queensland's third highest mountain.

The northern faces of these peaks have spectacular cliffs that drop hundreds of metres to forested slopes.

On the exposed eastern or seaward side of the island the slopes support Swamp Box, and eucalypts including White Mahogany.

On the western slopes are rainforests of Milky Pine, palms, figs, vines and hundreds of other species.

These forests have many animals in common with the adjacent mainland. Ten thousand years of separation, however, has resulted in some differences that the keen naturalist would find intriguing.

Creeks, fringed by lush vegetation, act as corridors for fauna. The flashing blue streak of the Azure Kingfisher in this environment is a common sight, along with many other birds.

In August, 1975, the Queensland Naturalists Club conducted a field trip to Hinchinbrook and over 11 days actually recorded 66 different species of birds.

Some of the many birds they spotted include the Satin Flycatcher, Fairy Warbler, Boobook Owl, Golden Bronze Cuckoo, Brown Honeyeater, Pale Yellow Robin and Yellow-breasted Sunbird.

1

2

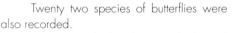

1. **Delicate fungi cling to the trunk of a tree in the rainforest.**

2. **A Giant Tree Frog, one inhabitant of the island's mangrove forests.**

3

4

3. **A Northern Jezebel butterfly, one of over 20 species of butterflies found on Hinchinbrook.**

4. **The wreckage of the "Texas Terror", an American B24 Liberator which crashed on Mount Straloch in December, 1942.**

Twenty two species of butterflies were also recorded.

Among Hinchinbrook's many biological treasures are the vast mangrove forests on the western side of the island.

There are 29 species of mangroves in Australia and all flourish on Hinchinbrook along the many kilometres of meandering waterways that flow into Missionary Bay.

The vibrant green mangroves are the breeding grounds of many varieties of fish and crustaceans - including Barramundi and Mudcrab, both considered seafood delicacies.

Hinchinbrook's mangrove forests are, in fact, second in intensity only to those found in the Amazon Delta.

Marine experts, botanists and geo-chemists from the Institute of Marine Science in Townsville have spent years studying the eerie jungle of mud and mangroves.

Their research has revealed that the varieties of mangroves found at Hinchinbrook (and elsewhere in Northern Queensland) are over 20 million years old.

Visitors to Hinchinbrook can actually view their entangled root systems by walking along a special boardwalk that has been built in one section of the mangrove forests.

A Bushwalker's delight.

So dense is the vegetation on the island that much of Hinchinbrook is inaccessible and still unexplored. There are a number of walks, however, that any reasonably fit person can enjoy.

Other walks are best tackled only by bush walkers who are both experienced and properly equipped.

Despite the size of the island - or perhaps because of it - there are very few well worn tracks on the island. Creek beds are often the best way to explore the island - they are nature's highway. Great care should be exercised, however, because these can often be very treacherous when wet.

If you are thinking of visiting Hinchinbrook as a back-packer who intends to camp on the island, then it is highly advisable to contact the Queensland National Parks and Wildlife office at Cardwell before your visit. (A camping permit is essential.)

They have very detailed information available on ideal camping spots and routes that have been previously negotiated by others.

Their postal address is P.O. Box 74, Cardwell, Queensland, 4816. Their phone number is (070) 66 8601.

If you intend to stay at the resort at Cape Richards there are several easy and well-marked walks that you will find most enjoyable. One walk that is well worth taking is the one to Shepherds Bay.

This walk takes some 40 minutes each way. Most of the walk is through rainforest.

From the moment you start walking along the well maintained track you are surrounded by a mass of vegetation. Within minutes you are in another world. You hear the sound of birds, hear the rustle of small creatures scurrying about unseen. You will also discover that the rainforest has very distinctive yet not unpleasant scents and odours of its own.

The sky is barely visible. Many of the trees are very spindly and tall. Their trunks may rise 10 metres in height before they branch out.

There are always sounds and noises around you. If you pause for a moment you may think you can hear the light and steady patter of rain. Usually it is leaves simply falling down through branches all over the forest, hitting other vegetation before they reach the floor of the forest.

Do not be surprised when lizards scamper across your path. You will probably see the occasional harmless goanna, too, measuring almost a metre in length.

You will also see colourful fungi protruding precariously out from tree trunks and branches. They often cantilever themselves out from a branch and grow in a flat circular fashion - not unlike a coin balancing on its rim. This example of nature's engineering appears to be rather fragile but the fungi seem to thrive quite happily.

At times you may be quite alarmed by the amount of movement you hear amongst the undergrowth. Fearful thoughts of dangerous animals stalking you may be safely banished from your mind. It will be nothing more than a wallaby or one of the very noisy Bush-hens which are native to the island.

As you near the end of this walk the lush rainforest suddenly gives way to more scrubby vegetation. The smell of salt air also replaces the dank smell of the rainforest.

Minutes later you will reach a small look-out which offers you a marvellous view of the Brook Islands.

Once you get to North Shepherd Bay you will find a beautiful beach that stretches south for perhaps a kilometre or more - and the chances are that you will have it entirely to yourself. It's ideal for swimming and, once again, there is a picturesque view of the Brook Islands from it.

At this point you have the pleasant option of either staying at North Shepherd Bay or walking another 15 or 20 minutes along to the far end of the beach where you will find another walking track.

This second track soon divides. The left fork will take you to South Shepherd Bay and another long and lovely sandy beach. The right fork will lead you to Macushla Bay on the western side of the island where mangroves abound. Either destination will add another 40 minutes or so to your journey each way.

As a guest at the small resort on Hinchinbrook Island, you can also enjoy any one of half a dozen casually organised day-trips, weather permitting. All involve a boat ride.

Zoe Bay, "the most beautiful place on the entire east coast of Australia".

Since Hinchinbrook is such a large island the quickest way of exploring some of its most interesting and beautiful features is to travel some of the way by boat.

An experience never to be forgotten is a visit to Zoe Bay and the waterfall nearby. Its beauty will linger long in your memory.

To get there, one must first travel by boat from Cape Richards for some 45 minutes. The boat trip itself is very interesting since you must travel about 25 kilometres along the seaward side of Hinchinbrook aboard "Reef Venture II", a powerful nine metre catamaran.

To see any island from the water gives you a totally different perspective of it, and Hinchinbrook is no exception. First of all, you pass the long, sandy beaches of Shepherd Bay. Then you round rocky Cape Sandwich and enter Ramsay Bay which boasts a superb beach that is strewn with shells. More about that shortly.

Travelling further south by boat the coastline gets quite rugged. This is hardly surprising since it is here that the mountainous backbone which bisects the island drops rapidly to meet the sea.

Needless to say, you get a wonderful, unimpeded view of Hinchinbrook's mountains from the water.

Before you know it, "Reef Venturer II" is then entering Zoe Bay. This bay is rather shallow, especially at low tide, so be prepared to wade in knee-deep water for 10 or 15 metres once the boat is anchored. Do not leave your shoes aboard. You will need them ashore.

As you reach the shore you will find a hard, sandy beach fringed by low native scrub, tropical foliage and palms.

Alan Lucas, who has spent many years sailing around Papua New Guinea and Australia gathering information and writing books for the cruising yachtsman, writes that Zoe Bay is "perhaps the most beautiful place on the entire east coast of Australia".

Do not use up all your camera film at this stage, however, because the best is still to come.

Once ashore the cheerful skipper of "Reef Venturer II" will guide you to a path near the entrance of South Zoe Creek.

Within moments you are walking inland through dense rainforest. It is extremely beautiful - but inhabited by mosquitoes that love to prey on intruders, so do remember to take insect repellent along or wear jeans rather than shorts.

Five minutes after you begin your walk you will find that the path leads you back to South Zoe Creek but places you further upstream. Here it is quite shallow, extremely clear and a very pretty sight.

Simply follow the track. It will eventually fork to the left so that it leads you onto the rocky bed of the creek itself. (If you fall behind the rest of your group, do not make the mistake of taking a steep fork to the right.) Walk along the creek bed and within 10 or 15 minutes you will reach your final destination.

You will then experience a scene that normally exists only in someone's imagination, movie or novel.

Having clambered up to the head of the rocky creek bed you will suddenly find yourself at the edge of a large, natural pool with a spectacular waterfall on the far side of it.

The water cascades 25 or 30 metres down what is almost a completely vertical drop into the deep pool below. The pool itself is about 15 metres in diameter and dense tropical foliage crowds its banks.

Normally, the schedule allows you to spend at least a couple of hours at this idyllic spot.

Because this is a favourite destination of theirs, too, several members from the resort

1

who have the day off usually volunteer to accompany the guests on this outing. They help the boat crew lay out a delightful picnic lunch, complete with liquid refreshments on a couple of large rocks.

Before or after lunch few people can resist plunging into the crystal clear water of the pool. It is particularly refreshing after the boat ride and walk on a hot, sunny day.

Overhanging the pool on one side is the branch of a large tree. Someone at some time has thoughtfully taken a large heavy rope up with them on their trek to the pool and waterfall, and then secured it around this branch. Even grown adults squeal with glee as they swing out over the pool and then drop into it.

At the edge of the pool the water is incredibly clear and you will see many small

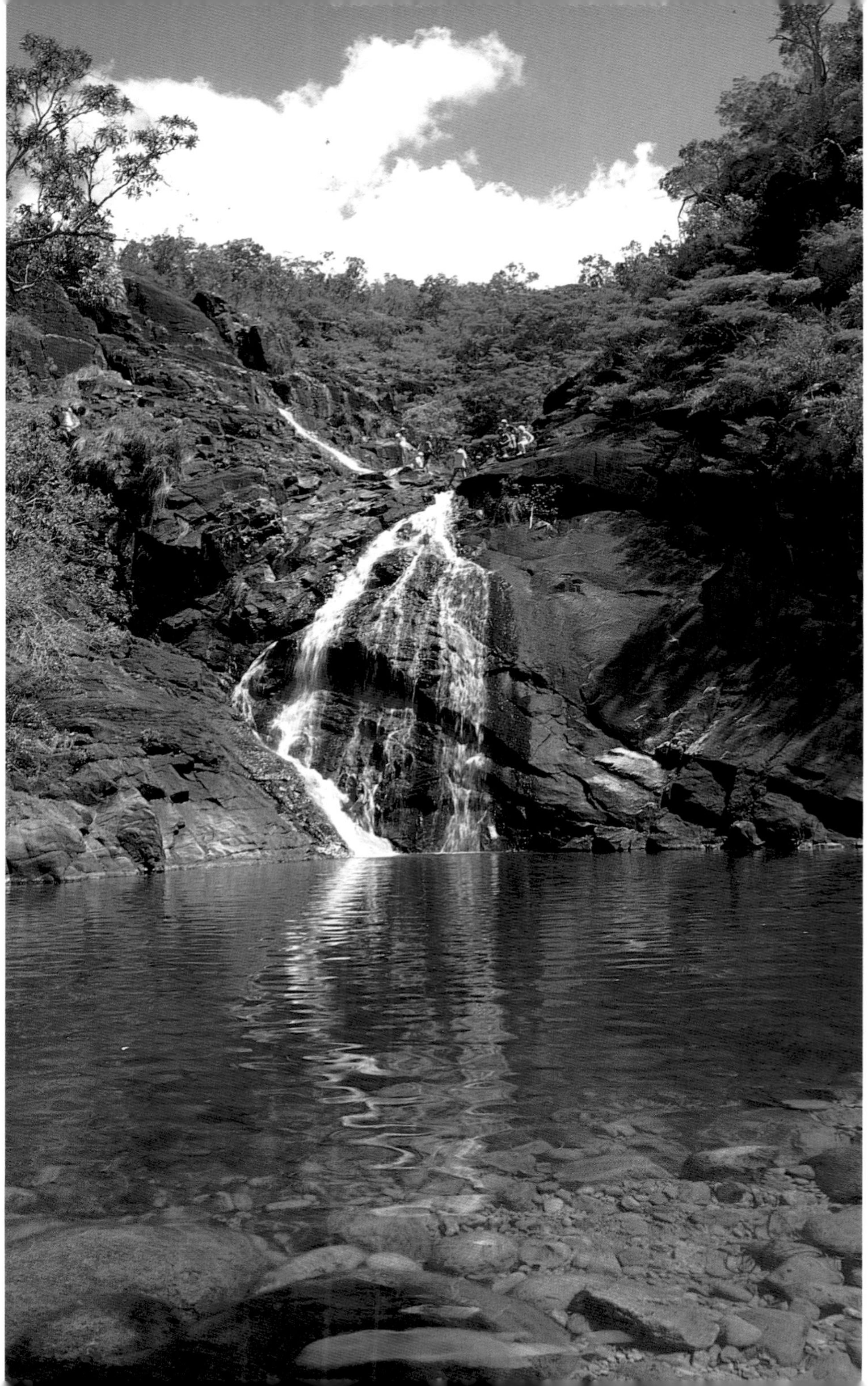

2

3

1, 2 & 3. Zoe Falls, one of the most spectacular sights on Hinchinbrook Island. This idyllic spot is about 20 minutes walk from Zoe Bay, which is near the far eastern corner of the island. Small fish live in the clear, cool waters of the pool and can be virtually hand-fed.

1

1. **Narrow waterways lead into the island's mangrove forests. Queensland's third highest peak, Mount Bowen, is part of the mountain range beyond.**

2. **Ramsay Beach, the long sandy beach on the north-eastern side of Hinchinbrook Island. It is strewn with many shells. Occasionally, beachcombers also find ancient petrified shells and crabs washed up on the beach.**

fish about 10 centimetres long - especially if you throw a little bread in.

When it is time to leave, everyone does so with great regret.

Unfortunately, access to Zoe Bay is very dependent on the weather. Very changeable conditions on the seaward side of Hinchinbrook mean that this trip cannot be easily scheduled - so if the trip is offered early in your stay, take it. You may not be offered a second chance.

Ramsay Beach, a shell collector's dream.

Another excursion that can be recommended is the one to Ramsay Bay. Although the boat passes Ramsay Bay on the way to Zoe Bay, it does not stop there on that occasion. Besides, access from the seaward side would be difficult at any time.

Fortunately, one can gain access to it easily from the western side of the island. Once again, the trip involves going some distance partly by boat and some by foot.

There are several aspects of this trip that make it well worthwhile. The first part of the journey which is by boat takes you around into Missionary Bay and then deep into a labyrinth of tidal rivers and creeks totally lined by mangroves. The area covered by these mangroves is immense and can truthfully be described as Australia's Everglades.

The wide waterway which "Reef Venturer II" ventures up gradually becomes narrower and narrower until the mangroves seem to be touching either side of the boat. Finally, the skipper ties the boat up to what must be one of the strangest structures ever built anywhere in the world for pedestrians. It is a narrow, roughly constructed wooden walkway a metre or two off the swampy ground that threads its way through the eerie, dimly lit jungle of mangroves for about a hundred metres.

This walkway gives you the opportunity to see first-hand the vast and intricate system that converts sunlight, water and mud into an immense canopy of luminous green foliage that seems endless even when you fly over the area.

The many leaves, when they fall, are eaten immediately or after decomposition by many of the teeming inhabitants below the water's surface. This source of nutrients is the beginning of an important cycle in the marine ecosystem.

In the mud flats around the mangroves, crabs and molluscs feed and breed. They, in turn, provide a food source vital to many fish.

The mangrove jungle and wooden walkway ends abruptly and ahead you suddenly see sand dunes. Five minutes later you climb over the crest of these to see ocean breakers rolling in to a sandy beach that would dwarf Bondi Beach in length. It is probably nine kilometres long.

An interesting feature of the beach is the varying colour of the sand. Most of it is very, very white but occasionally you will come across a patch which is almost black. It is quite an unusual sight.

Apart from swimming, a very pleasant way to spend time is to walk along the beach in either direction to look at and collect some of the countless shells that are constantly washed up on this part of Hinchinbrook Island.

There are literally thousands upon thousands of shells. All are different colours, different sizes.

If you are lucky you may come across petrified shells and crabs - each of which are many, many thousands of years old. These are found regularly by beachcombers here.

Once again, a picnic lunch is provided. This is usually an appetising choice of salads, chicken, salami and fruit. There is also a cold Esky full of beer, wine, fruit juice and soft drinks to quench the thirst of all and sundry.

Guests at the resort are normally offered this trip twice a week. The boat generally leaves the resort at 10:30 a.m. and returns to the resort by 3:30 p.m.

If you do not like boats, don't worry. There is still plenty to do and enjoy even if you never venture far from the resort at Cape Richards.

Firstly, there is Orchid Beach, which lies next to the resort. It is a superb, sandy beach which is not adversely affected by the tide. It is also completely safe to swim at all year round according to the management.

If you like to indulge in watersports, there are a couple of windsurfers and a small sailing boat.

In extremely light winds be cautious, however. If you venture out too far from the small bay that harbours Orchid Beach you may find that the currents off Cape Richards carry you around into Macushla Bay.

The resort on Hinchinbrook actually straddles the land lying between Orchid Beach and Macushla Bay. The jetty where one arrives from Cardwell is in Macushla Bay.

2

1

2

1. **Snorkellers view the coral and fish life on the fringing reefs around the Brook Islands. This cluster of small islands is about eight kilometres north-east of Cape Richards.**

2. **Beautiful Orchid Beach, at the northern tip of Hinchinbrook, is directly adjacent to the island's resort.**

3. **The Brook Islands can be easily seen from Orchid Beach.**

In the evenings, this is a great vantage point from which to view what is often a magnificent sunset.

Sometimes you can also see farmers burning sugar cane on the mainland and this adds a spectacular dimension to the beautiful sunsets.

The jetty is a great place to do a spot of fishing, too. Hand-lines and bait are provided free. The fish you can catch include Coral Trout, Cod, Bream and Mangrove Jack. Talk to the resort chef nicely and he will even cook your catch for you.

From the jetty, you will also see the occasional dolphin.

Another great vantage point is the very northern tip of Cape Richards which is just three or four minutes walk away from the resort's restaurant.

From the top of this headland you can look right out over Macushla Bay and Goold Island towards the mainland. Look due north and you can see the Family Islands. To the north-east you can see the Brook Islands. You also have a magnificent bird's-eye view of Orchid Beach.

Goold Island, to the north-west, is a national park that lies just 4.5 kilometres off Cape Richards. It is an island uninhabited by human beings but it does have a large population of noisy, Sulphur-crested Cockatoos residing there. Resort guests are sometimes offered the opportunity of picnicking on Goold Island.

The group of Family Islands, visible to the north, includes Bedarra - an island with two small, secluded resorts. Dunk, another resort island, just to the north of Bedarra, is also clearly visible. (Both these islands are covered in this volume).

There is a day cruise around the Family Islands about once a week and this includes a brief stopover at Dunk Island.

The Brook Islands lie about eight kilometres north-east of Cape Richards. There is a cluster of four small islands and around these is an extensive fringing coral reef which provides excellent snorkelling.

The Brook Islands are only 15 to 20 minutes away from Hinchinbrook by boat. Like the trips to Zoe Bay and Ramsay Beach this one really should not be missed.

If you snorkel you will have the chance to see some beautiful corals, especially those of the soft variety. You will be surprised by some of the colours to be seen - pinks, purples and blues. In addition, you will see

3

numerous tropical fish of varying colours and sizes darting in and around the outcrops of coral.

You will also have the chance to explore the beach on North Island. Do remember to take proper footwear, however, because it is a coral beach. Another tip - do not attempt to walk completely around the island, as some visitors have tried. One can only travel three quarters of the way around it with ease. You have to swim the final quarter!

As you walk around the island at low tide you will often see what appears to be coral clearly imbedded in rock. In fact, all the rock that you will be walking on has been formed from coral that has undergone a natural chemical process that solidifies and hardens it.

The Brook Islands are very important as a nesting place for the Torres Strait Imperial Pigeon. Up to 20,000 arrive in September to breed; then in February both parents and offspring return to New Guinea for the winter.

During the summer months Black-naped Terns also come to the Brook Islands to breed.

The utmost care should be taken by visitors to avoid nesting areas during the breeding season. Eggs can be unwittingly crushed or a disturbance can prompt young birds to desert their nest prematurely - only to perish.

If you are a diver and would like to explore the waters around the Brook Islands and Hinchinbrook itself then be sure to inform the resort before your arrival on the island. Diving gear is not usually available at the resort itself but they are very happy to make arrangements to supply it from the mainland.

If you want to snorkel at Hinchinbrook try the far end of Orchid Beach and nearby Turtle Bay. Whilst the snorkelling may not be quite as rewarding as that around the Brook Islands you will still enjoy the experience.

Comfortable accommodation, superb cuisine.

The resort on Hinchinbrook accommodates no more than 50 people. Partly because it is small, the resort is a very friendly place. Guests and staff mix very easily and this leads to a very relaxed and casual environment. It's like being part of one big, happy family.

Nor are guests expected to follow any kind of schedule. The resort management deliberately avoids anything that smacks of rigidly organised activities and entertainment. Instead, they allow guests to pursue their own pleasures and interests, at their own pace.

About 80% of the people who stay at the resort are Australians, the remaining 20% come from overseas.

From April, 1990, guests will have a choice of two grades of accommodation.

Fifteen new semi-circular "tree houses" with spectacular views towards the Family Islands will be available in addition to some of the existing bungalows which nestle unobtrusively in the dense forest directly behind Orchid Beach.

The new accommodation will be more luxurious than these but the bungalows are comfortable, although basic, and more than adequate for the little time you will find yourselves spending indoors. They are

1

2

1. The new "tree houses" at Hinchinbrook's resort will be ready for occupation by early 1990.

2. The complex housing the resort's new restaurant and bar.

3. The sun sets over Macushla Bay, Goold Island (to the right) and the mainland.

spacious, have their own sun-decks, and carry some of the names of birds which inhabit the island - Boobook Owl, Plumed Egret and Little Darter are just three.

Regardless of the accommodation you choose, at night-time you will fall asleep to sounds you are probably unaccustomed to hearing - yet there is something strangely pleasing about that. Instead of hearing cars or the television set of your noisy neighbours, you will hear the rhythmic pounding of the sea close by - and immediately around your cabin you will hear the nocturnal activity of various little creatures scurrying about.

In the morning, you will wake up to the sound of the sea and a symphony of birds. When you get up you may even discover a wallaby or two around the cabin. If you still have fruit left from the bowl thoughtfully provided by the management upon your arrival, try approaching one slowly and feeding it. They will normally take the bait.

From April, 1990, a new central complex including restaurant will also be open.

The social centre of the resort is currently a large, attractive, open-walled building which houses both the restaurant and bar. Cane and bamboo furniture, potted plants, driftwood and shells fill and decorate this spacious area. Only open timber trellis work and corrugated roofing comes between you and a lush tropical garden - so you always feel Nature close at hand.

At mealtime this fact is often highlighted by the impromptu visit of a tame and hungry wallaby known as "Mr. B".

On the subject of food, an unexpected and very agreeable surprise awaits guests at Hinchinbrook's resort. In short, the fare is outstanding.

Larger resorts may offer a greater variety of dishes but this is of no consequence to the people who have the pleasure to dine in the resort's restaurant on Hinchinbrook.

The menus are never the same but these are some examples of the mouth-watering dishes you can expect.

On one evening the first course was Gazpacho - a chilled Tomato, Onion, Sherry and Capsicum Soup. This was followed by Mushroom Feuilette - Mushrooms in layers of Puff Pastry with a Cognac and Cream Sauce. For the main course guests had to decide between Barramundi with Paw Paw and Mint, or Roast Loin of Pork with Apple and Raspberry Sauce.

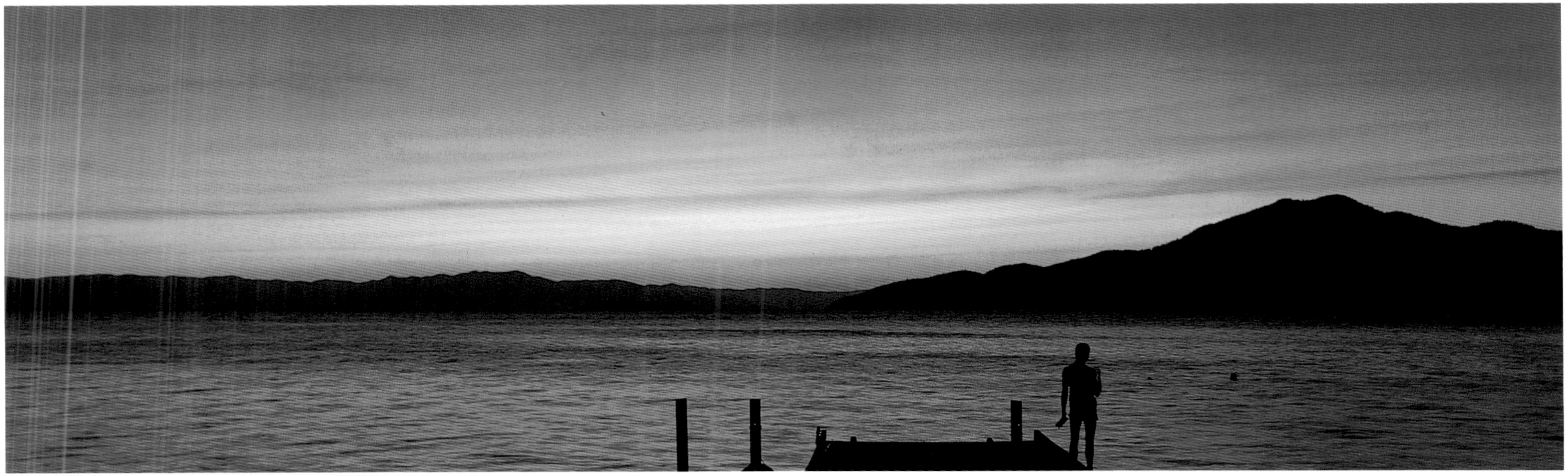

3

Needless to say, guests are offered a tantalising dessert that the chef has created as an encore.

The wine list offers an excellent choice of quality Australian wines, all reasonably priced. There is a choice of Australian and French champagnes, too.

Directly adjoining the restaurant and bar is a protected outdoor area around a swimming pool where you can enjoy a cocktail before lunch or dinner.

The resort also has a small shop. It carries a limited range of basic toiletries, photographic film and a small but excellent selection of quality souvenirs.

Just inside the door of the resort shop there are a few shelves of paperbacks left by other guests. If you want to read on your holiday, however, it is best to pack a few books of your own.

Do not expect daily newspapers. Newspapers arrive just once a week - and most guests seem to prefer it that way.

Nobody seems to mind that telephones are not constantly ringing, either. In fact, the resort has only one telephone but if you need to make the occasional call, you are welcome to use it.

Parents should note that children of any age are welcome at the resort on Hinchinbrook. As you can expect at a resort of this size, there are no formal baby-sitting facilities. However, if you ever feel the need for this service there is usually an off-duty staff member who will provide this for a small charge.

As a destination, Hinchinbrook is delightful and the resort's guest book best sums up what people think of the island and the resort itself.

Here are some of the comments you will find in it. "A place for thinking and peace." "Our third visit." A place for "renewal of body, mind and spirit". "Couldn't ask for more."

How to get to Hinchinbrook Island.

The quickest way is to fly direct from Cairns or Townsville aboard a Seair Pacific seaplane. The flight time from Cairns is 90 minutes, the time from Townsville is 60 minutes. Both flights give you a wonderful bird's-eye view of both the mainland and the Coral Sea.

Alternatively, you can travel by coach from Townsville to the small sleepy town of Cardwell, stay overnight there in a local motel and then transfer by boat at 9.00 a.m.

You can also arrive at Cardwell by car (storage facilities for cars are available there).

Should you wish to contact the island's resort their address is P.O. Box 3, Cardwell, Queensland, 4816. The resort's telephone and facsimile number is (070) 668585 and their telex number is: HNKIS 148971.

The closing words on Hinchinbrook come from a brochure on this resort. "We don't have miniature golf, mahjong, talent quests or treasure hunts. And we promise we will never, ever, hire an entertainment director. What we do have is the world's largest national park as our one and only neighbour. And miles of beaches where the only footprints you see will probably be your own."

It's all true.

HOOK ISLAND

2

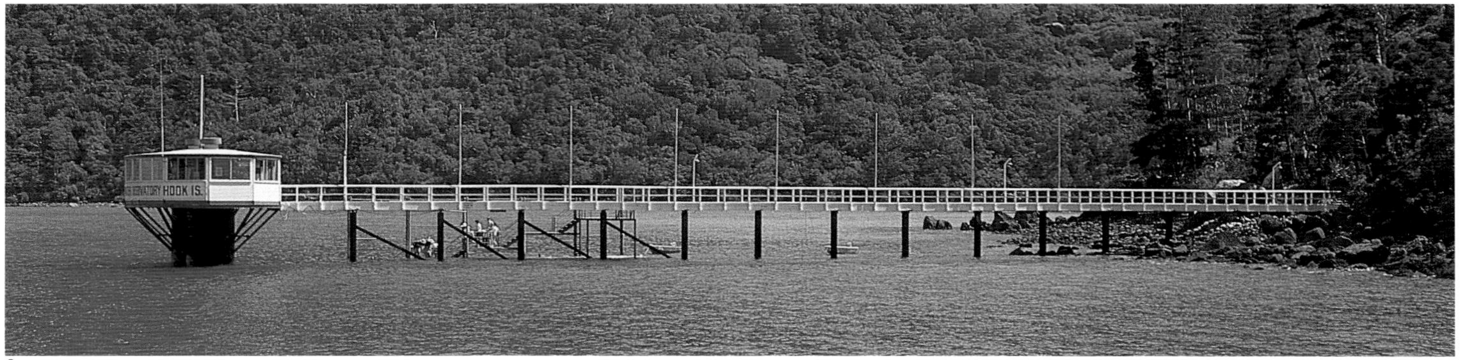

3

1. The southern end of Hook Island where an Underwater Observatory is located. Part of neighbouring Whitsunday Island is also visible.

2. Visitors to the Observatory can also see some of Hook's fringing reef aboard the "Coral Sub".

3. The Hook Island Underwater Observatory is a popular day destination for visitors staying on the mainland or other Whitsunday islands.

4. The famous 12 metre yacht "Gretel" brings a party of visitors ashore.

1

Hook Island is one of the largest islands in the beautiful Whitsundays. It also has the highest mountain of these islands, Hook Peak, which rises to 459 metres.

On its southern side Hook Island has two magnificent fjord-like inlets, Nara and Macona, which are favourite destinations for yachtsmen.

Aborigines once lived and hunted on the island - and their cave paintings can still be seen at Nara Inlet.

On the northern side of the island, there are some of the best diving sites in the Whitsundays.

Despite the size of the island, however, most of Hook Island is completely inaccessible by foot. It is heavily wooded but unlike the other Whitsunday resort islands, Hook does not have a network of trails.

Visitors must either explore it by charter or private boat, or be content with staying inside a relatively small area at the far south-eastern corner of the island where there is a very small resort.

The key attraction which draws most people to Hook Island is the Underwater Observatory which allows you to view both colourful coral and fish in their natural environment.

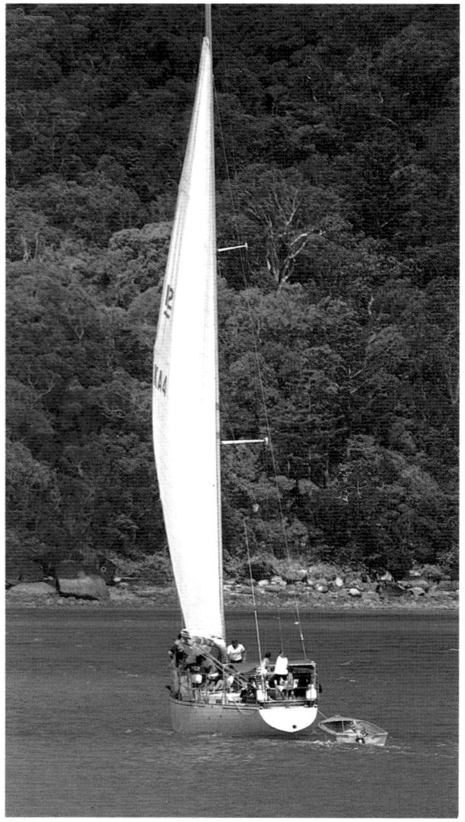
4

1

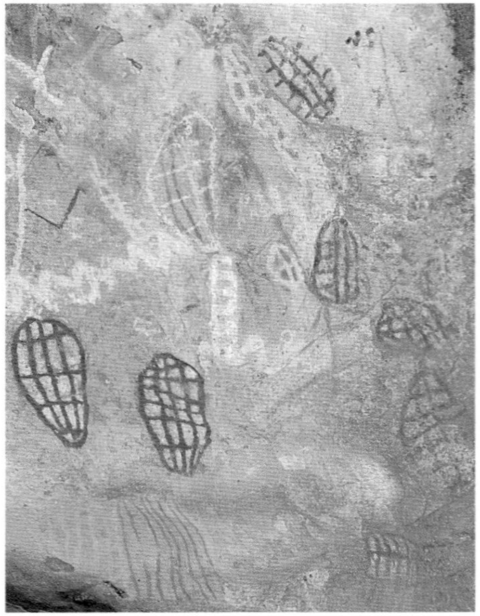

2

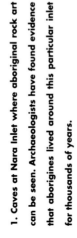

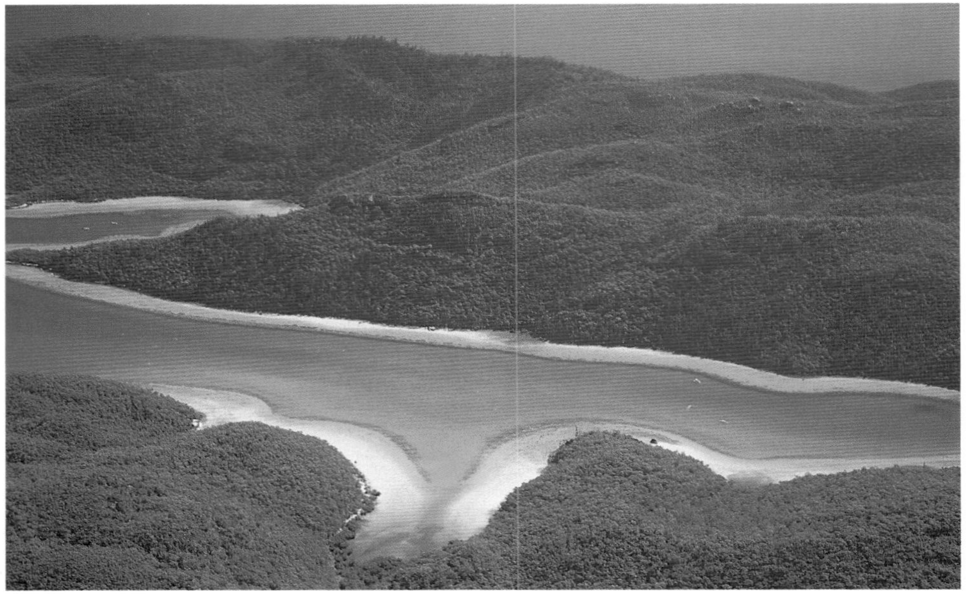

3

1. Caves at Nara Inlet where aboriginal rock art can be seen. Archaeologists have found evidence that aborigines lived around this particular inlet for thousands of years.

2. Examples of the aboriginal rock art at Nara Inlet.

3. An aerial view of Nara Inlet which is near the south-western corner of Hook Island. It is a popular anchorage for yachtsmen.

An area with a fascinating geological past.

If you explore Hook Island and observe many of its spectacular geographical features, you cannot help but wonder about the forces of nature that once created this island and others within the Whitsunday group.

The geological history of Hook Island and the rest of the Whitsundays is, in fact, fascinating.

One hundred million years ago, during the age of dinosaurs, the area experienced violent earthquakes and volcanic eruptions. At that time, Australia was much closer to the South Pole and New Zealand probably lay south of the Proserpine region.

The climate in the area then was far from tropical, too. The volcanoes were probably snow-capped.

Over hundreds of thousands of years, possibly millions, repeated eruptions built up layers of volcanic ash, boulders and lava until they were several thousands of metres thick.

Erosion has since resculptured this ancient landscape. The earth's sea level has also risen around a hundred metres since the last Ice Age, so the mountain peaks which were on a very wide coastal plain eventually became the islands we know today as the Whitsundays.

The most recent and significant rise in the level of the sea - which occurred within the last 10,000 years - has also enabled the existing fringing reefs to establish themselves.

A legacy of the turbulent volcanic period are the steeply inclined "dykes" formed from molten magma that can be seen around Hook and other Whitsunday islands. The "Woodpile", an unusual outcrop of pale, fine grained granite rising horizontally from the sea on the north-eastern tip of Hook Island, is one such formation.

A valuable source of timber last century.

During the 1860's Queensland had only two major ports. One was at Brisbane, the other was established at Bowen. All the timber that was used to build the growing town of Bowen came from the Whitsunday group of islands, including Hook Island.

A sawmill was established on nearby Whitsunday Island at Cid Harbour. This island and Hook Island were the main sources of the timber being milled, Hoop

4

Pine. The logs from trees cut down on Hook Island were pulled around to the mill on Whitsunday Island.

The timber was then loaded onto boats and shipped to Bowen.

The mill closed down around 1904 but its remains can still be seen today at Cid Harbour.

A second, smaller mill was also established for a time on the far north-eastern corner of Hook Island, directly opposite Hayman Island.

This was established by Thomas Abell, a gentleman who also held the grazing rights to Hayman Island for a number of years.

He shipped timber to the mainland aboard a boat which he purchased as a wreck for the handsome sum of £3 and subsequently returned to seaworthy condition.

An Underwater Observatory.

At Hook Island there is an Underwater Observatory which enables visitors to go down nine metres below the surface of the water to see many inhabitants of the Great Barrier Reef.

The Observatory was built in Mackay during 1967 and 1968. It was then transported in sections by barge and assembled on the sea-bed off Hook Island in 1969. It was opened officially to the public on April 13 of the same year by the Hon. John D. Herbert, Minister for Labour and Tourism.

Since then the Observatory has given thousands of people the opportunity to view coral and reef fish in their natural environment. It is a very popular attraction. Each day over 200 people visit the

5

Observatory. Most come to Hook Island for just several hours aboard boats that cruise out from Shute Harbour. People staying on Hamilton, South Molle and Daydream will find that they can also board day cruises to Hook Island.

Access to the Observatory is via a spiral staircase with 40 steps. This takes you down into what is essentially a giant steel tube with 36 windows around it that allow you to see a large variety of teeming marine life.

Visitors to the Observatory may also board a semi-submersible craft that lets you see even more of the life of the fringing reef around Hook Island. A marine biologist normally accompanies you on this trip to point out different features of the reef in detail.

6

4. Another popular anchorage for boats is Butterfly Bay which is at the northern end of the island.

5. A yacht sails through the passage dividing Hook and Whitsunday Islands.

6. Nara Inlet is renowned for the graffiti left by visiting yachtsmen.

A rocky but beautiful coastline.

The best place for guests staying at the Hook Island resort to snorkel is at Pebble Beach. This lies on the eastern side of the island and it takes no more than a 10 minute walk to reach.

This is also one of the few marked walks that one can take on the island. You start by walking up the small dirt road near the water tank directly behind the resort. Within several minutes you will reach what is called Back Beach or Stingray Bay where the resort's power plant and workshop is located. Near these you will see a sign directing you to Pebble Beach.

Within moments you will find yourself in rainforest. Vines as thick as ropes trail off trees and, depending on the time of year, you may encounter dozens of butterflies.

Five minutes later you will find yourself at Pebble Beach. It is very aptly named because the beach is strewn with pebbles and small rocks. It is normally a very sheltered area and the coral and fish life off the beach makes it very good for snorkelling.

At low tide you can return to the resort by following the shoreline. This will mean walking and clambering across rocks and large boulders - some wet and somewhat slippery - so only attempt this if you have good footwear and you are reasonably agile.

Along the rocks you will see many small shellfish attached to them. You will also enjoy a enjoy a wonderful view towards the north-eastern tip of Hook Island and a view of the rocky coastline on the seaward side of Whitsunday Island. Out to sea you will almost certainly see one or two sailing boats.

As you round the southern tip of Hook Island it is interesting to see how a number of trees have gained a precarious foothold on the bare and virtually horizontal surface of the rocky cliffs. In this area, too, you may well come across some rock oysters.

The walk around the shoreline will take considerably longer than by the short overland track - about 40 minutes.

Snorkelling should not be attempted at the very southern tip of the island, where a channel separates Hook from Whitsunday Island because of the strong currents.

For those who visit Hook Island by boat there are some other excellent spots for snorkelling and diving. On the western side of the island you will find a shallow coral reef off Stonehaven beach. Here the outer edge of the reef is worth exploring. The diving depth ranges between three and 10 metres.

Along the northern coastline of Hook Island there are at least five locations of interest. At Alcyonaria Point, which is at the north-western corner of the island, divers will find a ledge that runs towards Flat Rock. This drops off to form a vertical wall with both small caves and gullies. There is plentiful fish life in the area and many colourful soft corals can be seen at around 10 metres.

At Butterfly Bay, which is a popular anchorage for yachtsmen, there are bommies that provide good diving. The diving depth here ranges between five and 12 metres.

Heading further east there is another site called The Boulders where the shallow coral makes snorkelling very enjoyable. Divers will also find beautiful Fan corals at a depth of 10 metres, at the point which protrudes at this part of the coastline.

At the north-eastern corner of Hook Island there are two sites which attract both divers and snorkellers. The first is Manta Ray Bay which is regarded by many as the best site to dive within the Whitsundays. This small bay has beautiful coral gardens and a very large fish population. The best snorkelling is on the western side of the bay and off the beach itself.

The other good location is at Pinnacle Point. This has beautiful Plate and Staghorn corals along the western beach which is perfect for snorkelling. There is also excellent diving along the "Woodpile", the unusual rock formation rising out of the sea (mentioned earlier in this chapter).

Some of these locations, Manta Ray Bay in particular, may be visited aboard diving boats that operate out of Shute Harbour and from some of the other resort islands including Hamilton and Hayman.

A Dive Shop has recently been established at the resort on Hook Island and offers introductory dives, Open Water courses and advanced courses such as night diving and deep diving.

A good diving site for people staying at the Hook Island resort is The Gardens on the northern tip of Whitsunday Island where there are many varieties of soft coral. There are also several large bommies offshore with plenty of fish life around them.

Dive directly off the beach at Hook and you will also see a good variety of fish. Diving near the Observatory, unfortunately, is not permitted.

Twice a week, a boat takes guests from the Hook Island resort who wish to dive or snorkel to Manta Ray Bay.

A small, low-key resort.

The small resort on Hook Island caters mainly to back-packers, divers and school groups as well as families looking for budget accommodation.

The accommodation on Hook Island consists of 12 cabins, each with bunks for six to eight people. The air-conditioned cabins are basic but modern, and all guests share a central amenities block.

Campsites are also available.

In addition to the accommodation there is a restaurant/coffee shop, barbeque facilities, a small licensed bar, and a shop.

At lunchtime, guests staying at the resort and those who are visiting the island to see the Underwater Observatory may eat indoors or outdoors on a large patio area which has a splendid view overlooking the main beach and Whitsunday Island.

The main beach, incidentally, is called Yuengee Beach - aboriginal for Little Devil. The high peak almost directly opposite the resort on Whitsunday Island is Cairn Peak, which is 385 metres high.

To complement the view at lunchtime there is normally a barbeque and an array of salads for those with larger appetites; alternatively there is a good selection of sandwiches available.

The evenings are very homely affairs for the small number of guests staying at the resort. The fare served at dinner is simple but tasty with dishes like roasts and home cooked stews.

After dinner, guests and staff usually enjoy a few drinks together. Sometimes, you'll be joined by visiting yachtsmen who are welcome to take advantage of the moorings in Stingray Bay. (Provisions including bread, milk and groceries are available at the resort.)

The resort on Hook Island is actually leased by Ansett Airlines and is operated by the management of their larger Whitsunday resort, South Molle Island.

Bookings and more information can be obtained through the South Molle Island office at Airlie Beach. Their phone number is (079) 466900. The address of the resort, if you wish to write, is Hook Island, P.M.B. 21, Mackay, Queensland 4741.

Transfers to Hook Island are by boats leaving from Shute Harbour.

Hook Island is certainly one of the most beautiful and impressive islands in the Whitsunday group. As mentioned earlier in this chapter, however, it is also one of the most inaccessible unless you can explore it by boat.

For this reason and the fact that the resort has limited facilities most people would probably not wish to spend a full week or two on the island. Nevertheless, it is a very pleasant and inexpensive destination for a weekend or several days.

If you are travelling around the Whitsundays or staying on another island, a visit to the Underwater Observatory should, at the very least, be on your list. A visit to Hook Island is an absolute must for yachtsmen and Manta Ray Bay should also rate very highly amongst divers.

2

1. The small resort and facilities for daytrippers visiting the Underwater Observatory. These are located next to Yuengee Beach which is aboriginal for "Little Devil".

2. Guests can stay in cabins on Hook Island or camp.

1

LADY ELLIOT ISLAND

2

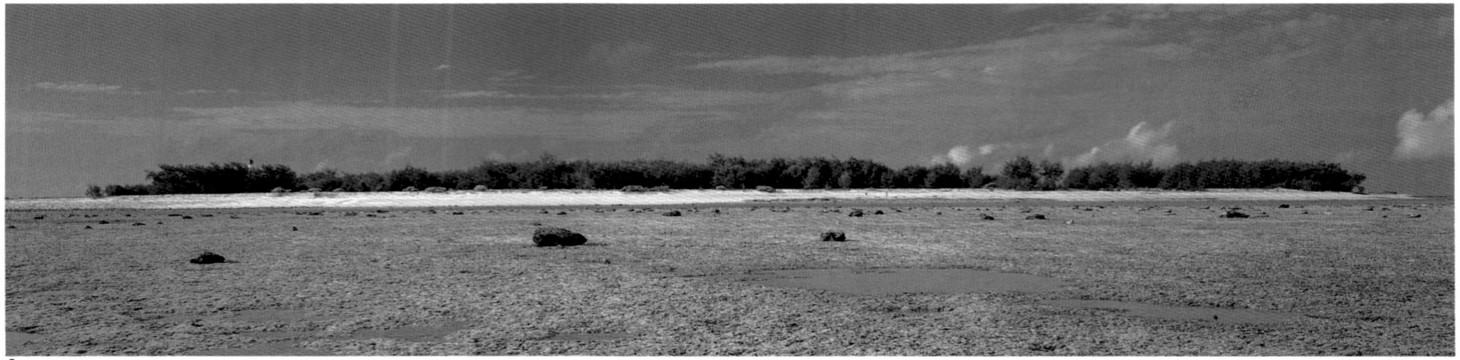

3

1. The sun rises over the reef flats around Lady Elliot Island.
2. One of the many boats that have been wrecked on Lady Elliot's reef.
3. Lady Elliot is a coral cay that began life as a sandbank on a reef about 3,000 years ago.
4. A visitor to the island relaxes on a strip of coral beach. In the background, two people can be seen reefwalking at low tide.

Lady Elliot is the most southerly island within the Great Barrier Reef Marine Park.

It lies 85 kilometres north-east of Bundaberg, a small but prosperous city in the heart of sugar cane territory.

The island is only 374 kilometres north of Brisbane, the capital of Queensland, and the flight time between the two places is just one and a half hours.

Lady Elliot is one of the few cays that one can actually stay on within the Great Barrier Reef region.

Like all cays, it is not large. If you decided to walk around Lady Elliot without pausing to appreciate the many features along its shores you could circumnavigate the island in less than an hour.

In the summer, temperatures on Lady Elliot range between 20°C and 31°C. During winter and autumn they range between 13°C and 25°C.

Late last century the island was mined for its valuable guano deposits.

For well over a hundred years the island has also been the site of many shipwrecks.

4

During the summer the island is the nesting ground for thousands of birds.

Humpback whales can often be seen cruising off-shore - a sight that nobody could ever forget.

Today, Lady Elliot Island is a popular destination for scuba divers and for those who like lazing around on deserted beaches, beachcombing, reef walking, and seclusion. There is a small resort - which is totally unsophisticated.

There is no disco, or evening entertainment and both the accommodation and facilities are quite basic. For the people who choose to go to Lady Elliot, however, this is a distinct plus and not a disadvantage.

In short, Lady Elliot is one of the most uncommercialised islands that you can stay on - and if you like that idea and getting close to nature, you will love it.

Named after a ship wrecked in 1816.

The first documented reference to Lady Elliot Island was made in 1803 by the captain of a whaling boat.

Two years later, in 1805, the island saw the brief establishment of a Bêche-de-mer station (see Chapter Two for more information about this early industry on the Reef).

Lady Elliot Island was officially named in 1816 after a ship bearing the same name. She was a cargo ship of 353 tonnes under the command of Captain Thomas Stewart and cruised the Pacific until she finally came to grief on a reef off Cardwell. Captain Thomas and all his crew were drowned.

The reef which was the cause of this tragedy is about 900 kilometres further north of Lady Elliot and also bears the ship's name.

LADY ELLIOTT'S ISLAND, ONE OF THE CAPRICORN GROUP.

The ship was originally built in India and registered in Calcutta. The vessel itself was named after the wife of a colonial governor who served in that country. This illustrious gentleman had previously served at the court of Frederick the Great of Prussia.

The island's location was first charted properly by Lieutenant Parker King when he was surveying much of Australia between 1818 and 1822.

Lady Elliot is also mentioned in the journals that were written when HMS "Fly" surveyed the eastern coast in the years 1842 to 1846 under the command of Captain Blackwood. Jukes, the naturalist on board, described the island at the time in quite some detail. Here are just a few extracts.

"On January 7, 1843, I landed for the first time in my life on a coral island... the beach was composed of coarse fragments of worn coral and shells, bleached by the weather... on the south-west or weather side of the island was a coral reef about two miles in diameter, having the form of a circle of breakers enclosing a shallow lagoon... (and) there were upwards of thirty fine turtle this morning when the boats first landed...

"The island was well stocked with birds... the trees were loaded with the nests of the noddies each of which was a small platform of sea-weed and earth, fixed in the fork of a branch..."

Almost 20 years went by and then a Mr. J. Askunas acquired a lease from the Queensland Government for £300 per annum which allowed him to mine the island for its guano deposits.

Guano is formed from dead leaves and bird droppings and is rich in phosphorus and nitrogen. Since Lady Elliot Island had been the annual nesting ground of many thousands of birds for countless years the deposits of guano were at least two metres deep - and very valuable because of its use as a fertiliser.

Unfortunately, the mining of guano was highly destructive to the natural environment. To mine the rich soil the natural vegetation was stripped bare. (Other islands along the Great Barrier Reef suffered the same fate including Lady Musgrave and North West Islands.)

Several Europeans worked on the island but most of the labour was done by about 25 Chinese and Malay workmen. They bagged the phosphate and loaded it

2

3

onto the ships. Most of the phosphate from Lady Elliot was apparently shipped to New Zealand.

Even today you can find old pieces of pottery and evidence of the diggings made by the guano miners. A number of wells were dug on the island and some are still visible and in use.

Askunas mined the island until 1846. The vegetation then started to regenerate but the government introduced goats to Lady Elliot Island (and others) in the early 1900's to provide food for future shipwrecked sailors.

About twenty years ago the goats were eventually removed and Casuarinas, Pisonias and other native plants were reintroduced. The vegetation of the island is now rapidly returning to its original state and thousands of birds have made the island their nesting grounds once again.

Often known as "Shipwreck Island".

Being at the gateway to the Great Barrier Reef, Lady Elliot Island and its reefs have caught many ships unawares. In fact, the remains of over 120 wrecks lie scattered around the island.

One of the oldest wrecks found off the island is that of the "Bolton Abbey". The wreck of this 620 tonne, timber built cargo ship, which sank in 1815, was discovered just recently.

Few people probably know that the famous explorer Matthew Flinders was wrecked on an isolated reef north-east of Lady Elliot in 1803.

Flinders was aboard the ship "Porpoise" and he was on the way home to England with the results of his Australian surveys. The "Porpoise" was travelling in convoy at the time and a second vessel, the "Cato", was also wrecked.

Unfortunately, a third vessel "Bridgewater" failed to assist but the survivors made it to a small cay. Flinders then set sail to Sydney in a small cutter - no mean achievement - and the seamen still stranded on the cay were subsequently rescued.

Another ship that was wrecked at Lady Elliot Island in the mid-19th century was the "Golden City". This clipper was American-built and was originally used during the Californian Gold Rush. Later she carried immigrants between England, Australia and New Zealand. She was wrecked at Lady

1. An engraving from a book printed in 1847 which details the voyage of HMS "Fly", a ship which surveyed the Reef between 1842 and 1846.

2. A photograph taken in 1938 shows the wreck of the ship "St. John" and the lighthouse keepers' homes. The bare landscape, a legacy of guano mining, is also clearly visible. The island's vegetation has since regenerated.

3. Several crew members of the wrecked "St. John" struggle ashore.

1

Elliot in 1865 whilst guano was being loaded aboard.

The biggest known vessel that was wrecked on the island was the steamer "Port St. John". It hit the island's outer reef in May, 1938, carrying a large cargo and crew.

Boats have also been wrecked on Lady Elliot in more recent times. The schooner "Thisby" was wrecked in February, 1980, after being caught for two whole days in horrific conditions caused by Cyclone Simon. "Thisby" and its crew of five were battered by gale force winds and rode waves 20 to 30 metres high.

The crew finally sighted Lady Elliot and threw out three anchors in the hope of halting the yacht's progress towards the island's outer reef. They failed, however, but made it safely ashore with the assistance of the men based at the lighthouse.

Rumours persist that drug-runners were aboard the "Thisby" for they left the island with undue haste. Nor was anything more heard of the crew.

Part of the small bar at the resort is actually built from the wreckage of the "Thisby". Its name, appropriately, is "Wreck Bar".

There was a more lucky ending for another vessel that ran aground on the reef in 1975. The "Vansittart" was heading north from Sydney to the Torres Strait to participate in a turtle farming project when it hit the coral reef on the north-eastern side of Lady Elliot at 1:15 a.m. on August 4.

The crew soon abandoned the vessel. Fortunately, they were able to refloat the "Vansittart" later that same day and were able to continue their voyage. The fact that the vessel was constructed from steel no doubt contributed to their good fortune.

A boat that came to grief on Lady Elliot during the same year was the cutter "Tahuna". It was wrecked on November 3, 1975. It struck the reef just before two o'clock in the morning. One of the crew managed to make it ashore to raise the alarm, and the remaining crew of two were rescued by 6:00 a.m.

The badly damaged vessel was washed up onto the beach the next day. "Tahuna", unfortunately, was burnt by sea vandals after they were warned about removing fixtures from the craft. Today, only its rusted steel ribs and a few heavy planks remain on the beach near the northern end of the airstrip.

The best known vessel to be shipwrecked on Lady Elliot was "Apollo 1". This famous 19 metre ocean racer was originally designed by Ben Lexcen for Western Australian entrepreneur Alan Bond. It was then bought and skippered by Jack Rooklyn, a Sydney millionaire, who won many major Australian yachting events aboard the sloop.

The disaster occurred during the 1980 Brisbane to Gladstone Yacht Race. There was a 20 knot wind and the seas were rough but "Apollo 1" was leading in the ocean classic.

Without warning or realisation from anybody on board that they were in grave danger the yacht slammed into the outer coral reef of Lady Elliot. Every wave then pounded "Apollo 1" and drove it further and further onto the reef. The yacht was badly holed and the crew were eventually forced to abandon it. With the help of holiday-makers staying on Lady Elliot they made it safely ashore in the resort's glass-bottom boat.

The crew later salvaged as much as they could from "Apollo" including her costly 24 metre aluminium mast. Then on Tuesday, May 13, they set her on fire.

Another vessel that was wrecked on the island in 1982 was "Gypsy Coin", a fishing trawler. She had the misfortune to become entangled on the anchor from the wreck of "Thisby".

Why so many vessels have come to grief on the island's reef is somewhat perplexing since the island's lighthouse operates day and night. The only explanation is that crew aboard the wrecked vessels have too often made the fatal mistake of thinking that the reef does not extend out as far as it does.

The lighthouse was one of the first steel-frame ones to be built in Queensland. It was built in 1873 after countless ships had encountered the treacherous reefs around the island.

The lighthouse and a cottage were built in prefabricated sections and then shipped to the island. The cost of construction for both was £749.

Whilst the lighthouse has withstood the test of time, the original cottage was replaced in the early 1900's. By the mid-30's, three comfortable houses had been built for the lighthouse keepers and their families.

The lighthouse is now fully automated but a lighthouse keeper lived on the island up until last year to maintain equipment and provide weather information for shipping.

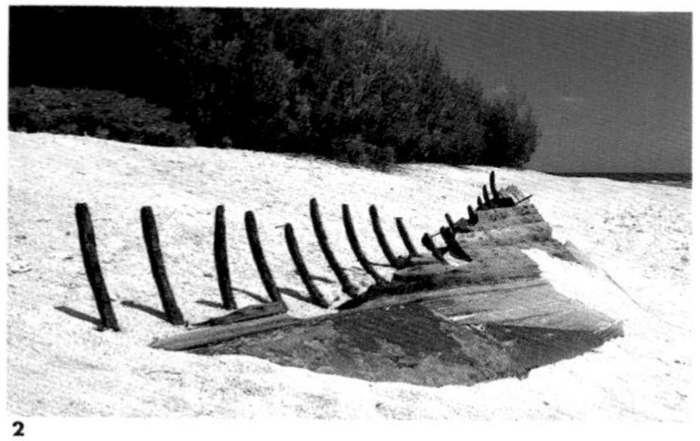

2

1. The well-known yacht "Apollo 1", which was wrecked on Lady Elliot's reef during the Brisbane to Gladstone Yacht Race in April, 1980.

2. The remains of the "Tahuna", a cutter that was wrecked in 1975.

Ian Walker, the island's last lighthouse keeper, lived on Lady Elliot Island with his family. His two older children, Peter and Jamie, belonged to the Charlieville School of the Air. Each day they spent half an hour on the radio listening to their teacher some 650 kilometres west and then worked their way through a correspondence course under the supervision of Heather, their mother.

Just close to the lighthouse you will find a small picket-fenced graveyard where two women lie buried. One is Phoebe Jane Phillips who was the daughter of James David Phillips, a lighthouse keeper posted to Lady Elliot Island in the late 1800's.

Phoebe died in August, 1896, after contracting a cold which quickly developed into severe pneumonia. It was a tragedy that could probably have been avoided if she had not been living in such an isolated situation.

Susannah McKee, who is buried alongside Phoebe Phillips, also died in tragic circumstances in 1907. It is believed that Susannah threw herself off the jetty and drowned. Apparently she was unable to cope with the isolation and loneliness of living on a small island.

Such were the perils for lighthouse keepers and their families in bygone days when communication and transport with the outside world were strictly limited.

In February, 1989, a Brisbane newspaper carried a strange story relating to one of the three houses once occupied by lighthouse keepers. Several staff from the island's resort who were using the house for temporary accommodation saw an object move mysteriously by itself and heard footsteps at night in the hall but could find nobody.

Finally, one staff member sighted a ghostly apparition silhouetted against an open doorway. One theory is that the house is haunted by the spirit of Susannah McKee.

One of the few Great Barrier Reef islands with an airstrip.

People were first able to visit Lady Elliot Island with ease in 1969. This was the year that an airstrip and accommodation were built for visitors. The new facilities were officially opened by Queensland's former Premier, Joh Bjelke-Peterson.

The person responsible for this venture was Don Adams who was undoubtedly a man of vision.

Don Adams was the son of a Queensland cane farmer. During World War II he joined the RAAF and maintained the engines of aircraft. After the war, Don learned to fly and began the first crop dusting and aerial seeding operation in the district of Maryborough.

Don Adams also flew over Lady Elliot many times and was greatly attracted to the island because of the beautiful coral formations around it.

As time went by he wondered why no one had built an airstrip on Lady Elliot to provide easy access to the island and its coral gardens - especially because it was at the southern end of the Great Barrier Reef and the closest island for any visitors from the south.

With this thought fixed firmly in his mind Don contacted the Commonwealth Department of Transport and agreed to build an airstrip in return for a lease over part of the island that would cater to tourists.

1

Don Adams was also largely responsible for restoring the vegetation of the island to its original state. After removing the last of the goats which were responsible for destroying so much of the natural flora Don Adams set about replanting many trees and shrubs.

In 1974 his valuable contribution was recognised when he received a conservation award from the Wildlife Preservation Society of Queensland.

Over a period of 15 years Don Adams and his pilots flew many visitors to Lady Elliot by planes purchased for that purpose. The facilities were far from plush but they allowed many people to view the wonders of the Reef.

In 1985 the original lease expired and the Commonwealth Government sought tenders from parties prepared to operate a small, low key resort which would not jeopardise the environment. The successful submission went to the couple who now run the new resort, John and Judy French.

A coral island on the Reef itself.

Originally, Lady Elliot Island was simply one of the many reefs along the north Queensland coastline that make up the Great Barrier Reef. That reef then slowly accumulated coral debris. As a sand bank gradually formed, birds began to visit it, leaving seeds behind, and vegetation started to take hold.

Geologists estimate that the cay or coral island began to develop about 3,000

SACRED
TO THE MEMORY
of
P J M PHILLIPS
WHO DEPARTED THIS LIFE
2 August 1896
AGED 30 & 6 MONTHS
2

years ago.

Being a part of the Reef there is much to see without going very far. Step off the beach a few metres from your cabin or tent and you will find an underwater wonderland awaiting.

There are several ways you can explore the colourful and fascinating marine life around Lady Elliot. You can go snorkelling or diving, and when the tide is out you can go reefwalking.

Every second day - tide permitting - a member of the resort's staff will take guests out on the reef flats and show them some of the interesting creatures that reside there.

This guided tour of the reef flats is excellent and should not be missed. You will learn some fascinating facts and if you decide to explore the flats by yourself you will

In Loving Memory
of
SUSANNAH
BELOVED WIFE OF
THOMAS McKEE,
DIED APRIL 23RD 1907
AGED 59 YEARS.
ON THE HOME YOU NOW INHERIT
MAY MY THOUGHTS FOR EVER
DWELL,
TILL WE MEET AGAIN IN HEAVEN,
BELOVED ONE, FAREWELL.
4

1. Ian Walker, the last lighthouse keeper to live on Lady Elliot, with his family. His children belonged to the Charleville School of the Air.

2. The grave of Phoebe Jane Phillips, the daughter of a lighthouse keeper who lived on Lady Elliot late last century. Phoebe died from pneumonia.

3. The lighthouse on Lady Elliot Island was built in 1873. It is now automated.

4. The grave of Susannah McKee. Her ghost has apparently been seen in the house she once lived in.

3

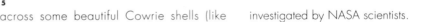

1

2

3

4

5

1. Small starfish like these are found on open reef flats or under boulders.

2. Pincushion starfish can measure up to 15 centimetres across.

3. A spiny sea urchin.

4. A delicate Brittle starfish.

5. A coral pool close to the edge of Lady Elliot's reef.

know exactly where to look for some of the local and often shy or well camouflaged inhabitants.

If you refer to the chapter on Heron Island you will discover in more detail what you can expect to find when you go reef-walking. There are three distinct zones to the reef flats and each has its own special characteristics and inhabitants.

Some of the creatures you will see include Bêche-de-mer or sea cucumbers, Blue Linkia starfish, Octopus and a wide variety of corals - including branching corals, colourful Staghorns and soft corals.

You will see clams - these have light sensitive cells in their "mantle" and if a shadow falls over them they automatically close as a form of protection.

You may also be lucky enough to come across some beautiful Cowrie shells (like everything else they may not be removed), Brittle starfish and Blue Swimmer crabs.

You should also come across Abalone which exude a bright purple dye when disturbed; this dye was used to colour the clothes of Roman emperors.

Keep a sharp eye out for the tiny Christmas Tree worms. These are attached to coral, are exquisite in form, brilliant in colour and retract with amazing speed when disturbed.

There is an interesting fact, incidentally, about the common Sea Urchin which you will undoubtedly see, too. Apparently its teeth, which are located in a central position on the underside of its body, are actually made from a substance harder than either diamonds or titanium. This unique property is now being investigated by NASA scientists.

Reef walks at night are also conducted on occasions and these allow you to see many creatures that are not normally visible during the day.

In the main Lodge you will also find a "Creature Feature" Tank. Inside this you will always find different forms of marine life that the staff have collected on a reef walk. They are placed in this aquarium for 24 hours before being returned to their natural environment. It is another chance to see some of the Reef's fascinating life close-up. Alongside the aquarium you will find notes that give details about each of the species on display.

As you walk around the island itself you will come across many different things of interest. You will, for example, see pumice

6

that has been washed up onto the shore. This came from a volcanic explosion in Tonga back in 1972.

You will also come across beach rock which has formed from sand, coral rubble and a natural chemical reaction with sea-water. In the beach rock you will often see perfect skeletons showing the growth of coral from the original single polyp.

Over 50 different species of birds.

The variety of species on Lady Elliot Island is such that keen bird-watchers now come to the island for only that purpose. At least 57 different species of birds have been recorded on the island and it is estimated that up to 200,000 birds nest on Lady Elliot during the summer months.

One very rare species that has been nesting on the island since 1985 is the Red-tailed Tropic bird. The only other nesting site of this rare species off the east coast of Australia is Raine Island which lies off the far northern tip of Queensland.

This sea-bird is predominantly white in colour and has both a red beak and long red tail-streamers. The Red-tailed Tropicbird lives on both squid and fish which it catches by diving into the sea. It is capable of staying submerged for as long as 25 seconds.

The Brown Booby which tends to rear its young on the north-eastern corner of the island is another sea-bird which dives for its food. In fact, they are considered the best bird divers in the world. Brown Boobies will often plummet 30 metres or more from the sky into the sea to catch fish or squid.

The Greater Frigate Bird, which is another local resident, has the largest wing-span for its body size in the world. During courtship a very noticeable feature is its red throat pouch which inflates like a large balloon.

Members from the Bundaberg branch of the Wildlife Preservation Society of Queensland visited Lady Elliot Island in 1973 and recorded 25 different species of birds in just 18 hours.

These species included the Wedgetailed Shearwater or Mutton bird, Reef Heron, Greater Frigate Bird, Brown Booby, Golden Plover, Greenshank, Black Naped Tern, Little Tern, Crested Tern, Roseate Tern, Bridled Tern, Common Tern, Common Noddy, Pied Oyster Catcher, Sooty Oyster Catcher, Bar Tailed Godwit, Mongolian Dotterel, Red Capped Dotterel, Silver Gull,

6. The Sooty Oystercatcher usually feeds on limpets, periwinkles and mussels.

Whimbrel, House Sparrow, Grey Tailed Tattle, Turnstone, Sharp Tailed Sandpiper and Sacred Kingfisher.

Even if you are not normally an avid bird-watcher remember to pack a pair of binoculars if you decide to visit Lady Elliot Island. The fact is that you cannot help but develop an interest in the many winged residents on the island.

As a visitor during the summer months you can also expect to see turtles at Lady Elliot Island. Three species visit the island - the Loggerhead, Hawk's Bill and Green turtle. The most common visitor is the Green turtle.

Only the female turtles come up onto the beaches - the male rarely leaves the water in his whole lifetime.

The nesting female Green turtle usually weighs anywhere between 90 and 140 kilograms and comes ashore to lay up to 120 eggs, each about the size of a golf ball. Green turtles actually lay up to eight clutches of eggs, at 13 day intervals.

The best time to see a nesting turtle is around high tide at night-time. Turtles are timid creatures, however, and there are some precautions you should take to avoid disturbing them (these are described in detail under the turtle watching section found in the chapter on Heron Island, another rookery for turtles).

A magical world awaiting scuba divers.

Divers will find Lady Elliot a very exciting destination. Many tropical species of fish inhabit the fringing reef around the island - and they are both tame and friendly. There is also a wide variety of beautiful and healthy

1

corals.

Divers will come across giant Manta Rays frequently - an experience which most find unforgettable. From tip to tip they can sometimes measure seven metres. Fortunately, they are completely harmless.

Visibility for diving around Lady Elliot Island is excellent - usually between 25 and 50 metres - and there are at least 10 different dive sites that you can look forward to.

Some of the dives are marked by star picket trails which means that it is also very difficult to get lost!

On the south-western corner of the island there is the Lighthouse Bommie. Visibility here is usually between 13 and 27 metres and sometimes well over 30 metres. Entry is from a beach.

On this dive you will see a wonderful variety of soft corals and certain fish that you will not see at other dive sites. You can also expect to see a very friendly Moray Eel, schools of Trevally and Mackerel, Leopard Sharks and probably more giant Manta Rays than you will see anywhere else in the southern section of the Great Barrier Reef.

Immediately north of The Lighthouse Bommie are the Coral Gardens. A picket trail once again guides you through the area. This is a good shallow dive with swim throughs and colourful corals and fans. You will see many of the species of fish common to the Reef here as well as Green turtles. This area is excellent for snorkelling as well because the currents here are seldom strong.

A little further north of the Coral Gardens there is a picket trail which weaves through coral canyons, around bommies, across sandy flats and past old shipwrecks.

2

3

4

5

1. Divers mark an underwater trail near Anchor Bommie.

2. A Clown fish and anemone.

3. Sunlight washes over a large formation of hard coral.

4. Four Batfish swim by in formation.

5. A Red-striped Fairy Basslet at Lady Elliot (shot at a depth of 30 metres).

Once again, you will see Manta Rays gliding by, Barracuda, large Potato Cod and countless smaller fish. Entry for this dive is straight off the beach.

Further north is another dive site, the Anchor Bommie. Here a massive coral bommie stands about seven metres high and this is completely surrounded by white sand. Two large anchors lie nearby, lost by guano boats that visited Lady Elliot back in the 1840's.

The visibility is generally very good and the marine life here is abundant. There are plenty of sharks, Shovel Nosed Rays, Manta Rays, Black Spotted Rays, schools of Trevally, Cod, Angel fish, and both soft and hard corals.

The next dive site is The Maori Wrasse Bommie, north-west of the island. This is approached from the Coral Gardens and here you will see soft colourful corals and many fish including Coral Trout, Mangrove Jacks, schools of Pike and Fairy Basslets.

The Canyons are almost directly north of Lady Elliot. Because the walk from the beach to the reef's edge is quite some distance this is usually a boat dive. It is a spectacular dive with narrow corridors between coral bommies, arches, caves and drop-offs to about 27 metres. You will see superb soft and hard coral formations - some very large - and plenty of marine life including banded Angel fish, Manta Rays and White Tip sharks.

Close by is another dive site called the Shark Pool. This is a drift dive and along the way you will see reef sharks, schools of Sweetlip, many turtles, schools of Eagle Rays, plus many other fish and beautiful coral formations.

On the eastern side of Lady Elliot there are several other great dives. Directly east of the resort is The Blowhole. This rather rare formation comprises a vertical shaft that plunges down through the reef to a depth of about 15 metres. A horizontal tunnel then leads off this into a large cave.

Outside the cave there are Maori Wrasse, sharks, Eagle Rays, Moray Eels and turtles. Inside the cave there is a myriad of fish, especially schooling Cardinal fish.

The Blowhole is a boat dive and so, too, is the next site south of it - The Docks. It received this name because a cutaway in the outer reef face bears a close resemblance to a shipping dock in its shape. Nearby there are soft corals, Gorgonia sea fans and many varieties of small but colourful fish.

The Tube, south of The Blowhole, consists of a tunnel about 15 metres in length that leads into a cave. On the walls and ceilings are many stinging hydroids. At the entrance there are many larger species of fish while the smaller varieties seek protection towards the rear of the cave.

The final dive, in the south-eastern corner of the island, is Hero's Cave. It lies at a depth of 26 metres. Gorgonia Fans flower around the entrance, soft corals cling to the walls and on the ceiling you will discover large numbers of Banded Coral Shrimp.

Near the cave's entrance there is also wreckage from a boat that came to grief on the reef surrounding Lady Elliot Island. The wreckage is believed to be from the ill-fated "Thisby".

1

2

3

If you have never dived before you can do an Open Water Diving Certificate Course during your stay on Lady Elliot Island. The course is conducted over five days. One day introductory dives are available, too.

All diving and snorkelling gear may be hired from the Dive Shop.

Another way to view the splendours of the island's coral gardens is from the resort's glass bottom boat.

A low key resort catering for just 88 people.

After John and Judy French took over the lease in 1985 they rebuilt the resort in just a few months and their first guests arrived in July of the same year. Ever since, the casual and relaxed atmosphere has attracted a steady flow of visitors.

About half of these are Australians and the rest are mainly Americans, Englishmen, Swedes and New Zealanders. Around 15% of the visitors are divers.

There are three different grades of accommodation. There are two types of cabins, each with their own verandah - or you can camp in spacious tents.

Both types of cabins are basic but comfortable. Reef Units directly overlook the island's lagoon and have their own shower and toilet.

Coral Cabins are just a stone's throw from the lagoon and beach.

Safari Tents are erected permanently and have beds and cupboards so you are hardly roughing it. Linen and towels are also provided.

Guests staying in the Coral Cabins and Safari Tents share amenities close to their accommodation.

The lodge which houses the dining room, Wreck Bar and recreation room is modern but unpretentious. The atmosphere is always relaxed with John French and his family usually acting as hosts along with several other members of the small staff.

There is always a hearty breakfast offered and lunch is an excellent buffet of cold and hot dishes (including seafood several times a week).

At dinner time you will be offered a three course meal that is always tasty. There may be Cream of Mushroom or Vegetable Soup (homemade, of course), a main dish like Chicken with Provencale Sauce or Pork Chops with Sweet and Sour Sauce, and a tempting dessert like Egg Custard Tart or freshly baked Apricot Tart and Cream.

A small but good selection of Australian wines is available.

In the evenings guests can relax in the Wreck Bar. Occasionally there is a Bush Dance, a Fancy Dress night or live musical entertainment.

Once or twice a week a video or slide show on some aspect of the island and Reef is screened in the recreation room. These are both informative and very interesting. In the recreation room you will also find a small library which contains some very interesting reference books on the Reef.

Generally speaking, though, the evening is a time to have a quiet drink and chat about the day's events with old and new acquaintances.

The resort has a small shop with basic

4

5

6

toiletries, souvenirs and casual clothing, and there is also a snack bar should you feel thirsty or hungry throughout the day.

There are no phones on the island so don't expect to phone home! There is a UHF Radio, however, which is used to contact the mainland when necessary. Mail is collected from the island each day.

How to get to Lady Elliot Island.

Lady Elliot is one of the few islands within the Great Barrier Reef region to have its own airstrip. This makes access to the island both easy and convenient.

A light aircraft flies from Bundaberg airport to the island. These flights connect with domestic flights on the mainland. Please note, however, that guests are allowed only 10 kg of personal luggage aboard the light aircraft which services the island (excess baggage will attract an additional charge).

For bookings or additional information about staying on Lady Elliot Island contact Sunstate Travel Centre, 188 Bourbong Street, Bundaberg, Qld. 4670. Their phone number is (071) 71 6077.

Incidentally, if you wish to drive to Bundaberg and then fly to Lady Elliot you will find that undercover parking is available at the airport itself. This may be arranged through Sunstate Travel Centre.

If you wish to write to the resort itself, address correspondence to Lady Elliot Island Holidays Pty. Ltd., Locked Mail Bag 6, Bundaberg Qld. 4670.

If you decide to visit Lady Elliot Island you may be assured of one fact. When you arrive on Lady Elliot, your hosts John and Judy French will provide you with a very warm welcome and do everything to ensure that your stay on this island is as enjoyable as possible.

Here are just two of the many entries from the visitor's book at the small resort. "Diving on Lady Elliot was just like a fantasy." "Very relaxing holiday and a great place to learn to scuba. Hope it stays simple."

For tranquil surroundings, an uncommercialised environment, seclusion, and a closeness to nature both above and below the sea, Lady Elliot has clearly won many hearts. And it will continue to do so.

1. Coral Cabins are only a short distance from the beach.

2. Permanently erected Safari tents have both beds and cupboards.

3. The coral beach close to the lighthouse.

4. The sun sets over the reef flats of Lady Elliot Island.

5. There is much to photograph on and around the island.

6. Divers leave the water in the late afternoon.

LINDEMAN ISLAND

2

3

1. The view from Hempel's Lookout at the southern end of Lindeman showing part of the island's resort and nearby Seaforth Island.
2. A clump of Umbrella trees in blossom. Photographed on the walk to Mt. Oldfield.
3. Two people relax on Seaforth Island which is directly off-shore from Lindeman Island's resort.
4. Verdant rainforest on the way to Boat Port Bay.

1

The first group of tourists visited Lindeman Island as far back as 1929. In the early days of the island's resort, accommodation was primitive - guests stayed in grass huts.

Established by Angus Nicolson, the resort was subsequently managed by his eldest son, Lachlan Nicolson, who was sent on secret missions with Allied Intelligence during World War II.

Lindeman Island is the most southerly resort island of the Whitsunday Group.

It is located approximately 900 kilometres north of Brisbane and 67 kilometres north of Mackay.

Covering an area of about 20 square kilometres, Lindeman Island is a National Park with 19 kilometres of walking trails.

Over 90 species of birds have been sighted on the island.

Lindeman was settled by Europeans at the turn of the century - although there is evidence to suggest that aborigines visited and lived on it long before that.

Today, there is a new resort on the island that accommodates around 300 guests. One feature enjoyed by many is its 9-hole golf course.

4

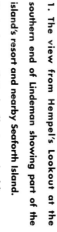

1

1. Billy Moogra, believed to be the last aborigine of the Whitsunday Tribe, lived and worked on Lindeman Island. This photograph was taken in 1928.

2. The island's original homestead and woolshed (later converted into accommodation for Lindeman's first guests) in 1923.

3. In the late 1930's guests stayed in these grass cabins.

4. A "Welcome to Lindeman" sign, c.1937.

5. View of the main beach and resort, c. 1937.

The Reef can also be visited - it is 30 minutes away by seaplane.

During the summer the temperature on Lindeman is between 22°C and 29°C. In the winter months it is normally somewhere between 13°C and 22°C.

Once visited by trochus luggers.

On the charts of Matthew Flinders, the island carries the name of Kowarra Island.

Lindeman Island apparently received its present name in 1866 from the captain of the HMS "Virago", a naval vessel surveying the Great Barrier Reef region at the time.

The captain was George Sidney Lindeman, the nephew of Dr. Lindeman who started the well-known winery in South Australia.

From all known accounts, the island was first settled in 1906 by Captain James Adderton who had previously worked aboard a ship plying between Townsville and Maryborough.

James Adderton retired to the island, stocked it with sheep, goats and cattle, and lived there with his wife until 1919. Between 1919 and 1923 it was owned by two different owners, Mathew Fredericks and then Billy Nicklin.

Billy Nicklin - along with a "Doctor" Frank Wylde - planned to grow papaws with the intention of manufacturing a cure for cancer. This dubious plan fell through, however, and Billy became a beachcomber instead.

The lease was subsequently purchased by Angus Nicolson, a man with a colourful background.

Early in his adult life, Angus worked as a linesman around the top end of Cape York and Thursday Island. Dynamite was an essential part of a linesman's kit - it was used to blow up ant beds which threatened telegraph poles and as an easy way to stun and catch fish.

Unfortunately, Angus blew a hand off on one such fishing expedition. Needless to say, this brought his career as a linesman to an abrupt end and he moved to Bowen.

It was years later, after Angus had married and was rearing three children, that a Captain Farmer put the idea into the head of Angus to lease Lindeman Island. Captain Farmer was master of a British India vessel which called into Bowen regularly for beef, and he was constantly talking to Angus about the potential of the Whitsundays as a wonderful tourist destination.

Angus took up Captain Farmer's suggestion and although the facilities he provided initially were very basic - an old woolshed was converted into accommodation - Lindeman soon attracted guests. The first visitors came from Melbourne and fishing was the major attraction.

Huts were also constructed from Coconut branches and grass but as time went by many improvements were made and Angus Nicolson's eldest son Lachlan took over the management of the growing resort.

Incidentally, during World War II, Lachlan Nicolson left the island and served with Allied Intelligence. Although many of his secret and dangerous missions are still shrouded in mystery it is known that he entered Japanese controlled waters aboard a boat disguised as a native Malayan prau to gather information vital to the Allied Forces.

Lachlan is no longer alive but his wife, Thora Nicolson, is still living on the island in a house next to the resort.

Decades ago, Lindeman Island sometimes had unexpected guests. On one occasion Mrs. Angus Nicolson discovered a trochus boat from Thursday Island moored just off the island. The native crew were ashore, cooking a large turtle.

They had heated stones in a hole scooped out on the beach, placed the turtle on its back along with bananas and potatoes, and then covered everything with palm leaves and grass. They had then packed sand on top until the impromptu oven was sealed like a pressure cooker.

An hour later the native boys uncovered the turtle and invited the curious onlookers to join them in a feast which was enjoyed by all.

Other luggers dropped in from time to time and the Torres Strait crew boys on some of these boats would often come ashore and dance for the guests on Lindeman.

A few aborigines lived on Lindeman until the late 1920's and possibly a little longer. Early photographs show a Gunyah or native hut at the end of the main beach in 1929. The last aborigine to live on the island was an aborigine by the name of Billy Moogra.

Bushwalk trails and seven beaches.

There are almost 20 kilometres of excellent walking tracks on Lindeman Island. These are maintained in conjunction with the National Parks and Wildlife Service and all lead to places well worth seeing.

The most rewarding walk is probably

2

4. Grass Cabins Lindeman Island. N.Q

3

WELCOME
LINDEMAN

4

11. View of Lindeman Is, Tourist Resort. N.Q

5

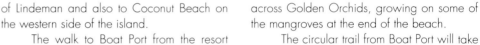

1

2

the one to the top of Mount Oldfield, 212 metres (695') above sea level, and the highest point on the island.

The track to Mount Oldfield runs alongside the airstrip towards the northern end of the island and then winds to the east. Along the way you will pass through tracts of eucalypt trees, rainforest and grasslands.

The walk, which only takes about 35 minutes each way, takes you to the top of Mount Oldfield where you can enjoy uninterrupted and spectacular 360° views. Directly to the north you can see rugged Pentecost Island and in the distance, on a clear day, you can see Hamilton, Whitsunday and Haslewood Islands as well as some smaller islands.

To the south and east you can enjoy good views of Shaw Island. At its northern tip you can see Maher Island. Both are National Parks and uninhabited.

From Mount Oldfield you can see some of the ten beautiful beaches on Shaw Island which you can visit easily by a dinghy with an outboard on a good day.

Directly to the west of the look-out on Mount Oldfield you also overlook Whitsunday Passage which James Cook sailed through and named in 1770, and opposite on the mainland is Conway National Park.

Occasionally, you can see Humpback whales passing through Whitsunday Passage, a sight not to be forgotten. Dolphins also frequent the area.

Two tracks fork off the main one to Mount Oldfield. The first is a circular one that leads to Boat Port on the north-western corner of Lindeman and also to Coconut Beach on the western side of the island.

The walk to Boat Port from the resort will take you about 30 minutes. Along the way you will pass a large number of Pandanus Palms. The vegetation then changes and you enter rainforest with delicate Maiden Hair ferns fringing the path.

Boat Port is so named because this was where boats were once repaired and painted, and the remains of an old slipway can still be seen. Today, people visit this bay because of the sandy, protected beach. Check the tides before you go, however, for the water recedes quite some distance at low tide.

A permanent picnic table under the shade of a large tree makes it an ideal spot for lunch. At Boat Port you may also come across Golden Orchids, growing on some of the mangroves at the end of the beach.

The circular trail from Boat Port will take you to Coconut Beach and then back to the resort.

Coconut Beach is a long, sandy beach and another beautiful place to visit. Directly mid-point off the beach, snorkellers will also find Giant Clams up to 45 centimetres long. Like Boat Port, the water at Coconut Beach is very shallow at low tide so plan your trip accordingly.

A second fork on the main track to Mount Oldfield - close to the northern end of the airstrip - leads to Gap Beach, a destination which is another 10 minutes walk.

Within minutes of taking this second track you will enter Butterfly Valley, a lush

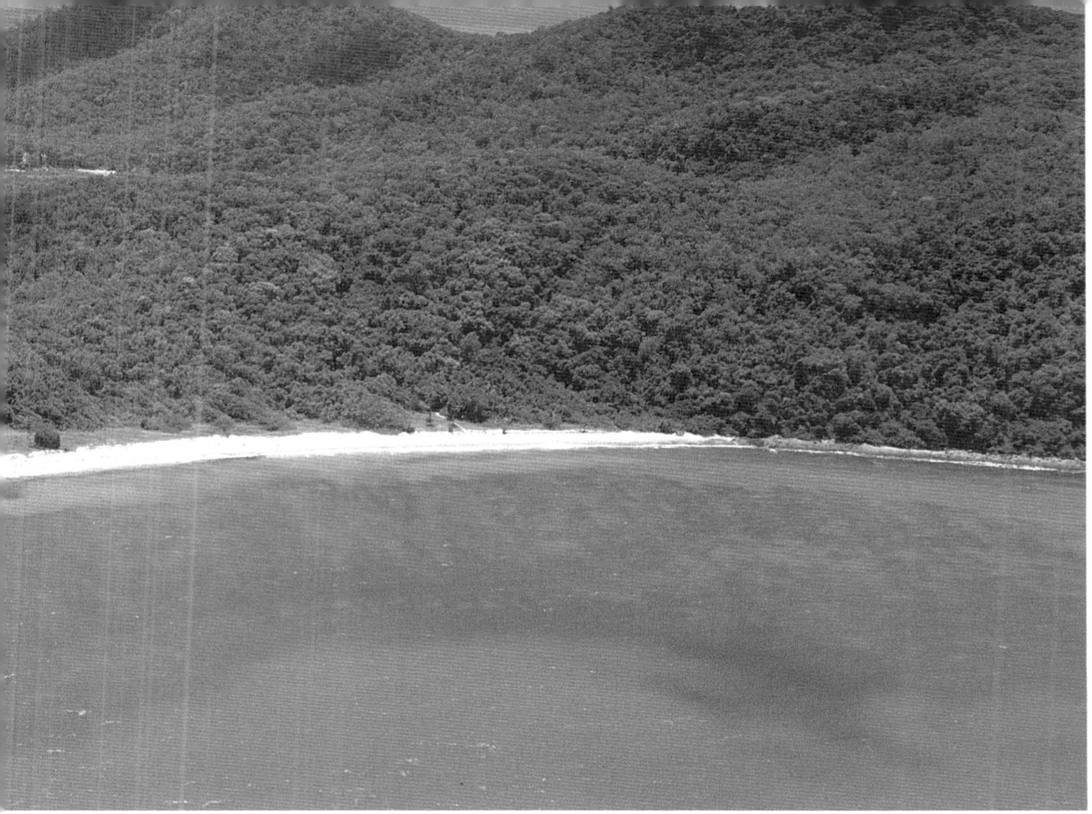

3

pocket of rainforest that is filled with ferns, twisted vines and towering trees that block out much of the sunlight.

As the name suggests, many butterflies can be observed here. These delightful creatures are usually present from October through to May. The most striking example is the Blue Tiger butterfly which is a powerful flyer (this species is also found on many islands in the Pacific including Fiji and Samoa).

Gap Beach itself is a rather rocky beach but people often go oystering and snorkelling here.

The coral and marine life in Turtle Bay - which is to the north-east of Gap Beach - is apparently better. Unfortunately, Turtle Bay is not easily accessible by boat because it is too shallow and it is something of a hike by foot (there is no walking trail to Turtle Bay).

A short distance from the resort itself - just five minutes walk from a signpost close to the staff quarters on the eastern side of the airstrip - is Hempels Look-out. From here you will enjoy a bird's-eye view of the resort on the terraced hillside below, as well as panoramic views of Seaforth Island which is close by, and Shaw Island.

You will also get a glimpse of Plantation Beach, a secluded beach which is another 20 minutes walk away from the signpost referred to above.

There are no native animals on Lindeman but as you walk around the island you will be able to observe many different species of birds. In fact, over 90 different varieties have been sighted on Lindeman.

The most common birds you are likely to see are brightly coloured Rainbow Lorikeets, noisy Brush Turkeys and Jungle Fowl, high flying White Breasted Sea Eagles and Sulphur Crested Cockatoos.

Some of the other birds you may see include four different varieties of both Finches and Kingfishers, Pied Currawongs, Stone Curlews, Noddy and Crested Terns, Honeyeaters, six varieties of Pigeons, Pied and Sooty Oystercatchers, and Herons.

Cruise around the Whitsundays and see the Reef.

Various half day and full day trips are available to guests staying on Lindeman. All these are subject, of course, to good weather conditions.

Once a week, there is usually a trip by boat to Whitehaven Beach. This is a

1. The beach and picnic area at Boat Port Bay.

2. Thumb Point and Coconut Beach.

3. The view from the top of Mt. Oldfield looking towards Pentecost Island, a rugged and uninhabited island directly north of Lindeman.

1

1. **A Black-backed Butterfly fish, a species commonly seen at Bait and Hardy Reefs.**
2. **The easiest way to visit one of the outer reefs from Lindeman is to fly. This Seair Pacific seaplane has landed at Bait Reef. Here guests can snorkel, dive, and view coral from a semi-submersible craft.**

2

magnificent beach of pure white sand over five kilometres long on the eastern side of Whitsunday Island.

Those who love sailing will find that they can also visit Whitehaven Beach or Thomas Island (which lies to the south of both Lindeman and Shaw Islands) aboard the "Lindeman Pacific", a beautiful motor cruiser. A smorgasbord lunch is included and there is also plenty of time to swim and sunbake.

A pleasant half-day excursion is a three hour visit to Seaforth Island, the small uninhabited island that lies to the south of Lindeman and is just several minutes away from the resort by boat.

This island is a National Park and the home of many species of birds as well as thousands of fruit bats.

Whilst on the island you can explore its rainforest, enjoy a barbeque, swim and snorkel. (You can also rent a dinghy with outboard and explore Seaforth Island by yourself at any time.)

If you would like to see more of the Whitsundays you can take a three island cruise to Hamilton Island, South Molle Island and Hook Island. Hamilton has the largest resort in the Great Barrier Reef region and a popular attraction on Hook Island is the Underwater Observatory where you can view many varieties of coral and colourful fish.

Lindeman - beautiful as it is - does not have any extensive coral formations itself but it is easy, nevertheless, to enjoy the wonders of two large outer reefs that lie just 80 kilometres away from the island.

Access for people staying on Lindeman Island is by one of Seair Pacific's small seaplanes. These take guests to either Hardy or Bait Reef several times a week.

The seaplanes are almost like airborne taxis - a very common form of transport around the Whitsundays - and the flights themselves are spectacular. From the air you get an amazing bird's-eye view of both the nearby islands and the Reef. You will find that the pilots are very likeable, friendly individuals who also act as guides.

Hardy Reef has 7,500 acres of coral and is just half an hour away from Lindeman by plane. Once there, you can view coral gardens and the teeming marine-life around them in a semi-submersible craft that is not unlike a small submarine. You can also go snorkelling. About two hours is spent at Hardy Reef.

At Bait Reef, a smaller reef that lies to the west of Hardy Reef, the plane lands inside another lagoon where you can view gardens of coral from a glass bottom boat, snorkel and go reef walking. One and a half hours is spent at Bait Reef.

If you are interested in diving, you will find a Dive Shop at the resort. Diving trips to Hardy Reef by boat are organised once a week. You can also fly out with Seair Pacific with gear and have time to enjoy one dive on either of the excursions mentioned above.

Another trip made is to Langford Reef at the northern end of the Whitsunday Group. Langford Reef lies just south of Hayman Island and west of Hook Island - an area where there are some superb snorkelling and diving sites.

There are beautiful soft and hard corals to see and a wide variety of fish including colourful Parrot fish, large Maori Wrasse, big Bat fish and small Sargeant Major fish which have distinctive stripes, hence their name.

If you have never dived before you can do a one day Introductory Dive Course which includes instruction in the resort pool and the thrill of one dive at Langford, Hardy or Bait Reef.

Alternatively, you can complete a P.A.D.I. Course over five days and enjoy two local dives and another two out on the Reef.

If you like to fish you can hire a dinghy with outboard and try your luck around the southern end of the island.

Half day fishing trips are also organised regularly and a game fishing boat can be chartered.

For those who enjoy water sports, there are catamarans, sailboards and paddle skis available at no charge at the main beach alongside the resort. Only activities which use fuel like water-skiing, parasailing and jet skis attract a charge.

Also free is the use of the resort's tennis courts and the 9-hole golf course from which you have magnificent views of other Whitsunday islands.

Other activities for guests include cricket, aerobics and archery.

Parents should be pleased to learn that there are supervised activities for children between the age of three and eight between 9:00 a.m. and 12 noon every morning, all year round.

Children between three and fourteen can also enjoy their own dinner and activities until 9:00 p.m. Babysitting facilities are available, too (for a small charge).

During school holiday periods, supervised groups of children are taken camping to Plantation Beach for two days where they fish, snorkel and learn the art of bushcraft. It's a great adventure for them, and also gives parents a chance to relax by themselves.

A new resort which accommodates 300 guests.

Although there has been a resort on Lindeman for over 50 years, it has been upgraded at various times and just recently it was almost totally rebuilt at a cost of over $30 million. The result is a resort that is modern and luxurious in an understated way.

All the facilities in the main resort complex are new. There are also 104 new rooms.

There are two grades of accommodation for guests - the new Seaforth rooms and 48 older style Whitsunday rooms. Together they can accommodate just over 300 guests.

Some of the new Seaforth rooms are virtually beachfront, others overlook the pool but are still within a stone's throw of the main beach. All have a balcony.

Seaforth rooms have either a double bed or twin single beds. Each Seaforth room also has a comfortable sofa as well (which converts to two single beds) in a small but comfortable lounge area. There is also a very attractive en-suite bathroom. All rooms are air-conditioned and have ceiling fans in addition to a television, telephone, refrigerator and mini-bar.

The 48 Whitsunday rooms are older and more basic but the tariffs reflect this. All Whitsunday rooms have a double bed and two single beds. They do have an en-suite bathroom and ceiling fans but are not air-conditioned. They also have a refrigerator but no mini-bar or television.

As budget accommodation, however, the Whitsunday rooms represent extremely good value. They have been recently refurbished and all have magnificent views over Kennedy Sound and Shaw Island.

Tariffs for both Seaforth and Whitsunday rooms include all meals.

The resort has two restaurants for guests in the new complex. The main restaurant is called "The Islander". This has sweeping views over Kennedy Sound with Seaforth Island in the foreground and Shaw Island in the background.

"The Islander" is open for breakfast, lunch and dinner. Breakfast and lunch are normally buffet style.

Three or four evenings a week "The Islander" has a small but imaginative menu which varies daily with a choice of four starters, three main courses and several desserts.

On one evening the menu offered guests these starters - Cream of Pumpkin Soup, Consomme Royale (Clear Beef Soup garnished with a Savoury Egg Custard), Duck Liver Terrine with Cumberland Sauce or Smoked Salmon Rosette with Horseradish Sauce.

They could then enjoy a Seafood Stew of Fresh Queensland Seafood with Pernod Sauce, Pork Medallions Calypso (served with a Sauce of Orange, Pineapple and Jamaican Rum) or Ped Oob Mor Din (Casseroled Duck Breast cooked with herbs in traditional Thai style).

The three delicious desserts offered were Strawberries and Kirsch with Wafer

1

2

3

4

5

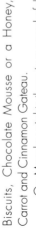

Biscuits, Chocolate Mousse or a Honey, Carrot and Cinnamon Gateau.

On Monday nights there is a wonderful Seafood Smorgasbord and on Wednesday there is a mouth-watering Oriental buffet. On Friday night there is a Barbeque (around the pool, weather permitting) and on Sunday night there is either a Bavarian Night with traditional German fare or an appetising menu of Italian dishes.

A second restaurant called "Nicolsons" is open three to five nights a week, depending on the season. Meals in "Nicolsons" are not included in the tariff.

This intimate a la carte restaurant offers a menu with half a dozen entrees like a Seafood Trilogy (Fresh Prawns, Mud Crab and Moreton Bay Bugs served on assorted Fruit Coulis with an Avocado Sauce) and a Veal and Prawn "Moneybag" (Fillet of Veal and Prawns sauteed with Leeks and Basil, wrapped in a Filo Pastry and presented on a Walnut Sabayon).

Main Courses include Coral Trout "Virago" (Coral Trout flavoured with Brandy, enclosed in Filo Pastry and presented on a Green Ginger and Leek Sauce), and Supreme of Chicken en Cage (Breast of Chicken with a Liver Farce enclosed in a Puff pastry cage accompanied by a Raspberry Sauce).

Guests then have half a dozen desserts to choose from like a Hot Grand Marnier Souffle or Pistachio Bavorois (served with an Orange flavoured Vanilla Sauce).

Both the "Islander" restaurant and "Nicolsons" have an excellent wine list with Australian whites and reds as well as local and French champagnes.

Usually once a week guests can also enjoy a special Gourmet Night at "Nicolsons" where the talented chef tries to outdo his own high standards with a small set menu that he has created for the occasion. Each dish is even accompanied by a specially selected wine and these are included in the cost of the dinner.

Apart from the restaurants there is a coffee shop alongside the pool area that serves light snacks.

Next to the coffee shop there is an excellent shop stocked with a good range of casual wear, footwear, jewellery, souvenirs, toiletries, magazines and a small selection of books for holiday reading.

Mention should also be made of the entertainment in the evenings. Almost every night there is light live music in the main cocktail lounge adjoining the restaurants.

Five nights a week there is also live music after dinner. In addition, there are Games Nights, a Casino Night, and an evening when there is a Talent Quest and Bush Dancing.

Three times a week there is a late night disco at Juliet's Nightspot.

How to get to Lindeman Island.

There are several ways of getting to Lindeman Island. The quickest way for most visitors is to fly into nearby Hamilton Island with Ansett. They operate direct flights from Sydney, Melbourne, Cairns, Rockhampton, Townsville and the Gold Coast.

You then catch a local Seair Pacific plane for a short 15 minute flight to Lindeman

Island which is the only other Whitsunday island apart from Brampton to have its own airstrip.

Seair Pacific also have flights from Mackay and Proserpine which connect with those of Australian Airlines and East West Airlines.

If you arrive by coach or want to drive to the beautiful Whitsunday area you would head for Shute Harbour, the busy port which services most of the local islands.

From here you would then fly to Lindeman, once again with Seair Pacific. There is security parking at Shute Harbour for those with cars.

Three times a week you can also transfer to Lindeman Island aboard one of the Roylen boats which cruise out from Mackay.

The telephone and facsimile numbers of the resort on Lindeman Island - should you wish to contact it direct - are (079) 469333 and (079) 469598 respectively. The postal address of the resort is simply Lindeman Island, via Mackay, Queensland 4741.

No camping on Lindeman is permitted but yachtsmen are welcome to visit the island. Those who want moorings or use of various amenities including the pool, coffee shop and restaurants should first check with Reception.

Lindeman Island has long been a popular destination and its appeal should be even greater with its new resort. Lindeman's natural features are well summed up in "Summer Days", one of the many poems written by Thora Nicolson who has lived on the island for over 40 years. Here are several verses from it.

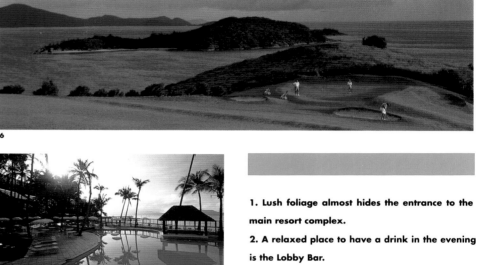

6

7

"I paddle along the shelly shore,
The sun so warm and bright.
Gathering clams and cuttlefish shells,
A sleeping stingray I sight.

Gently the breeze brings the scent of the sea,
Sparkles of sun on blue.
Trees on the shore offer patterns of shade,
Like lace, where the leaves are strewn.

Green are the ferns growing under the trees,
Orchids in flower above.
Sunbirds are singing, my heart is at ease,
These summer days I love."

1. Lush foliage almost hides the entrance to the main resort complex.

2. A relaxed place to have a drink in the evening is the Lobby Bar.

3. The resort's new Seaforth Units.

4. The interior of a Seaforth Unit.

5. Lindeman Island Resort and Home Beach.

6. The resort's 9-hole golf course. Golfers also enjoy sweeping views over Whitsunday Passage.

7. The sun rises over the resort's pool and Pool Bar.

LIZARD ISLAND

2

3

1. Lizard Island's magnificent Blue Lagoon. The uninhabited island on the far side of the lagoon is South Island. The smaller ones are called Bird Islets.

2. From the island's Lodge, you enjoy water views and a glimpse of Prince Charles Island, formerly Osprey Island. The small island received its new name after Prince Charles visited Lizard Island in 1974.

3. Turtle Beach, one of 24 beautiful beaches on Lizard Island.

4. Game fishing attracts many visitors to the island.

1

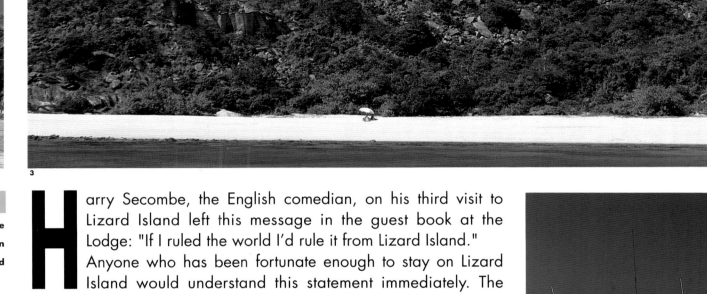

Harry Secombe, the English comedian, on his third visit to Lizard Island left this message in the guest book at the Lodge: "If I ruled the world I'd rule it from Lizard Island." Anyone who has been fortunate enough to stay on Lizard Island would understand this statement immediately. The truth is that Lizard Island is one of Australia's best kept secrets.

Although it does not have the same amount of lush vegetation of some Great Barrier Reef islands, Lizard Island is still exceptionally beautiful.

What this island does have is very extensive fringing coral reefs, a stunning Blue Lagoon, and superb beaches. As a backdrop to these features, the island has a stately mountain peak.

Lizard Island is probably best known amongst game fishermen. The waters around the island are considered by most as the world's best fishing grounds for Black Marlin.

The island is also close to some of the best diving spots in the world.

Lizard Island lies about 270 kilometres north of Cairns, the "capital" of tropical North Queensland, and is 93 kilometres north-

4

east of Cooktown.

This makes it the most northerly resort island on the Great Barrier Reef.

The first Europeans to make a recorded visit to Lizard Island were James Cook and his crew aboard the "Endeavour" in August, 1770

Cook named the island after the large but harmless Monitor lizards that still inhabit it.

In the 1870's Captain Robert Watson established a plant on Lizard Island to process Bêche-de-mer or sea cucumbers - with tragic results, as you will discover.

Today, most of the island - which covers about 2,500 acres - is classified as National Park.

On the island there is an important Marine Research Station and a small resort.

This exclusive yet low-key resort has seen many notable guests - including royalty, heads of state, business tycoons and movie stars.

Throughout the year the temperature on Lizard Island ranges between 23°C and 32°C.

An island visited by a succession of famous explorers.

Whilst the Great Barrier Reef is undoubtedly one of the great natural wonders of the world, it has also proved very hazardous to seamen. The further north a ship travels, the narrower the channel becomes between the mainland and the Reef.

James Cook, on his historic journey of exploration up the coast of Australia, eventually became trapped in the maze of reefs around Lizard Island. This prompted the intrepid explorer to land on the island and twice climb to the tip of the highest peak in an attempt to survey a route of escape.

The "Endeavour" anchored off Lizard Island on Sunday, August 12, 1770. Cook's Journals describe the visit in detail. He wrote that "we saw several turtle and chased one or two, but caught none it blowing too hard and I had no time to spare being otherwise employ'd."

On landing, he immediately climbed to the top of what is now known as Cook's Look, a peak some 1,200 feet or 359 metres above sea level.

Cook found the view rather hazy and this hampered his efforts to sight an escape route through the surrounding reefs. Unfortunately, it was just as hazy when he repeated the exercise later in the day.

Finally, a small boat which he sent out towards the seemingly impenetrable barriers of coral managed to find a narrow break in the Reef and Cook subsequently named it Providence Passage (see Chapter Two for the full story of this escape).

Amongst his observations of Lizard Island, Cook noted that the party did not see any local inhabitants. However, they did come across ruins of several huts and heaps of discarded shells which clearly suggested that aborigines or "Indians", as the naturalist Joseph Banks described them, visited the island regularly.

In following years, Lizard Island was visited by a succession of famous explorers, including Commander J.L. Stokes who surveyed the Great Barrier Reef in 1839 aboard the H.M.S "Beagle", and Captain Blackwood who surveyed the Reef aboard the H.M.S "Fly" in 1843.

Lizard Island is also mentioned in the Diary of Thomas Henry Huxley - surgeon, naturalist, anthropologist and philosopher - who visited Lizard Island aboard the H.M.S "Rattlesnake", which surveyed the inner passage of the Great Barrier Reef in 1848.

The tragic story of Mary Watson.

Mary Watson was the wife of Robert F. Watson. He was in partnership with P.C. Fuller in a Bêche-de-mer fishing venture that was based on Lizard Island.

In May, 1881, the H.M.S. "Alert" anchored at Lizard Island and Dr. R.W. Coppinger, the Ship's Surgeon, happened to record life on the island at the time.

He observed that "the Bêche-de-mer industry seems simple enough to conduct. The sluggish animals are picked off the reefs at low tide, and at the close of each day the produce as soon as landed is transferred to a huge iron tank, propped up on stones, in which it is boiled. The trepangs are then slit open, cleaned, and spread out on gratings in a smokehouse until dry, when they are ready for shipping to the Chinese market."

Fuller occupied a wooden hut on the island and the Watsons lived in a small stone cottage along with Ferrier, their three month old son.

Two Chinese were employed by the Watsons. One was Ah Leong, the gardener, and the other was a houseboy called Ah Sam.

In September, 1881, Watson and Fuller left Lizard Island in search of more Bêche-de-mer. Since they had already cleared the Bêche-de-mer off the more accessible reefs Watson and Fuller planned to go further afield and expected to be away for several weeks.

At the time of their departure there was no indication at all that Mrs. Watson, her baby and the two Chinese servants would be in any danger on the island.

Not long after the men left, however, a number of aborigines arrived on Lizard Island by canoe. What happened next, as Dr. Coppinger wrote later as a postscript to his visit to Lizard Island, was a "horrible catastrophe".

Mrs. Watson, who kept a diary over the following few days, made an entry on September 29 that is both short and descriptive. "Ah Leong killed by the blacks. Ah Sam found his hat, which is the only proof."

The only other evidence of Ah Leong's murder was discovered later on the mainland. His pigtail was found at the site of an abandoned aboriginal camp.

On September 30, aborigines appeared again near the small habitation on Lizard Island. They quickly retreated when Mrs. Watson fired both her rifle and revolver but the trouble was far from over. The very next day Ah Sam, the houseboy, was speared a number of times in the shoulder and right side.

There was no spare boat so on Sunday, October 2, the brave Mrs. Watson improvised and launched a small iron tank about one and half metres square in a desperate attempt to escape from the island and the marauding aborigines. The tank was one normally used for boiling Bêche-de-mer.

1

2

3

Mrs. Watson took her son along with her as well as the wounded Ah Sam. She also took some food, clothing, personal trinkets and an umbrella to shade the baby.

On October 20, the cutter "Neptune" passed Lizard Island and the crew saw eight canoes and about 40 aborigines on the main beach.

The authorities in Cooktown immediately began a search for the missing inhabitants but the matter remained a mystery for almost three months.

Then, on January 19, 1882, the schooner "Kate Kearney" visited No. 5 Howick Island - and the captain discovered the bodies of all three castaways. They had died from exposure and thirst.

Also found was Mrs. Watson's diary which chronicled the tragic train of events.

During the first four days the small party either drifted or were stranded on reefs. They then landed on No.1 Howick Island to replenish their water but the presence of aborigines on that island was enough to scare them away. The next day the unlucky threesome headed for No. 5 Howick Island.

It was here that Mrs. Watson made the final entries in her diary. The last one was written on October 11, 1881, nine days after the initial escape from Lizard Island. This is how it read:

"Still all alive. Ferrier very much better this morning. Self feeling very weak. I think it will rain today; clouds very heavy; wind not quite so hard.

No rain. Morning fine weather. Ah Sam preparing to die. Have not seen him since 9. Ferrier more cheerful. Self not feeling at all well. Have not seen any boat of any description. No water. Nearly dead with thirst."

The funeral of Mrs. Watson, her baby and faithful servant took place in Cooktown on January 29, 1882. It included a huge procession of some 650 people including the Mayor, the whole Municipal Council, most of the local schoolchildren, bandsmen, firemen and Chinese merchants.

After the funeral of Mrs. Watson and her son, the procession accompanied the remains of Ah Sam to his final resting place.

A Chinese band played, volleys of firecrackers were fired, and candles and charm papers were burned at his grave.

The tank that Mrs. Watson tried to escape in was retrieved. It is now on display in the Brisbane Museum.

1. An engraving of Mary Watson, known as "the heroine of Lizard Island".

2. The remains of the stone cottage which was once the home of Mrs. Watson.

3. The grave of Mrs. Watson and her son Ferrier. They were buried in Cooktown. Hundreds attended their burial.

Mrs. Watson's original diary is also in Brisbane, at the John Oxley Library.

The motive for the aborigines attack was not clear until recently. In 1972 a group of documentary film-makers stayed on Lizard Island for five months. They discovered evidence of an aboriginal ceremonial ground with religious significance close to the place that Mrs. Watson lived.

The attack directed at her was undoubtedly prompted by the fact that aborigines did not tolerate women near sacred ground such as this.

Beaches with postcard views.

There are few islands that can offer the idyllic surroundings, comforts and secluded privacy that Lizard Island can.

The island has 24 glorious, unspoiled beaches for a total population of about 100 people.

Walk along most of them and you are unlikely to see another person in sight.

The beautiful sandy beaches are probably unequalled by those on any other resort island with the possible exception of Great Keppel.

There are several superb beaches within easy reach of the resort. The first is at Anchor Bay where the resort is located. The beach here is ideal for both swimming and snorkelling.

If you don a mask and flippers you need go only a very short distance from the water's edge in order to see small outcrops of coral and interesting marine life.

On one occasion the author had barely swum a few metres out from the beach, only to notice that a large turtle was nonchalantly swimming along just a metre or so below him. It continued to do so, until the temptation to touch it proved too great, and it then shot away at an amazing speed for a creature that appeared so cumbersome and ungainly.

Lying just a hundred metres or so off Anchor Bay is Prince Charles Island. This was named after the heir to the British throne following his visit to Lizard Island in 1974. The snorkelling between this tiny island and the beach is excellent.

Another beach worth visiting is the next one north of Anchor Bay. This is Mrs. Watson's Beach.

Some 40 metres back from the beach at the southern end you can see the crumbling remains of the stone cottage where this brave lady once resided.

The beach itself is both long and sandy. The bay that encompasses it is a favourite anchorage for yachtsmen and it is often the final port of call for those bound for Port Moresby.

If you snorkel off the northern end of Mrs. Watson's Beach you can see a remarkable garden of giant clams. Many are well over a metre long and some of these giant clams are reputed to be up to 120 years old.

Mrs. Watson's Beach is about twenty minutes walk from the resort and only a few minutes away by boat.

At the northern end of the beach you will also find the beginning of the trail which will take you up to the top of Cook's Look. More about that in a moment.

There are at least two other wonderful beaches where you can laze away the day in total seclusion and marvellous surroundings. Both are reached by boat. If you are staying at the resort all you have to do is book one of the aluminium runabouts the day before, order a picnic hamper and you are then guaranteed one of the most enjoyable days of your life.

Both beaches are further north again from Watson's Beach. The first is Turtle Beach and it takes just five or ten minutes to reach it by boat.

You will find that it is perfect for both swimming and snorkelling.

If you go past Turtle Beach you will approach a headland near the northern tip of Lizard Island. Round it and you will enter Mermaid Cove.

The scene that greets you is postcard material at its best.

You must take care as you approach the beach, however, because this small bay with its clear turquoise water is also quite shallow and there are many outcrops of coral.

If you keep a sharp eye out once you land you will see some of the large Monitor lizards that the island was named after. They can usually be heard and seen amongst the rocks at each end of the beach.

If you plan to go to Mermaid Cove ask the kitchen at the resort to provide you with a small container with pieces of red meat. With a little patience you will tempt one or two of the lizards out onto the beach with these juicy morsels. They move with surprising speed despite their ungainly gait. Monitor lizards are harmless so do not be alarmed by their size (they can be as long as one or two metres).

2

1. Mrs. Watson's Bay is a favourite anchorage of yachtsmen. In the bay there are also giant clams reputed to be over 100 years old. Both Lizard Island Lodge and Prince Charles Island are visible in the bay beyond.

2. One of the harmless Monitor lizards after which the island was named.

Follow in the footsteps of James Cook.

There are some wonderful walks on Lizard Island. The best one leads you to the top of Cook's Look. It was from this craggy peak that the explorer James Cook sought a safe passage through the Reef over 200 years ago.

In all honesty, it is more than just a leisurely walk. At times the trail seems more akin to a training ground for goats but if you persist you will be handsomely rewarded.

The track starts at the northern end of Watson's Bay and as you ascend you quickly enjoy panoramic views stretching back to Anchor Bay and the resort. Directly below the surface of the water in Watson's Bay, you will clearly see patches of coral and the beds of giant clams mentioned a little earlier.

As you climb still higher you will encounter a variety of wildflowers. The most noticeable will be the yellow flowers of the native Kapok tree. You will see these on other parts of Lizard Island, too.

About half way up the trail - just as you may be wondering if your legs and lungs can take any more - the gradient eases off. You will also know when you are a few hundred metres from the top of Cook's Look when you come across a small stone cairn that someone has thoughtfully constructed. It has the message "Not far now!" on it, which does give you a feeling of hope as you enter the last phase of this somewhat arduous journey.

Finally, you will reach the top and a very large boulder which James Cook undoubtedly rested on two centuries earlier. From this vantage point the 360° view is truly magnificent.

In the foreground you will see Watson's Bay and the remains of Mrs. Watson's house, the airstrip, the Marine Research Station, and the remarkable Blue Lagoon on the southern side of Lizard Island. Further afield you will see other reefs, cays and islands including Poultry Island which has an unmanned lighthouse. You can also see the mainland which is 25 kilometres away.

On the top of Cook's Look there is both a stone cairn and a plaque that records the distances to various places around the world. New York is 15,200 kilometres away, London is 14,900 kilometres away. Sydney lies exactly 2,210 kilometres to the south.

A little book is kept at the top of Cook's Look and the comments made by those who actually reach the peak and then revel in the spectacular views are well worth reading before you add your own.

The joys and tribulations are captured in comments like these. "Made it at last, the mountain grew as we climbed!" "This is the pot of gold at the end of the rainbow which is at this very moment stretched across the bay of the early morning rain."

The visitor's book contains the names of many famous people. One royal visitor simply signed himself as "Charles".

Making it to the summit has one additional bonus. It entitles you to an impressive certificate back at the Lodge which documents your visit to the top of Cook's Look. It is a pleasant momento worth claiming.

The round trip to Cook's Look will take you about three hours.

A second walk which is not quite so demanding is the one to Lizard Head, the

1

most southerly tip of the island. From the ridge here you will get a bird's-eye view of the Blue Lagoon, a spectacular feature of the island.

Inside the lagoon a tangle of coral links three smaller islands to Lizard Island. The brilliant clear blue water within the lagoon itself completes a picture that is breath-taking.

Coral and marine life abounds in the lagoon - so it is also a wonderful place to go snorkelling.

When you snorkel on the fringing reefs around the island you are likely to see a wide variety of hard corals such as colourful Staghorn, Plate, Mushroom and Brain corals as well as huge waving fans of Gorgonia and other beautifully coloured soft corals.

There is also an infinite variety of tropical fish that draw upon all the colours of the rainbow - ranging from Angel and Butterfly fish to Parrot fish and Coral Trout.

If you go for a reefwalk at low tide you will find everything from sea cucumbers, starfish and crabs to many different species of algae in the rock pools.

If you are feeling adventuresome you can scale down the eastern side of Lizard Head on a sturdy rope securely anchored for that purpose and walk along Coconut Beach. Towards the northern end of this beach a short track will take you up to a small area of lush tropical rainforest known as the Hidden Valley.

If you decide to go on this walk you should allow at least a full morning or afternoon for it.

On your walks around the island you will sight many different species of birds.

2

At least 20 species of birds reside on Lizard Island including the brightly coloured Sunbird, White Breasted Sea Eagle, Bar Shouldered Pigeon, Coucal Pheasant, Eastern Golden Plover, Sooty Oystercatcher and eight different members of the Tern family.

In addition to these residents there are over 30 different species that visit Lizard Island.

A few of the visiting birds you may see are the Rainbow Bird, Sacred Kingfisher, Satin Flycatcher, White-tailed Tropicbird and White Ibis.

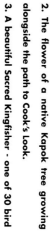

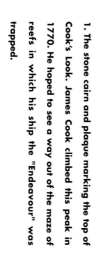

4

1. The stone cairn and plaque marking the top of Cook's Look. James Cook climbed this peak in 1770. He hoped to see a way out of the maze of reefs in which his ship the "Endeavour" was trapped.

2. The flower of a native Kapok tree growing alongside the path to Cook's Look.

3. A beautiful Sacred Kingfisher - one of 30 bird species that visit Lizard Island.

4. White Breasted Sea Eagles can often be seen high in the sky searching for prey.

3

1

In search of the big Black Marlin.

Lizard Island is a fisherman's paradise because of the large variety and size of fish that abound in the area.

In fact, the waters around Lizard Island are acknowledged as some of the finest game fishing grounds in the world. And each year, between the end of August and December, fishermen come from all around the globe to do battle with the largest fish of them all - the giant Black Marlin.

Bookings are particularly heavy at the Lodge during this period so make your arrangements for accommodation well in advance if you wish to join in the action.

The island even has its own angling association - the Lizard Island Game Fish Club, with members from 18 different countries including the U.S.A., Canada, Brazil, Kenya, Switzerland and Thailand.

Every year specimens weighing over 450 kilograms or 1,000 pounds are regularly taken or tagged and released by boats operating from the island. In fact, it has been estimated that 200 Black Marlin weighing 454 kilograms or over have been weighed in at Lizard Island since 1966 and thousands more have been tagged and set free.

According to Peter Goadby, a well-known angler and fishing journalist, "these reefs provide grander action than anywhere else in the world".

Seven World and two Australian Black Marlin Records have been weighed at Lizard since 1975. The largest Marlin was taken on November 1, 1979, by Morton "Buster" May at No.10 Ribbon Reef. This reef - along with No Name, Yonge, Carter, Day, Hicks, Hilder and Jewell - is legendary amongst Black Marlin fishermen.

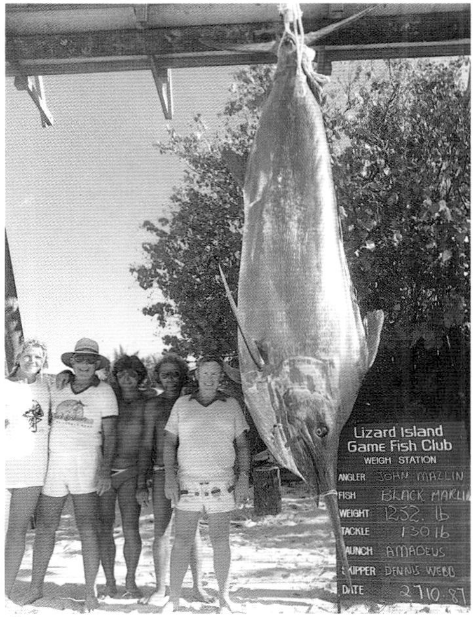

2

"Buster" May's catch weighed a massive 611 kilograms or 1,347 pounds.

More details about the annual Black Marlin tournament at Lizard Island may be obtained by writing to the Lizard Island Game Fish Club, P.O. Box 5740, Cairns Mail Centre, Cairns, Queensland, 4871.

The area around Lizard Island is also one of the best in the world for light and medium tackle game and sport fishing. Yellowfin, Dogtooth Tuna, Sailfish, Dolphin fish (Mahi Mahi), Spanish Mackerel, giant Trevally, and Cobia are just some of the many species of fish providing excitement in these waters.

Day trips for light and medium tackle angling can be arranged through the Lodge aboard charter vessels. All tackle is provided.

3

The action does not stop there. You can cast from the beaches and headlands. You will also find it very rewarding to fish by simply drifting across some of the expanses of coral reef around Lizard Island in a dinghy at high tide.

The best places for dinghy fishing are between South Bay Point and Palfry Island, and on the northern side of Mermaid Cove. You can expect to catch anything from Coral Trout, Sweetlip and Red Emperors to Cod, Bass and Trevallies.

If you decide to go fishing remember to ask at the Lodge about the areas where you may fish. There are some restricted areas where no fishing is permitted.

Needless to say, one of the delights of fishing at Lizard Island is also enjoying your

4

1. A massive Black Marlin that finally eluded capture. It was thought to weigh somewhere between 1,400 lbs and 1,600 lbs.

2. One of three record-breakers. This specimen weighed in at 1,252 lbs.

3. The largest Black Marlin ever caught by a Japanese visitor to the island. It weighed 1,245 lbs.

4. This Black Marlin, weighing 1,271 lbs, was caught by Alan Turnbull, President of the Lizard Island Game Fish Club.

1

2

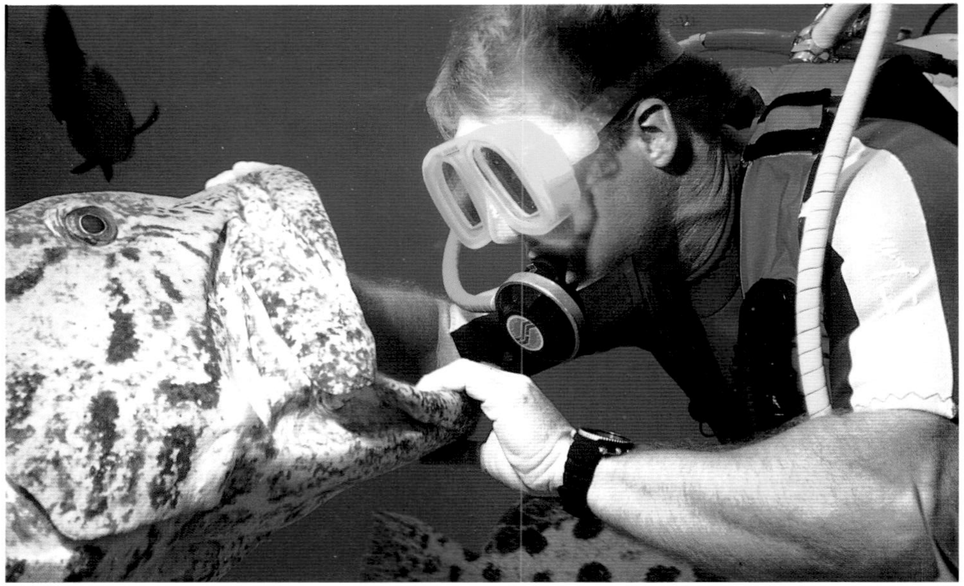
3

1. Turret Coral.

2. A colourful array of Feather stars and soft corals.

3. Large and friendly Potato Cod, a major attraction at The Cod Hole.

fresh catch. Take it to the kitchen at the Lodge on your return and the chefs will happily serve it up to you that very same evening.

The "Cod Hole", one of the world's most exciting dives.

Some mention has already been made of the wonderful snorkelling around Lizard Island. Lizard Island also attracts scuba divers and with the rich marine life in the waters around the island it is not hard to realise why.

You can dive all the year round from Lizard Island but September through to December are considered the best months because this is when the trade-winds die down a little.

There are some outstanding dive sites around the island. These include North Point, Cobia Hole, The Caves, The Galleries, The Staghorn Gardens and Chinaman's Alley. All these dives are between six and 20 metres. Some divers claim that there are better corals to be seen at some of these locations than at the nearby outer reefs.

There is no doubt, however, that the outer reefs provide some of the most spectacular dives known to man. Perhaps the best known one is The Cod Hole at the top end of No.11 Ribbon Reef. This is about 50 minutes by boat from Lizard Island.

The visibility here is usually anywhere between 20 and 30 metres and like many dive sites, snorkellers will also find this spot an exciting place to be.

There are hundreds of varieties of coral to be seen as well as a myriad of colourful tropical fish, Manta rays, Moray eels, turtles and giant but friendly Potato Cod.

The fish are well accustomed to being hand-fed and as soon as a diver enters the water with a food bucket there are scores of fish hovering around expectantly. The large Cod which are well over a metre in length (and weigh about 100 pounds) naturally take the lion's share but Maori Wrasse, Coral Trout and other smaller fish manage to get a feed as well. Two large Moray eels - about two metres in length - live at the Cod Hole and they, too, appear for their share.

For either a diver or snorkeller the experience is unbelievable. Quite frankly, you should not miss it if you are staying at Lizard Island. A trip to The Cod Hole will undoubtedly be one of the highlights of your visit.

On the Reef divers can also look forward to a number of other great dives at

4

5

4. **This is not the landscape of some alien planet but a vast formation of hard coral.**

5. **A brightly coloured Butterfly fish.**

6

7

6. **A diver takes a closer look at a Giant Clam.**

7. **Although they look like plants, Feather stars are animals. Their delicate arms filter plankton from the water around them.**

the Grottos, Shark Alley, Wall Dive, The Lookout and Dynamite Passage. All are in the vicinity of The Cod Hole.

Another very good place for diving and snorkelling is Bank's Bank, a small sandy cay exposed at low tide just a few kilometres east of Lizard Island.

Full diving facilities are provided by the resort and each party is accompanied by a Dive Master Instructor. All diving equipment may be hired if you have not brought your own.

If you wish to learn to scuba dive this can be arranged.

You can do a one day Resort Course with a single dive on the Reef or complete a four day course and qualify for an Open Water NAUI Certificate which entitles you to dive anywhere in the world.

Underwater cameras are available for hire and if you go on a dive a VHS cassette recording all the fun and activity of the day is usually available. It's one "home movie" that your friends will definitely watch with eyes wide open.

Investigating the love life of coral.

It is quite astonishing to contemplate the fact that the Great Barrier Reef - all 2,500 kilometres of it - was created by billions of organisms, some of which are barely visible to the naked eye.

Learning how coral actually reproduces is just one of the subjects under study at the Research Station on Lizard Island.

This Station was established in 1974 and is a facility operated by the Australian Museum, Sydney.

Each year it accommodates up to 100 visiting scientists who come to study the biology, geology, ecology, oceanography or hydrology of the Great Barrier Reef. Many of these scientists come from overseas.

At the Station there is a fully equipped laboratory, an aquarium constantly supplied with fresh sea water, darkroom for underwater photographers, workshop, and a 14 metre research vessel.

Research work conducted at the Lizard Island Research Station has led to over 190 different scientific publications.

In more recent times a considerable amount of effort has been dedicated to locating chemical compounds from Reef marine life that may have medicinal qualities.

Some of the other subjects scientists have recently been studying at the Research Station include the structure and behaviour of fish communities, giant clams, jelly fish, the presence of heavy metals in the sea, plus the nesting behaviour and feeding of sea-birds.

You are welcome to visit the Research Station and learn more about the work of scientists there but this must always be done by prior arrangement. To arrange a visit simply contact the Lodge Reception.

The "Silver Service" Resort.

The Lizard Island Lodge is unquestionably one of the premier resorts on the Great Barrier Reef. Many of the visitors who holiday here are regulars who return time and time again from destinations all around the world.

The resort, which is operated by Australian Airlines, has always catered to a

1

1. The resort's pool.
2. The main building of the Lodge which houses a restaurant, bar and small shop.
3. One of the 16 bungalows which accommodate guests.
4. The luxurious interiors of the bungalows.
5. A view of the Lodge and its beach.

2

3

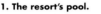

4

small number of guests and this has enabled the management to ensure that the standards are exceptionally high in every respect.

The Lodge was judged as "Best Resort" in the 1986 National Tourism Awards and "Best Resort" in the 1986 Queensland Tourism Awards.

The resort accommodates up to 64 people in 16 bungalows, each with two suites. The bungalows are built in Australian homestead style with timber walls, high ceilings, and verandahs overlooking the Coral Sea. The bungalows are air-conditioned and the interiors are both spacious and very tastefully decorated.

The accommodation reeks of quality right down to the marble bathrooms with twin vanities. The bathrooms have baths as well as showers - a feature not common on many islands because water is often in short supply.

Two de luxe suites are also available - these have a large lounge as well as a separate bedroom.

Fresh flowers are placed in each suite - a thoughtful touch which really is another example of the attention which goes into making a guest's stay on Lizard Island as pleasurable as possible.

Each suite also has a well stocked mini-bar and ice is delivered nightly at 5 p.m.

One of the most enjoyable features of the resort are the meals. The standard of the cuisine is excellent, especially in the evenings.

Before dinner you can relax around the bar adjoining the restaurant. Because of the small number of guests at the resort the atmosphere is more like a club. In the evening there is no other entertainment - simply good conversation with new found friends and then a wonderful dinner.

The menu each day is never the same but you could well expect a meal like the following. To start with you could be offered Pumpkin and Crab Soup and Lobster Terrine with Tomato Couli as entrees. You would then have a choice of three main dishes - such as Reef Fish in Banana Leaves and Coconut Sauce, Lamb Wellington, or Steak Pappilotte with Caviar Butter. The chef will then tempt you with a choice of desserts like Baiser Romanoff or Tree Cake with Tropical Fruit Salad.

The wine list offers a selection of some 15 quality Australian whites and about 18 reds.

5

The tariffs for staying at the Lizard Island resort include virtually everything except liquor. All meals are included, as are picnic hampers, the use of the outboard dinghies, windsurfers, catamarans, water skiing and glass bottom boat trips.

Boat trips to the outer reefs, diving equipment and game fishing charters are the only additional costs you should have.

Some further information about the resort - it also has a swimming pool, a tennis court that can be used day or night, a library for the use of guests, a boutique which offers a small but good range of swimwear, resort wear, souvenirs and toiletries, and a daily mail service.

Please note that if you wish your children to accompany you to the Lodge, they must be over the age of six.

To give people the seclusion and privacy they wish to enjoy you will also find no phone, television or radios in your suite. If you do wish to make contact with the outside world - which is most unlikely once you have sampled the joys of staying on Lizard Island - all you need do is visit Reception.

How to get to Lizard Island.

Lizard Island is about four hours flying time from Sydney. Overseas visitors can shorten their trip by arriving at either of the international airports at Townsville or Cairns. The connecting flight from Cairns to Lizard Island is about one hour. This is a spectacular scenic flight, since the aircraft flies up the coastline and over many of the individual reefs which help make up the Great Barrier Reef.

Private and chartered aircraft may land on Lizard Island.

Yachtsmen, incidentally, may moor at Lizard Island and ask permission to land and dine at the Lodge.

The telephone number of the resort on Lizard Island is (070) 603999. Their facsimile and telex numbers are (070) 603991 and 146177 respectively. The postal address of Lizard Island Resort is P.M.B. 40, Cairns 4870.

Holidaying at the Lodge on Lizard Island is certainly more expensive than staying on most other islands in the Great Barrier Reef region. With the standards and facilities the resort offers, however, the cost is unlikely to be a deterrent to the well-heeled people it is obviously catering to.

One of the resort's original founders, Sir Sydney Williams, swears that an Arab sheik once came ashore from a chartered yacht and wanted to book a suite for the night. When he was informed that none were available, he promptly pulled his cheque book out and offered to buy the resort on the spot.

Such is the irresistible appeal of Lizard Island.

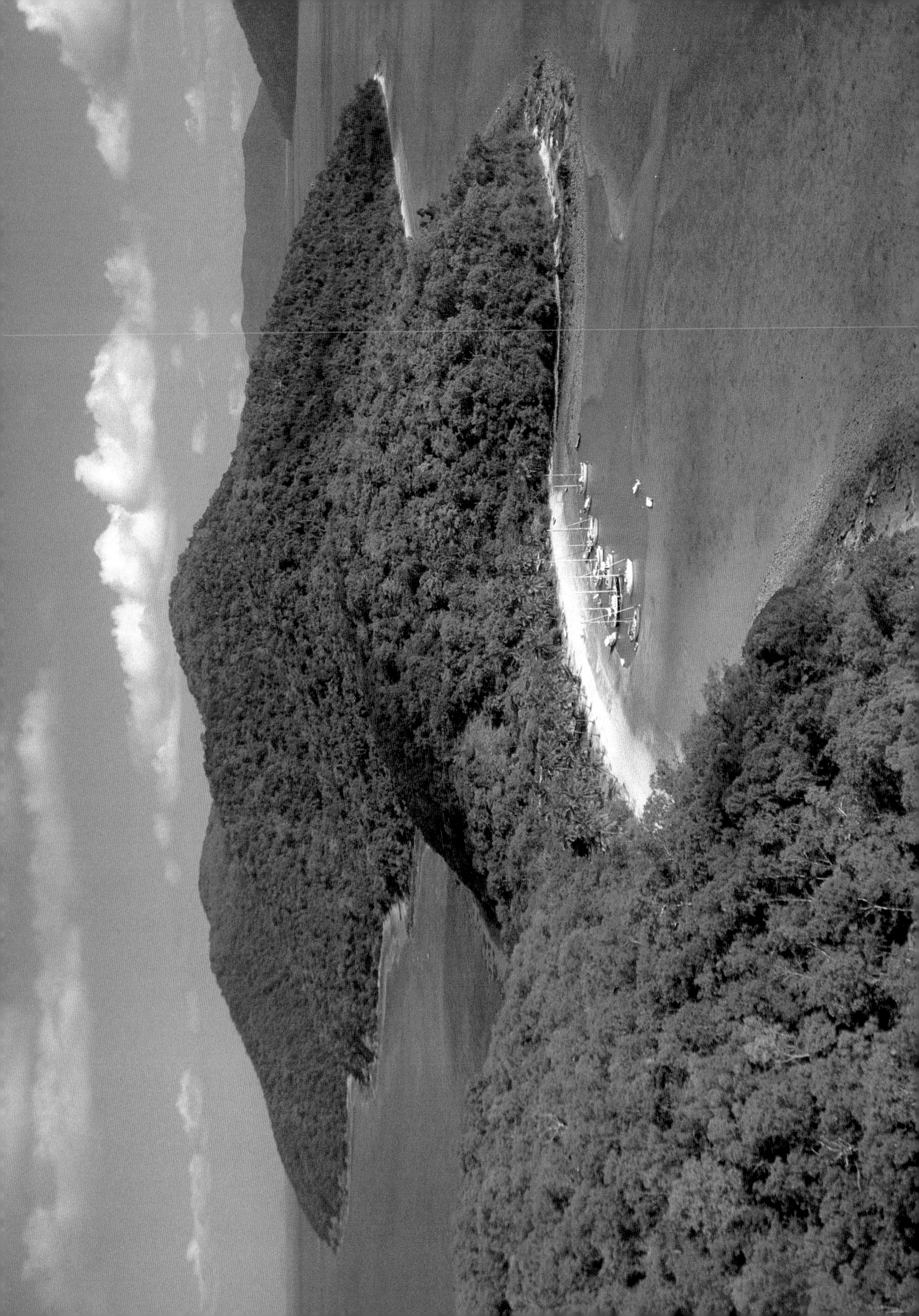

LONG ISLAND

2

3

Long Island is the closest resort island in the Whitsundays to the mainland. Both are separated by a deep channel about one kilometre wide.

As the name implies, the island is long and narrow. It is nine kilometres in length and about two kilometres in breadth at its widest point.

It is also one of the prettiest islands within the Whitsundays.

The vegetation on it is extremely dense with patches of lush rainforest in protected gullies with pines and eucalypt forest in more exposed areas. Indeed, much of the island – particularly the southern end – is inaccessible by foot because of the dense vegetation.

Fortunately, there are some excellent walking trails on Long Island which are maintained by the National Parks and Wildlife Service since the island is classified as a National Park with the exception of three resort areas.

Two of these resorts are quite small. The simple, unpretentious nature of both resorts is not unlike those of the early resorts established in the Great Barrier Reef region decades ago.

4

1. An aerial photograph of Palm Bay. A small, unpretentious resort here has attracted visitors for over 40 years.

2. Palm Bay is a favourite destination of yachtsmen sailing in the Whitsundays.

3. At Happy Bay, near the northern end of Long Island, there is a resort which caters exclusively to 18 to 35 year olds.

4. Half a dozen people relax on a catamaran at Happy Bay.

1

1

2

3

4

5

1. Moss covers a fallen tree in rainforest near Sandy Bay.

2. Delicate fungi are a common sight in the rainforest.

3. Dense rainforest covers much of Long Island.

4. Plants and trees with strange and twisted shapes can often be seen in the rainforest.

5. As you walk along trails you will often see wild goats.

6. East Rock is an islet on the eastern side of Long Island. Whitsunday Passage lies beyond it.

7. Pelican Island.

One is at Palm Bay which is also a favourite port of call for yachts and motor cruisers. The second is at Paradise Bay, at the southern tip of Long Island.

The third resort is at Happy Bay. Called Contiki Whitsunday Resort, it is the only resort in the Great Barrier Reef region which caters exclusively to those in the 18 to 35 year old age group.

The scant remains of a wooden ship - once believed to be an ancient Spanish galleon - lie at Happy Bay.

On the seaward side of Long Island you will often see turtles and the island itself is home to many birds.

Walks through lush rainforest.

Long Island has about 13 kilometres of walking trails. These all run through the top half of Long Island. A circular track runs north of the Contiki Resort. Another - with one or two side tracks - runs between the Contiki Resort and the Palm Bay Resort. A third track runs south from the Palm Bay Resort to Sandy Bay on the south-western side of the island.

The track from the Palm Bay Resort to Sandy Bay is 4.3 kilometres long. As you walk along it (and any of the other tracks) do not be surprised if you occasionally see wild goats. These were introduced to some of the Whitsunday islands decades ago but are gradually being removed so they will have no further detrimental effect on the natural habitat.

The track first wanders over to the eastern side of Long Island and from it you can catch some wonderful panoramic views of Whitsunday Passage and the islands beyond.

As the track meanders back towards the western side of Long Island you will soon find yourself enclosed by a canopy of dense rainforest. Vines are draped off towering trees. Light or brightly coloured fungi cling to some trunks and countless ferns line the track. At times, the path itself seems just like a tunnel - with light barely visible at the end.

About two thirds along the track you will come across a very large mound, over two metres in diameter and about one and a half metres high. The mound is made mainly from dirt and leaves and is the nest of the native Scrubfowl. This bird builds the mound high to protect its eggs from reptiles and incubates them in the warmth of rotting organic material.

Once you reach Sandy Beach you will

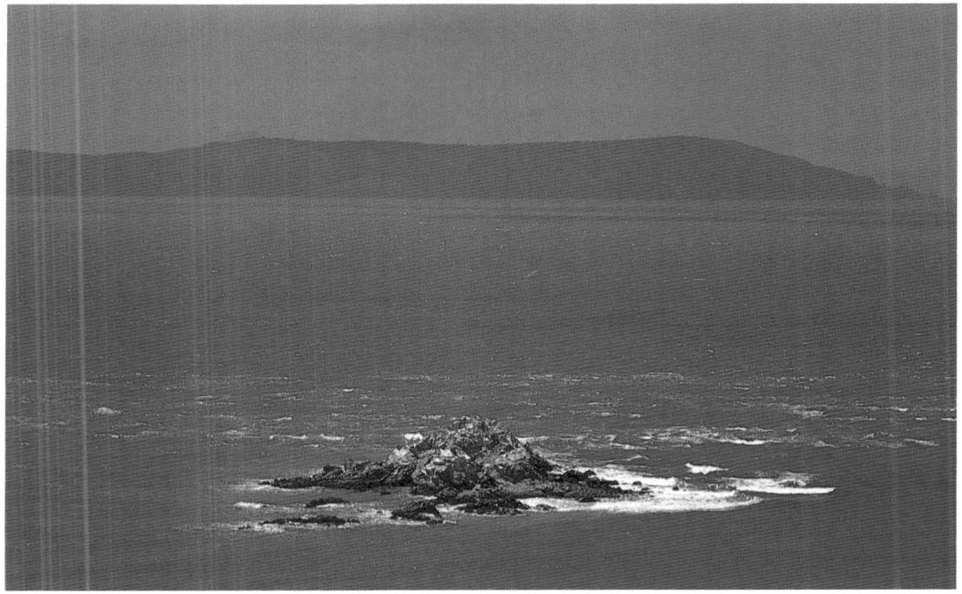

6

7

come across patches of mangrove and a very shallow beach. At high tide you could swim here but at low tide the water retreats some 100 metres or more.

It is an enjoyable and interesting walk - but it is worthwhile taking some insect repellent along since the area directly around Sandy Bay seems to be a favourite spot for mosquitoes.

On your walk to Sandy Bay or on the way back to the Palm Bay Resort you can deviate off the main track onto another called the Panoramic Circuit. This rejoins the main track after a kilometre. A look-out on this route gives excellent views of the more rugged coast on the eastern side of Long Island.

The walk to Sandy Bay and back will take you about three hours. If you wish to go to the look-out only on the Panoramic Circuit you will find the turn-off to this just half a kilometre from the resort.

The track between the resorts at Palm Bay and Happy Bay is 2.2 kilometres long. A few minutes from the Palm Bay resort you will come to a "cross road". To the left there is a short path down to Fish Bay and to the right there is a short track down to Pandanus Bay.

Fish Bay is a small cove and its main feature is mangroves. It no doubt received its name because of the plentiful fish life that usually thrives around mangroves. When aborigines lived on Long Island this was apparently one spot where they often fished.

Further along the track you will come to yet another turn-off. Whereas the vegetation has been mainly rainforest up until this point, Australian eucalypts begin to dominate the landscape.

A fork to the left takes you to Humpty Point which gives you a lovely, elevated view of Palm Bay - with several cabins visible amongst the palms and yachts dotted along the waterfront. This diversion is well worth taking, especially if you have a camera.

The fork to the right leads to Happy Bay. Just before reaching this you will also see a short Round Hill Circuit sign-posted.

Probably the most interesting walk is the Whitsunday Circuit which runs in a circular fashion north of the Contiki Resort. It is about 3.5 kilometres long and will take you an hour to complete in leisurely fashion.

If you walk anti-clockwise you will soon gain elevation and enjoy sweeping views over Whitsunday Passage. Immediately in the foreground - just off-shore from Long Island - you will see a small island called Pelican Island and a rocky islet named East Rock.

On the other side of Whitsunday Passage you will clearly see Dent Island, Henning Island, Whitsunday Island, Cid Island and Hook Island. All of these are uninhabited with the exception of Dent.

On the north-eastern side of the island you will see quite a rugged coastline. The vegetation here is also more sparse because the area is exposed to the prevailing winds. Nevertheless, you will encounter small pockets of rainforest in protected gullies - and as you move away from the eastern side and head towards the western side of Long Island you will enter an uninterrupted area of lush rainforest.

On your walk you may be lucky enough to catch a glimpse of an eastern-grey

1

2

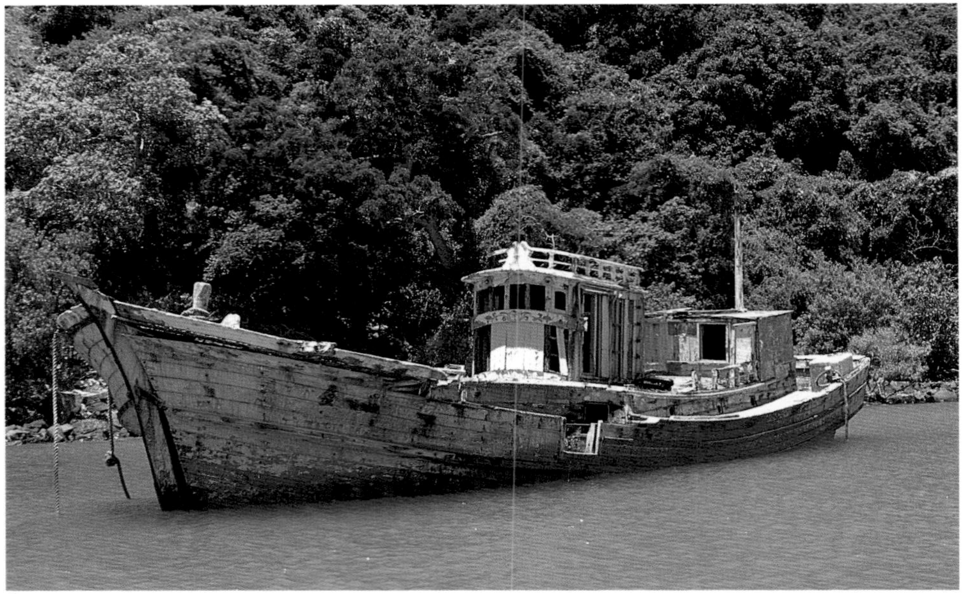
3

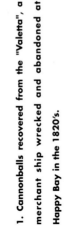

1. Cannonballs recovered from the "Valetta", a merchant ship wrecked and abandoned at Happy Bay in the 1820's.

2. Little remains of the "Valetta". A section of its keel, however, is clearly visible at low tide. More of the hull lies buried under mud.

3. The wreck of a junk also lies in Happy Bay. It was bought by a previous owner of the resort but was sunk during a storm.

kangaroo, a creature you will not see on other islands nearby. Most Whitsunday islands once had kangaroos and wallabies but these were hunted out long ago by the aborigines that once inhabited the area. Long Island seems to be the exception.

On the western side of Long Island you will follow the shore line of Happy Bay. As you do so you will see the wreck of an old burnt out junk. This vessel was originally confiscated from illegal fishermen in the 1950's, auctioned and subsequently bought by a former owner of the resort at Happy Bay.

A much older wreck lies in Happy Bay. At low tide part of a timber keel is partially exposed on the sand flats and for a long time it was thought to be the remains of an ancient Spanish galleon.

Decades ago, an old aboriginal inhabitant of Whitsunday Island told a story handed down by his parents that was thought to relate to this wreck. According to tradition, a large boat once sailed in from the direction of the Reef. Aborigines approached the strange craft and bartered fish but as they left the ship one was stabbed.

The other aborigines returned to shore and then plotted their revenge. At midnight they approached the ship with stealth and murdered all aboard her. According to the story, the ship finally drifted into shallow water where it eventually became buried in mud.

In the late 1890's a sheep-farmer who had settled on a nearby island apparently investigated the wreck. Digging through the sandy slush the wreck was buried in, he found several pieces of silver plate and cutlery.

Some distance from the beach he also found gold and silver coins of Spanish origin. Some were in bad condition but others looked as if they had just been minted.

In 1983, the wreck was excavated by Ron Coleman of the Queensland Museum and subsequently identified as the "Valetta", a private merchant ship with an interesting history. She was built in India in 1821, reportedly carried a cargo of opium to China in 1824, and carried a cargo of tea to Sydney in 1825.

On her return to Calcutta, however, she was damaged on a coral reef near the Cumberland islands. After repairs, the ship continued north but as she was leaking badly the "Valetta" was beached at Happy Bay and

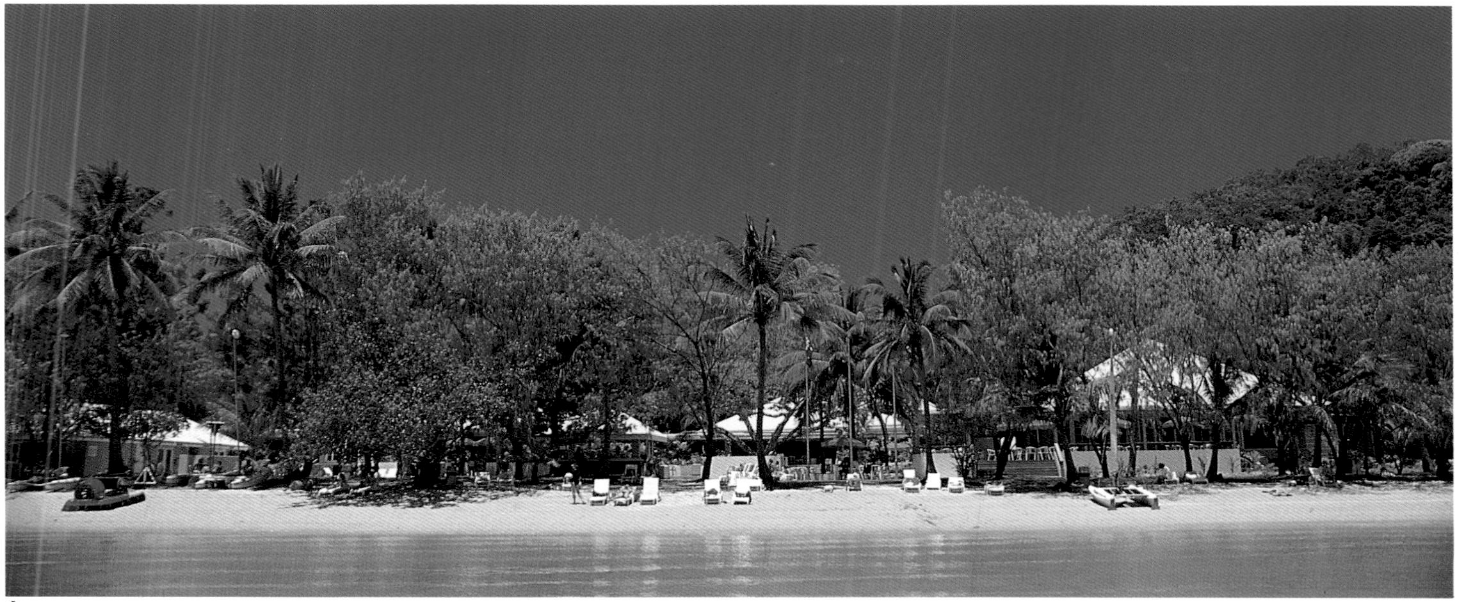

4

5

here she was eventually abandoned.

A resort at Happy Bay for those under 35.

The Contiki resort at Happy Bay has only been open since 1988. It caters exclusively to people between the ages of 18 and 35.

About ninety per cent of the guests are Australians with Canadians and Swedish tending to make up the other ten per cent. The resort can accommodate up to 400 guests.

Two grades of accommodation are available. There are 145 hotel rooms, each with a king sized double bed or two single beds. These rooms have their own en-suite bathrooms, radios, ceiling fans and balconies.

In addition, there are two lodges with 32 rooms for back-packers. Each room has four bunks and people in the lodges share communal amenities.

The accommodation overall is of excellent standard, with the hotel rooms comparing very favourably with those of more expensive resorts on some other Great Barrier Reef islands.

The facilities are also very good. The resort is laid out over a large area and the central complex has a restaurant, cafe, boutique, an entertainment lounge, disco and bar, a swimming pool with its own bar, and a games room with snooker tables and an irresistible range of video and pin-ball machines.

For those staying in hotel rooms, meals are included in the tariff. Back-packers pay for their meals separately.

Guests may eat in either the main restaurant, the Poinciana Room, or Pelican Bill's Cafe. The main restaurant offers a varying smorgasbord of hot and cold dishes with vegetables and salads for both lunch and dinner. Twice a week there is also a barbeque - one in the evening, one at lunchtime.

Breakfast is buffet-style.

Pelican Bill's is a cafe which is open from 9:30 a.m. to 4:00 a.m. next morning. As well as offering drinks, fruit, and hot and cold snacks it also has a special meal each day, often a pasta dish.

Overall, the standard of food is excellent without pretending to be of gourmet standard.

As you can probably imagine, a resort

4. The Contiki Whitsunday Resort at Happy Bay. It was opened in 1988 after being totally rebuilt.

5. Guests at the resort find a cool way to play volleyball.

1

2

3

1. The standard hotel-style rooms offered by the resort.

2. Although the beach is just metres away, the pool is a popular place to relax.

3. The resort's pool, spa and bar.

4. Yachts moored in the small lagoon at Palm Bay.

which caters exclusively to this age group has a wide range of activities to occupy and entertain guests. There are all the usual watersports like windsurfing as well as jet-skiing and parasailing.

Once a week you can board the yacht "Apollo" and sail to beautiful Whitehaven Beach on Whitsunday Island.

Three times a week, weather permitting, you can go out to the Reef itself by boat to snorkel or dive. You can also go reef-walking and view coral from a glass bottom boat. The destination is Hardy Reef which covers over 3,000 hectares and is the home for hundreds of species of coral and fish.

You can go out to Hardy or Bait Reef by seaplane as well (details follow in the Palm Bay section of this chapter).

Another excellent excursion by boat is to Manta Ray Bay on the northern side of Hook Island which has some of the best fringing reefs in the Whitsundays. A wonderful place to snorkel or dive, Manta Ray Bay is about 50 minutes away by boat from Long Island.

If you are staying at the Contiki resort and wish to dive for the first time, you have two choices. You can do a one-day introductory course and enjoy a single dive at Manta Ray Bay or out at the Reef with qualified instructors. Alternatively, you can do a full five-day P.A.D.I. course during your stay.

Another boat trip is aboard the Contiki Cat. This is a half day trip to various uninhabited islands where you can swim, snorkel and go oystering.

If you wish to explore more of Long Island by water you can also rent motor powered dinghies for either a half or whole day. Bait and tackle are available for those who like fishing.

At the resort there are other activities during the day including volleyball on the beach, cricket, water aerobics and tennis. There is even a gymnasium for the those who are serious about keeping fit.

Throughout the day there are often other more light-hearted activities. These vary from egg-throwing contests to Contiki's own Iron Man contest with somewhat different rules than normal. They're all fun and highly entertaining - at least for the onlookers!

At night-time the fun begins at 6:00 p.m. with Happy Hour and always continues after dinner. Sometimes there are duos, live bands or theme nights. Joke Night is

4

particularly outrageous but the atmosphere is like a party on many evenings. After the live entertainment finishes the discotheque opens.

The success of the evening can easily be gauged - by simply counting the number of people who manage to make it to the dining room for breakfast.

Many guests regain their strength by sunbaking on the main beach which lies directly adjacent to the resort. This is a safe, sandy beach - it is affected, however, by low tides when the water recedes quite some distance. Those who wish to cool off, however, may then use the swimming pool which is just metres away.

Contiki has a number of resorts elsewhere in the world catering exclusively for people between the ages of 18 and 35. With their experience they have established a resort on Long Island that will certainly have great appeal for those within that age group who wish to visit the Great Barrier Reef region.

Palm Bay, a place where time has stood still.

The resort at Palm Bay is a far cry from the stylish, sophisticated resorts on some of the other islands nearby and elsewhere on the Great Barrier Reef. Therein lies the appeal of Palm Bay because not everyone wants or needs all the comforts and facilities available elsewhere.

People first started to visit Palm Bay back in the 1940's and possibly beforehand. In many respects time has stood still at Palm Bay and the current management make no apology for this - indeed, they are rather proud of the fact. Even the cabins bear a remarkable resemblance in design to those built originally at Palm Bay over 40 years ago.

They know that there will always be a number of people who want to leave "civilisation" behind along with most of its trappings. Life at Palm Bay is refreshingly simple.

There are nine rustic cabins each set well apart to ensure privacy. All overlook a small lagoon on the western side of Long Island. The cabins each have a double bed and four bunks. They are also equipped with a refrigerator, electric stove, sink, cooking and eating utensils, crockery, linen and towels.

The two larger "Lamoo" cabins have private bathrooms and the slightly smaller "Koobala" cabins share a central amenities block. Naturally, the tariff differs for each type of cabin but both are very affordable.

In addition to the cabins there are a number of permanently erected Camp-o-tel tents overlooking Pandanus Cove. These have an electric light, a radio, a raised wooden floor, regular beds, a storage locker, as well as a table and chairs. Needless to say, this basic but adequate accommodation is even less expensive than the cabins.

The cost of staying at Palm Bay in 1958, incidentally, was £1/15/- per person - about $3. A full day's cruise around the Whitsundays cost $3 and dinner was about $1.

Today, a set and inexpensive two course meal - which changes daily - is available in the evenings. Guests can also

1

2

1. Palm Bay, a place to write home about.

2. Yachtsmen and landlubbers alike enjoy the simple facilities of Palm Bay's resort.

3. Two visitors soak up the sun on Palm Bay's coral beach.

4. Guests have the choice of staying in one of 11 cabins or in Camp-o-tel tents.

cook their own meals either in their cabins or at the excellent barbeque facilities alongside the "Palm Trader" kiosk. This small store has a selection of meats, fresh fish, dairy produce, vegetables, and other basic items including toiletries.

Once you have cooked some fish or a juicy steak outdoors you can then dine with other guests under the stars at wooden tables and benches. It's a little like being part of one big family.

Before or after dinner guests can relax in an open walled "lounge" complete with stone fireplace directly adjacent to the "Palm Trader" kiosk. Here you can have a quiet drink - in front of a fire in cooler weather - chat, read or play pool. Drinks are served from a very small and limited bar at the "Palm Trader". Guests are also free to bring their own supplies.

On some evenings a large camp fire is built and lit down near the beach. Then there may be an hour or so of games that always brings enjoyment and laughter from everybody, regardless of their age. Modern entertainment such as television, radio, discos and floor shows are long forgotten as people just enjoy good old fashioned fun and sometimes a sing-song together - plus a beer or glass of wine, of course, to add to the conviviality of the occasion.

If you are staying at Palm Bay you are welcome to dine at the restaurant at the Contiki Resort, 15 or 20 minutes walk away. You may also go to the bar and discotheque there, too. Just remember to take a torch for the walk home!

Some of the new friends you will probably make at Palm Bay will be visiting yachtsmen or people off motor cruisers. Palm Bay is a popular spot for people who have chartered or are sailing their own boats around the Whitsundays.

They are drawn to Palm Bay because of the friendly nature of the place and the fact that there is a safe anchorage here. A channel through the fringing coral reef gives access to a small deep-water lagoon that gives boats excellent protection.

Boats are secured side by side by rather unconventional means. Once an anchor has been dropped over the bow yachtsmen use long ropes looped around some of the sturdy palm trees along the beach in order to secure their sterns.

During the day adults and children alike play and swim in the small lagoon. It is

3

4

a safe swimming place all year round. The resort has an in-ground swimming pool, too.

Guests can also hire sailboards, canoes, paddle skis and dinghies. These are ideal if you wish to do a little fishing. Waterskiing and parasailing can be enjoyed by guests as well.

If you wish to snorkel, try the eastern side of the island, just a moment's walk from the resort (snorkelling gear is available for hire).

The coral is not nearly as extensive as that around some of the other islands - and will in no way match the coral gardens found at outer reefs, but there is still underwater marine life to be seen.

On the eastern side of the island you will often see turtles mating off-shore during the summer months. From time to time you will also see whales passing through Whitsunday Passage, a sight that few will ever forget.

If you wish to visit one of the outer reefs like Hardy or Bait to either snorkel or dive, you can travel to Shute Harbour by launch in the morning and return late in the afternoon.

At Shute Harbour you can then board boats that go daily to the Reef. Others - including yachts like the famous 12-metre "Gretel" - will take you through the Whitsundays and stop off at other islands like South Molle, Hook (which has a popular Underwater Observatory), Hamilton and Daydream.

Another way to see the Reef is by seaplane. Seair Pacific have small seaplanes that will land at Palm Bay, pick you up and fly you over the Whitsundays and to the Reef. The flight takes about 30 minutes and is spectacular.

Their seaplanes land at either Hardy Reef or Bait Reef. At Hardy Reef there is a semi-submersible craft that will enable you to view this vast natural aquarium teeming with tropical fish. You will also have the opportunity to snorkel and get an even closer look at dozens of colourful soft and hard corals. It is an experience that is quite magical. About two hours is spent at Hardy Reef.

At Bait Reef you can view coral from a glass bottom boat, snorkel or go reef walking. One and a half hours is spent at Bait Reef.

The service Seair Pacific provide is excellent and the pilots are very friendly. In short, their service is highly recommended. Seair Pacific is based close to nearby Shute Harbour and their phone number is (079) 469 133.

Scenic flights around the Whitsundays are available too.

How long Palm Bay will stay as the small low-key place it currently is nobody can really say. There is probably little doubt that Palm Bay will be totally redeveloped at some point in the future.

Until then, however, this pretty spot will be a relaxing hideaway for both landlubbers and visiting yachtsmen who enjoy its very down-to-ground charm.

One visitor to Palm Bay compared it to "Gilligan's Island" and considered it to be one of her favourite destinations within the Whitsundays.

A small leaflet for Palm Bay, printed just over 30 years ago, has a short poem on the

1

1. Life at Palm Bay in 1954. Note the tame wallaby.
2. Paradise Bay, a secluded spot at the southern end of Long Island.

front of it. The words still encapsulate the attractions of this delightful place.

"I must go down to the sea again,
To the lonely sea and sky,
To the swaying palms,
To the rippling waters,
To the glorious sunshine,
Palm Bay."

Another small resort at Paradise Bay.

An even more secluded spot than Palm Bay is Paradise Bay at the very southern tip of Long Island. Here there is an even smaller resort that attracts both families and back-packers seeking budget accommodation, often for just several days, amidst tranquil and uncrowded surroundings.

There are six self-contained units at Paradise Bay which accommodate up to four people. There is also a bunkhouse with six bedrooms, each with four bunks. Campers are welcome as well.

Both the cabins and bunkhouse offer very basic accommodation and facilities, but the tariffs reflect this.

Guests must bring their own food and liquor although the Trading Post offers basic food items like canned vegetables, milk, tea and coffee, as well as some toiletries.

You can cook either on the gas stoves in the units or at a barbeque area.

At Paradise Bay there is an excellent beach. There are paddle skis for hire and also dinghies (bait is available at the Trading Post for fishing).

There are no true walking trails at this end of Long Island but it is still possible to explore the shoreline and wooded areas behind the resort.

The tiny resort - which is run only by one couple - is not geared up for boat trips to the Reef and so forth. Guests who wish to see the coral gardens of the Reef itself usually take day trips from nearby Shute Harbour prior to their arrival at Paradise Bay or fly out by seaplane with Seair Pacific.

Like the Palm Bay resort, the one at Paradise Bay does not pretend to cater for those who want luxury accommodation, a large range of activities and night-time entertainment.

However, for those who enjoy the basic things in life - including beautiful, unspoiled surroundings - Paradise Bay will prove to be a peaceful and affordable destination far from the maddening crowds.

How to get to Long Island.

Direct access to Palm Bay is by launch or seaplane. The launch departs from Shute Harbour - which is just eight kilometres away - at 9:15 a.m. and 3:15 p.m.

If you wish to travel by air you may fly into Proserpine Airport where there are coach connections daily to Shute Harbour - or you can fly to nearby Hamilton Island with Ansett and then transfer to Palm Bay by launch (this transfer should be arranged with the resort prior to arrival). You may also fly from Shute Harbour by seaplane with Seair Pacific.

The postal address of the Palm Bay Resort is P.M.B. 28, Mackay, Queensland, 4740. Their phone number on Long Island is (079) 469233. Facsimiles can be sent to the same number.

To travel to the Contiki Whitsunday Resort at Happy Bay the arrangements are similar. If you arrive via Hamilton Island you will be automatically transferred to the resort's launch for a 30 minute boat trip to the island. You may also catch a water taxi to Happy Bay from Shute Harbour morning and late afternoon.

The postal address of the Contiki Whitsunday Resort is P.M.B. 26, Mackay, Queensland, 4741. Their telephone and facsimile numbers are (079) 469400 and (079) 469555 respectively. Their telex number is 48117.

Access to the small resort at Paradise Bay is by the boat "Escape", which departs from Shute Harbour four times a week. At other times you can reach Paradise Bay by seaplane or water taxi.

The resort cannot be contacted direct by telephone but more information and bookings may be made through the office of Airlie Beach Travel. Their telephone number is (079) 466255.

Long Island, as you have probably realised by now, has various attractions. If you want a low-key, inexpensive holiday there are the small resorts at Palm Bay or Paradise Bay. If you are between 18 and 35 you can enjoy yourself at The Contiki Resort, the only resort in the Great Barrier Reef region that caters exclusively to this age group.

The belief that a Spanish galleon was once wrecked at Happy Bay provided the island with a special feeling of romance and adventure for many years. Many visitors would agree, however, that although that legend has been dispelled you can still find adventure and romance on Long Island.

2

ORPHEUS ISLAND

2

3

1. The resort's beach at Hazard Bay.

2. Sir Ninian Stephen, former Governor General of Australia, arrives on Orpheus Island for a holiday, accompanied by his wife and bodyguard.

3. Visitors to Orpheus picnic on uninhabited Havannah Island, another island within the Palm Group.

4. A Sea Eagle's nest occupies a precarious position at Iris Point, the northern tip of Orpheus Island.

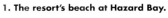

1

Orpheus Island has attracted travellers from all over the world since the late 1930's, including the rich and famous. The American author of many classic westerns, Zane Grey, and the actress Vivien Leigh were among the first to visit the island decades ago.

Orpheus Island lies about 80 kilometres north of Townsville and is 24 kilometres from the mainland.

This small, volcanic island - which is surrounded by coral reefs - is about 11 kilometres long, one kilometre wide and covers some 3,400 acres.

The island is now designated as a National Park. Over 50 varieties of birds have been recorded on Orpheus Island, and turtles nest regularly on its beaches.

Orpheus is the second largest island in the Palm Group of islands. This group of islands was discovered and named in 1770 by Captain Cook after the cabbage-palms that are native to the area.

Orpheus Island itself was named in 1887 after a naval survey ship.

4

1

1. The cover of an old brochure advertising the attractions of Orpheus Island.

2. In a photograph taken 35 years ago, "Kingy", a local aborigine, prepares to harpoon a fish.

3. "Kingy" holds up a prize catch.

4. The resort's Dining Room back in 1954. Locally caught fish were usually served to the 20 or 30 guests.

5. The resort in 1954. A number of aborigines including "Kingy" worked at the resort.

It was first settled in the late 1800's and stone-walled sheep pens over a hundred years old can still be seen on the southern end of Orpheus. There are no sheep on the island today but you will sometimes catch a glimpse of wild angora goats.

During World War II a U.S. naval installation on the island serviced submarines. At Yankee Bay, submarines used to be demagnetised - and old generators, cables and other equipment can still be found there.

At Pioneer Bay there is a Marine Research Station. This was established by the James Cook University in 1980.

Today, a small exclusive resort at Hazard Bay caters to no more than 80 guests at a time. In 1985 it received the Award for Best Island Resort in Queensland.

Seclusion, fine cuisine, luxurious accommodation, game fishing, snorkelling, and island hopping are just some of the attractions awaiting those who visit Orpheus Island.

A tourist destination before World War II.

Orpheus Island was named by Lieutenant G.E. Richards who was surveying the waters of this region in 1887. He gave the island its name after a Royal Navy ship called "Orpheus" which was wrecked on the Manakau Bar in New Zealand on February 5, 1863. The ship's captain and 187 men perished with the vessel.

Orpheus himself, of course, was a legendary musician and poet of ancient Greece. Playing music on a lyre presented to him by the god Apollo, Orpheus enchanted both men and beasts.

There is no doubt that the island that bears his name has also enchanted many visitors over the years.

Tourists first began to visit Orpheus Island before World War II when George Morris, a local in the area, started a small resort. In 1951 it was taken over by the Taylors, a New Zealand couple, who ran it for 20 years.

Mr. Keith Benjamin, now living in Caloundra, visited Orpheus 40 years ago when George Morris was the proprietor and has fond memories of his visit.

"My lifelong friend Dick Richards and myself wanted to visit an off-shore island which had the best coral. We wrote to the director of the Brisbane Museum and he advised Orpheus so in February, 1948, in the middle of the cyclone season, we set out. We boarded a DC3 at Archerfield aerodrome and after a six hour flight arrived in Townsville.

We caught the last train to Ingham before a big train strike started, and then with the help of the local mailman we agonised the last few miles in his canvas hood Dodge Tourer before being deposited at Lucinda Point.

We were then met by the son of Pop Morris and boarded his fishing boat "Sapphire" for the two hour journey to the island.

We spent a delightful two weeks there - no rain and no cyclones. The board charge was three pounds and three shillings a week ($6.50) and we were the only guests.

The bunkhouses, I believe, were put together from wartime materials left on the island.

We slept in army style beds and candles lit us to bed.

Pop Morris was quite a character and would play cards from daylight till dark. His Chinese cook would deliver some delightful meals - then he asked if we liked the meat which turned out to be goat.

The island had a colony of goats and whenever he wanted fresh meat he would pop one off.

Fishing was extra good. Pop would fire a round into a school of Hardy-heads, which stunned would float to the surface where he gathered them for bait. We would row out to the edge of the reef and collect enough rock cod and red emperor in 30 minutes to keep us going for a week...

The superb reef was viewed by holding a glass bottom box over the side of a rowing boat...

The whole holiday cost me £100 ($200) of which £80 ($160) was Australian National Airways air-fare. I was 23 years old at that time and was earning a salary of £5 ($10) a week."

Needless to say, the long travel times and spartan conditions have long since disappeared but the beauty of the island has remained unchanged.

One well-known person who visited the island in September, 1961, was the actress Vivien Leigh.

She had various engagements on the stage in Melbourne, Brisbane and then Sydney. Vivien Leigh (also Lady Olivier at that time) had 12 days free after her engagement in Brisbane and before her appearance at the Theatre Royal in Sydney, so she and Lord Olivier holidayed on Orpheus.

2

3

4

5

1

2

Other guests who have visited the island include Mickey Rooney, Helen Reddy, Cheryl Ladd, Michael Parkinson, Maggie Tabberer, Elton John, the Duke and Duchess of Westminster, and Sir Ninian Stephen, former Governor-General of Australia.

One oil-rich sheik who visited the island brought with him an entourage of thirteen. Whether he considered this to be an unlucky number is uncertain but he left with fourteen, having added one of the island's waitresses to his crew.

Both the island and resort have been featured in a television drama series. The very first episode of the successful Australian mini-series "Return to Eden" was filmed on Orpheus.

Orpheus Island has also featured in the TV series "Lifestyles of the Rich and Famous".

An island with eucalypts, rainforest and grasslands.

Orpheus is the second largest island in the Palm Group. It has a craggy terrain rising to 172 metres above sea level. A series of beautiful sheltered bays with a total of seven sandy beaches border the island.

Geologists estimate that the granite base of Orpheus Island was formed around 270 million years ago. An interesting geological feature that can be seen along parts of the island's rocky shoreline are "ring dykes" where molten rock once filled cracks in the granite, resulting in an unusual spider-web effect.

Orpheus Island has a wide range of vegetation. In many of the gullies and around the sheltered bays you will find lush, green rainforest. Fig trees and Syzygium, a large tree which bears fruit and flowers on its knobbly trunk, are just two of the distinctive trees you will come across in the rainforest along with tangled vines and dozens of ferns. You may even see some of the spectacular wild orchids that grow in this tropical environment.

Some of the most luxuriant rainforest can be found on the western side of Iris Point which is at the northern tip of Orpheus Island. This spot can only be reached by boat.

Other areas of the island are covered in dense eucalyptus woodland comprised mainly of Moreton Bay Ash and Acacias. On the island there are also small bands of grassland. These can be seen in photographs taken in the late 1800's by Saville Kent, a naturalist, which suggests that they are a natural feature of the island and are not areas that were cleared by early settlers.

These areas are now favoured by the wild angora goats that were introduced to the island last century as a food source for wrecked sailors. You will almost certainly see some if you go for a walk, although they are somewhat timid. The goats - which have adapted to life on the island exceedingly well - are white, black, brown or a variation of all these colours.

Orpheus Island is home to countless birds as well. In the forest you will see brilliant yellow-bellied Sunbirds. You will also come across mounds of vegetation as high as three metres, built by the Orange-footed Scrubfowl to incubate their eggs. Several other species commonly seen around the forests are Spangled Drongos, Friarbirds and Crested Cockatoos.

3

4

Along the shoreline of Orpheus Island you will see birds like Reef Herons and Egrets. Soaring high above the bays you will often spot large Ospreys and Brahminy Kites on the look-out for prey.

If you wish to explore the island you will find that there are several walks you can take from the resort itself. A path near the southern end of the main beach will lead you up to the top of the ridge which bisects Orpheus and then down to Picnic Bay on the eastern side of the island.

From the top of the ridge you will be treated to a marvellous panoramic view of the Coral Sea and some of the other islands within the Palm Group. These are all uninhabited except for the largest one which you can see clearly in the distance as you face south-east. This is known as Great Palm Island and a large community of aborigines live there.

The population consists of aborigines who are descendants of the original inhabitants of Great Palm Island; there are also descendants of various mainland tribes who were brought forcibly to the island early this century but who now regard it as their home. Occasionally, you will see several fishing off Orpheus.

Picnic Bay is quite small and rocky so it is not ideal for swimming. However, as the name suggests, it is a perfect place to take a picnic and enjoy the spectacular scenery. You may order a picnic hamper at the resort (without charge) for an occasion such as this.

A feature of the landscape at Picnic Bay are the Black-boys. These plants are so named because of the high black stalks that protrude from them which, from a distance, bear a remarkable resemblance to the spears that aborigines once carried.

The walk to Picnic Bay will take you no more than 20 minutes. If you wish to walk further south on Orpheus Island you will find no marked track. That should prove no deterrent, however, since this part of the island is covered only by low grass and a rocky terrain that is quite negotiable - providing you have some good footwear.

Another short walk worth taking is up to the top of the hill directly behind the resort. Here you can look towards the outer reefs in one direction and enjoy a magnificent view of the mainland in the other direction.

The view of the mainland can be spectacular from this vantage point, particularly at sunset when fields of sugar

1. Black "ring dykes" are an unusual feature along parts of the rocky coastline on the eastern side of Orpheus.

2. A view of Picnic Bay with other islands within the Palm Group visible in the background.

3. A stone cairn built by a passing yachtsman in memory of Mr. Nicholson, his pet terrier.

4. The remains of an old shepherd's cottage at Pioneer Bay.

1

1. **Outcrops of coral at Havannah Island, another island in the Palm Group often visited by guests staying on Orpheus.**

2. **Colourful Staghorn coral at nearby Falcon Island. Holiday-makers on Orpheus can enjoy a day cruise to Falcon and Havannah Islands, both uninhabited.**

cane are being burned prior to harvesting.

Right at the top of the hill where you can enjoy these sights you will discover a small stone cairn. This was built in memory of Mr. Nicholson, a black and white terrier who sailed these waters with its master aboard the "Wandoo" between 1953 and 1966. For some inexplicable reason, this stone cairn has also become the final resting place of countless old shoes.

Because of the dense vegetation over much of the island the quickest way to explore Orpheus properly is by boat. Dinghies with outboards are available from the resort.

One destination worth visiting by boat is the northern end of Pioneer Bay. There is not only a lovely, sandy beach here. A track from the beach will take you up to the stone ruins of an old shepherd's cottage constructed in the 1920's.

A Research Station at Pioneer Bay.

Another place of interest to visit is the Research Station at the southern end of Pioneer Bay. This was established nine years ago by James Cook University, Townsville, and can cater for up to 20 visiting scientists.

The station is equipped with its own laboratory and sea-water aquariums and these are used to study the different marine species that are found around Orpheus. Scientists and students also stay at the Research Station to study the flora, fauna, birds and insects of the island.

Perhaps the most important project being conducted at the Research Station is the study of clams. These are seen as a valuable food source for the future. Scientists have already established that one hectare could yield six tonnes of nutritious food.

Although you are welcome to visit the Research Station you should first make an appointment through the resort office.

Marine life around Orpheus.

One reason that the Research Station was established on Orpheus is that it has some of the best coral anywhere in the Great Barrier Reef region.

Coral dislikes fresh-water sediment and the waters around Orpheus are much clearer than those immediately to the north or south.

The fringing reefs on the north-eastern and south-eastern ends of the islands are regarded as being especially good. Iris Point and Cattle Bay at the north-eastern end, and Harrier Point at the south-eastern end, are best reached by a dinghy with outboard.

Naturally, these are ideal locations for those snorkelling or diving.

The narrow channel directly between Orpheus Island and Fantome Island is considered to have the largest range of soft corals on the Great Barrier Reef. A good protected spot to snorkel is usually Juno Bay at the northern tip of Fantome Island. Here you will see a stunning array of hard and soft corals in brilliant colours including yellow, blue, green and purple.

You can snorkel directly off the main beach in Hazard Bay as well. Unfortunately, the live coral in this particular area is not abundant and this is evident when you walk out on the reef flats at low tide.

Apart from the excellent snorkelling and diving at the south-eastern and north-eastern ends of Orpheus Island, there is usually a trip at least once a week to an outer reef.

Incidentally, if you are interested in learning to dive, the resort offers a one-day introductory dive course or you may qualify for a PADI or NAUI Open-Water Certificate over five days.

If you are staying on Orpheus Island there are at least two other boat trips that you should consider taking.

The first is to Zoe Bay at Hinchinbrook Island. The highlight of this trip is a walk up to a spectacular spot, Zoe Falls.

The boat trip to Zoe Bay also includes an hour of superb snorkelling at Iris Point, the northern tip of Orpheus Island.

The other boat trip which you should not miss is a cruise to two of the beautiful and uninhabited islands within the Palm Group.

The islands visited may vary but often include Havannah and Falcon, lying to the south-east of Great Palm Island.

When the boat reaches Havannah there is time to sun-bake, beachcomb for shells or view some of the wonderful coral that lies immediately off-shore.

As you do this, the crew of the boat are unfolding chairs and preparing a wonderful luncheon on the beach.

As you gaze out over the turquoise waters of the Coral Sea and enjoy the feast with half a dozen new friends, it is very hard to imagine a more enjoyable experience.

After lunch, the next stop is Falcon Island. This is another totally uninhabited island which the small party has completely to themselves. The main attraction here is the profuse and brilliantly coloured corals which abound around the edge of the island.

2

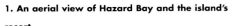

1

2

1. An aerial view of Hazard Bay and the island's resort.

2. A picturesque scene of Hazard Bay and the resort's jetty.

3. The resort's restaurant where guests enjoy meals of a very high standard.

4. The interior of a Studio unit.

5. Beautiful gardens surround guest accommodation.

6. Six luxury villas are also available for rent.

7. The resort's pool area.

On the way home, hand-lines are dispensed and lures are attached in the hope of catching a decent sized fish. All in all, it's a memorable day, and worth every cent.

Game fishing is a key attraction for some who visit Orpheus. Trunk and Bramble Reefs, two outer reefs, are 50 kilometres away and large schools of small Black Marlin congregate in these areas. The waters near Orpheus are also the spawning and breeding grounds for Spanish Mackerel.

Winner of several prestigious Awards.

Few resorts offer the same standards as those found on Orpheus Island. In 1984 it was selected as "The Pacific Resort Sanctuary of the Year", and in 1985 the resort won the Queensland State Tourism Award.

The resort, which is situated on the protected western side of the island, has a very European flavour to it. The architecture is very Mediterranean in style and complements the island and environment perfectly.

There are two bungalows and 23 studios that are finished in white stucco. The windows, doors and eaves are all made from handsome Australian redwood and Queensland pine. Cool terracotta tiles from Italy line the floors.

All contain queen size beds with gossamer white mosquito nets looped up on bamboo frames, a comfortable lounge area, refrigerator and mini-bar, radio, air-conditioning, ceiling fans, and an en-suite bathroom.

Both the bungalows and studios are situated just a stone's throw from the beach and are situated in beautiful gardens with colourful and fragrant hibiscus, bougainvillea and poincianas. The bungalows are a little larger than the studios, contain king-size bath tubs and have a private courtyard off the bathroom.

Set up on the hill directly behind the resort are six luxury villas. These are available for letting through the resort too, and accommodate up to four people.

Because of the way the resort has been designed and the fact that it accommodates no more than 80 guests you will never get the feeling of being hemmed in. There is a separate indoor/outdoor area with comfortable cane furniture where one can lounge, read, play backgammon or simply sip coffee or drinks, a bar and a very spacious restaurant.

In the restaurant the guests are tempted

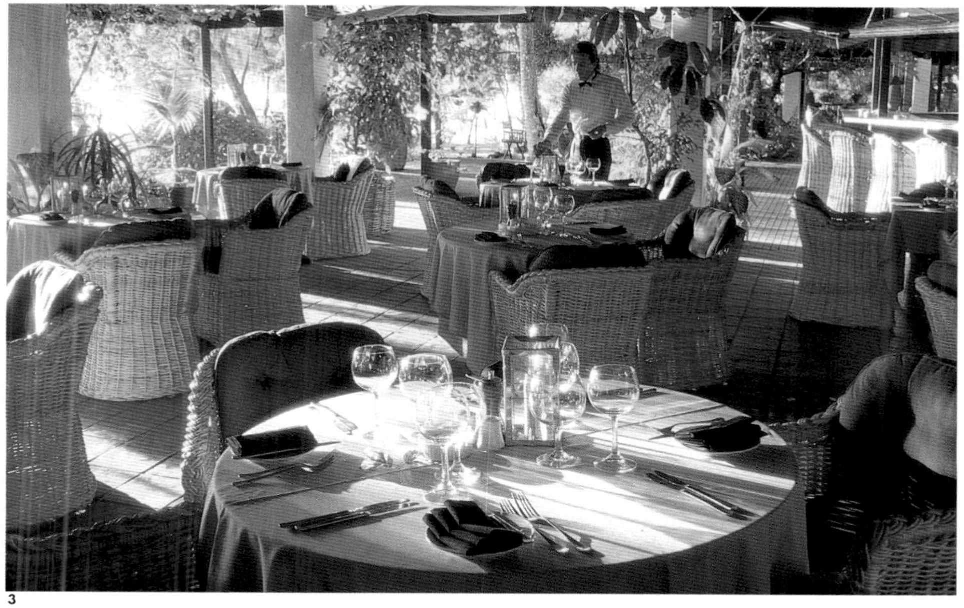
3

4

5

6

7

with one culinary delight after another. Much time and great effort is taken to serve meals of the highest standard. In this respect, few other resorts on the Great Barrier Reef would match Orpheus.

The evening's menus are never the same but here is an example of what guests were offered on one occasion. For soup, Cream of Artichokes and Coconut. Entrees were Garfish in Vinaigrette or Vegetables in Filo Pastry.

For the main course there was a selection of three dishes - Scallops with Mango Puree and Capsicums, Chicken Breast with Prawn Farce, or Veal Kidney in Pepper and Mustard Sauce. Accompanying vegetables were Pommes Lyonnaise, Pumpkin Puree and Braised Lettuce. The main course was followed by a choice of Tamarillo Sorbet or a Frozen Lemon dessert.

The restaurant has an extensive wine list of both Australian and imported wines.

Needless to say, both other meals - breakfast and lunch - are also worth writing home about. Breakfast is a la carte, and for lunch there is usually a small but wonderful menu of hot and cold dishes.

All these meals are included in the tariff, as are activities like tennis and watersports such as catamaran sailing, sail-boarding, paddle boards, snorkelling equipment, the use of runabouts and glass-bottom coral viewing cruises.

To help ensure that you enjoy a quiet and peaceful stay you will find that no day-trippers are permitted to visit the resort. Nor are children twelve years and under catered for at the resort.

How to get to Orpheus Island.

Should you wish to contact the resort direct, write to Orpheus Island Resort, Private Mail Bag, Ingham, Qld. 4850. The telex number is 47434 REEFIS. Their telephone and facsimile number is (077) 77 7377.

The easiest way to get to Orpheus Island is by seaplane. Seair Pacific flights leave Townsville International Airport every day except for Tuesday and Thursday. This scenic flight takes approximately half an hour.

Seair Pacific also has flights from Cairns to Orpheus three times a week which take one hour and 35 minutes. Helicopters can be chartered from Townsville.

Orpheus Island is one of the least publicised islands on the Great Barrier Reef. The select group of people to whom it caters, however, are very well aware of its existence and many return to the island again and again.

A recent survey conducted amongst visitors to this exclusive hideaway asked the respondents what they would like to change or add. Most replied, "Absolutely nothing".

It should be noted that Orpheus Island is not just restricted to those people staying at the resort. Camping is permitted in three areas on Orpheus Island. Permits are needed, however, from the Queensland National Parks and Wildlife Service prior to visiting the island.

The music of Orpheus, the legendary poet and musician of ancient Greece, won the hearts of all who heard it. The island that bears his name on the Barrier Reef has also won countless hearts - and there is little doubt that it will continue to do so in the future.

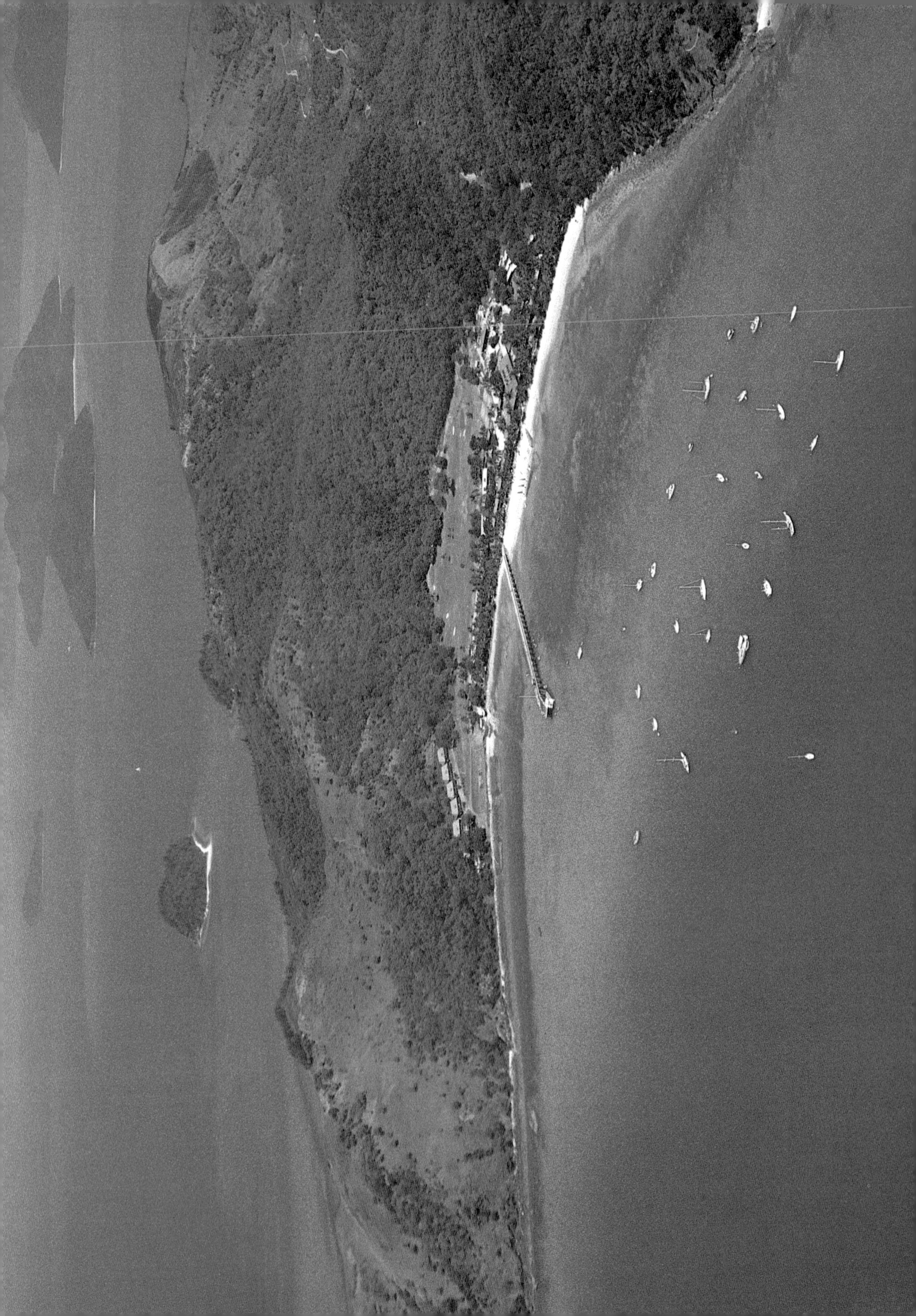

SOUTH MOLLE ISLAND

2

3

South Molle Island was named after an early Lieutenant-Governor of New South Wales, George James Molle, a friend and later a foe of Governor Macquarie.

The island itself is in the magnificent Whitsunday Group of islands - about eight kilometres north-east of Shute Harbour.

This places it about 900 kilometres north of Brisbane and 500 kilometres south of Cairns.

South Molle is a hilly and picturesque island that is four kilometres long and two and a half kilometres wide. It is lightly timbered, has pockets of lush rainforest and undulating grasslands on the western side. The island also has a number of secluded bays, and fringing reefs.

The temperature in the summer ranges between 24°C and 30°C, and in the winter is a comfortable 20°C to 24°C. The water temperature remains constantly warm all the year around, staying around 20°C to 22°C.

Aborigines once lived on the island but the recorded history of the island began when Cook sailed through the Whitsundays in 1770.

4

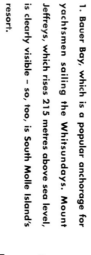

1. Bauer Bay, which is a popular anchorage for yachtsmen sailing the Whitsundays. Mount Jeffreys, which rises 215 metres above sea level, is clearly visible – so, too, is South Molle Island's resort.

2. Every day hundreds of colourful Lorikeets congregate near the island's golf course to be hand fed.

3. One of the large and fast catamarans which take guests from South Molle Island to the outer reefs.

4. Spion Kop is the second highest peak on South Molle Island. From the top you can enjoy spectacular views over Whitsunday Passage and many islands in the Whitsunday Group.

1

Back in the late 1800's the island was developed as a sheep property. Today, it is classified as a National Park and has a well-run resort at Bauer Bay which caters to people of all age groups. Because of the excellent facilities and activities during both the day and evening, it is a very popular choice for those with families.

There are some excellent walks on the island, and guests can enjoy regular cruises to the Reef and several other islands within the Whitsundays.

Known as "Whirriba" to the aborigines.

Aborigines used to both visit and inhabit South Molle Island long before any European ventured into the area. It was known to the local aborigines as Whirriba, after the basalt stone that they gathered on the island to make axes and cutting tools.

The island received its present name from Lieutenant Charles Jeffreys of the brig "Kangaroo" in 1815 - although the name was first given to Port Molle, the sheltered area of water between the island and the mainland.

George James Molle was commanding officer of the 46th Regiment when it arrived in New South Wales in 1814. Molle was soon appointed Lieutenant-Governor and was a friend of Governor Macquarie until they clashed on a number of public issues. When his regiment was relieved in 1817 by the arrival of the 48th Regiment, Molle departed for Madras.

South Molle was not settled by people of European stock until 1883. This was the year that Mr. D.C. Gordon took up a leasehold on the island and ran sheep and cattle on it. He lived in a small dwelling on the site where the resort now stands.

By 1901 the station on South Molle was being managed by Joseph William Hawkes. Since there were few settlers in the area in those days, life was rather lonely and Hawkes befriended an aborigine who had lived on nearby Whitsunday Island. His name was Goolgatta and he told Hawkes of many aboriginal legends and stories.

Before too long the lease on the island was bought by William Cooke of Runnymede, Cannonvale, a small seaside town on the mainland. In the year 1911 he experienced a week of drama that is well worth retelling.

Cooke was betrothed to an English girl and the marriage was to take place on the island itself. On the wedding day Cooke rowed a small dinghy across to Cannonvale to collect a wedding guest and the parson who was to conduct the ceremony. Elfreda Squires, his bride, and two relatives had already arrived on South Molle.

Unfortunately, Cooke and his two guests encountered a gale on their return trip to the island. Due to the groom's great determination and skilful boatmanship, however, they eventually arrived on the island by 7.p.m. that night - somewhat damp but safe.

The wedding ceremony took place that very evening. The bride wore a Japanese silk gown with a coronet of orange blossoms and the ceremony was conducted by the parson, still in wet trousers.

This was not the end of the story. The gale worsened and the wedding party were stranded on the island for another week. They were eventually picked up by the government steamer "Relief" which had been despatched after anxious friends on the mainland wondered if the party of three had ever crossed the channel from Cannonvale in safety.

South Molle changed hands several more times before it was acquired by Henry Lamond. He and his family left a property in outback Queensland, after a severe drought in 1927, to settle in the Whitsundays.

Lamond also purchased the leases on six other islands in the group including West Molle, better known today as Daydream Island.

Despite the fact that there was no electricity and little contact with the mainland the family enjoyed their self-sufficient lifestyle on South Molle immensely. They grew all their own vegetables and tropical fruits including papaws, guavas, custard apples and passionfruit. Wild goats provided them with meat, their cows supplied milk and butter. Of course, there was also plenty of fresh fish and oysters, too.

Lamond actually wrote about his life in the Whitsundays and became a well-known author world-wide because of his stories. Indeed, they undoubtedly encouraged many people to visit the area.

By 1936 there were a number of people living on other Whitsunday islands and some started to provide some very basic accommodation for holidaymakers but Lamond had no desire to share his "little Eden".

In 1937, however, Lamond put South Molle up for sale. Ernie Bauer, a sugar farmer from Bundaberg, heard about it and casually offered to exchange it for a dairy farm that he owned in Brisbane. Bauer's proposition was accepted and the new owner, along with his wife and eight children, arrived on the island in May of the same year.

Bauer saw that the holiday accommodation on other islands was basic, to say the least. Guests were often expected to stay in timber shacks that did not even have glass windows. Bauer decided he could offer much better facilities and set about building them.

The tourist trade in the thirties was small with guests arriving by coastal steamer. Most of Bauer's visitors came from Mackay and Townsville.

During the war, Bauer was often embarrassed by the scarcity of supplies, particularly drinks. This prompted him to visit Proserpine and purchase two empty casks.

He made ginger beer in an old wine cask, and beer in an old rum cask. When his daughter Irene and a friend were the first to sample the ginger beer they both ended up drunk - and Bauer had a bit of explaining to do.

Apparently the wine in the timber of the cask had mixed with the ginger beer. Likewise, the rum in the other cask mixed with the beer with equally potent results! He was subsequently nick-named "Bauer the Brewer".

With a lot of hard labour and a very small budget Bauer installed a diesel engine to provide electricity (previously kerosene provided the lighting), constructed a large water tank for fresh-water, built a lounge, dining room and kitchen, and added an

1

extra cabin one at a time made from timber and fibro.

He used to take guests out to the Reef aboard "Pearl", a 33' launch. The trip took four hours each way in those days and more than once they almost came to grief during bad weather.

Since it was still wartime Bauer felt compelled to take appropriate precautions. "In case the Japs invaded and burnt the settlement," he once wrote, "I dug a cave in a hill hidden in the centre of the island, and packed all tin fruit, etc., in it. Also bought a tank to store wheat, and having cattle, sheep and pigs on the island, we could hold out for years."

Fortunately, no invasion of South Molle ever took place but Bauer did once go to assist an American boat that got wrecked on Pine Island. He rescued the crew, took them back to South Molle Island and fed the grateful seamen.

On another occasion he towed a Catalina seaplane 60 kilometres to Bowen after it had developed engine problems.

When the war ended the number of visitors to South Molle grew and grew, and very soon the island catered for up to 200 people every Christmas and Easter. Bauer's philosophy was simple. He treated everyone alike - family, staff and guests - and provided an atmosphere of fun and informality that people found irresistible. In the evening his daughter Ruth entertained the guests by singing, dancing, games and jokes.

Bauer, who was known affectionately to everyone as "Pop", once said that his greatest satisfaction was meeting past guests in Brisbane, Melbourne and Sydney and hearing what a great time they had had on South Molle.

Walking trails to each part of the island.

In those early days, guests often got lost on the island because there were no established tracks. Search parties were despatched regularly to find them.

On one such occasion Bauer related that a black boy going with them was carrying a tin. Bauer asked him why he was carrying the tin. He said: "Suppose it rains, I put my clothes in the tin."

Today, guests may run the risk of getting a soaking from time to time but they need not worry about getting lost. There are a number of excellent, well-marked walking

1. An old photograph showing holiday-makers on South Molle Island decades ago. Guests first stayed on the island in the 1930's. They arrived by coastal steamer.

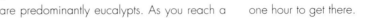

1

2

3

tracks and all are worth exploring.

The resort is situated at Bauer Bay which is on the northern side of the island. There are essentially five different walks from the resort - one takes you to Spion Kop, a high peak that is in the far north-eastern corner of South Molle; a second leads you to pretty Paddle Bay on the north-western corner; another takes you to Oyster Bay directly to the west; a fourth path winds up to Mount Jeffreys in the south-eastern area of the island; and then there is a track that takes you to Pine Bay and Sandy Bay, both secluded coves in the far south-western corner.

The destinations of these tracks are all very different and you will find something of interest along all four. All have scenic views that are picturesque, to say the least.

All the walks start near the first hole of the golf course, located behind the tennis court. At the beginning of the trail is a small stone monument. On it is an inscription dedicated to one of the first settlers on South Molle: "This island was the home of author Henry G. Lamond, his wife Eileen and family Hal, Amy and Bill, 1927-1937."

Several hundred metres further on, the track branches out to the different destinations, all sign-posted.

If you take the trail to Spion Kop you will find that it ascends fairly quickly - and within five or ten minutes you will have a magnificent bird's-eye view of Bauer Bay and the resort. You can also enjoy a beautiful view of Paddle Bay, which is the next one around from Bauer Bay.

The trees you will see along the way are predominantly eucalypts. As you reach a ridge that leads up to the peak you will come across a large grassy area and here you will find many colourful wild flowers.

As you near the top of Spion Kop the vegetation changes suddenly and you encounter trees and plants common to rainforest. The sunlight, in fact, is almost blocked out by the dense umbrella of trees and vines. Tucked in under large rocks and boulders you'll see many Maidenhair ferns.

Having reached the top of Spion Kop you will enjoy spectacular 360° views over the Whitsundays and the mainland. You can see a number of other islands including Hamilton Island (another resort island), Whitsunday Island, and Hook Island. The walk to the top of Spion Kop is 2.2 kilometres long and will take you a leisurely one hour to get there.

Another wonderful vantage point is Mount Jeffreys which is 215 metres above sea level. The walk to this look-out takes about one hour and, once again, gives you panoramic views of the Whitsundays and the mainland.

From Mount Jeffreys you can enjoy a wonderful view of Daydream Island - a small resort island lying to the west - and you can even see some of the boats moored close to busy Shute Harbour.

The two small uninhabited islands lying just off-shore to the south-east of South Molle are Goat Island and Denman Island.

You will discover that the southern side of South Molle is quite different from the northern half. There are undulating hills here with high grass that ripples in the breeze and

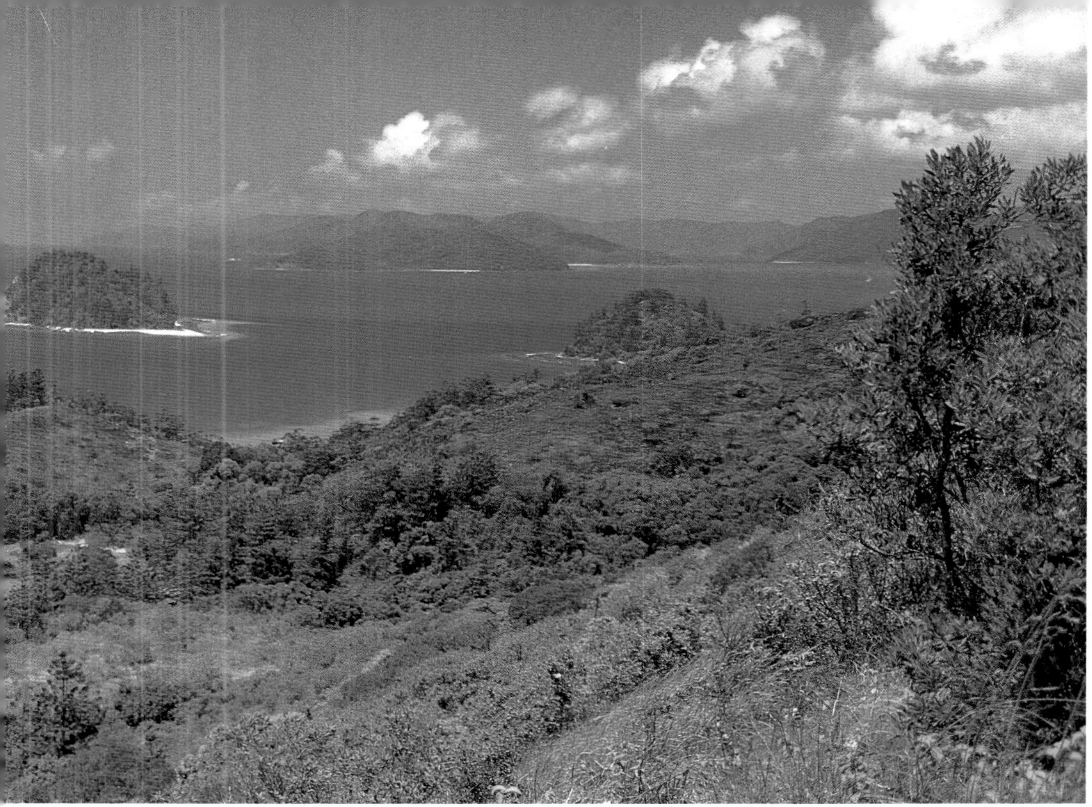

4

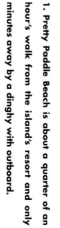

5

trees are far fewer in number.

The walk to Pine Bay or Sandy Bay at the very southern tip of the island will take you about one and a half hours (they are 3.8 kilometres away from the resort). Pine Bay is a fairly rocky little inlet whilst Sandy Bay is precisely that. Sandy Bay is undoubtedly the most enjoyable of the two and perfect if you wish to take a picnic and have a swim.

Incidentally, there is no track to Sandy and Pine Bay from Mount Jeffreys although the trail to these two places is clearly visible from the top of the peak. If the grass is not too long it is possible to walk along the ridge sloping down towards the south and join up with the other track in about ten minutes. This shortcut is not advisable, however, if you wish to stay spotless or if you are with children. If you do decide to try this shortcut be careful since the long grass can hide rocky obstacles and some very uneven ground underfoot.

When you take the marked trail from the resort to either Pine Bay or Sandy Bay you will pass through a place called the Hidden Valley. This is a small valley covered in dense rainforest. Here the vegetation is lush and green and you will see many ferns, colourful fungi and butterflies galore.

The walk from the resort to Oyster Bay, which is about 1.2 kilometres long, will take you about forty five minutes. This is to the west and is considered one of the best two places to do a spot of snorkelling at South Molle. The island directly off-shore from Oyster Bay is named Planton Island.

The best place for snorkelling is probably Paddle Bay. This is just half an hour's walk from the resort and has a lovely secluded beach with acres of coral off-shore. More often than not you will find that you have the whole beach to yourself.

Each week there are also several organised bushwalks including a night-time one and these last for an hour or two. An ex-National Parks and Wildlife Ranger usually accompanies guests on these and points out flora and wildlife on the island.

A resort that accommodates 600 guests.

About 75% of the visitors to South Molle are Australian and the remainder are from overseas - those being mainly Americans and Japanese.

Most of the visitors are either families or honeymooners, although some 5% of guests

1. Pretty Paddle Beach is about a quarter of an hour's walk from the island's resort and only minutes away by a dinghy with outboard.

2. Denman Island is a small and uninhabited island which lies to the south-east of South Molle Island.

3. The views from the eastern side of South Molle Island overlooking Whitsunday Passage.

4. Grassy, undulating hills in the south-western corner of the island.

5. Hoop Pines line one of the island's walking trails.

1

1. A spectacular way to see the outer reefs is aboard a Seair Pacific seaplane.

2. One regular destination of Seair Pacific flights is Bait Reef where you can view coral from a semi-submersible craft, and snorkel. Bait Reef is half an hour's flight from South Molle Island.

are singles. Depending on the season there are anywhere between 100 and 220 staff to look after guests.

Camping on South Molle Island is not permitted but yachtsmen are welcome - although there is a mooring fee - and it is a popular destination for them (particularly on weekends when they seek the lively entertainment on shore, as well as cool refreshment and company at the Endeavour Bar). Water and fuel are available to visiting yachtsmen (there is also a small bottle shop where they can replenish their alcoholic supplies!).

The activities and sports to be enjoyed on the island by visitors are varied. Apart from the 9-hole golf course there are tennis and squash courts, a gymnasium, archery, and watersports including windsurfing, sailing and paddle skis.

All these activities are included in the tariff. The only activities that are extras are water skiing, parasailing, hire of dinghies with outboards, and scuba diving.

There is also a large 25 metre swimming pool (swimming off the main beach at Bauer Bay is not possible at low tide because of the shallow water and coral).

There are cruises to an outer reef three times a week on South Molle's large air-conditioned catamaran which is capable of carrying 350 passengers and travelling at 37 knots. The destination is Hardy Reef which has 7,500 acres of coral. Out at the Reef you can swim, snorkel, scuba dive and go for a reef walk (when tides permit).

You can also marvel at the profuse and colourful underwater marine life of the Reef from a semi-submersible craft. In total, you spend a wonderful three hours exploring Hardy Reef. Snorkelling gear, the trip aboard the Coral Sub, plus an excellent smorgasbord lunch, morning and afternoon tea are included in the cost of the cruise.

You can go scuba diving as well if you are an experienced diver, since South Molle has its own Dive Shop with full facilities. If you would like to learn to dive you may do so.

Divers can explore Hardy Reef and Bait Reef - both outer reefs - in addition to some of the excellent fringing reefs of several Whitsunday islands.

Another excellent cruise, departing only on Sundays, takes you around Whitsunday Island which has a number of very beautiful inlets. The cruise also takes you past Hamilton Island, the largest resort island in the Whitsundays. You make a stop at Whitehaven Beach as well which must be one of the most beautiful beaches in Australia, and at the Hook Island Underwater Observatory. A smorgasbord lunch is included.

On Sundays there is a half-day cruise to Hamilton Island (see Chapter 10). A trip to the Fauna Park there is included.

Another wonderful way to see both the Whitsundays and the Reef is by seaplane or helicopter. If you can afford it, do not hesitate. A flight over the islands and the Reef gives you a view of the area that is absolutely spectacular.

Two companies offer these flights. The first is Seair Pacific, which operates small seaplanes. Helicopter flights are offered by the chopper fleet operating out of nearby Hamilton Island. Both companies pick up passengers from South Molle and return them there.

The craft of both operators land at the Reef where you can go reefwalking, snorkelling or diving.

The seaplane flight offered by Seair Pacific lasts about half an hour each way and you will spend about two hours out on the Reef. They offer various scenic flights around the Whitsundays, too.

The helicopter flight to the Reef takes about 40 minutes (the chopper lands on a large pontoon permanently moored on the Reef). The duration of the stay out on the Reef is about two hours.

Regardless of who you fly out with you can also see the wonders of the Reef from a semi-submersible craft. Either flight cannot be too highly recommended. Bookings for these trips can be made through Reception at the resort.

Back at South Molle you can always see more of the island by hiring a dinghy with outboard. One of these will take you quickly to secluded bays that might be difficult to walk to, and to North Molle Island which is both rugged and beautiful. Do not be tempted, however, to go too far and keep an eye on the weather.

You can also use these dinghies to go fishing. Tackle is available free of cost at the resort Gift Shop (although there is a small deposit). Around South Molle you can catch a huge variety of fish including Mackerel, Red Emperor, Coral Trout and Cod - and the chefs will happily serve your catch up for dinner. Many people have also had success fishing off the main jetty.

In addition, trips can be arranged aboard a professional game fishing boat.

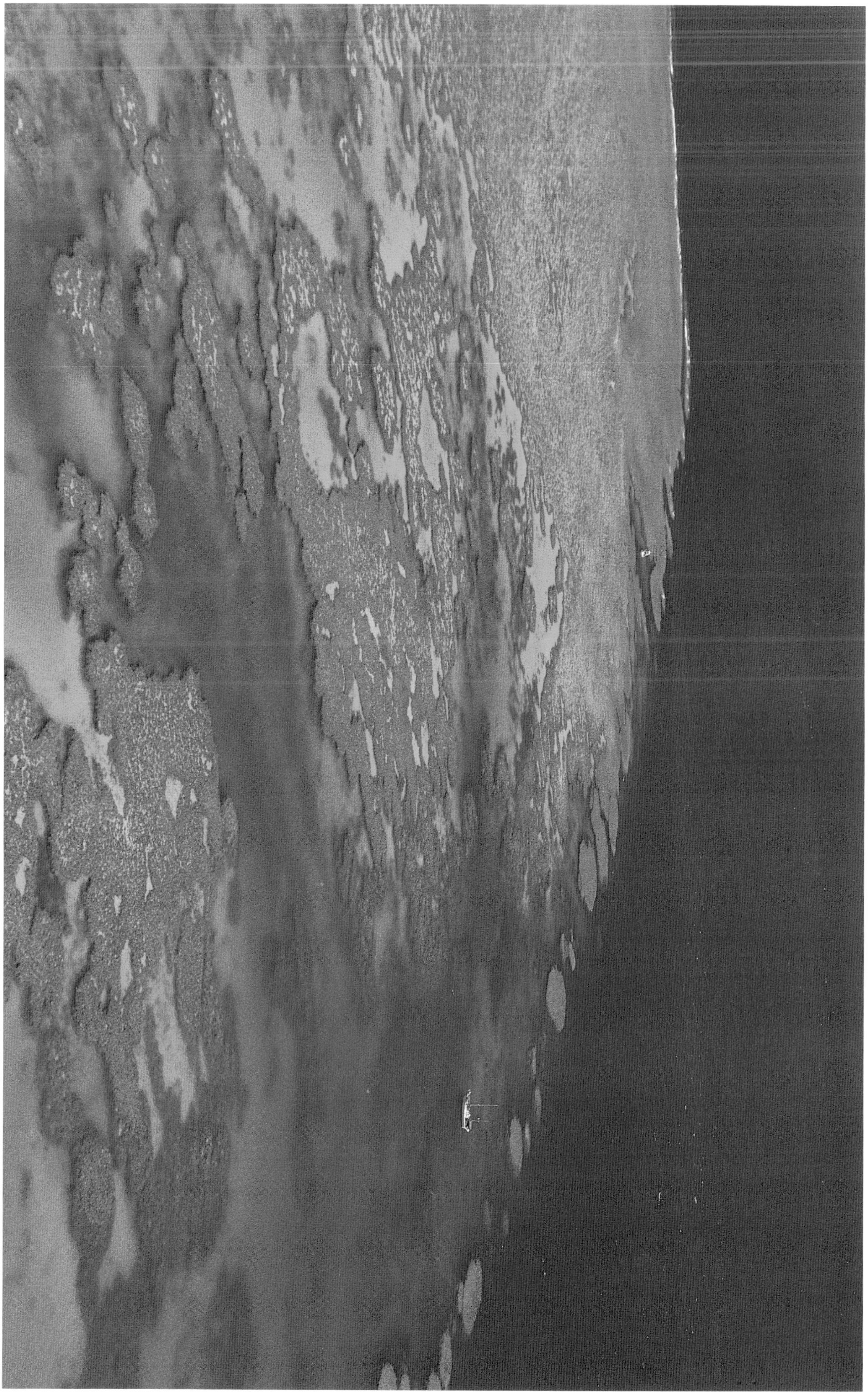

2

1

2

3

4

1. Whitsunday Units are situated just a few metres from the main beach.

2. Beachcomber Units lie on the western side of the resort and overlook Bauer Bay.

3. Most Reef Units enjoy views over the resort's golf course as well as Bauer Bay.

4. Bauer Bay, a sheltered stretch of water where resort guests can enjoy water skiing, sailing and windsurfing.

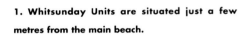

If you enjoy sailing, you can also spend a day aboard the first America's Cup Challenger "Gretel". This historic and graceful yacht cruises through the Whitsundays. Lunch is provided.

There is at least one other event worth noting. Each day at 3:00 p.m. hundreds of colourful Lorikeets congregate in and around the trees opposite the Golf Club, with the knowledge that they will receive a hearty meal. Each of these beautiful birds are a brilliant splash of colour and are a delight to see and hand-feed.

A variety of accommodation and restaurants.

There are three grades of accommodation available on South Molle Island - Whitsunday Units which directly overlook the main beachfront, Beachcomber Units which have uninterrupted views of Bauer Bay and the Whitsunday Passage, and Reef Units which are set in delightful garden settings just 30 or 40 metres from the beachfront.

The Whitsunday Units are the newest and are very attractively decorated. The age of the Beachcomber and Reef Units vary, some being older than others but the interiors of all are very pleasant and comfortable.

All units have air-conditioning, a colour television, radio, telephone and mini-bar.

The tariffs include all meals. Lunch at the resort is like most - an extensive smorgasbord of hot and cold dishes.

In the evening you have two choices. You may dine in the main resort restaurant called the Island Restaurant or in a smaller, intimate a la carte restaurant. The normal tariff does not cover a meal in the a la carte restaurant, but a credit of $10 applies for house guests.

Although the menu in the Island Restaurant would not compete with that of a premiere restaurant you will find that the dishes are, nevertheless, of very good standard - and are clearly enjoyed by most guests.

The menu of the Island Restaurant changes nightly but here is a sample of the dishes you might expect. There is always a Soup of the Day, followed by an appetiser such as Chicken and Ham Cutlets served with Mushroom Sauce.

You would then be offered a choice of four main courses such as Poached Fillets of Reef Fish (served in a White wine and Lemon

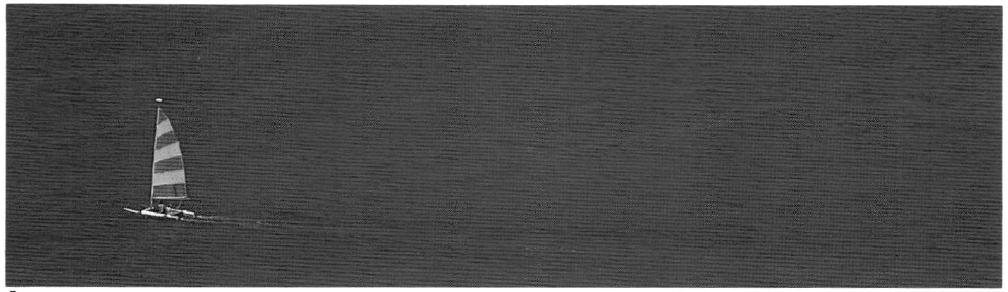

5

6

5. A catamaran skims across Bauer Bay on a perfect summer's day.

6. An unexpected obstacle sometimes encountered on the island's golf course.

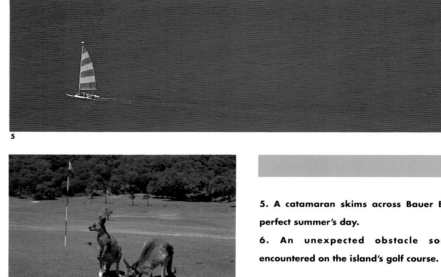

juice sauce enriched with cream), Roast Duckling, Veal Escalopes (served with a sauce of demi-glace, capers, sour cream and lemon zest), and Cold Roast Turkey Salad.

You will then be tempted with desserts like Fresh Tropical Fruit Salad, a selection of Pastries and Gateaux, Ice Cream, and a Cheese Board.

On Saturday evenings the Island Restaurant always features an Italian menu.

The wine list in the Island Restaurant features a good selection of Australian red and white wines which are very reasonably priced. House wines are also available by the carafe.

The menu of the a la carte restaurant is more extensive. There is a selection of entrees like Mushrooms and Crab Mousse (Crab Mousse moulded into Button Mushrooms, crumbed in sesame seeds, fried and served with Honey Soy sauce), a Russian Omelette (an omelette filled with strips of Smoked Salmon, diced Tomato, Avocado, sour cream and a touch of horseradish) and Pork Vindaloo (served with Banana, Apples and Toasted Coconut).

Main courses to choose from include dishes like Mignon Madagascar (Mignon of Prime Fillet topped with sauteed Bugs and served with a creamy green Peppercorn sauce), Fresh Fillets of Fish (grilled with Macadamia ground nuts or pan-fried with Lemon Butter), and Chicken Spion Kop (Chicken Breast filled with Crab Meat and Camembert Cheese, crumbed, pan fried and served with a Hollandaise sauce).

The wine list in the a la carte restaurant has an excellent and reasonably priced selection of Australian reds and whites plus some imported wines.

After dinner you can look forward to excellent entertainment in The Discovery Bar. Not all of the resorts on the islands feature extensive entertainment at night-time but South Molle is certainly one of the exceptions.

Throughout the week there are live shows with different themes presented by very talented and versatile resident singers and musicians. There are also talent quests, Polynesian dancing, toad racing (a unique Queensland sport!), Fancy Dress evenings and a disco most nights. All these are very popular and a lot of fun for young and old.

Around lunchtime the band often plays around the pool, too, much to the enjoyment of most guests.

Should you ever feel hungry between

1

1. A rocky but beautiful cliff on the north-west side of nearby North Molle Island. North Molle, which is uninhabited, can be easily visited by boat.

2. A view of Spion Kop, South Molle's second highest peak, at dawn. The boat moored at the jetty is the "Roylen Endeavour" which cruises the Whitsundays and its outer reefs from her home port of Mackay.

mealtimes you will find a Coffee Shop alongside the pool area that offers snacks, drinks and ice-cream.

There is a large Gift Shop that stocks everything from biscuits to toiletries and casual clothes to souvenirs and daily newspapers. Film and 24-hour processing is available. You may also rent VHS recorders and movies from the Gift Shop.

In addition, the resort has a hair salon, Westpac Savings Bank agency, dry cleaning and laundry facilities.

Children well looked after.

Parents who visit South Molle with their family will find that their children are well catered for, especially during school holidays. During these times, there are some six hours of supervised activities each day.

The list of activities for children ranges from nature walks and aerobics to face painting, treasure hunts and kite flying. There are games and videos for them through to 8:30p.m., too, which allow parents to dine by themselves if they wish to.

For pre-school children there is childminding in the resort's own nursery between 8:00 a.m. and 4:30 p.m., four days a week, during school holidays - and every night between 5:30 p.m. and 6:30 p.m. you can leave your children to enjoy a meal together with other kids. Baby-sitting is available, free of charge, until 9:00 p.m.

Even outside of school holidays, there is childminding for pre-school children on several days to give their parents a welcome break - and the staff in the nursery always includes a fully trained nurse.

During the periods outside of school holidays there are two hours of activities each day to keep children both entertained and out of your hair.

Unlike some island resorts, children of all ages are welcome to stay at the resort on South Molle.

How to get to South Molle Island.

The resort - especially considering its size - is extremely well run. It is hard to imagine that there could be too many complaints from any guest because of the obvious desire by management to ensure that your visit to South Molle is as enjoyable as possible.

Overall, it represents extremely good value for money (particularly for those with families).

The telephone and facsimile numbers of the South Molle Island Resort are (079) 469433 and (079) 469580. Their postal address is South Molle Island Resort, Whitsunday Passage, P.M.B. 21, Mackay, Queensland 4741.

To reach South Molle Island by plane, rail or coach you will go via Proserpine which is about an hour inland on the mainland.

Coach connections will then take you to Airlie Beach and nearby Shute Harbour. From Shute Harbour you will board a high speed catamaran which will take you out to South Molle Island in about 30 minutes.

People who wish to drive to the area will find that security parking is available at Shute Harbour.

In 1936 Henry Lamond, who lived on South Molle Island at that time, wrote an article for "Walkabout" magazine.

In it he describes his life on the island and this is how he finally concluded the article. "Perhaps some day I will leave here. That brings a whole heap of restrictions into view: trousers instead of shorts, collars, hats, and greatest abomination of all, boots and shoes. I presume it is only fair to my youngsters that I should give them a chance on the mainland, and some day, perhaps, I may motor to sea and wave farewell to my island home."

Henry Lamond considered South Molle his "Eden" and obviously contemplated his future departure from it with deep regret.

Today, it is hardly surprising that many visitors also harbour the same feelings of regret as they leave this beautiful tropical island.

2

ACKNOWLEDGEMENTS

The photographs in this book were taken by David Heenan with the exception of those listed here.

The author would like to give special thanks to all the photographers, museums, companies and individuals who provided this additional material.

Sources of historical black-and-white material and illustrations are listed separately.

The numerals in brackets following the page numbers refer to the respective plate on that page.

COLOUR PHOTOGRAPHS

G. Anderson (National Photographic Index of Australian Birds): 29 (1)

Australian Resorts Pty. Ltd: 30/1 (1-3, 5), 32/3 (2 & 4), 44 (3), 66/7 (2, 4-6, 8)

Max Beck: 200

Clifford and Dawn Frith: 55 (2), 72/3 (2-4), 153 (2-4)

Neville Coleman (Sea Australia Resource Centre): 10 (2 & 3), 179 (5), 188 (1)

Daydream Island Resort: 47 (3), 53 (18)

Great Adventures Pty. Ltd: 77 (2), 78 (1-3), 92 (1), 103 (1-3)

Great Barrier Reef Marine Park Authority: 4 (1), 13 (2), 73 (6), 197 (2), 199 (4), 240 (1-4)

Hamilton Island Resort: 105 (3), 108 (3), 115 (2 & 3), 118/9 (2-6 & 8), 240

Peter Harrison: 6 (1-3), 8

Hayman Island Resort: 130/1 (2 & 3), 132 (3 & 5)

Dean Lee: 5 (2)

Lindeman Island Resort: 183 (3), 190 (2, 4-7)

Ian Mariner: 7 (5), 9, 202/3 (1-7), 204 (4)

Orpheus Island Resort: 226/7 (1-3, 6 & 7)

P & O Resorts: Front Cover, 143 (6), 145 (4), 147 (5), 148/9 (1-4, 7)

Premier's Department, Queensland: 121 (2)

Queensland Department of Environment and Conservation (formerly the Queensland National Parks and Wildlife Service): 98 (1), 101 (4), 163 (3), 164/5 (1-4 & 6), 176 (5), 178/9 (1-3), 180/1 (2, 4-6), 233 (5)

Queensland Museum: 18/19 (1-4 & 6)

Queensland Tourist & Travel Corporation: 39 (2), 42 (1), 67 (9 & 10), 111 (4 & 5), 112 (2), 118 (1), 140 (2), 236/7 (4)

Seair Pacific: 51 (5), 188 (2), 234 (1)

Ron and Valerie Taylor: Dust-jacket (Underwater), 3 (2-4), 6/7 (4, 6 & 7), 10/11 (1, 4 & 5), 77 (4), 109 (5 & 6), 110 (3), 135 (2 & 4), 141 (4), 142/3 (1-5), 145 (2), 179 (23)

B. Wells: 199 (3)

HISTORICAL PHOTOGRAPHS/ ILLUSTRATIONS

Douglass Baglin: 221 (2-5)

James Cook University: 16 (1), 95 (1 & 2), 96/7 (1& 2), all from the Hayles Collection

Courier Mail: 96 (3), 171 (2 & 3)

Gladstone Observer: 182 (1)

John Hopkins: 57, 59 (3 & 4)

Bill Lamond: 49 (3 & 4)

Pam Land: 136 (2)

Thora Nicolson: 184/5 (1 & 2)

P & O Resorts: 137 (4, 5 & 6)

John Oxley Library: 15 (3 & 4), 21 (1 & 2), 39 (1), 48/9 (1, 2 & 5), 59 (2 & 5), 70 (1), 83 (2, 3 & 5), 97 (5), 122/3 (1-5), 136/7 (1 & 3), 151 (2), 170 (1), 185 (3-5), 195 (1), 216 (1), 220 (1)

National Geographic Magazine: 19, Illustration of the "Pandora" by Roy Anderson.

National Library of Australia: 14 (1) Portrait of James Cook after a portrait by Nathaniel Dance Holland held in the National Maritime Museum, Greenwich; 15 (2) Tinted lithograph, hand coloured, Artist unknown; 17 (3) An engraving from a volume written by John Hawkesworth and published in London, 1773 - Artist, Sydney Parkison; Engraver, William Byrne

Rockhampton Library: 83 (4)

Derek Scott: 96 (4)

South Molle Island Resort: 231 (1)

MAPS

Sunmap: Base map of the Great Barrier Reef region.

Great Barrier Reef Marine Park Authority: Map showing different zones of Marine Park, 13.

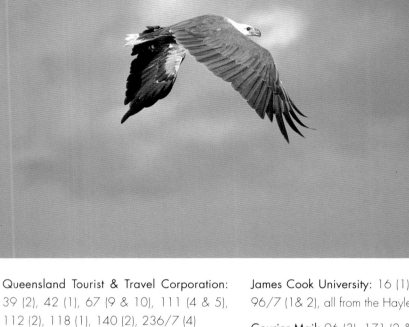

THE ULTIMATE CRUISE

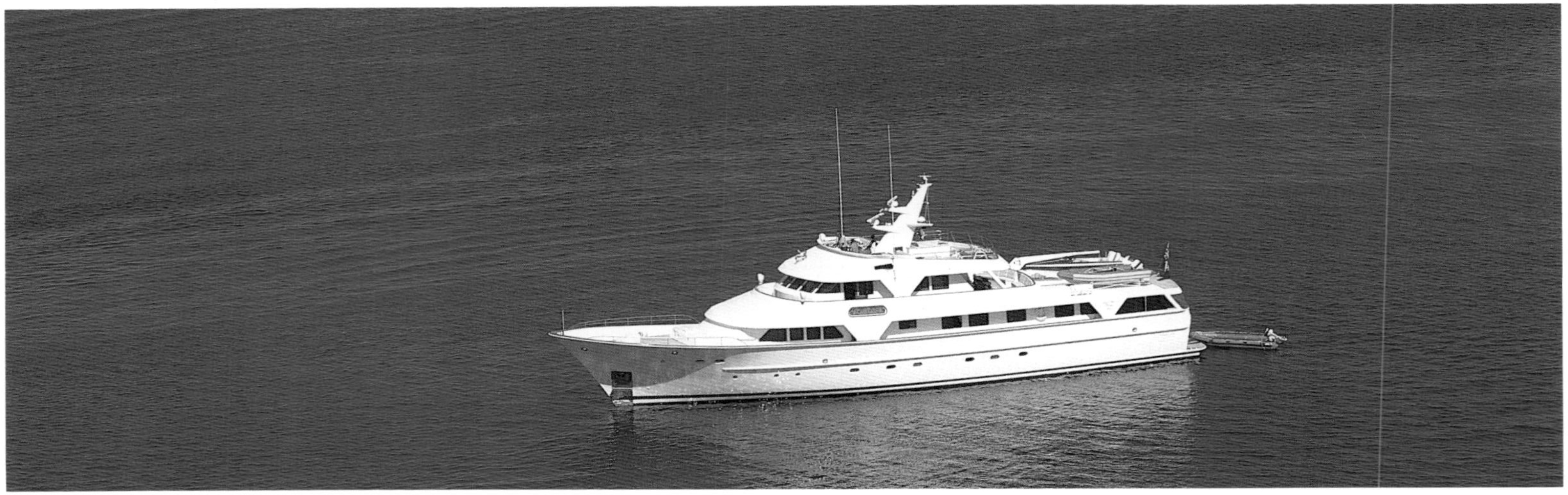

Each year, the author David Heenan will be hosting a special Great Barrier Reef cruise for no more than 10 guests aboard a luxury motor yacht comparable to the one above. If you wish to visit the Great Barrier Reef, it will give you the opportunity to combine a relaxing holiday on one of the resort islands with the cruise of a lifetime. During this cruise, the author of "The Great Barrier Reef" will share his intimate knowledge of the Reef with you - taking you to the secluded bays and beaches of the uninhabited islands he considers to be the most beautiful. You will visit the best places to snorkel and dive. And you will learn of the Reef's rich history, first-hand. This small party will also be accompanied by a marine biologist who will give you additional insight into the amazing marine life on the Reef. Each evening, you will enjoy a dinner party where only the finest cuisine and wines are served.